PERSPECTIVES ON THE ACADEMIC DISCIPLINE OF PHYSICAL EDUCATION

A TRIBUTE TO G. LAWRENCE RARICK

EDITED BY
George A. Brooks

PUBLISHED BY

Human Kinetics Publishers
Champaign, Illinois

Library of Congress Catalog Card Number: 80-85203

ISBN: 0-931250-18-8

HUMAN KINETICS PUBLISHERS, INC.
Box 5076
Champaign, Illinois 61820

TRIBUTE

The work included in this volume is a tribute to Professor G. Lawrence Rarick: the man and his career. Dr. Rarick has devoted his working life to research and instruction on the motor and physical development of children. In particular, he has focused on the needs and characteristics of atypical children, especially the mildly and moderately mentally retarded.

Dr. Rarick received his bachelor's and master's degrees from Fort Hayes, Kansas State College. Later, he studied with C.H. McCloy and W.W. Tuttle at the University of Iowa where he obtained his PhD. Following the award of his doctorate, Professor Rarick instructed at the University of Wichita, Boston University, the University of Wisconsin, and the University of California at Berkeley. He retired from Berkeley in June 1979.

In support of his work on the development of normal and atypical children, Dr. Rarick has received several significant extramural research and training grants. The efforts associated with those grants have illuminated many aspects of child development. Professor Rarick's achievements have also nurtured and supported numerous graduate students; many of these students have also gone on to make significant contributions in the field of child growth and development.

Professor Rarick has been the preeminent worker in his field, distinguished both nationally and internationally. His scholarly efforts have also been complemented by professional activities. Dr. Rarick has served on university, regional, and national committees in service to youth. In addition, he has lectured widely on the topics of his expertise.

Beyond all his scholarly and professional achievements, G. Lawrence Rarick is known for his distinguished character and manner of conduct in his dealings with colleagues, associates, and professional, scholarly and public agencies. Dr. Rarick's wife Mary Alice, is a person of like capacity and character. They have three children: David, Thomas, and Janet.

G. Lawrence Rarick

CONTENTS

TRIBUTE   **iii**

THE AUTHORS   **xi**

PREFACE   **xv**

PART 1. INTRODUCTION TO THE DISCIPLINE   **1**

Chapter 1   **3**

What is the Discipline of Physical Education?
G.A. Brooks

The Academic Discipline	3
Inter- or Cross-disciplinary?	5
The Role of Methodology	5
Challenges to the Discipline	6
What to Call It	7

Chapter 2   **10**

Physical Education: An Academic Discipline
F.M. Henry

Chapter 3   **16**

The Domain of Physical Education
G.L. Rarick

Chapter 4   **20**

The Emergence of the Academic Discipline of
Physical Education in the United States
R.J. Park

From Classical Antiquity to the 19th Century 22
Physical Education Becomes a Profession: 1885-1929 26
Efforts to Stimulate Research: 1930-1959 31
Organized Efforts in the 1960s and 1970s 35

PART 2. PHYSIOLOGY OF EXERCISE 47

Chapter 5 55

The Emergence of Exercise Physiology in
Physical Education
E.R. Buskirk

Trends 56
Politics and Support 57
Responsibility 58
Participation 60
Research Interpretation 60
Scope of Involvement 61
Sources of Information 62
General Contributions 63
Research 65
Chronological Bibliography of Books
    and Review Articles 67

Chapter 6 75

Current and Future Topics in Exercise Physiology
J.A. Faulkner and T.P. White

Current Areas of Emphasis 76
Future Prospects 89

Chapter 7 97

The Physiological Bases of Elevated Postexercise
Oxygen Consumption
G.A. Brooks

Basic Terminology 98
The Classical Research 101
Other Experimental Approaches 105
The Contemporary Case for the "Lactacid O_2 Debt" 110
Towards a Contemporary Interpretation 111
Selection of a Term 115

PART 3. BIOMECHANICS OF SPORT   121

Chapter 8   124

The Emergence of Human Biomechanics
R.F. Zernicke

Biomechanics/Kinesiology	125
A Historical Milieu	126
Recent Developments	132

Chapter 9   137

Biomechanics of Sport: The State of the Art
P.R. Cavanagh and R. Hinrichs

The Measurement of Motion	138
Errors in Data Collection	139
Kinematic Analysis	140
Body Segment Parameters	143
Kinetic Analysis	145
Modeling and Simulation	152
Sports Equipment	153

PART 4. MOTOR DEVELOPMENT   159

Chapter 10   163

The Emergence of the Study of Human Motor
Development
G.L. Rarick

Methodological Approaches in Motor Development Investigations	164
Genetic and Maturational Factors in Motor Development	165
Differential Effects of Age, Sex, and Maturity	172
Physique and the Development of Motor Abilities	179
Ethnic and Cultural Factors in Motor Development	181
Stability and Change in Motor Abilities	182
Intellectual Factors	184

Chapter 11   190

Growth, Maturation, and Human Performance
R.M. Malina

Overview of Postnatal Growth, Maturation,
    and Performance   191
Factors Influencing Growth and Maturation   192
Factors Influencing Physical Performance   193
Selected Developments and Directions   194

Chapter 12   211

A Movement Development Framework and a
Perceptual-Cognitive Perspective
J. Keogh

Movement Development Framework   211
Movement Skill Development: A Perceptual-Cognitive
    Perspective   214
Role of Vision   221

Chapter 13   234

Time Passages in Adapted Physical Education
G.D. Broadhead

Features of Adapted Physical Education   234
A Traditional Route to Adapted Physical Education   236
The New Adapted Physical Education   238
Current Forces and the Future   239

PART 5. MOTOR BEHAVIOR   253

Chapter 14   257

The Emergence of Research in Motor Control
and Learning
W.W. Spirduso

What is Motor Learning Research?   257
Telegraph Keys and Reflexology: 1890-1931   259
Describing, Measuring, and Applying: 1931-1959   261
Ushering in the "Discipline" with a "Memory
    Drum-Roll": 1959-1969   263
Peering Into the Black Box: 1970-   266

Chapter 15   273

Current and Prospective Issues in Motor Behavior
*G.E. Stelmach, V.A. Diggles, L.D. Szendrovits,
and B.G. Hughes*

Control Theory 275
Specification of Action 281
Automation 289

Chapter 16 **301**

The Evolution of the Memory Drum Theory of
Neuromotor Reaction
F.M. Henry

The Memory Drum Concept 301
Emergence of a Tentative Theory 302
Emergence of an Experimental Design 304
Factual Results Confirm the Theory 306
Another Line of Evidence: The Psychological
    Refractory Period 307
Independence of Reaction and Movement Times 312
Experimental Results at Other Laboratories 317
Current Status of the Memory Drum Theory 318

PART 6. SPORT PSYCHOLOGY AND SOCIOLOGY **323**

Chapter 17 **327**

The Emergence of Psychological Research as
Related to Performance in Physical Activity
E.D. Ryan

Earliest Studies 328
First Emergence 329
Second Emergence 332
Sustained Contributions 333

Chapter 18 **342**

Current Research and Future Prospects in
Sport Psychology
D.L. Gill

Personality 342
Motivation 347
Social Influences on Motor Performance 352
Social Interaction 357
Applied Sport Psychology 361

Chapter 19   **379**

Emergence of and Future Prospects for Sociology
of Sport
S. Greendorfer

Issues Related to the Development of Sociology of Sport   384
Future Prospects   390

THE AUTHORS

Geoffrey D. Broadhead, PhD, is a professor in the Department of Human Development as well as in the School of Health, Physical Education, Recreation and Dance at Louisiana State University. Dr. Broadhead's research is primarily focused on physical activity for handicapped children, including movement screening of preschool-aged "at risk" children. When not at work, Dr. Broadhead enjoys classical music, hates jogging, gardens reluctantly, and likes all sporting events.

George A. Brooks, PhD, is a professor of physical education at the University of California, Berkeley, where he has built the Exercise Physiology Laboratory. His research interests involve studies of lactic acid metabolism during and after exercise. Dr. Brooks enjoys carpentry and mechanics in his spare time, but mainly, he and Suzanne Brooks enjoy the company of their sons Danny and Timmy.

Elsworth R. Buskirk, PhD, is a professor of applied physiology at the Pennsylvania State University, director of the Laboratory for Human Performance Research, chairman of Penn State's Graduate Program in Physiology, and chairman of the Biomedical Committee for Use of Human Subjects in Research. He is involved in appraisals of the physiological consequences of obesity as well as in a study of exercise in the primary prevention of coronary heart disease. In his free time, Dr. Buskirk swims, plays tennis, cross-country skis, hikes, and ice skates.

Peter R. Cavanagh, PhD, is an associate professor of biomechanics at the Pennsylvania State University. His research focuses on human locomotion, particularly for the study and development of footwear for walking, running, and other sport activities. Dr. Cavanagh is an avid runner, and his best marathon time was 2 hours and 44 minutes at the Avenue of the Giants Marathon in 1980 in Eureka, California.

John A. Faulkner, PhD, is a professor in the Department of Physiology at the University of Michigan. He is interested in the fatigability of skeletal muscle and is investigating the mechanisms by which regenerating skeletal muscle revascularizes as well as the operative procedures that improve the structure and function of transplanted muscle. In his free time, Dr. Faulkner enjoys playing tennis and skiing, and he has completed the 100-mile Canadian Ski Marathon.

Diane L. Gill, PhD, is an associate professor in the Department of Physical Education and Dance at the University of Iowa. She is interested in the psychology of sport, particularly group performance and motivation, confidence in sport, and psychological skills training. When she is not working, Dr. Gill enjoys running 10 kilometer races.

Sue Greendorfer, PhD, is an associate professor in the Department of Physical Education at the University of Illinois. Her research focuses on race and gender differences in socializing children into sport and professional socialization of undergraduate physical education majors. Outside of her academic interests, Dr. Greendorfer plays tennis and golf, and enjoys watching professional football.

Franklin M. Henry, PhD, is a professor emeritus at the University of California, Berkeley. Dr. Henry developed the pioneering "Memory Drum" theory and was among the first to establish physical education as an academic discipline. His current research interests are the stability-instability of the motor memory trace, which is a derivation of his earlier theory, as well as programmed control of learned motor skill. Dr. Henry also photographs desert landscapes and wildflowers, and studies American Southwest archeology.

Richard N. Hinrichs, MA, is a doctoral student in biomechanics at the Pennsylvania State University and expects to receive his PhD this year. He is interested in human body rotation in free fall and in human locomotion, particularly in the area of upper extremity function. Mr. Hinrichs is a former All-American swimmer who still competes, and he also enjoys cycling, trampolining, and basketball.

Jack F. Keogh, EdD, is a professor in the Department of Kinesiology at the University of California, Los Angeles. He is interested in several aspects of movement skill development, including movement dysfunction and related measurement problems, knowledge of movement effort, role of vision in movement development, and development of movement confidence. Dr. Keogh is a wine connoisseur and makes his own wine in his spare time.

Robert M. Malina, PhD, is a professor of anthropology and of physical and health education at the University of Texas, Austin, as well as associate director of the Institute of Latin American Studies. Dr. Malina's research interests include the study of the growth of school children in several urban and rural communities of southern Mexico, analysis of sibling similarities in growth and physical performance, growth and maturity characteristics of age group swimmers, and physique and body composition of women athletes at the university level. Dr. Malina is also an avid noon-hour squash player.

Robert J. Park, PhD, is a professor in the Department of Physical Education at the University of California, Berkeley. She is interested in attitudes toward the body in 18th and 19th century Western thought as reflected in changing conceptions of health, hygiene, physical education, and sport; the interrelationships of play, games, and sport and moral lessons as reflected in 19th and early 20th century children's literature; and the institutionalization and bureaucratization of play from 1890-1915. Dr. Park also enjoys backpacking, opera, and cooking.

E. Dean Ryan, PhD, is a professor in the Department of Physical Education at the University of California, Davis, and editor of *Quest,* a scholarly journal for physical educators. Dr. Ryan is interested in sport psychology and in the psychosocial factors in physical activity. He also investigates the use of mental imagery in sport. In his free time, Dr. Ryan enjoys backpacking and fishing.

Waneen W. Spirduso, PhD, is chairman of the Department of Physical and Health Education at the University of Texas, Austin. She is involved in a 3-year research project in which the longitudinal effects of exercise on reactive capacity are examined. In her free time, Dr. Spirduso jogs, studies Spanish, and is interested in numismatics.

George E. Stelmach, PhD, is a professor of motor behavior and director of the Motor Behavior Laboratory at the University of Wisconsin, Madison. His research interests include the study of skill acquisition, motor control, and response determination and response selection processes for motor programming. Dr. Stelmach enjoys playing golf, racquetball, and cycling. **Virginia Diggles**, **Barry Hughes**, and **Les Szendrovits** are all graduate students in motor behavior working toward their doctorates.

Timothy P. White, PhD, is an assistant professor at the University of Michigan. He is interested in the structural and functional changes in normal skeletal muscle and in regenerating skeletal muscle to different types of activities. Dr. White sails an 18-foot catamaran, jogs, and plays racquetball; he is also an avid cross-country skier and has completed the 100-mile Canadian Ski Marathon.

Ronald F. Zernicke, PhD, is an associate professor of biomechanics in the Department of Kinesiology at the University of California, Los Angeles. His research interests include the biomechanics of both normal and pathological locomotion, determination of the mechanical and physiological factors to affect the control of coordinated movement, and the assessment of the injury mechanisms of the musculoskeletal system. Outside of his academic interests, Dr. Zernicke enjoys reading, playing the piano, cross-country skiing, and running.

PREFACE

This volume is directed to beginning graduate students of the discipline of physical education in the United States. We all are students in the discipline of physical education as well as other disciplines, and we remain students as long as we learn and grow in knowledge. Should we stop, or even slow down in our intellectual pursuits, the world will pass us by. It is a difficult job being a student. Basic uncertainty in the nature of information with which we shape our concepts, as well as the continually expanding limits of the data base we need to consider, are trepidations with which serious students must live. Considering the diversity and complexity of physical education research, it is particularly difficult for the student initiate to acquire a working knowledge of the discipline and to become aware of the major issues in the discipline. It is for these beginning students that this volume is intended.

After approximately fifteen years as a serious student in the discipline, I can honestly state that I am beginning to comprehend the scope of the discipline. I have also made some progress in terms of being able to identify the major issues and personalities in the discipline. Why my university professors did not strive to insure that I was aware of these obvious elements in the discipline, I do not know. There may have been several reasons: my professors may have assumed students were aware of the many issues within the discipline. Or I may have been too immersed in studies related to my specialization within the discipline to be receptive to an education on the broader aspects of the discipline. My professors may also have assumed that some things are best learned through experience. In retrospect, I believe I would have gained from a discussion of the organization, scope, and direction of the discipline; a book like this one would have been helpful. Certainly those of you who are beginning students must focus on one or two areas in the discipline for advanced study and research. However, take time at the outset of your career to obtain a grasp on the discipline as a whole.

The basis of the discipline of physical education is the "body of knowledge." This body is comprised of facts and concepts developed by physical education academicians or borrowed from other disciplines. Together, these facts and concepts are used to understand the human body during exercise. Because of a commonality of subject matter and for convenience, parts of the body of knowledge are sometimes classified by particular terms. Frequently, detailed study of a particular part of the body of knowledge results in specialization.

A Summary of the Text

Major specializations in the discipline of physical education are often identified by the terms: history of physical education, exercise physiology, biomechanics, motor development, motor learning, sport psychology, and sport sociology. In the text, an attempt is made to provide two chapters on each of these specialized areas. One chapter describes the emergence of study in the area of specialization, and the second chapter describes the current status of the field as well as suggests areas for future research. The history of physical education as a subarea is an exception to this two-chapter approach. By definition, the study of history deals only with the past; therefore, the volume contains a single chapter on this aspect of the discipline. The events and persons responsible for influencing emergence of the academic discipline in the United States are highlighted by Roberta Park. Susan Greendorfer, in her chapter on the relatively new area of sports sociology, describes both the emergence of, and future prospects for, study in sociology of sport. In addition to covering the various subareas of the discipline, the volume also includes chapters dealing with specialized topics encompassed within several of the larger subareas. These special chapters are included to give the student an appreciation of the experimental approaches used for solving problems in physical education research. The metabolism of lactic acid, and its involvement with recovery from strenuous exercise has represented one of the major questions in exercise physiology. Regarding this question, I have contributed a chapter on metabolism during the postexercise ("O_2 debt") period. Concerning the specialization of motor learning, Franklin Henry, the pioneer of the field, has contributed a chapter describing evolution of the "memory drum" theory. In the area of movement development, Jack Keogh describes the perceptual-cognitive development of motor skills. The importance of physical education as contributory to development of physically handicapped individuals is discussed by Geoff Broadhead in his chapter on adapted physical education.

These are but a few of the papers included in the text.

It is a well-deserved tribute to Larry Rarick that scholars of international repute have contributed to this work. Contributions have come from major universities in all areas of the United States. They have been made out of respect for Larry Rarick and out of respect for the beginning graduate student. Future advancement of the discipline depends upon the success of its students. By nurturing new students, our progress in the future is insured.

The Nature of Graduate Study

When students reach the graduate level, they cross a major threshold. At the graduate level, students are usually expected to contribute to the body of knowledge as well as to assume a command of that body as a whole. In assuming the roles of scholar and researcher, students take on a responsibility, not only for themselves, but also for their past, present, and future colleagues. It is this responsibility for scholarship which perhaps most distinguishes the graduate from the undergraduate student.

The nature of graduate study is so vastly different from undergraduate study, that without benefit of much experience in research, most beginning graduate students usually find themselves asking, "What is this all about?" One common characteristic of new graduate students is that they are enthusiasts—they are believers. There has been some set of events in their undergraduate experiences (in studying exercise physiology, in working with the handicapped, or whatever), which has stimulated their interest to undertake advanced study. However, success in graduate work requires students to change from believers to skeptics. The ability to evaluate your own research, as well as that of others, depends upon critical evaluation of experimental design, technical application, and data analysis and interpretation. The capacity for critical evaluation is, perhaps unfortunately, developed only by research experience. Indeed, research experience at some point, may limit not only the ability to do research, but also the ability to critically read and evaluate the work of others.

A turning point in the research careers of many students sometimes coincides with a disasterous episode in the laboratory or library. For instance, you may bungle your work so completely that you wonder, "How does anyone ever do anything correctly?" When you get to that point in your career, you may decide that this business is too much for you. Or because of interest or determination, you may decide to continue on. You must then become extremely discerning with every aspect of your own work and with the work you are presented with. You simply must know the literature, analytical techniques, experimental design, and statistical evaluation. Furthermore, you must maintain a perspective of the field as a whole, continually evaluating your role in the discipline and profession. Therefore, an aim of this volume is to assist you in becoming the kind of accomplished student our discipline needs.

PART 1

Introduction to the Discipline

What is the Discipline of Physical Education?

1

G.A. Brooks

The Academic Discipline

In addition to serving as an introduction to scholarly aspects of physical education, this volume is also intended to present students with the proposition that the material encompassed within the classification of "physical education" represents an academic discipline. Students of the discipline must be aware that discussion over the scope and depth of the discipline persists (Henry, 1964; Locke, 1977; Rarick, 1967; Ross, 1978). The proposition that there is an "academic discipline of physical education" has not been without controversy (Ross, 1978). Further, the position that emphasis in physical education in colleges and universities should be placed upon acquisition of theoretical concepts, rather than on acquisition of pedagogical skill, has been challenged (Locke, 1977).

The position for an academic discipline of physical education was started by Franklin M. Henry (1964). Because Henry's article on the subject is so important, it is reproduced in this volume (Chapter 2). To paraphrase Henry, the academic discipline of physical education is an organized body of knowledge collectively embraced in a formal course of learning; the acquisition of such knowledge is assumed to be an adequate and worthy objective as such without any demonstration or requirement of practical application; the content is theoretical and scholarly rather than technical and professional (Henry, 1964). Several aspects of this typically precise statement of Henry need mention. The "organized body of knowledge" is comprised of those facts and hypotheses arranged around the understanding of the function of the human body performing exercise. This knowledge has been developed by individuals in physical education and related disciplines, but it has been collected and used by physical educators for their own specific purposes.

The relationships among physical education and other disciplines were described by G. Lawrence Rarick (1967). Again, because of the importance of his statements on the discipline, an article by Rarick is also reprinted (Chapter 3). According to Rarick, "with the advent of the scientific method, knowledge accumulated rapidly" (Rarick, 1967, p. 49). Separate disciplines began to emerge when scholars concentrated on particular matters. Each of the individual disciplines became recognized as distinct entities when, over time, the scope of each field of study was identified and recognized. As the various disciplines attempted to extend the scope of their knowledge, branches of the various disciplines necessarily overlapped. Consequently, new disciplines were formed and others disappeared.

Today the efforts of individual scientists in many fields overlap. Consequently, identifying and defining the boundaries of individual disciplines can be difficult. Since knowledge belongs to no one, let alone to a particular discipline, it is inevitable that each discipline borrows and uses the knowledge of other disciplines. Just as the physical educator, to understand the limits of physical performance, borrows on results of studies by physiologists, the physiologist, to understand basic physiology, borrows on results obtained by physical education-exercise physiologists.

Pursuit of knowledge in the academic discipline of physical education is a worthy objective in and of itself. In this context, the study of physical education is consistent with the philosophy of liberal education. That is, knowledge pursued for the sake of knowledge is an established principle which colleges and universities operate upon. It has been established that results of scholarly efforts ultimately give rise to the practical applications upon which society advances. It is assumed that results of scholarly activities in physical education have an impact on professional education and physical education instruction in schools.

The theoretical and scholarly pursuits of members of the academic discipline are distinguished from the professional efforts of other physical educators. Of course, this is not to say that the scholarly efforts of professional physical educators are better or worse, higher or lower, than pedagogical efforts of the physical educators involved in primary, secondary, and higher education. Certainly, pedagogy in general, and pedagogy in physical education are worthy and essential pursuits. Professional physical educators are involved in the application of knowledge; efforts of academics result in the creation of knowledge. The discipline of physical education is concerned with the latter, rather than with the former.

As work in physical education can vary from either the academic (theoretical) to the professional (practical), so can the efforts of higher education institutions vary. The emphasis within a particular department need only be consistent with the mission of that institution. In the United States, state colleges have most often been identified with professional preparation, whereas universities have tended to focus on academic pursuits. Some larger state universities have attempted to offer both professional and academic courses of study. Both are important, and both need to be done well.

Inter- or Cross-disciplinary?

With much of the academic discipline's content taken from many other fields, it is easy to wonder if the discipline of physical education is interdisciplinary or cross-disciplinary in nature. Interdisciplinary means that the discipline is based upon knowledge supplied by several other disciplines (e.g., anatomy, physiology, psychology). Therefore, students of physical education take courses in, and study material of, other disciplines. These students then bring their knowledge back to physical education. In a cross-disciplinary approach, it is realized that each of the courses in the other disciplines may contain only bits of information directly relevant to human performance in a physical education setting. A cross-disciplinary approach to physical education means that courses exist within physical education which focus on various aspects of the discipline (e.g., exercise physiology, motor learning, sport psychology, motor development).

The academic discipline of physical education is both interdisciplinary and cross-disciplinary in nature. Undergraduate students are required to take courses such as anatomy, chemistry, physiology, physics, statistics, history, psychology, anthropology, and sociology to prepare them for advanced, upper-division course work in physical education. Taking courses outside the major makes very good sense; a college or university faculty includes experts in a variety of fields related to physical education. Having those experts instruct physical education students allows the students to obtain quality instruction efficiently. The taking of courses outside the major promotes the general education of physical education students. It also allows the physical education faculty and resources to be focused on particular interests, rather than on developing courses like anatomy and physiology which are already offered by other departments. When students apply the knowledge of other disciplines to understand human movement, then the approach is cross-disciplinary.

The Role of Methodology

In addressing the issue of whether physical education is cross- or interdisciplinary, graduate students frequently find that semantics have little to do with practice. In the scientific method, ideas (hypotheses) are put forth, and implications of those hypotheses are tested by the systematic (experimental) collection of information (data). A researcher's interest may influence the choice of hypothesis, but once a hypothesis is stated, testing it follows the scientific method. Should two researchers, (e.g., a kinesiologist and a mechanical engineer) independently ask the same question about movement of body segments during locomotion, then the two investigators should solve the problem in very similar ways. The two individuals' success in finding the solution to their question will probably depend on their ability to state the problem at hand in a way which can be tested experimentally. Therefore, it matters little to researchers with an orientation in physical education whether physical education is cross-disciplinary, interdisciplinary, or nondisciplinary; what matters is that they can be effective in solving the problem at hand. The questions to you as a researcher are: "What is the question? Can you pose the question? Can you answer it?" To the extent that the experimental techniques of physical education are borrowed from other disciplines, students of physical education must then obtain a solid grounding in those other disciplines. This is most likely the only way that students can acquire the conceptual, factual, and technical skills necessary to be effective researchers.

It is possible that with the necessary emphasis on course work outside the major field, physical education students may lose their interest in physical education. However, it is more probable that students will instead broaden their horizons. Interest in physical education has followed the course of civilization (Chapter 4); thus, there is no worry that physical education will disappear. Colleges and universities are marvelous institutions, and faculty in physical education are wise to encourage students to use laboratories and study with professors from several departments. Frequently, a requisite step in becoming a researcher is seeing research done. Since effective research often depends upon technology, it is of great benefit to have first-hand experience with a variety of analytical procedures.

Challenges to the Discipline

The perspective expressed here, as well as by Henry (Chapter 2) and Rarick (Chapter 3)—that scholarship is the basis of physical education at the college and university level—is not supported by Lawrence Locke (1977). According to Locke and many others in the profession, pedagogy should be the main concern of physical education.

According to Locke, it is assumed:

> ...that the central role of the physical educator is to help students learn
> how to play and to love physically active games, to dance, and to exercise.
> The principal 'valuable' that we have to give our client is motor skill. The
> principal target for our service is youth. The principal locale for our oper-
> ation is the public school, and the main reason our role exists is because
> society so values active play that it arranged to pass the subject matter on
> to the next generation.

According to Locke, teacher preparation should be the role of physical education at the college level.

The premise that physical education is an autonomous discipline, comprised of a body of knowledge which can be subdivided into specializations or subdisciplines, has been challenged by Saul Ross (1978). He believes the absence of a paradigm (central, unifying theory) precludes physical education from being a proper discipline. What Ross believes to exist under the label "physical education," is a cooperative amalgamation or association of subdisciplines. In Ross' view, the lack of cohesiveness in contemporary physical education reduces it to the level of a "prediscipline" (p. 11). Regardless of personal opinions, graduate students in physical education must be aware of the various issues and arguments surrounding the nature and purpose of the field.

What to Call It

The title of this volume is *Perspectives on the Academic Discipline of Physical Education: A Tribute to G. Lawrence Rarick*. The nature of the discipline was previously presented here, and it was pointed out that acceptance of the disciplinary nature of physical education is not universal. But what of this term "physical education," and use of the term in conjunction with an "academic discipline"? With development of a slightly wider perspective, it soon becomes apparent that the term physical education may be far from appropriate. The term implies education of the physical being, or education by or through the physical being. As important as these practical objectives are, they are inconsistent with the objectives of an academic discipline which are, by definition, theoretical in nature. Perhaps the best that can be said for the term when used in an academic context is that it pertains to the pursuit of knowledge applicable to physical education instruction. It is equally likely also that this knowledge could be applied in recreational, industrial, athletic, or other endeavors.

Because of the inappropriateness of the term "physical education," there have been several attempts to find an alternative, such as kinesiology, kinesiological sciences, ergonomics, and exercise science. In fact, some departments in colleges and universities have elected to change their names. Because of the inherent problems with the designation "physical education," movement away from the term is most likely inevitable. Yet an inhibiting factor may be the lack of concensus regarding which of the alternatives to adopt. Whereas most people rightly or wrongly think they know what "physical education" is, very few know what the other terms mean. A further problem is that changing the name gives the impression that the reference is to a new, evolving discipline, rather than to an established discipline. Whereas "physical education" has roots in American and other educational systems, terms like kinesiology do not.

Use of an alternative to "physical education" does, however, partially escape association with those unfortunate instructional programs in schools, colleges, and universities which maximize athletic competition by minimizing the physical education instruction. Certainly overemphasis on success in athletics remains one of the major problems in the physical education profession. Appropriation of facilities, funds, and personnel for athletics, emphasis on games of little carry-over values, unjustified influence of nonacademicians on school activities, and lack of emphasis on basic education are a few of the problems associated with interscholastic and intercollegiate athletics. Emphasis on the so-called "major sports" only occasionally affords athletes, their country, or their institution any international recognition. Consequently there is little wonder why academicians do not want to be identified with the problems of the profession. However, while using an alternative term to "physical education" does afford academicians a degree of status, it remains to be demonstrated that changing the name of the discipline will improve the profession.

The widely accepted term "physical education" will be used for this volume. In my opinion, the term used to denote the discipline really does not matter. What matters is what, and how well, things are done within the discipline. The discipline will stand or fall on its accomplishments, not on its name.

References

Henry, F.M. Physical Education: An Academic Discipline. *Proceedings of the 67th annual conference of NCPEAM,* 1964, p. 6-9.

Locke, L.F. From Research and the Disciplines to Practice and the Profession: One More Time. *Proceedings of the NAPECW/NCPEAM National Conference,* 1977, 34-45.

Rarick, G.L. The Domain of Physical Education. *Quest,* 1967, **9**, 49-52.

Ross, S. Physical Education: A Pre-Discipline in Search of a Paradigm.
International Journal of Physical Education, 1978, **15**(2), 9-15.

Physical Education: An Academic Discipline

2

F.M. Henry

College physical education in America owes much of its genesis to the concept that exercise and sports are therapeutic and prophylactic. In fact many directors of physical education of the last generation were M.D.'s. The school program probably received its greatest impetus as an effort to reduce draft rejects and improve the fitness of youth for military service in World War I. This objective was of course re-emphasized in World War II. It is understandable that our professional concern has tended to center on what physical education can do for people rather than the development of a field of knowledge.

The majority of the present senior generation of physical educators received their doctorates in education; thus it is understandable that their orientation has been toward the profession of education rather than the development of a subject field of knowledge. In fact, physical education has the doubtful distinction of being a school subject for which colleges prepare teachers but do not recognize as a subject field, since the typical physical education department is unique in being under the jurisdiction of or closely related to the school or department of education. Some schools or colleges of physical education exist in large universities, and are patterned after the schools or colleges of education.

When a young person planning a high school teaching career begins his college or university degree work with a major, for example, in chemistry, he starts out with freshman chemistry, which has as a prerequisite a course in high school chemistry. He then takes other lower division chemistry courses, to which the first course is prerequisite. In his junior and senior years, he completes an upper division major in chemistry, in order to qualify for the bachelor's degree. This major consists entirely of course content far more advanced than anything he will teach in a high school. Similarly, the student who majors in mathematics must have an upper division major in advanced mathematics, and even his

This article is reprinted with the permission of the author and the publisher.

most elementary freshman course in mathematics will be at an advanced level in comparison with the usual high school mathematics courses. In marked contrast, the student who obtains a bachelor's degree in physical education typically has a major that is evaluated and oriented with respect to what he is to teach in the secondary schools, and how he is to do the teaching or how he is to administer the program. Many physical education major programs, for example, do not even require a course in exercise physiology.

Actually, it is both possible and practical to offer a degree with an academic major in the subject field of physical education, and several universities actually have such a degree. If the person obtaining this degree plans to teach in the schools, he supplements the academic major with the necessary courses in methods and other professional topics. Academic vs. professional is not an issue of having either one or the other, since the two are not mutually exclusive. However, the present discussion is not concerned with the merits of one or the other or the nature of the best combination. Rather, it is concerned with defining, at least in a general way, the field of knowledge that constitutes the academic discipline of physical education in the college degree program.

An academic discipline is an organized body of knowledge collectively embraced in a formal course of learning. The acquisition of such knowledge is assumed to be an adequate and worthy objective as such, without any demonstration or requirement of practical application. The content is theoretical and scholarly as distinguished from technical and professional. (This statement is a synthesis of the appropriate definitions found in several lexicons, and is probably acceptable to most college faculties.)

There is indeed a scholarly field of knowledge basic to physical education. It is constituted of certain portions of such diverse fields as anatomy, physics and physiology, cultural anthropology, history and sociology, as well as psychology. The focus of attention is on the study of man as an individual, engaging in the motor performances required by his daily life and in other motor performances yielding aesthetic values or serving as expressions of his physical and competitive nature, accepting challenges of his capability in pitting himself against a hostile environment, and participating in the leisure time activities that have become of increasing importance in our culture. However, a person could be by ordinary standards well educated in the traditional fields listed above, and yet be quite ignorant with respect to comprehensive and integrated knowledge of the motor behavior and capabilities of man. The areas within these fields that are vital to physical education receive haphazard and peripheral treatment, rather than systematic development, since the focus of attention is directed elsewhere.

Thus, the academic discipline under consideration cannot be synthesized by a curriculum composed of carefully selected courses from departments listed under A, H, P, and S in a university catalog. True, the student who would master the field of knowledge must first be grounded in general courses in anatomy, physiology, physics, and certain of the behavioral and social sciences. But upper division courses need to be specialized, or else the development of the subject field will be haphazard, incomplete, and ineffective. Twenty-four semester units, in fact, may well be insufficient to cover adequately the available body of knowledge. The areas to be covered include kinesiology and body mechanics; the physiology of exercise, training, and environment; neuromotor coordination, the kinesthetic senses, motor learning, and transfer; emotional and personality factors in physical performance; the relation of all these to human development, the functional status of the individual and his ability to engage in motor activity. They also include the role of athletics, dance, and other physical activities in the culture (both historic and contemporary) and in primitive as well as "advanced" societies. Consideration of the relation of these activities to the emotional and physical health and aesthetic development of the individual constitutes an application of the field of knowledge, but may well be presented and integrated with it, provided that priority is given to the basic knowledge rather than its application to health.

This field of study, considered as an academic discipline, does not consist of the *application* of the disciplines of anthropology, physiology, psychology, and the like to the study of physical activity. On the contrary, it has to do with the study, as a discipline, of certain aspects of anatomy, anthropology, physiology, psychology, and other appropriate fields. The student who majors in this cross-disciplinary field of knowledge will not be a physiologist or a psychologist or an anthropologist, since there has necessarily been a restriction in breadth of study within each of the traditional fields. Moreover, the emphasis must frequently be placed on special areas within each of these fields; areas that receive little attention in the existing courses. There is far more material in any of these disciplines than can be included in the usual courses that constitute the major in anthropology, physiology, psychology, etc.

This is comparable to the situation in a number of the disciplines. A biochemist, for example, is necessarily deficient in his breadth of training as a chemist, and he is also necessarily narrow as a biologist. Nevertheless, he is a more competent biochemist than is a chemist or a biologist.

Special hazards and special responsibilities are connected with the introduction of any new field of study. In a major that is made up of courses
in a cross-disciplinary department, there is a danger that normal academic
standards of depth may be relaxed. For example, an upper division course
in exercise physiology will not be respected, and in fact will not ordinarily
be authorized in a college of exceptionally high standards, unless a
thorough elementary course in human or mammalian physiology is required as a prerequisite. This reasoning holds for all upper division courses
in any major that is accepted as a discipline in such a college.

Problems certainly occur in delimiting the field of knowledge outlined
above. The development of personal skill in motor performance is without question a worthy objective in itself. But it should not be confused
with the academic field of knowledge. Similarly, technical competence
in measuring a chemical reaction, or computational skill in mathematics,
are not components of the corresponding fields of knowledge. Learning
the rules and strategy of sports may well be intellectual, but it is highly
doubtful if a course on rules and strategy can be justified as a major
component of an academic field of knowledge at the upper division college or university level. There simply is not enough time for such specifics within the undergraduate years.

One may well raise such questions as where, for instance, is the borderline between a field such as physiology and the field of physical
education? No simple definitive statement is possible, but it is not difficult to show examples that illustrate the region of demarcation. The
existence of oxygen debt is physiology; the role of oxygen debt in various physical performances is physical education. We do not know why
a muscle becomes stronger when it is exercised repeatedly. The ferreting
out of the causal mechanism of this phenomenon can be considered a
problem in physiology, although the explanation, when available, will
be appropriate for inclusion in a physical education course. On the
other hand, the derivation of laws governing the quantitative relation
between an increase in strength and the amount, duration, and frequency
of muscle forces exerted in training is surely more physical education than
physiology. Determination of the intimate biochemical changes in a muscle during fatigue would seem to be a problem in physiology, although
of direct interest to physical education. Here again, the quantification of
relationships and the theoretical explanation of their pattern as observed
in the intact human organism is more physical education than physiology.
This is not mere application—it only becomes application when such laws
are applied to practical problems. The physiology of athletic training is
not really application of physiology—rather it *is* physiology, of the sort

that is part of the academic discipline of physical education, and only becomes applied when it is actually applied to practical problems. Unfortunately, in this particular area, what is called "physiology of training" consists to a large extent of over-generalized and speculative attempts to apply the incomplete and fragmentary fundamental knowledge currently available. It is to be hoped that this is but a temporary situation.

The study of the heart as an organ is physiology, whereas determining the quantitative role of heart action as a limiting factor in physical performance in normal individuals is perhaps more physical education than physiology. (Certainly the physiology textbooks consider such limitation chiefly with respect to the diseased rather than the normal and physically gifted individuals.) Thus quantitative elucidation of the role of such variables in causing individual differences in performance in the normal range of individuals is of particular concern to physical education but evidently of little interest to physiology. (All of these examples are, of course, borderline by intent.)

Textbooks on exercise physiology are written for physical education courses. Much of the research they describe was done by physiologists. On the other hand, a standard textbook on physiology written for physiologists may not even have a chapter on exercise, and if it does, the treatment is notably incomplete. Similar examples are to be found in the field of anatomy. Textbooks on psychology have at best a sparse treatment of such topics as reaction time, the kinesthetic sense, and motor performance. These are not matters of fundamental interest to present-day psychologists, although they did occupy a position of importance in the first two decades of the present century. Even though anthropologists have long been aware of the role of physical games and sports in all cultures, one cannot find any comprehensive treatment of the topic in anthropology textbooks.

It would be unfair to say that scholars in various fields such as those mentioned above feel that it is unimportant to study man as an individual engaging in physical activity. Rather, the neglect is because this aspect is of peripheral rather than central interest to the scholar in that field. To borrow a figure of speech (not to be taken too literally), anthropology and other fields mentioned approach the study of man longitudinally, whereas physical education proposes a cross-sectional look at man as he engages in physical activity.

It would perhaps not be overly presumptuous to suggest that there is an increasing need for the organization and study of the academic discipline herein called physical education. As each of the traditional fields of knowledge concerning man becomes more specialized, complex, and detailed, it becomes more differentiated from physical education. Physiology of the first half of the century, for example, had a major interest in the total individual as a unit, whereas present-day physiology focuses attention on the biochemistry of cells and subcellular structures. While the importance of mitrochondria in exercise cannot be denied, there is still need to study and understand the macrophenomena of exercise. Furthermore, the purely motor aspects of human behavior need far more attention than they currently receive in the traditional fields of anthropology and psychology. If the academic discipline of physical education did not already exist, there would be a need for it to be invented.

The Domain
of
Physical Education

3 *G.L. Rarick*

Man's curiosity about the unknown is probably as old as man himself. Yet it is only in relatively recent times that man has been able to offer plausible explanations of what he observed in nature. True, scholars in some ancient civilizations sought logical explanations of what they observed. They noted that there was order in the universe. They observed relationships and were concerned with causes and predictions. But it was not until well after the Dark Ages that science as we know it today began to flourish. Systematic observation provided data against which hypotheses could be tested. Theories were developed and scientific laws established. The scientific method was born.

With the advent of the scientific method, knowledge accumulated rapidly. From the very beginning, scientists classified like things together for systematic and detailed study. Thus separate fields of knowledge began to emerge on which scholars concentrated their attention. Some probed the mysteries of the universe, others examined the nature of matter, some studied living things. Each in his own field sought to extend the scope of knowledge. Knowledge thus gained has become part of our cultural heritage, passed from generation to generation in formal courses of study, each dealing with a closely related body of knowledge. Thus we have come to recognize segments of knowledge as disciplines.

As knowledge and technical skill advanced, new disciplines began to emerge. Today any first-class American university will offer an imposing list of courses in from seventy-five to a hundred fields of study. The last two decades have witnessed a marked increase in the number of fields of study, each with its own courses. What, then, does constitute the domain of a discipline? Fifty years ago the answer would have been relatively simple. Today it is highly complex except for the longstanding disciplines. We have come to realize that even though we live in an age of specialization, it is difficult to isolate one branch of knowledge from

---

This article is reprinted with the permission of the author and the publisher.

another. This is true even for such well-established disciplines as physics and chemistry. On the surface it would seem that the lines here are neatly drawn. Yet there is some overlap, for the chemist must be informed about the intimate structure of matter, and the physicist must be informed about the transformations which matter undergoes. In fact today every self-respecting chemistry department offers at least one course in physical chemistry.

How have new disciplines emerged, and how have they been able to stake out their respective domains? Most often this has been done by developing a clearly defined segment of knowledge from an already existing discipline. Such, for example, occurred in microbiology, molecular biology, and, in the early days, botany and zoology. Each owed its origin to biology—the parent. Some disciplines of relatively long standing came into being without any apparent break from a parent discipline, such as astronomy, anthropology, psychology, and physiology.

Other fields have the dubious distinction of just now being on the threshold of becoming disciplines. For example, a brief commentary in a recent issue of *Science* points out that professors of computer science are sometimes asked whether there is a computer science, and if so, what it is. According to these professors, it is a science which studies computers, investigating them with the same intensity that others have studied natural phenomena, using the intellectual curiosity which is characteristic of all scientific inquiry. It is pointed out that while computers themselves belong to engineering and hence have a professional orientation, there is a difference between the study of computers and the application of the resulting knowledge (Newell, Perlis, & Simon, 1967). In a sense this is the problem facing physical education today: the professional as against the disciplinary orientation.

In many quarters there has been a genuine concern about overspecialization and a recognition of the need for a synthesis of knowledge. Proponents of this viewpoint hold that students and scientists must view natural phenomena not in isolation, but in relation to other areas of inquiry and to the world at large. This has resulted not infrequently in a merger of disciplines, a breakdown of traditional disciplinary boundaries. We now see broad areas of study, such as geophysics, biochemistry, medical genetics, and medical physics. Similarly, the trend toward interdisciplinary research is gaining momentum rapidly. With this trend, the traditional concept of a discipline may have to be abandoned.

Physical education today is generally identified as a profession in much the same way as engineering, law, and medicine are. Just as Webster defines medicine as "the science or art concerned with prevention, cure or alleviation of disease," physical education is defined as "education in its application to the development and care of the body, especially with reference to instruction in hygiene and systematic exercise." In both, the major emphasis is on application of knowledge rather than on scholarship. How the knowledge is used is of little concern to a discipline. As Henry points out, the content of a discipline is "theoretical and scholarly as distinguished from technical and professional." (Henry, 1964). Over the years this has not been our orientation in physical education. We have for the most part been doers, not thinkers.

It is nevertheless evident that physical education has within its scope a body of knowledge which is not the concern of any other academic discipline. It is equally clear that there is much that is borderline (handled in part by other disciplines). Most certainly human movement is a legitimate field of study and research. We have only just begun to explore it. There is need for a well-organized body of knowledge about how and why the human body moves, how simple and complex motor skills are acquired and executed, and how the effects (physical, psychological, and emotional) of physical activity may be immediate or lasting.

The question is sometimes raised: Is one justified in including the execution of a motor skill in and of itself as an integral part of a discipline? The mechanics of the skill can be observed and studied, the physiological responses monitored, the feeling states noted. These are areas of legitimate study and research. On the other hand, do we need to clarify for ourselves the level of cognition that is required in learning and executing semi-automatic motor skills? Perhaps we need to ask what level of insight and of understanding is required in a behavioral response in order for it to qualify as a part of an academic discipline. Can we justify as a part of our discipline behavioral responses which are for the most part automatically controlled even though there is conscious direction of certain aspects of the movement and interpretative and affective controls which give to the movement refinement, meaning, and beauty?

All would agree that physical education is concerned essentially with exercise, active games, sports, athletics, gymnastics, and dance. Yet one would be hard pressed to build a case to support this categorization as a logical framework within which to develop concepts, hypotheses, theories, and laws. Reference to the organizational framework of a long-established discipline might be useful here. The classical organizational pattern of physics is straightforward and logical. Its focus is on matter and energy. It is developed around core ideas, theories, and laws, neatly categorized into five distinct areas: namely, mechanics, heat, light, sound, and electricity. This provides a systematic approach in the search for orderliness in nature.

Physical education needs to come of age. As yet there is no agreement as to its focus. Nor does it have a clearly defined body of knowledge or scope of inquiry. Physical education does, however, have a focus: namely, human movement (i.e., bodily movements in sports, active games, gymnastics, and dance) and its correlates. This aspect of man's experience is our domain. No other discipline explores it. Thus we may state the following:

1. Physical education as a discipline is concerned with the mechanics of human movement, with the mode of acquisition and control of movement patterns, and with the psychological factors affecting movement responses.

2. Physical education is concerned with the physiology of man under the stresses of exercise, sports, and dance and with the immediate and lasting effects of physical activity.

3. The historical and cultural aspects of physical education and dance occupy a prominent place in our discipline. The roles of sports and dance in the cultures which have preceded ours and in our own culture need to be fully explored.

4. Lastly, in physical education we are aware that man does not function alone. Individual and group interactions in games, sports, and dance are an important area, one which needs our attention. As yet we have no rationale for explaining the diversified behavior patterns of individuals and groups as either participants or spectators.

We have a considerable body of knowledge to draw upon. However it is widely scattered and at the moment not well-structured. An immediate need is to bring order out of chaos. If, in fact, we are serious in our belief that there is an identifiable body of knowledge which belongs to what we call physical education, we need to begin at once to build the general framework for structuring this body of knowledge. With this accomplished, we can perhaps more clearly pinpoint the future direction of our research and other scholarly efforts.

References

Henry, F.M. Physical education: An academic discipline. *Journal of Health, Physical Education and Recreation,* 1964, **35**, 32-33.

Newell, A., Perlis, A.J., & Simon, H.A. Computer Science. *Science,* September 1967, **157**, 1373-1374.

The Emergence of the Academic Discipline of Physical Education in the United States

4

R.J. Park

A discussion of the historical development of the phrase "academic discipline of physical education" necessitates some clarification. Of the several standard dictionary definitions of *discipline,* the one which appears most suitable is "a field of study." *Academic* is usually associated with theoretical and scholarly, as opposed to technical and vocational, areas of study. *Physical education* is a term for which it has become increasingly difficult to find an exact and broadly accepted definition. "Instruction in sports, exercises, and hygiene, especially as part of a school or college program"—the definition offered by most contemporary dictionaries—falls far short of describing what modern physical education is all abou

In their attempts to clarify the nature of physical education as an academic discipline, some authors have described what *established* disciplines are concerned with. Although a considerable variety of opinion exists, most writers agree that, at the least, established disciplines have: (a) identified a pool of significant and related questions which form the focus of their investigations, and (b) a significant body of knowledge to draw upon when attempting to answer these questions. Physical education, many contend, is still in the process of defining its questions, establishing the framework for structuring its body of knowledge, and determining the scope of its inquiry. What is the "body of knowledge?" What are the fundamental disciplines which today constitute the discipline called "physical education?" As of Spring 1980, there were 10 AAHPERD[1] National Association for Sport and Physical Educa-

---

[1] There have been seven official titles of the professional organization: Association for the Advancement of Physical Education, 1885; American Association for the Advancement of Physical Education, 1886-1902; American Physical Education Association, 1903-1937; American Association for Health and Physical Education, 1937-1938; American Association for Health, Physical Education and Recreation, 1938-1974; American Alliance for Health, Physical Education and Recreation, 1974-1979; American Alliance for Health, Physical Education, Recreation and Dance, 1979- (the present).

tion Academies: Exercise Physiology, History, Kinesiology, Motor Development, Psychology, Sociology, Philosophy, Adapted, Sport Art, Curriculum. The first six of these reflect the general areas set forth by the Big Ten Body of Knowledge Project in Physical Education in 1965 (McCristal, 1975; Zeigler & McCristal, 1967).

Two important points must be mentioned in connection with efforts to trace the emergence of an academic discipline of physical education. The first is the fact that professional physical education has traditionally called upon quite diverse fields of study for both its content and its methods of inquiry. This has led some commentators to maintain that since physical education has no methodology of its own, its claim to status as a discipline is seriously impaired. While it must be recognized that one of the hallmarks of a discipline is the existence of a pool of significant and related questions, it is not necessary that all researchers attack these questions with the same *methodology.* The only subject which relies upon a single unitary methodology is pure mathematics (Best, 1978); all others, to a greater or lesser degree, utilize not only the methodologies but parts of the *content* of other disciplines (e.g. biochemistry, anthropology, physiology).

The second point relates to the explosion of knowledge within each of the academic areas which comprise modern physical education. Some individuals argue that physical education has become so fragmented, colleagues in one area (e.g. motor learning, sport sociology, exercise physiology, biomechanics, or sport history) can neither understand nor appreciate the research interests and/or efforts of others. The rapidly growing sophistication within each of the "subdisciplines" is making it difficult for physical educators to achieve both the needed depth and the desired scope in their field. Efforts to address this problem have been made. The best-known have centered about the issue of whether physical education is, or should be, *interdisciplinary* or *cross-disciplinary* in nature (see chapters 1 and 2), or various combinations of these two positions.

There is one other point which deserves mention. This is the matter of the *disciplinary* versus the *professional* orientation, sometimes referred to as the theoretical/research versus the practical/applied issue. Most, but not all, commentators agree that both orientations are important, but on questions of where emphases should be placed and what the relationships between the two should be, there has been, and still is, a good deal of disagreement (see chapter 1). From 1885 to the present, American physical education has directed the majority of its efforts to the professional orientation. During the last two decades, however, there has been increasing criticism of what many believe has been an excessive preoccupation with the practical/applied approach, to the detriment of scholarly/research endeavors, and there is a growing concern that many individuals interested in research and scholarship are affiliating more with the "parent-disciplines" than with physical education.

Insofar as physical education draws upon a variety of other disciplines for both content and methodology, some familiarity with the history of these contributory disciplines is important. Obviously, it would be impossible to provide more than the briefest outline here. However, a few observations should help to illustrate the evolution of physical education as an academic discipline.

From Classical Antiquity to the 19th Century

Long before the famous Greek historians Heroditus (ca. 484-425 B.C.) and Thucydides (ca. 460-400 B.C.) began to record events of the past, people had been interested in "what one age finds worthy of note in another."* Homer's epic poems *The Illiad* and *The Odyssey* gave to athletic events a place of considerable importance. Pausanias included accounts of the origins of the major pan-Hellenic festivals in his *Description of Greece,* written in the 2nd century A.D. Over the millenia, there have been scores of works which devoted attention to the history of games, athletics, therapeutic exercise, and/or physical education. Joseph Strutt's *Sports and Pastimes of the People of England* anticipated the 20th century interest of sports historians and sociologists in observing that sport might be an aid in attempts "to form a just estimation of the character of any particular people" (Strutt, 1801/1810). In recent decades, considerable interest has been given to investigating ways in which play, games, and sport are reflections of and/or commentaries on culture (Loy, 1980; Schwartzman, 1978).

Philosophy, from the Greek *philos* (loving) and *sophia* (wisdom), has also been of enduring interest. The works of Plato and Aristotle are remarkable for their philosophical as well as political and literary qualities. Their theories of ethics, aesthetics, politics, and knowledge have been of profound influence to Western thought for 25 centuries. Many philosophers have devoted attention to such matters as the mind/body dilemma, ways of knowing, aesthetics, and ethics by discussing questions which revolve around physical education. Among them, Locke in the 17th century, Rousseau, Kant, and Schiller in the 18th century, and Dewey, Santayana and Whitehead in the 20th century are worthy of note (Harper, Miller, Park, & Davis, 1977).

Although it would scarcely be correct to claim that a "discipline of physical education" has existed since 500 B.C., it can be argued that the outlines of both the field and the discipline are located in classical antiquity. According to the tradition of Hippocrates (ca. 460-360 B.C.), the *body,* the primary object of the physician's concern, was to be studied as one would study any other natural object, and an exact regimen of health for each person could be determined "if it were possible to discover for each individual a due proportion of food to exercise, with no inaccuracy either of excess or defect" (Hippocrates, trans. 1967, p. 229). Among Hippocrates' important observations was that of the relationship of exercise and fatigue, although an exact scientific understanding of the physiological and chemical processes would have to await the improved instrumentation and experimental techniques of the 19th and 20th centuries.

Hippocrates' concern with *physis* (body) rather than *psyche* (soul) was criticized by the greatest of all Greek philosophers, Plato (427-347 B.C.), who believed the individual must be regarded as a whole. His voluminous writings contain many observations on the value of physical education, both for the individual and for society. Plato's opinions regarding the role of *exercise* in growth and development, *play* in the formation of proper habits, and the *social benefits* of a fit population could be considered distant antecedents of those aspects of motor development, social psychology and sociology which are of concern to modern physical education. Defense of one's city-state constituted the primary basis of the "social good" in Plato's day, and it is largely for this reason that he and his contemporaries, Socrates and Aristotle, criticized *athletics,* which aimed at the production of victory in a specialized contest, rather than at the balanced development of the entire body: it was all-around, harmonious development, not a specialized athletic skill, which the citizen-soldier and the socially responsible man was to attain (Plato, trans. 1967; Plato, trans. 1969).

Plato's pupil Aristotle (384-322 B.C.) shared his mentor's views concerning the importance of physical education. He was extremely interested in all scientific phenomena, and considered *gymnastics* (in antiquity the term meant something akin to modern conceptions of physical education) to be a complete science: one which sought to learn which exercises are best for each individual and what types of training would be best for the majority of men. His *Movement of Animals* and *Progression of Animals,* albeit lacking in experimental evidence, contain descriptions of phenomena which still form the basis of kinesiology: flexion/extension, stabilization, action/reaction, resistence, center of gravity/base of support, etc. His ideas anticipated the mechanics of the lever, the transformation of rotatory to linear motion, and Newton's laws of motion. Aristotle also made a distinction between *gymnasts* (those who understand the science of exercise) and *paedotribes* (those whose work is limited to the practical, often uninformed, application of training techniques) (Aristotle, trans. 1968; Aristotle, trans. 1978). A similar distinction was made by Claudius Galen (ca. 130-200 A.D.), who was probably the most famous physician and authority on athletic training in the Greco-Roman world. Galen drew from the best of all medical knowledge of his day, adding to it his own vast experience with both medicine and athletics. Although Galen's knowledge of physiology, like that of every researcher until the 19th century, had to be largely speculative (he was, for example, intrigued by the relationship of exercise to heat production), his anatomical descriptions were remarkably advanced (Green, 1951).

The Middle Ages offered little encouragement to the systematic study of nature, and it is precisely *systematic* investigation which is the basis of the modern scientific attitude. According to Medieval belief, knowledge was supposed to agree with the teachings of the Church, considered supreme in all spiritual matters, or with Aristotle, who was considered the authority on nature. With the beginning of the Renaissance in the 15th century, there was a renewed interest in the writings of classical antiquity and in learning about the world of nature. The detailed anatomical drawings of Leonardo da Vinci (1452-1519) were based upon knowledge gained through dissections. Galileo's (1564-1642) discoveries were important to emerging studies of the mechanics of human motion and circulation. Vasalius' *De Humani Corpus Fabrica (The Structure of the Human Body),* published in 1543, opened a new era in anatomy and helped overturn Galenic theory. In 1628, William Harvey's *De Motu Cordis (On the Motion of the Heart)* established the theory that the blood *circulated* through the body, a discovery of the utmost importance to physiology. Closely tied with the concept of circulation is that of respiration. In the mid-1600s, John Mayow demonstrated that aerated blood changes appearance and that breathing involves an exchange of gases. It was in the 17th century, the so-called "Age of Scientific Experimentation," that the microscope was improved. The vastly improved instrumentation in the 19th century made possible much more sophisticated advances in physiological research (Castiglione, 1951; Foster, 1901/1970; Park, 1976).

The 17th century was also important in fostering embryonic theories of developmental play and perceptual-motor learning. The Moravian theologian and educator Jan Comenius (1592-1670) advocated the psychological and sociological benefits of play, and held that children should have "daily exercises and amusements." The English philosopher John

Locke (1623-1704) denied the existence of innate ideas and insisted that sense-experience and reflection upon sensible data formed the basis of knowledge. A trained physician, his *Some Thoughts Concerning Education* (1693) opens with one of the most famous declarations in the history of physical education: *mens sana en corpore sano* (a sound mind in a sound body). Locke also saw that in order for an activity to be re-creative, individuals must engage in it as a matter of their own free choice—an idea which has come to occupy a central position with some 20th century psychologists and philosophers of play. In the 18th century, Jean Jacques Rousseau's *Emile* (1762) expanded the concept that play could be an important cognitive, developmental, motor-skill activity, and provided a surprisingly modern concept of the relationship of sensory input to motor output. His ideas anticipated the early 20th century theories of "natural" activities and "The New Physical Education" advocated by Thomas Denison Wood, Clark W. Hetherington and others (Aires, 1962; Gerber, 1971).

In the late 1700s, the English anatomist and surgeon John Hunter described muscular function in great detail, emphasizing the value of observation and experiments based on *live* subjects rather than cadavers. Galvini described the electrical potentials of nerve and muscle in 1791. These and similar discoveries were of the utmost importance to the future of kinesiology, as well as to exercise physiology. During the 19th century, science made an enormous leap forward, prompting a number of discoveries which would prove to be of major importance to the discipline of physical education. Duchenne investigated the effect of electrical stimulation on muscles, writing *Physiologie des Mouvements* in 1865. Du Bois-Reymond and Marey illuminated the concepts of electrical charges, motor force contraction and heat production in muscle fibers, opening the way for the work of Hill and Meyerhof on the role of carbohydrates and lactic acid formation in muscular work in the 1920s, and the work of Margaria Dill and others in the 1930s. The function of the liver in storing carbohydrate, the demonstration that the *cell* was the site of metabolism and energy exchange (as well as the foundation for integrative behavior), and the relationship of chemistry to physiology are all products of 19th century scientific investigations. The role of oxygenated blood in the process of respiration, which had been brilliantly sketched by Lavoisier's researches in 1777, was expanded in the 1850s by the work of Mayer. In 1872, Pflüger ascertained that even slight differences in pressure permitted a rapid transfer of oxygen across cellular membranes. Advances in the study of kinesiology and biomechanics were further enhanced in the 1880s by the work of Eadweard Muybridge, who devised a means for taking a controlled sequence of photographs of animals and men in motion (Castiglione, 1941; Coleman, 1977; Foster, 1901/1970).

Discoveries during the second half of the 19th century also had an impact on psychology, which for centuries had been considered a branch of philosophy (metaphysics). In 1830, Charles Bell specified in his book *The Nervous System of the Human Body,* that the ventral roots of the spinal cord were composed of motor nerves whereas the dorsal roots and spinal gaglia were composed of sensory nerve fiber, a discovery which enabled subsequent psychological theories to present mental life as a stimulus-response relationship in place of the traditional theory of "mental faculties." Von Helmholtz's studies of the speed of neural conduction from 1856 to 1866 opened the way for studies of "reaction time." By the 1870s, laboratory experimentation had begun to replace speculation and inference, and improved instrumentation further enabled those who sought to locate a physiological basis for mental functioning to pursue their research (Coleman, 1977; Rosen, 1959; Wolman, 1960).

Sociology also evolved as a formalized discipline in the last decades of the 19th century. In *Cours de philosophie positive,* August Comte declared sociology to be the penultimate science. Emile Durkheim argued that social phenomena should be analyzed in terms of the *functions* they serve in maintaining the social order. Max Weber maintained that the context for socially relevant behavior was the *institutional structure* of society. In recent years, the study of sport as a social institution, and of the functions of sport in reflecting and maintaining the complex structure of modern society, has received attention from sociologists, social psychologists, and physical educators. Karl Groos' monumental works *The Play of Animals* (1898) and *The Play of Man* (1901) emphasized the instinct-practice theory and set the stage for later elaborations of the functional theory of play. Ethnologists began to compile reports of the spontaneous play of children, and psychologists and educators argued in favor of the importance of play as a developmental activity. The study of the sociocultural meaning of play, games, and sport both within and across cultures recently has again begun to attract the scholarly attention of some anthropologists and physical educators (Becker & Boskoff, 1957; Coleman, 1977; Wolman, 1960).

Physical Education Becomes a Profession: 1885-1929

Interest in health, hygiene, sport, and physical education had been growing in America since the early decades of the 19th century, but it was the founding of the American Association for the Advancement of

Physical Education (AAAPE) in 1885 which provided the much-needed focus for the many disparate efforts. The enormous range of interests which wouid come to be housed under the rubric "physical education" was made evident early in the history of the professional organization, and a persistent problem has been how the conflicting interests and claims of the diverse elements of the field can be resolved and welded into a comprehensive and integrated whole.

At the first convention of the AAAPE, study groups were set up to "improve technical techniques"—which largely meant taking anthropometric measurements—and the first committee appointed was one on statistics and measurements. As early as the 1890s it was possible to discern the broad outlines of what might be called the disciplinary direction of physical education. The program of the 9th Annual Meeting in 1894 is illustrative, for it included sessions and papers dealing with tests and measurements, exercise and cardiovascular function, reaction-time and memory-time, kinesiology, correctives, history, and the educational use of play. The 1899 AAAPE meeting included papers which discussed compulsory physical education, qualification and certification of teachers, the inadvisability of permitting gymnastics to become subordinated to play and games, the establishment of more training schools, and the procurement of textbook materials. (Few texts existed, which obliged professional physical educators to rely upon articles scattered throughout various journals and periodicals.) After several years of discussion, the AAAPE Council voted to establish its own professional journal, and the first issue of the *American Physical Education Review* was published in 1896. The *Review* served for thirty-six years as both the research and professional journal for the physical education association. It was not until 1930 that a separate research journal, *The Research Quarterly*, was established; the *Journal of Health and Physical Education*, established the same year, became the professional journal and centered its efforts on practical and informational items.

The AAAPE Proceedings between 1885 and 1895, and the early issues of the *American Physical Education Review,* reflected the young profession's initial interest in several of the scientific advances which had occurred during the second half of the 19th century; they also pointed to a growing rift in the profession between theoretical/scientific research interests and the demand for immediate practical solutions to the day-to-day problems of teachers, coaches, recreation directors, athletic directors, and others working in the field. Those who sought to establish physical education on a sound scientific basis found ample reason to be concerned as the immediate exigencies of convincing schools to include physical education in the curriculum, preparing teachers, and endeavoring to establish athletics on an educational footing soon consumed a majority of the time and energies of the profession. Edward M. Hartwell, President of the AAAPE (a medical doctor, like many early leaders), opened the 1892 annual meeting with a speech entitled "The Condition and Prospects of Physical Education in the United States." The revolutionary advances of the last 60 years in both physiology and psychology, Hartwell lamented, had been largely ignored by the vast majority of those engaged in physical education; he called upon the membership to place the field on a more scientific footing (AAAPE, 1892).

During the late 1800s and early 1900s, advocates of the German, Swedish, and various indigenous gymnastic systems (especially that designed by Dudley Allen Sargent, M.D., Director of Physical Training at Harvard University) vied with each other over which system was to take precedence in school and college curricula. (In the late 1800s, athletic sport developed largely outside of physical education departments, and different philosophies have, to a considerable extent, undergirded physical education and intercollegiate athletic programs for a century.) At the 1892 AAAPE annual meeting, George Fitz, M.D., of the Lawrence Scientific School at Harvard University, criticized the lack of scientific evidence upon which most of the various claims were based. (The Lawrence Scientific School would gain attention in the 1930s as the famous "Harvard Fatigue Laboratory" at which Margaria, Dill, and others conducted studies on the relationship of oxygen utilization and oxygen debt.) At the 1894 annual meeting, Thomas Denison Wood declared that what was needed was a "science" of physical training, noting that the term "physical education" was so misleading that another must be found. (Wood's observation seems especially prophetic, for in the 1960s and 1970s a growing number of departments have deemed the title "physical education" inappropriate for the nature and scope of their programs and have adopted names like Kinesiological Sciences, Ergonomics and Sports Studies.) A paper at the same 1894 convention entitled "Reaction-Time and Time-Memory in Gymnastic Work" criticized physical training teachers for their failure to learn the experimental laboratory methods of either experimental or clinical psychology (AAAPE, 1892-1894).

Although there was a clear foundation for such criticisms, it would be a distortion of historical fact to suggest that scientific/scholarly progress was not being made. Early issues of the *American Physical Education Review* contain a considerable number of quite respectable studies. For example, Theodore Hough (1902) reported on his work on neuromuscular fatigue at the M.I.T. Physiology Laboratory; C. Ward Crampton's (1905-1907) series of eight articles on the vascular effects of exercise appeared soon after, followed by William Skarstrom's (1908-1909) lengthy series on kinesiology. Fred E. Leonard contributed a number of historical studies of physical education and sport from Greco-Roman to modern times. These formed the basis for his history text, published two decades later (Leonard, 1923). The work of G. Stanley Hall, who founded the Psychology Laboratory at Johns Hopkins University in 1884, along with that of John Dewey and William James, did much to stimulate early 20th century physical educators' interest in questions dealing with developmental play and attendant questions of interest, effort, and the psychology of learning.

Precise measurement and the careful recording of data is an important contributor to the advancement of scientific knowledge. In the late 1800s, Galton's work on heredity and mental intelligence (1889) resulted in one of the most important measures in statistics—the correlation. Anthropometric studies focused upon body measurements and proportions, documenting increases in the size and strength of muscles and body segments. Before long it became apparent that statistical procedures could and should be applied to physiological, psychological, and motor ability investigations. It also became apparent that improved tests and measurements procedures were needed if more sophisticated research was to follow (Beyer, 1901; Boas, 1901).

The 1910s and 1920s saw a marked, and much needed, increase in the number and variety of books devoted to topics of interest and importance to physical education. Many should be viewed as landmarks on the path of the development of the academic discipline. William Skarstrom's *Gymnastic Kinesiology* was published in 1909; Wilbur Bowen's *The Action of Muscles in Bodily Movement and Posture,* which pointed out the interdependence of anatomy, mechanics and therapeutics in study of kinesiology, appeared in 1912. In 1923, Fred Leonard's *A Guide to the History of Physical Education* was published as part of the Lea & Febiger "Physical Education Series." Although there had been earlier works (e.g., Fernand Lagrange's *Physiology of Bodily Exercise,* published in 1889, and George Fitz's *Principles of Physiology and Hygiene,* 1908), it was not until the 1920s that a dramatic increase in textbooks dealing with exercise physiology appeared. *Physiology of Muscular Exercise,* published in 1923 by F.A. Bainbridge of the University of London, included the topics: sources of muscular energy, respiratory changes during exercise, mechanical efficiency of the heart, fatigue, second wind, effects of training, and exercise under emotional stress. Schneider's "A Cardiovascular Rating As A Measure of Physical Fatigue and

Efficiency" was published in the *Journal of the American Medical Association* in 1920. In 1923, A.V. Hill published his classic studies on "oxygen debt," setting forth basic concepts of oxygen utilization and the accumulation of lactic acid (Brown & Kenyon, 1968; Hill & Lupton, 1923).

Physical examinations, posture work, and corrective exercises, all closely related to kinesiology, have been of considerable interest to physical educators for more than a century. In fact, at the turn of the century, the greatest number of textbooks in the field dealt with posture and exercise. Nils Posse's *Special Kinesiology of Educational Gymnastics,* published in 1890, is an early example. Lovett's *Lateral Curvature of the Spine and Round Shoulders,* based on work done in the Anatomical Department of Harvard University and the Scoliosis Clinic of the Boston Children's Hospital, was first published in 1907. Recognition that therapeutic exercise was of concern to both physical education and the emerging field of physical therapy was made clear in Mary McMillan's *Massage and Therapeutic Exercise,* published in 1921. Although once closely allied through their mutual interest in corrective exercises and kinesiology, physical education and physical therapy have emerged over the decades as two distinct fields.

At the beginning of the 20th century, a considerable amount of interest was turned to the socializing and educating potential of play, culminating in the establishment of the Playground Association of America in 1906. This organization fostered an immense number of projects and programs. "A Normal Course in Play," which reflected contemporary views regarding the biological, psychological, social, and cultural theories of play, was outlined in the *Proceedings of the 3rd Annual Congress* (1909): Play was to promote physiological health, develop nervous coordination, establish social morality, develop social responsibility, and teach respect for work. Interest in the social, cultural and psychological aspects of play resulted in the publication of the number of books in the early decades of the 20th century. Clark Hetherington's *A Normal Course in Play,* Joseph Lee's *Play in Education,* and Luther Halsey Gulick's *A Philosophy of Play* are but a few of the scores of books which were written on this subject. Whereas biological, sociological, and psychological considerations predominated, some authors were concerned with more philosophical questions reminiscent of those raised a century earlier in Schiller's *On the Aesthetic Education of Man,* published in 1795.

The years from 1915 to 1930 have been referred to as "a period of growing pains" for physical education (Lee & Bennett, 1960). Numerous organizations (e.g., Camp Directors' Association; Directors of Physical Education in Colleges; Therapeutic Section; Y.M.C.A. Section) affiliated with the American Physical Education Association (APEA). In 1925, the Athletic Research Society (founded in 1907 to study problems in interscholastic and intercollegiate sport) affiliated with the APEA, becoming the Research Section in 1928. The Research Section soon declared its desire to stimulate interest in scientific research among members of the profession, and its secretary C.H. McCloy prepared an article in which he stated that increasing attention to research would do much to transform physical education into a more "mature science," (McCloy, 1929; Park, 1980). In 1927, a widely circulated pamphlet published by the APEA, "The Objectives of the American Physical Education Association," specified that four things were necessary for the continued growth of the profession: (a) more conferences where differences of opinion could be discussed and settled on a *scientific* basis; (b) an adequate standard of undergraduate work; (c) more postgraduate research in the fundamental problems of physical education (specifically, the laws of growth, chemistry of the blood and urine, animal mechanics, physiology of growth, physiology of exercise, psychology of learning, social psychology, character training and administrative problems); (d) the establishment of a *Research Quarterly* through which those interested in scientific/ scholarly research could make the results of their investigations accessible to others.

Efforts to Stimulate Research: 1930-1959

In 1930, the APEA launched its two new publications, the *Journal of Health and Physical Education* (JOHPE), formed by the merger of the *American Physical Education Review* and the *Pentathlon*, and the *Research Quarterly*. Initially, quality articles were difficult to obtain, but research activity among faculty and graduate students expanded during the 1930s, especially in tests and measurements and exercise physiology. R. Tait McKenzie's *Exercise in Education and Medicine,* originally published in 1909, was reissued in 1923 and 1939. McCurdy's *The Physiology of Exercise,* originally published in 1924, was revised in 1928 and again in 1939. Gould and Dye's *Exercise and Its Physiology* was published in 1932. Schneider's *Physiology of Muscular Exercise,* first published in 1933, became a popular textbook and was revised in 1941, and again in 1948 by Peter Karpovich. The publication of kinesiology and corrective textbooks continued, with Bowen's *Applied Anatomy and Kinesiology* enjoying a 5th edition in 1934, and Steindler's *Mechanics*

of Normal and Pathological Locomotion in Man appearing in 1935.
Whereas in the 1920s and early 1930s the interest of physical educators
had centered on *general motor ability,* later studies began to emphasize
the multidimensional nature of motor performance. McCloy's *Measurement of Athletic Power,* published in 1932, and Bovard and Cozens'
Tests and Measurements in Physical Education, published in 1930, were
among the large number of tests and measurement texts which appeared.
Blanch Trilling of the University of Wisconsin aptly summed up the
growing interest in all kinds of testing in the May 1935 *JOHPE:* "If in
the 1880s the profession was already using tests and had statistical evidence of the outcomes of our work, why today do we feel that testing
is new? The answer lies in the changes in the objectives of physical
education. . . .the teacher of today must be skillful. . .with frequency
distributions, normal probability curves, coefficients of correlation, probable errors, standard deviations, and T-scale scores" (pp. 5-7). Trilling also
pointed to another highly significant change which had occurred since
1885. Whereas a teacher in the late 1800s could probably state with
reasonable accuracy the profession's objectives, by 1935 this was far
from an easy task (Trilling, 1935). In the 50 year period, physical education had taken an interest in so many different things that it was becoming
difficult to grasp where the profession was going—and what its central
research questions should be. The APEA affiliated with the National
Education Association in 1937 and became the American Association
for Health and Physical Education (AAHPE); in 1938 the term Recreation was added to the official title. The increasing diversity of interest
which confronted the professional organization, and a suggestion of the
tensions this diversity might cause, was apparent when AAHPER President Frederick W. Cozens asked all members to work together harmoni-
ously and try to learn what others in the profession were doing (Cozens,
1939).

In the 1930s, research in exercise physiology took an important step
forward when D.B. Dill and his associates at the Harvard Fatigue Laboratory extended Hill's work in describing the mechanisms of the removal
of lactic acid (Brown & Kenyon, 1968; Margaria, Edwards, & Dill, 1933).
The immediate and pressing concerns of military defense prompted by
America's entry into World War II resulted in a temporary decline in
research as many of those engaged in such endeavors joined the
armed forces or turned their attention to issues which had a direct bearing on national security. Important investigations did continue, however. Franklin Henry, working at the University of California's Donner Laboratory, continued cardiovascular and endurance

research and engaged in important high altitude studies in the 1940s (Henry, 1946). Henry's (1951) work on the kinetics of oxygen consumption in recovery contributed to the understanding of the metabolic responses to exercise. At the same time, work at the Harvard Fatigue Laboratory focused on the environmental stresses of heat and cold exposure. During the late 1940s and 1950s, the work of Henry and his students in motor learning at the University of California was instrumental in demolishing the older general motor ability theories and replacing them with an understanding that motor skills and large muscle psychomotor abilities are far more specific than previously had been realized (Henry, 1953, 1958; Henry & Rogers, 1960).

It was in the 1940s when interest in motor development studies of children and youth expanded, spurred by the investigations of Harold E. Jones, Nancy Bayley and Anna S. Espenschade of the University of California (Espenschade, 1940; Jones, 1949), and the publication of the widely used text *The Child from Five to Ten* by Gesell and Ilg (1946). The publications by Jones and Espenschade, derived from data collected as part of the California Adolescent Growth study, were of particular importance as they represented the first longitudinal investigation of consequence on the motor development of school age children.

Endeavors to better understand human life in its social context, new discoveries in the fields of psychology and sociology, and an unexpected increase in leisure time during the 1930s, combined to stimulate further publication of books and monographs on the subject of play. A revised edition of *The Theory of Play* (originally published in 1923) was issued in 1937. Particular attention was given to the theory that play was an important form of self-expression. The work also sought to bring order to the multitude of definitions associated with the term. A distinction was made between the older theories which had considered work and play as diametric opposites and the newer interpretations. Play was not to be viewed as an "activity," the authors believed, but as an "attitude of mind which may pervade any given human activity" (Mitchell & Mason, pp. 48-85). (This important distinction would be elaborated in the 1940s and again in the 1970s.) *Homo Ludens: A Study of the Play Element in Culture*, written by the Dutch humanist-historian Johan Huizinga, stimulated renewed interest in the cultural significance of play. In his introduction Huizinga declared: "anthropology and its sister sciences have so far laid too little stress on the concept of play and on the supreme importance to civilization of the play factor" (1938/1950, pp. i-ii). Since the 1950s, Huizinga's interpretation of the nature and significance of play in human culture has been of considerable importance to researchers in physical education.

With the cessation of hostilities in 1945, research activity increased. The Research Section and the Research Council of AAHPER approved the preparation of a monograph designed to help guide graduate students and other investigators with research methods appropriate for their work. This was published as *Research Methods Applied to Health, Physical Education, and Recreation* (1949). It included sections on history, philosophy, anthropometry and body mechanics, experimental kinesiology, physiology laboratory research, factor analysis, statistical prediction, and errors in measurement. Its steering committee pointed out that research methods in physical education had been applied mainly to solving practical problems rather than toward developing fundamental knowledge. Although much progress had been made, it could not be claimed that the field had "reached maturity or stability in the study of its problems by the scientific method" (AAPHER, 1949, p. 3). A second and completely revised edition appeared in 1952, and had gone to 10 printings before it was revised and a third edition published in 1973.

In the late 1940s, three major conferences dealt with facilities, professional preparation, and graduate education. The last is of particular interest to the development of the concept of an academic discipline. The *Report of the National Conference on Graduate Study in Health, Physical Education and Recreation,* January 1950, set forth three major purposes of graduate work: (a) prepare better teachers, leaders, administrators, and creative scholars; (b) improve the quality of research and its use; (c) develop specialists in particular lines of endeavor. Nine areas of concentration were suggested: history and philosophy, sociology, psychology, aesthetics (i.e., dance), tools of research, physical growth and development, analysis of body movement, nature of kinesthetic perception, and physiological effects of exercise. Recommendations were also made concerning the necessary quality of faculties, libraries, and laboratories.

Research in health, physical education, and recreation increased in volume during the 1950s; more importantly, it increased in quality. The topic of physical fitness, dramatized by the publication of the results of the Kraus-Weber tests which alleged that European children were more "fit" than American children, received the major attention of the profession. The September 1956, 1957, and 1958 *JOHPER* were devoted entirely to this topic and a number of projects (e.g., the Youth Fitness Test Project; Operation Fitness—USA) were undertaken. The successful orbiting of the Soviet Union's "Sputnik" created not only a scientific but a political and technological furor in the United States.

Physical science and mathematics were elevated to a position of prominence and other studies took steps to assert their scientific and scholarly dimensions. As might be expected, the interest in physical fitness spurred research efforts, especially in physiology of exercise, tests and measurements, and growth and development. In May 1960, the *Research Quarterly* published a supplement entitled "The Contributions of Physical Activity to Human Well-Being" which included papers on the contributions of physical activity to physical health (emphasis on exercise physiology), social development (psychology, sociology, history), skill learning (motor performance, motor learning and measurement), growth (motor development), and rehabilitation (neurophysiological, anatomical and cardiovascular considerations).

Organized Efforts in the 1960s and 1970s

Research areas during the 1960s, especially in exercise physiology and motor learning, were more clearly defined, and refinements in methodology and instrumentation made possible increasingly complex and specialized studies. In exercise physiology, intensive investigations of cardiovascular response to exercise, the effects of training, and strength and endurance showed a steady progression from the macroscopic to the microscopic level, and more attention was devoted to questions of a biochemical nature. In motor learning, researchers investigated increasingly complex psychological and physiological variables related to the learning and performing of motor tasks.

Beginning in the 1950s, H. Harrison Clarke at the University of Oregon initiated a longitudinal investigation of the physical growth and motor performances of boys in the 7-18 year range. The results of this study were published as *Physical and Motor Tests in the Medford Boys' Growth Study* (1971). Robert J. Francis and G. Lawrence Rarick at the University of Wisconsin published the results of their investigation of the motor characteristics of educable mentally retarded children in special classes in the public schools (1959). During the 1960s and the 1970s, Rarick and associates, first at the University of Wisconsin and then at the University of California, continued research on the basic components of motor performance of educable mentally retarded children and the effect of individualized versus group-oriented physical education programs on educable mentally retarded and minimally brain-injured children (Rarick & Broadhead, 1968; Rarick, Dobbins, & Broadhead, 1976).

In the 1960s, and especially after the widespread availability of computer programming, biomechanical analyses greatly extended the kinesiological study of human movement and sports skills. In fact, by the 1970s biomechanical research, like many of the other areas of physical education research, required a multidisciplinary effort. In order to produce sophisticated research in kinesiology and biomechanics today, a researcher must be competent in calculus, physics, human anatomy, engineering, and computer science. In the opening paper of *Kinesiology IV* (1974), by the Committee on Kinesiology of the Physical Education Division of the AAHPER, David L. Kelley of the University of Maryland, pointed out that the traditional undergraduate kinesiology courses needed to be augmented by rigorous studies of a mechanical and mathematical nature, and noted that some of the knowledge and instrumentation currently available through engineering departments might be put to excellent use. Other authors writing for *Kinesiology IV* emphasized the importance of a more profound understanding of neural integration. The detailed papers included more recently in the *International Series on Biomechanics* publications (which have evolved from various International Congresses of Biomechanics) are indicators of the growing importance and sophistication of this area of research. Anne Atwater (1980) has recently discussed the evolution of both kinesiology and biomechanics in the United States, making particular note of the important distinctions which must now be made between the two.

A number of important events aimed at defining physical education as an academic discipline took place in the 1960s. From 1962 to 1965, the American Academy of Physical Education conducted an informal study in an effort to determine what constituted the body of knowledge implied by the term *physical education.* The Academy, the Physical Education Division of the AAHPER, and the Athletic Institute explored the question of "a research design which would permit more systematic analysis of the conceptual dimension of physical education as an area of scholarly study and research" (Metheny, 1966, p. 6). The topic also received considerable attention from the Big Ten Body of Knowledge Symposium Project, which decided that a longitudinal effort should be made to establish the body of knowledge of the field of physical education. By 1966, six areas of specialization had been identified: exercise physiology, biomechanics, motor learning/sports psychology, sociology and sport education, history and philosophy of physical education and sport, and administrative theory in athletics and physical education. However, some hesitancy regarding the appropriateness of the last item was recorded. Small working groups for each of the areas were given the following charge: (a) identify the related disciplines; (b) list in topical form the primary concepts in each related discipline; (c) supplement the primary concepts with any which seem unique to physical education; (d) state the prerequisites to the study of these concepts. This original effort led to a series of six body-of-knowledge symposia (one in each area) designed to "develop and clarify the basic scientific concepts of physical education" and to enrich the graduate programs (Zeigler & McCristal, 1967). Proceedings from each of these conferences were subsequently published by the Athletic Institute. In 1975, an additional symposium was held at the University of Iowa on the topic "Physical Education for the Handicapped: Implications for Research."

Franklin M. Henry's often-quoted and highly influential article "Physical Education—An Academic Discipline" (first delivered at the January 1964 NCPEAM meetings and reprinted in this volume) was published in the September 1964 JOHPER. The author concluded that there was indeed a "scholarly field of knowledge basic to physical education[which] . . .is constituted of certain portions of such diverse fields as anatomy, physics and physiology, cultural anthropology, history and sociology, as well as psychology" (p. 32). This field, Henry stated, was *cross-disciplinary*, as opposed to interdisciplinary. The distinction between these two, further explicated by Henry in his paper "The Academic Discipline of Physical Education" (1978), is an extremely important one and should be read carefully by anyone interested in the discipline of physical education. Recent commentators have cogently argued that the explosion of knowledge within each of the many traditional disciplines from which physical education draws has made it impossible for researchers to keep abreast of all the latest developments. In an effort to help remedy the problem, some individuals have suggested that the academic content of physical education should be grouped into "areas of study" which draw upon related parent disciplines for their subject matter. Those areas most frequently mentioned are: (a) exercise sciences/biodynamics, (b) motor control/motor integration, and (c) sport studies/sociocultural bases of sport and physical education (Lawson & Morford, 1979).

The December 1967 issue of *Quest* was devoted to the theme "The Nature of a Discipline." In this issue, G. Lawrence Rarick observed that the emergence of most acknowledged disciplines had involved "developing a clearly defined segment of knowledge from an already existing discipline" (p. 50). While 50 years ago it would have been relatively simple to identify what constituted the domain of a discipline, by the 1960s the volume of new knowledge, a splintering into new and more specialized disciplinary orientations, and an ensuing realization that in the end it was often difficult to isolate one branch of knowledge from another had often made classification a highly complex matter. If physical education was to become an academic discipline, Rarick noted, its excessive emphasis "on application of knowledge rather than on scholarship" would have to be abandoned (Rarick, 1967, p. 50). It was also in 1967 that the AAHPER National Conference on Graduate Education in Physical Education, Health Education, Recreation Education, Safety Education and Dance defined nine areas of study for the advanced degree. These areas were similar to the current ten NASPE Academies.

The expansion of interest in identifying the "academic discipline" was accompanied by a rising interest in research during the 1960s and 1970s, and by an increase in the number of journals devoted to specialized scholarship. Warren R. Johnson, editor of *Science and Medicine of Exercise and Sports,* aptly summed up the situation at the beginning of the 1960s:

> Slowly, as carefully gathered data has accumulated, a mosaic of the entire field of exercise and sports seems to be forming. At present, the amount of work that has been done which throws light upon various phenomena related to exercise and sports is impressive and encouraging. But it is also bewildering. Research workers have of course published their findings in their own journals, with the result that information pertinent to exercise and sports is scattered through a vast literature ranging from the anthropological, chemical, physiological, and nutritional to the psychological, physical educational, and medical. The problem is further complicated by the diversity of technical language found in this literature. Serious students of the subject are confronted with a truly formidable problem if they address themselves to the task of achieving a reasonable grasp of the entire research field associated with exercise and sport. (1960, p. xiv)

Two international publications reflect the directions which scholarly/ research interests in physical education would follow in the 1960s and 1970s. *International Research in Sport and Physical Education* (1964), edited on behalf of the International Council of Sport and Physical Education of the United Nations Educational, Scientific and Cultural Organization (UNESCO), included papers on cultural anthropology, psychology, sociology, physique, body composition and growth, physiology of exercise, fitness, clinical sports medicine, pharmacology, sports surgery, rehabilitation, and school health. The two-volume report of the 1976 Pre-Olympic International Congress of Physical Activity Sciences, also sponsored by UNESCO, included papers on growth and development; aging; exercise physiology (including biomechanical and pharmacological concerns); sociology and political science; social, behavioral and humanistic psychology; anthropology; history; philosophy, and aesthetics (Landry & Orban, 1978). The research areas enumerated by the Big Ten Body of Knowledge Project and the other conferences of the 1960s are now represented by at least one national and/or international scholarly organization, each holding its own convention, and often publishing its own journal or journals (e.g., *Medicine and Science in Sport, Arbeitsphysiologie, Journal of Motor Behavior, International Review of Sport Sociology, Journal of Sport History, Stadion, Journal of Sport Psychology, Journal of Biomechanics, International Journal of Sport Psychology, Journal of Applied Physiology).* Many scholars located in departments of physical education publish their research in journals of the so-called "parent-disciplines." As necessary and beneficial as it has been for researchers in physical education to go to the parent-disciplines to develop and refine their scholarly techniques, there are some misgivings that these individuals are likely to remain more allied with the parent-discipline than with the broad field of physical education. Indeed, there is substantial reason for concern that such specialization may actually impede the development of an academic discipline of physical education.

Anyone who would search the professional literature from 1896 through the 1970s cannot fail to be impressed by the increasing volume and sophistication of the research and the scholarship in several areas which today comprise the discipline. This trend is exemplified by the research in exercise physiology undertaken by Buskirk at Pennsylvania State University, Gollnick at Washington State University, Faulkner at the University of Michigan, and Tipton at the University of Iowa. Also, in the 1970s, Brooks and others conducted important studies on the metabolic fates of lactic acid during recovery from heavy exercise (Brooks, Brauner, & Cassens, 1973; Brooks, Hittelman, Faulkner, & Beyer, 1971; Segal & Brooks, 1979). These and related studies of exercise and recovery cast doubt upon classical theories of "the O_2 debt."

During the past decade, research studies and theoretical papers have increased markedly in the sociocultural area of the discipline. Except for the pioneering work of Stumpf and Cozens (1947) little attention had been paid to anthropological considerations until the 1970s. The extent of the interest which has recently developed concerning play, games, and sport within and across cultures has been demonstrated by the founding of The Association for the Anthropological Study of Play in 1974. Another indication of the growing interest in examining play, games, and sport in human culture has been the founding of the North American Society for Sport History in 1972, and the establishment of several sport history journals. Since the mid-1970s, historical research in physical education has moved away from chronological, descriptive, and reportorial studies toward an interpretive analysis of historical data within conceptual frameworks. The more frequent themes have included industrialization, urbanization, socioeconomic changes, religion, ethnic pluralism, and "class."

The recent article by Loy (with McPherson and Kenyon) which appeared in the 50th Anniversary Issue of the *Research Quarterly* sums up the present state of research in sport sociology. The authors conclude that although notable advances have been made in the last 25 years, "the sociology of sport has yet to be perceived as a legitimate sub-field . . .owing to factors associated with critical mass, academic status, and ideological orientations" (Loy, 1980, p. 106). The *Journal of Sport Psychology,* established in 1979, is ". . . designed to stimulate and communicate research and theory in an emerging multidisciplinary area of specialization" (Landers, 1979, p. 2). Regardless of their academic roots (e.g., social, clinical, experimental, and physiological psychology, child development, physical education, sociology, cultural anthropology), Landers contends that those investigators to which the *Journal of Sport Psychology* is addressed share an interest in similar questions pertaining to sport. Helen B. Schwartzman of the Institute for Juvenile Research, University of Chicago, has sought "to illustrate how the discipline of anthropology provides students of play with a broadened perspective on their topic and also to suggest that the study of play provides anthopologists with a new perspective on their discipline" (Schwartzman, 1978, p. 325). Such recent efforts fit most compatibly with the philosophy of the *cross-disciplinary* approach explicated by Henry and others.

In the final analysis, it may be philosophy, man's oldest scholarly concern, which will provide the key to achieving a new synthesis and help to clarify the uniqueness of physical education as an academic discipline. Although it is by no means the only field of study which does so, philosophy's emphasis on *reasons* rather than *causes,* logical rather than experimental methods of substantiation, and its dedication to eliciting presuppositions which lie behind questions, may provide a useful corrective for such limitations as may exist in more dominant modes of modern 20th century thought. The founding of the Philosophic Society for the Study of Sport in 1972 and the publication of the first issue of the *Journal of the Philosophy of Sport* in 1973 are, perhaps, steps in this direction. Certainly, the Greeks of the Age of Pericles would have found the effort admirable.

References

Aires, P. *Centuries of childhood: A social history of family life.* New York: Alfred A. Knopf, 1962.

American Association for the Advancement of Physical Education. *Proceedings of the American Association for the Advancement of Physical Education.* 1885-1895.

American Association for Health, Physical Education and Recreation. *Research methods applied to health, physical education, and recreation.* Washington, DC: AAHPER, 1949.

American Association for Health, Physical Education and Recreation. *Kinesiology IV.* Washington, DC: AAHPER, 1974.

Aristotle. *Movement of animals* (E.S. Forester, Ed. and trans.). Cambridge, MA: Harvard University Press, 1968.

Aristotle. *Politics* (E. Barker, Ed. and trans.). London: Oxford University Press, 1978.

Atwater, A.E. Kinesiology/biomechanics: Perspectives and trends. *Researcu Quarterly,* 1980, **51,** 193-218.

Becker, H. & Boskoff, A. (Eds.). *Modern sociological theory in continuity and change.* New York: Dryden Press, 1957.

Best, D. *Philosophy and human movement.* London: George Allen & Unwin, 1978.

Beyer, H.G. The value to physiology of anthropometric tests and measurements in the form of statistics and their importance to education. *American Physical Education Review,* 1901, **6,** 181-193.

Boas, F. Statistical study of anthropometry. *American Physical Education Review,* 1901, **6,** 174-180.

Brooks, G.A., Brauner, K.E., & Cassens, R.G. Glycogen synthesis and metabolism of lactic acid after exercise. *American Journal of Physiology,* 1973, **224,** 1162-1166.

Brooks, G.A., Hittelman, K.J., Faulkner, J.A., & Beyer, R.E. Temperature, skeletal muscle mitochondrial functions, and oxygen debt. *American Journal of Physiology,* 1971, **220,** 1053-1059.

Brown, R.C. & Kenyon, G.S., (Eds.). *Classical studies on physical activity.* Englewood Cliffs, NJ: Prentice-Hall, 1968.

Castiglione, A. *History of medicine* (E.B. Krumbhaar, trans.). New York: Alfred A. Knopf, 1941.

Clarke, H.H. *Physical and motor tests in the Medford boys' growth study.* Englewood Cliffs, NJ: Prentice-Hall, 1971.

Coleman, W. *Biology in the nineteenth century: Problems of form, function and transformation.* Cambridge: Cambridge University Press, 1977.

Cozens, F.W. A unified organization. *JOHPE,* 1939, **10,** 323-324.

Crampton, C.W. Blood pressure. *American Physical Education Review,* 1905, **10,** 275-283; 1906, **11,** pp. 12-18; 105-120; 199-210; 258-263; 1907, **12,** pp. 41-48; 144-153; 256-271.

Espenschade, A. Motor performance in adolescence including the study of relationships with measures of physical growth and maturity. *Monographs of the Society for Research in Child Development,* 1940, **5,** 1-126.

Foster, M. *Lectures on the history of physiology during the 16th, 17th and 18th centuries.* New York: Dover Publications, 1970. (Originally published, 1901.)

Francis, R.J. & Rarick, G.L. Motor characteristics of the mentally retarded. *American Journal of Mental Deficiency,* 1959, **63,** 792-811.

Galton, F. *Natural inheritance.* London: Macmillan, 1889.

Gerber, E.W. *Innovators and institutions in physical education.* Philadelphia: Lea & Febiger, 1971.

Gessell, A.L. & Ilg, F.L. *The child from five to ten.* New York: Harper, 1946.

Green, R.M. *A translation of Galen's Hygiene.* Springfield, IL: Charles C. Thomas, 1951.

Groos, K. *The play of animals.* New York: D. Appleton, 1898.

Groos, K. *The play of man.* New York: D. Appleton, 1901.

Harper, W.A., Miller, D.M., Park, R.J., & Davis, E.C. *The philosophic process in physical education* (3rd ed.). Philadelphia: Lea & Febiger, 1977.

Henry, F.M. The role of exercise in altitude pain. *American Journal of Physiology,* 1946, **145,** 279-284.

Henry, F.M. Aerobic oxygen consumption and alactic debt in muscular work. *Journal of Applied Physiology,* 1951, **3,** 427-438.

Henry, F.M. Dynamic kinesthetic perception and adjustment. *Research Quarterly,* 1953, **24,** 176-187.

Henry, F.M. Specificity vs. generality in learning motor skills. *Proceedings of the College Physical Education Association,* 1958, **61,** 126-128.

Henry, F.M. Physical education—an academic discipline. *Journal of Health, Physical Education, and Recreation,* 1964, **35**(7), 32-38; 69.

Henry, F.M. The academic discipline of physical education. *Quest,* 1978, **29,** 13-29.

Henry, F.M. & Rogers, D.E. Increased response latency for complicated movements and a "memory drum" theory of neuromotor reaction. *Research Quarterly,* 1960, **31,** 448-458.

Hill, A.V. & Lupton, H. Muscular exercise, lactic acid and the supply and utilization of oxygen. *Quarterly Journal of Medicine,* 1923, **16,** 135-171.

Hippocrates. *Regimen.* (W.H.S. Jones, trans.). Cambridge, MA: Harvard University Press, 1967.

Hough, T. Ergographic studies in muscular soreness. *American Physical Education Review,* 1902, **7**, 1-17.

Huizinga, J. *Homo ludens: A study of the play element in culture.* Boston: Beacon Press, 1950 (Originally published, 1938).

Johnson, W.R. (Ed.). *Science and medicine of exercise and sports.* New York: Harper, 1960.

Jokl, E. & Simon, E. (Eds.). *International research in sport and physical education.* Springfield, IL: Charles C. Thomas, 1964.

Jones, H.E. *Motor performance and growth.* Berkeley: University of California Press, 1949.

Landers, D. Sport psychology today. *Journal of Sport Psychology,* 1979, **1**, 2-3.

Landry, F. & Orban, W.A.R. (Eds.). *Physical activity and human well-being* (2 vols.). Miami: Symposia Specialists, 1978.

Lawson, H.A. & Morford, W.R. The cross-disciplinary structure of kinesiology and sports studies: Distinctions, implications and advantages. *Quest,* 1979, **31**, 222-230.

Lee, M. & Bennett, B. This is our heritage, part 1: 1885-1900—a time of gymnastics and measurement. *Journal of Health, Physical Education, and Recreation,* 1960, **32**(4), 26-33.

Leonard, F.E. *A guide to the history of physical education.* Philadelphia: Lea & Febiger, 1923.

Locke, J. *Some thoughts concerning education.* London: A. & J. Churchhill, 1693.

Loy, J.W. The emergence and development of the sociology of sport as an academic speciality. *Research Quarterly,* 1980, **51**, 91-109.

McCloy, C.H. Methods of research in physical education. *American Physical Education Review,* 1929, **34**, 10-16.

McCristal, K.J. Meanings in the realm of academic disciplines. *The Academy Papers,* 1975, **9**, 2-11.

Margaria, R., Edwards, H.T., & Dill, D.B. The possible mechanisms of contracting and paying the oxygen debt and the role of lactic acid in muscular contraction. *American Journal of Physiology,* 1933, **106**, 689-715.

Metheny, E. The "design" conference. *Journal of Health, Physical Education and Recreation,* 1966, **37**(5), 6.

Mitchell, E.D. & Mason, B.S. *The theory of play.* New York: A.S. Barnes, 1937.

Park, R.J. Concern for health and exercise as expressed in the writings of 18th century physicians and informed laymen (England, France and Switzerland). *Research Quarterly,* 1976, **47**, 756-767.

Park, R.J. *The Research Quarterly* and its antecedents. *Research Quarterly* 1980, **51**, 1-22.

Plato. *The laws* (R.G. Bury, trans). Cambridge, MA: Harvard University Press, 1967.

Plato. *The republic* (P. Shoey, trans.). Cambridge, MA: Harvard University Press, 1969.

Playground Association of America. *Proceedings of the 3rd annual playground congress,* 1909, pp. 92-228.

Rarick, G.L. The domain of physical education as a discipline. *Quest,* 1967, **9**, 49-52.

Rarick, G.L. & Broadhead, G.D. *The effects of individualized versus group oriented physical education programs on selected parameters of the development of educable mentally retarded and minimally brain-injured children.* U.S. Office of Education, Department of Health, Education and Welfare, 1968.

Rarick, G.L., Dobbins, D.A., & Broadhead, G.D. *The motor domain and its correlates in educationally handicapped children.* Englewood Cliffs, NJ: Prentice-Hall, 1976.

Rosen, G. The conservation of energy and the study of metabolism. In C.M. Brooks & P.F. Cranefield, (Eds.). *The historical development of physiological thought.* New York: Hafner, 1959.

Rousseau, J.J. *Emile.* Amsterdam: J. Neaulme, 1762.

Schwartzman, H.G. *Transformations: The anthropology of children's play.* New York: Plenum Press, 1978.

Segal, S.S. & Brooks, G.A. Effects of glycogen depletion and work load on post exercise O_2 consumption and blood lactate. *Journal of Applied Physiology,* 1979, **47**, 514-521.

Skarstrom, W. Kinesiology of the trunk, shoulder and hip applied to gymnastics. *American Physical Education Review,* 1908, **13**, pp. 67-75; 163-167; 253-262; 335-344; 409-419; 442-450; 515-523; 1909, **14**, pp. 17-26; 157-167; 233-243; 390-401.

Strutt, J. *Sports and pastimes of the people of England: Including the rural and domestic recreations, May-games, mummeries, pageants, processions, and pompous spectacles from the earliest period to the present time.* London: T. Bensley, 1810. (Originally published, 1801.)

Stumpf, F. & Cozens, F.W. Some aspects of the role of games, sports and recreational activities in the culture of modern primitive peoples. *Research Quarterly,* 1947, **18**, 198-218.

Trilling, Blanche M. A twenty-five-year perspective on physical education needs. *Journal of Health and Physical Education,* 1935, **6**(5); 3-7; 55-58.

Wolman, B.B. *Contemporary theories and systems in psychology.* New York: Harper, 1960.

Zeigler, E.F. & McCristal, K.J. A history of the Big Ten Body of Knowledge project in physical education. *Quest,* 1967, **9,** 79-84.

PART 2

Physiology of Exercise

For centuries it has been obvious that physical exercise has immediate as well as long-term effects on the individual. Because physical education activities usually result in some form of exercise, the study of exercise physiology has been a central part of the physical education curriculum. Improvements in functional capacity due to exercise training, effects of exercise on growth and development, and the effect of exercise training on minimizing the consequences of degenerative diseases—in short, the health-related aspects of exercise—frequently form the bases upon which programs of physical education are built and maintained. The links between physical education—physiological research, and physiology have been strong, so strong that in fact it is sometimes difficult to discern the boundaries between the disciplines. In general, advances in exercise physiology have followed advances in basic physiology. At times, however, interest in human performance during exercise has been part of or has even led advances in the basic science.

"Exercise physiology" as a subdiscipline is the systematized study of body function during exercise. Because exercise, immediately or ultimately, may affect most body parts, many basic physiologists have good reason to use exercise as a means to study body function. Just as one turns up the volume when considering stereo equipment for purchase, so the physiologist amplifies physiological responses by means of exercise. Exercise is an excellent way to study the body.

The wide range of effects of exercise on the body exacerbates the problem of precisely defining exercise physiology or of locating all the individuals studying it in one department or discipline. For instance, one physiologist may be concerned with the mechanisms of muscle contraction and another with the control of breathing, yet they may work in the same department of physiology. Both could use exercise to study these processes, and thus, each many have more in common with the campus physical education-exercise physiologist than with each other.

So what then is the difference between an "exercise" physiologist and a "proper" physiologist who uses exercise to study physiology? This depends on the placement of the term "exercise." Exercise physiologists use physiology to understand exercise, and their primary interest is to understand human movement. Proper physiologists' main objective is to understand basic body function. Therefore, physiologists ask questions which are influenced by the category of physiology, and the solution to the problems is determined by the scientific method. Both types of scientists can have different motives and yet study similar problems in similar ways.

The previous description of an exercise physiologist involved the phrase "systematized study." It was intended that the reader refer to the scientific method as the "system of study." Moreover, the statement was intended to include others who systematically study exercise. Many coaches, including many contemporary swim coaches, are fine students and practitioners of exercise physiology.

In Europe, but also in the United States, the terms "work physiology" and "ergonomics" are frequently used. Usually, these terms refer to the study of physiological response in industrial labor situations. The terms can also be used as a substitute for "exercise physiology." This is because exercise involves physical work. In Germany, the term "arbeits physiologie" (arbeits meaning work) is used.

As mentioned previously, interest in exercise physiology has at times been at the forefront of advances in basic science. The greatest respiratory physiologist of all time was the 18th century Frenchman Lavosier, who used exercise as a means to study physiology (Grimaux, 1888). Lavosier contributed more to the understanding of metabolism and respiration than anyone will again have the opportunity to contribute. In Germany, during the late 19th century, great strides were made in studying metabolism and nutrition under conditions of rest and exercise. Zuntz and his associates (including Schumburg and Geppert) were particularly important. Tables developed by Zuntz and Schumburg (1901), relating metabolic rate to O_2 consumption, CO_2 production, and amount of carbohydrate and fat used, are essentially the same as those frequently referred to today by respiratory physiologists, exercise physiologists, and nutritionists. In Germany, work in exercise (arbeits) physiology continued and centered at the Max-Planck Institut für Arbeits Physiologie. The Nazi regime and the events of World War II resulted in the emigration of many scientists to the United States; among these were E. Simonsen (University of Minnesota) and B. Balke (University of Wisconsin).

In the early 20th century, F. Benedict and his associates, including E. Cathcart and H. Smith at the Carnegie Nutrition Laboratory in Boston, performed detailed studies on metabolism in people at rest and during steady-rate exercise. The precision, thoroughness, and insightful interpretation of results by the Carnegie Nutrition group is seldom matched today. The works by Benedict and Cathcart (1913) on efficiency of the body during cycling exercise, and the similar work of Smith (1922) on the efficiency of walking should be required reading for all graduate students specializing in exercise physiology.

The giant in the field of exercise physiology is the English physiologist, A. V. Hill. Hill's tremendous understanding of physiology was coupled with a similar stamina for work and the technical capacity for originating experimental devices. Throughout his career, Hill performed detailed studies on the energetics of muscles isolated from small animals. He ever sought, however, to relate those results of detailed studies to the functioning, intact human. Hill and his associates (see Hill, Long, & Lupton, 1924) performed many studies on athletes and other individuals engaged in severe exercise. These studies were performed on both sides of the Atlantic ocean. In 1926, Hill was a visiting lecturer at Cornell University where he studied acceleration in varsity sprinters. His influence was so great that he inspired a nucleus of American scientists who later participated in the development of the Harvard Fatigue Laboratory (Dill, 1967).

The Harvard Fatigue Laboratory, established for the study of exercise and environmental physiology at Harvard University in the late 1920s, became a center for the study of applied physiology in the United States. Moreover, scientists from around the world went to Harvard to work in the Fatigue Laboratory. In the realm of exercise physiology, the Laboratory is perhaps best known for its attempt to understand the metabolic responses to "nonsteady-rate" exercise (Margaria, Edwards, & Dill, 1933). As noted previously, earlier work in Germany and the United States had laid a foundation for understanding the metabolic responses to continuous exercise of moderate in intensity. The problems of understanding the nonsteady-rate metabolism were, and remain, far more difficult. In tackling problems, the Harvard group carried on in the tradition of A. V. Hill. Resolution of these problems has not yet been achieved (see Chapter 7), however, revealing the enormity of the task taken on by the Harvard group. When the Laboratory was dissolved following World War II, its members were dispersed throughout the universities of the United States. Even though the Harvard Fatigue Laboratory no longer existed per se, its seed was scattered upon fertile ground. The result was perhaps a wider and more vigorous proliferation of work in exercise and environmental physiology than if the Laboratory had continued to exist as a discrete entity.

Many other sites for the study of exercise-related problems existed as contemporaries or followed the Harvard Fatigue Laboratory. Of note were departments of physical education and physiology at Springfield College, the University of Iowa, the University of Texas, the University of Oregon, and the University of California. The Laboratory of Physiological Hygiene at the University of Minnesota also deserves special mention for its faculty of internationally distinguished scientists. They and their proteges have continued to produce outstanding work on physiology, nutrition, and health-related aspects of exercise.

In Copenhagen during the early 20th century, A. Krogh established a laboratory for the study of zoological physiology. Although Krogh's range of physiological interests was very wide, he and his associates (J. L. Lindhard, E. H. Christensen, E. Asmussen, and M. Neilsen) became known as exercise physiologists. The contemporary laboratory in Copenhagen is named the Krogh Institute. The long tradition of excellence of physiological investigation in Scandanavia, the deep interest in studying exercise physiology, and the direct links to physical education have resulted in many contributions to understanding human movement.

In the following chapter, "The Emergence of Exercise Physiology in Physical Education," E.R. Buskirk describes the thrust of the development of science and technology in the world today. He portrays the study of exercise physiology in the United States as tied in with the evolution of science as a whole, the structure of support for science and biomedical research, the nation's approach to health and health maintenance, the nation's image in international politics, and the roles of physical education in this milieu. Dr. Buskirk notes that the development of physiological research is similar to that of biomedical science, and thus, he states that if the latter prospers, the former will probably prosper as well. Dr. Buskirk considers it unlikely, however, that exercise science will ever be given special treatment.

Even though exercise has been a means to study physiology, and although the physiological responses to exercise have been a major interest of physical education researchers, exercise physiology has not been, and probably shall not evolve into, a discrete discipline, or even a major branch of physiology. As previously mentioned, several of the early great physiologists were known as exercise physiologists. The current trend in departments of physiology, mostly located in schools on medicine, has moved away from gross mammalian and exercise physiology, and toward cellular physiology and biophysics. As time passes, fewer departments of physiology have an exercise physiologist on the faculty. Therefore, research in exercise physiology is increasingly becoming a responsibility of schools and departments of physical education. This trend has at least two consequences: First, the pool from which the scientists studying exercise physiology are drawn is narrowing. Second, opportunities for funding research are limited because such funding in the United States is organized around solving biomedical problems. As pointed out by Dr. Buskirk, opportunities exist to obtain support for exercise research which has implications for basic biology or applied medicine. Despite a popular, even worldwide, interest in solving practical problems related to exercise, no national organization or agency exists to support solution of practical problems of exercise physiology. Many problems related to athletics or recreational sports are simply not addressed.

Public Law 95-626, passed by Congress in 1978, called for the establishment of an office of Health Information, Health Promotion, Physical Fitness, and Sports Medicine for fiscal year 1980-1981. No funds were appropriated for that office, and it does not appear that funds will be allocated in the foreseeable future. The National Collegiate Athletic Association (NCAA) and the United States Olympic Committee (USOC) have taken no major role in supporting research in exercise physiology or sports medicine.

As pointed out by Dr. Buskirk, exercise physiology is emerging: emerging as biological science develops, emerging into national and world politics, emerging in a way to change the roles of physical education practitioners, and perhaps, also emerging from physiology into physical education.

In their chapter, "Current and Future Topics in Exercise Physiology," Dr. J.A. Faulkner and Dr. T.P. White identify nine major current areas of emphasis in exercise physiology. Because of the current "state of the art," research competence in each of those areas requires a great degree of specialization. Although budgets for research in departments of physical education are often small compared to the monetary commitment to research in other departments of the biological sciences, and although funding sources are organized to support biomedical research, physical education-exercise physiologists are building sophisticated laboratories and making significant contributions to the field. As noted by Dr. Buskirk, well-trained and energetic researchers in physical education are now effectively competing for biomedical research grants. Techniques involving determination of ventilatory gas exchange, blood metabolites and hormones, radioactive and nonradioactive tracers, cellular constituents including enzymes and organelles, muscle structure and ultrastructure, muscle contraction characteristics, muscle electrical potentials, and brain electrical potentials are used routinely in physical education-exercise physiology laboratories where efforts are under way to solve problems such as those delineated by Faulkner and White.

The question of the metabolic factors underlying the elevated O_2 consumption (O_2 debt) observed after exercise (Chapter 7) has been an important question since the early 1920s when A.V. Hill and his associates addressed it. At the Harvard Fatigue Laboratory, Margaria et al. (1933) studied the recovery process from exercise, and since that time, several scientists have addressed the question of O_2 debt. A significant part of the applied physiological research in physical education (Henry & DeMoor, 1956) and in medicine (Wasserman, Whipp, Koyal, & Beaver, 1973) has been concerned with effects of lactic acid, anaerobiosis, and the O_2 debt on performance. The contemporary explanation of the mechanisms of and relationships among these factors has emerged as has the study of exercise physiology. Much of the contemporary research is technically detailed and involves many of the methods indicated previously. The techniques have come from physiology and biochemistry, but the impetus for study has come from physical education. The work has involved time, effort, and financial support. Chapter 7 is therefore included to provide students with a contemporary view of the mechanism of the O_2 debt and with an impression of how advances in technology have allowed progress in the understanding of processes.

References

Benedict, F. G., & Cathcart, E. P. *Muscular work. A metabolic study with special reference to the efficiency of the human body as a machine* (Publ. 187). Washington: Carnegie Institute of Washington, 1913.

Dill, D. B. The Harvard Fatigue Laboratory: Its development, contributions, and demise. *Circulation Research* (Suppl. 1), 1967, pp. 161-170.

Grimaux, E. *Lavosier: 1743-1794.* Paris: Ancienne Librairie Germer Bailliero et Cie, 1888.

Henry, F. M., & DeMoor, J. Lactic and alactic oxygen consumption in moderate exercise. *Journal of Applied Physiology,* 1956, **8**, 608-614.

Hill, A. V., Long, C. N. H., & Lupton, H. Muscular exercise, lactic acid and supply and utilization of oxygen. *Proceedings of the Royal Society of London* (Series B), 1924, pp. 96-97.

Margaria, R., Edwards, H. T., & Dill, D. B. The possible mechanisms of contracting and paying the oxygen debt and the role of lactic acid in muscular contraction. *American Journal of Physiology,* 1933, **106**, 689-715.

Smith, H. M. *Gaseous exchange and physiological requirements for level and grade walking* (Publ. 309). Washington: Carnegie Institute of Washington, 1922.

Wasserman, K., Whipp, B. J., Koyal, S. N., & Beaver, W. L. Anaerobic threshold and respiratory gas exchange during exercise. *Journal of Applied Physiology,* 1973, **35**, 236-243.

Zuntz, N., & Schumburg, Dr. *Studien zu einer physiologie des marsches.* Berlin: Verlag von August Hirschwald, 1901.

The Emergence of Exercise Physiology in Physical Education

5

E.R. Buskirk

As world population increases and travel time between countries and continents decreases, human cross cultural involvement proceeds both constructively and destructively—but nevertheless proceeds. Science has, for the most part, contributed to society in a constructive way. Of course, there have been scientific findings which have aided and abetted warfare causing destruction and human suffering. In the biomedical research arena, few destructive elements have arisen other than scientific abuses such as in Nazi Germany.

Today, people from all cultures are making significant research contributions to the rapidly expanding field of biomedical science. International exchange of scientific information is at an all-time high, including relatively free circulation of scientific publications, abundant international meetings, and numerous collaborative projects. It is the rare scientist who is not involved in international travel and/or joint enterprise with some frequency. The recent change of government in mainland China bodes well for the rapid development and expansion of research there, since the Chinese have made numerous research contributions in the past and should continue to do so in the future. While there are pockets of minimal research activity, particularly among third world or developing countries, the trend of research activity around the world is ever upward (Handler, 1979).

The USA's disproportionate contribution to growth of scientific understanding is lessening, for science abroad is expanding rapidly. The totality of research endeavor in Western Europe virtually equals our own and has had a continuing impact on significant developments, particularly in biomedical research. Japan's research enterprise is about one-half that of the USA, but because of minimal military involvement, their

The assistance of Calvin Shearburn and Vincent Rabatin is acknowledged for their assistance with the chronological bibliography, and that of Becky Nilson for typing the manuscript.

commitment to basic research has been comparatively extraordinary. Scientific endeavor in the USSR and in the Eastern European countries nearly matches our own. In the area of athletics and sports medicine, their effort surpasses ours—particularly in applied areas geared to the improvement of performance in world class competition. Such research is not always considered innovative or productive when dedicated to peripheral, single-minded, and arbitrary goals. Nevertheless, the effort remains intensive even if not well understood in the West. Following World War II, expansion of research in the regions mentioned above has proceeded rapidly, for the respective countries have acquired the latest and most powerful instruments of science. Although American research effort had a tremendous post-World War II growth spurt, research support has recently declined in real purchasing power and our instrumentation is becoming old and outmoded. Avid competition in the future can be expected from both India and China as well as from Central and South America and Africa. Hopefully, the USA will retain a commitment to preeminence; it is important for us to maintain a front-line research capability in order to appropriately utilize the findings from world science (Handler, 1979).

Unfortunately, science keeps getting more expensive, and with undiminishing inflationary trends, expenses will continue to mount. Thus, hard choices will have to be made in the future regarding research support. Society will judge how much it wishes to spend for research but this judgment is best rendered when based on informed opinions (Cohen & Rothshield, 1979): thus, the need for continuing science education of society as a whole. Physiological research, a part of exercise science, has followed essentially the same path as biomedical science. It is strongly hoped that biomedical science will continue to receive enough support to sustain the various aspects of exercise science. It can be anticipated that if biomedical science prospers, exercise science and the exercise physiology component will follow suit; however, it is unlikely that exercise science will ever be established as sufficiently unique to be given priority or other special treatment.

Trends

What trends have we seen in recent years in physical education? To what extent has physiological research aided development of these trends? As the prominence of farming and heavy manufacturing work involving considerable manual labor gradually shifted to light industrial and office jobs, so too has our interest shifted in recreation and associated exercise. The change from manual to automated labor has provided us with more free time. Thus, sports like tennis, racquetball, golf, swimming, and jogging take more of our time than ever before. This trend has been supported by the accumulating evidence that physical activity is necessary for maintaining a healthy body. The major research impetus has come from work related to the prevention of atherosclerosis and coronary heart disease as well as rehabilitation following myocardial infarction. The implication that physical activity and health are interrelated is not a new postulate, particularly in physical education circles. What *is* new is the accumulation of hard data in support of the postulate. While these data are not overwhelming, the hypotheses being investigated in physiological and epidemiological research should lead to more convincing answers within the next decade or two. Additional research for development and control of chronic diseases, such as diabetes and hypertension, may well help to implement an educational philosophy of lifelong, regular physical activity.

There is a growing awareness that successful physical education involves establishing in children the concept that exercise and health are related, and that habits established early in life may well remain for a lifetime. Children can be "sold" the idea that regular activity is important, and that strength, endurance, and flexibility are complementary capabilities which can be developed and maintained with regular exercise. Thus, physical education is evolving to mean education for lifelong physical activity.

Politics and Support

To some extent, politics has entered the physical education and exercise science arena, and its impact is still only partially known. The President's Council of Physical Fitness and Sport has been in existence for some time, serving largely a promotional function. Department of Health, Education and Welfare operating regulations such as Title IX have provided a boost for women's sports. A new Department of Education has been formed, but its influence on physical education remains to be seen. An appropriation for support of the Olympic program has been passed by Congress and more funds have been requested. Therefore, the administrative and legislative oars are in the water, but the propulsive force remains undetermined. Hopefully, the result of such political activity will be support for continuation of significant research efforts.

A source of pride for exercise physiology researchers is their success in the competition for federal and private research funds. Many of the proposals submitted to the National Institutes of Health, the National Science Foundation, the Department of Defense, the Department of Education, the American Heart Association, the Muscular Dystrophy Association, etc., have been favorably reviewed and the projects funded. The responsible investigators have been trained well enough to compete successfully for limited available funding.

Of concern is the virtual absence of support from those organizations vitally involved with development and support of the best possible programs of physical education and athletics. Although the National Collegiate Athletic Association has sponsored a small amount of research, this research has been funded at a near poverty level. Other comparable sources of funds are even more sparse. For example, a football game could be played for the support of exercise science research or special fund-raising events put on—events, comparable to those for cancer and heart disease, which secure funds for research on health promotion and disease prevention. It is fair to say that much of the research for physical education, particularly for athletics or sports has been "bootlegged" in the past, and it is time for the responsible organizations to support research for physical educators, coaches, trainers, and other similarly involved participants.

Despite the fact that humankind is increasingly free of the shackles and drudgery of manual labor, awareness of the contributions of basic and applied research to physical welfare and psychosocial well-being is not very extensive. The physical educator has part of the story to tell the public, much of which emanates from underlying research. Hopefully, success in telling the story may yet generate a more substantial research base.

Responsibility

During his term in office, President Lyndon B. Johnson suggested that important scientific discoveries remained sequestered in laboratories and that it was time to rectify this situation. The same idea has frequently been suggested by physical education teachers and coaches. But is this supposition accurate? I think not—it is a rare scientist indeed who locks up discoveries. Normal scientific procedure is to ensure that observations and measurements are as correct as possible for preparing a manuscript for publication. The usual publication choice is the most prestigious and widely read journal in the respective area of research. This is not to say that a scientist may make a significant observation and not know it or make a potentially major discovery and not notice it. "Missing the boat" in this way is unintentional but nevertheless unfortunate.

As I recall, Eric Hoffer, the longshoreman turned philosopher, was once reported to have said something like "There are educated nobodies who want to be somebodies and end up being mischief-making busybodies." In another vein, Winston Churchill is reputed to have said, "Men occasionally stumble over the truth, but most of them pick themselves up and hurry off as if nothing had happened." These images may apply to some physical fitness promoters, but they do not legitimately project to the serious scientists who work in the area of exercise physiology. For the most part, these scientists have a distinguished record, for their important observations have been made readily accessible through the scientific literature.

Whose duty is it to disseminate this knowledge to the general public? Normally, the role should be reserved for the scientific writer and for the health and physical education teacher. Thus, the physical educator has an obligation to be well enough versed in science to be able to interpret pertinent science for students. Books and review articles in exercise physiology that summarize existing knowledge play a vital role in education, and physical educators should be expected to read many of them. They should also refer to the original literature in order to gain perspective in areas of primary interest. Interpretative journals, such as *Medicine and Science in Sports* and *The Physician and Sports Medicine,* help provide both knowledge and perspective. Perhaps it is time for a comparable journal to appear in physical education literature. The ascendancy of the Research Division within the reorganized American Alliance for Health, Physical Education, and Recreation (AAHPER), may well provide the impetus for the developing of pertinent publications. Certainly, the annual meeting and scientific program of the Research Division has grown in scope and prestige. Special symposia proceedings from these meetings could provide the basis for a new journal.

Other sources also contribute information for physical education. For example, the President's Council on Physical Fitness and Sports provides the *Physical Fitness Research Digest,* and AAHPER has developed a series on *What Research Tells the Coach about . . .,* as well as the *International Monograph Series in Physical Education.* These publications are well written and provde important interpretive presentations. Currently, the various specialty publications, such as *Runner's World*, have articles with considerable reference to basic exercise science prepared by knowledgeable people.

Participation

In a recent paper prepared for the Department of Health, Education and Welfare's National Conference on Disease Prevention Objectives, the President's Council on Physical Fitness and Sport presented a summary of participation in exercise and sport in the USA (PCPFS, 1979). They contended that participation has reached unprecedented numbers during recent years. Approximately 55% of adults over the age of 18 participate regularly in exercise or sport. This means about 90 million men and women. Participation over the past 15 years has increased twofold. Thirty million children, aged 6 to 21, take part in organized sports such as age-group swimming, track and field, basketball, volleyball, baseball, and football. In addition, some 6.45 million boys and girls and 538,000 intercollegiate athletes participate in competitive athletic programs. College intramural participation is estimated at 4.34 million persons, with college club and recreational sports programs involving 1.41 million more. Thus, more active people in a recreational and athletic context may well characterize the future as contrasted with the pattern of sedentary living so common in the 1940s, 50s, and early 60s.

The trend toward increased participation means that the colleges and universities of our country need to prepare physical educators differently than in the past. The emphasis should be on health promotion and disease prevention with particular focus on the importance of regular physical activity. In addition, more emphasis needs to be placed on out-of-school programs.

Research Interpretation

In 1953 D.B. Dill wrote a most interesting introduction to the textbook by Morehouse and Miller (1953) (see bibliography).

> Until the pioneering work of A.V. Hill little was known about the physiology of strenuous muscular exercise. The sober school of physiologists in Germany had preferred to study exercise in a steady state and American students trained in that school continued to shy away from anaerobic work at least in studies on man. The bold attack of A.V. Hill on the physiology of sport inspired. . . others. From that beginning arose the Fatigue Laboratory and many happy years of association with physiologists coming from far and near to carry on research on the physiology of man in sport, at work, and at war. The reader will be impressed with the arduous experiments upon which our present understanding of the physiology of muscular exercise rests. It is not enough to make neat studies of frogs' nerve-muscle preparations, of swimming rats and of panting dogs. Man himself must be the subject;

many of the advances in exercise physiology have come from self-experimentation.

It should be added to Dill's comments that such research has contributed to human well-being, largely through interpretation of such research by those involved with physical education. There have been many important physical educators who have elucidated physiological research for their field. Some of those include:

D.K. Brace	C.H. McCloy	D.A. Sargent
H.H. Clarke	J.H. McCurdy	E.C. Schneider
F.A. Hellebrandt	E. Metheny	G. Scott
F.M. Henry	H.J. Montoye	A. Steinhaus
S.M. Horvath	L.E. Morehouse	W.W. Tuttle
P.V. Karpovich	G.L. Rarick	W. Van Huss

Scope of Involvement

Present day physical educators must, through instruction, furnish accurate information about the effects of exercise on the body. Also, they must provide opportunities for participation in exercise programs and sport and skill development.

When costs for teachers and facilities are considered, the question is frequently raised, "is it essential for children to have physical education?" From the physiological viewpoint, the answer is yes! If a sufficient number of physical activity alternatives were viable in our culture, the response might then be different.

Simultaneous development of mind and body is essential. One aspect of that development which could well receive more attention is the important role physical education should play in teaching care of the body, for throughout life, the body serves as a vehicle for the mind. Thus, developing and maintaining a reasonable level of physical fitness poses an important challenge, not only for concerned individuals, but also for those involved with physical education.

Regular exercise habits are most easily developed in the young whose bodies can best be physically conditioned. The early development of strength, flexibility, speed, skill, and endurance enhances children's self-confidence and self-image—two important components of the personality which favor intellectual and social development. Because most children today are driven or bussed to school, it is important to establish programs that supply regular opportunities for physical activity in addition to an educational background that teaches the value of regular exercise.

There are various physical activities available for regular participation regardless of age, sex, disability, or infirmity. The scope of physical education has expanded from simply school programs, to include community recreational organizations, clubs, churches, corporations, foundations, private and public agencies, governments, etc. More people than ever before want to enjoy physical activity, motivated perhaps, by the possibilities for improved health, well being, and productivity. Age group programs have expanded to include the elderly. Despite this growing interest in sport, many schools are cutting back on programs because of inflation and the associated diminution of resources. Whereas Title IX and legislation related to support of the Olympics has provided an impetus for expanding activity, such countering influences as product and program liability suits and tax-related citizen revolts have curtailed progress. Nevertheless, "the band marches on." National training centers have been established and staffed with top-flight coaches, laboratory investigators, and technicians as well as sports medicine physicians and their assistants. A national sports festival has been initiated, and there has been expansion of the number of community sponsored road races distancing anywhere from six to 100 miles!

Sources of Information

Physiological research has provided much of the factual knowledge used in laboratory assessment programs, treatment, and therapy rendered in sports medicine, and information used in the preparation of physical conditioning and training regimens. Although related educational progress has been made, the need for better training of physical education teachers remains. The knowledge gained in the research laboratory needs to filter down more rapidly to the classroom and to training programs.

In this regard, an impressive list of excellent manuals and books are available, covering a variety of topics related to physiology and its impact on the understanding of physical activity through physical education. One can perhaps best appreciate the scope and availability of such information through the listing in the attached bibliography arranged alphabetically by year (see *Books* section of bibliography). Similarly, the list of many of the important review articles provides a conception of not only the type of work completed, but also a notion of the importance attached to it by the physiologically oriented research community—simply by virtue of the fact that it was published. Exercise physiology has been of considerable interest to this community for several decades (see *Reviews* section of bibliography).

A summary of publication by decade appears as Table 1. It should

Table 1

Number of Contributions to Physiological Literature by Decade

Decade*	Books**	Reviews***
1920s	5	7
1930s	12	13
1940s	3	14
1950s	7	9
1960s	21	3
1970s	52	4

*Only frequently cited publications are listed.

**Includes tally of subsequent editions.

***Only includes those reviews that appeared in the Annual Review of Physiology or Physiological Reviews.

also be stressed that the tabulation in Table 1 lists publications such as *The Exercise and Sports Sciences Reviews* under books rather than reviews. Considering the number of books, it is apparent that publication of topics related to the physiology of exercise increased dramatically during the 1960s and particularly the 1970s as compared to earlier years. A book publication lull occurred during the 1940s largely because of the impact of World War II. In contrast to the considerable growth in book publication, the number of reviews published in the 1960s and 70s decreased—probably because the same material was replaced to a large extent by symposia proceedings and edited volumes.

There are a variety of other sources of information. The *American Journal of Physiology* first appeared in 1898 and contained most of the original investigative papers on the physiology of exercise until the *Journal of Applied Physiology* was started in 1948. *Physiological Reviews* was first published in 1921, and the *Annual Reviews of Physiology* appeared in 1939. *The Physiologist* was first published in 1957 (Fenn, 1963). Also, there is the AAHPER publication *Research Quarterly* as well as several in Europe, such as *Arbeitsphysiologie* and the relatively new *European Journal of Applied Physiology*. Through these publications, original investigations have become available to physical educators for their evaluation and use.

General Contributions

Because this paper is general in nature and contains only "broad brush" information about the contributions of physiology to physical education, a summary listing areas in which contributions have been made should prove helpful. These contributions may broadly be identified as the following (also see Brotherhood, 1978):

1. The addition of functional characteristics to those of age, sex, morphology, etc., such as aerobic capacity, anerobic capacity, skeletal muscle fiber types and their enzymatic complements.

2. Knowledge of the impact of acute exercise on the body including various types, intensities, and durations of exercise.

3. Specific knowledge of tissue and organ system reactions and interactions in response to exercise.

4. Knowledge of control mechanisms and neurohumoral sensing and response system interactions.

5. Knowledge of the fatigue process and factors limiting performance, including limits set by genetic endowment.

6. Knowledge of environmental effects on specific activities including the effects of heat, cold, hypoxia, ambient pressure, etc.

7. Knowledge of adaptation and de-adaptation to regular exercise, i.e., the effects of physical conditioning and training contrasted with the effects of sedentary living, particularly bedrest.

8. Knowledge of conditions leading to excessive physiological strain and possible injury.

9. Knowledge of the effects of special treatment or tampering, such as the use of drugs, dietary adjuncts, blood doping, etc.

Despite the many contributions already made, there remains much to be learned. Based on current knowledge, fitness for regular exercise is generally enhanced if individuals have a high aerobic capacity per unit of body weight, can deliver an optimal mixture of energy-yielding substrates to working muscle, and have the ability to appropriately thermoregulate. These capabilities are achieved through regular participation in a planned, physical conditioning program that will supplement genetic endowment with conditioning advancements. Similarly, such programs facilitate achievement of greater strength, flexibility, speed, skill, endurance, and improved performance as well as enhanced enjoyment of activity.

The importance of such findings for physical education is that students can be given a more complete description of physiological processes. With knowledge of skeletal muscle functions, students are likely to recognize the significance of regular exercise and to include it is their regimen for daily living.

Research

One example of the type of research applicable to physical education is the investigations of the structure and function of skeletal muscles, a subject which has advanced considerably in recent years. Because physical education invariably involves skeletal muscular activity, it is important to understand the contractile process, including effective stimuli, shortening, relaxation, and fatigue. This knowledge has developed rapidly along with the characterization of fiber types and their specific properties. The chemistry of contraction has been partially worked out, and although it is not completely understood, there is reason to hope that important interactions will soon be definitely described among activating elements such as Ca^{++}, contractile components such as actin and myosin and energetic components such as adenosine triphosphate (ATP), adenosine diphosphate (ADP), and creatine phosphate (CrP). Understanding the processes will not only aid in structuring physical activities for normal individuals, but should also increase the number of people eligible to benefit from participation in regular exercise by helping to correct skeletal muscle problems.

Muscle is the most abundant cellular tissue in the body; skeletal muscle tends to be somewhat uniform in composition within a given individual. The profound biochemical changes that occur with exercise in skeletal muscle have been investigated in the last two decades, largely because of the development of the needle biopsy procedure which provides small samples of muscle (10-100 mg) for analytical purposes, relatively atraumatically (Bergström, 1962; Fisler & Drenick, 1972; Hendriksson, 1979). Both morphological and biochemical studies have been accomplished with muscle samples obtained in this way. These studies have documented specific tissue changes in metabolic substrates, enzymes, and cellular elements with exercise, as well as the adaptive changes that occur with physical conditioning or training (Bergström, 1975).

Today much more is known about the metabolic fuels needed to support different types of exercise. During heavy exercise, free fatty acids, glucose, and glycogen are utilized, and muscle glycogen and blood glucose can decrease to levels which force the exerciser to either slow down or stop. Liver glycogen is the main source of blood glucose although a small amount can come from gluconeogenesis, i.e., from protein. Muscle glycogen is usually regarded as an important metabolic substrate during exhausting work.

Following the introduction of the muscle biopsy technique, a method for glycogen determination was developed, and numerous studies were conducted which identified lack of glycogen as a limiting factor in exercise. During these investigations, the role of carbohydrate-rich or carbohydrate-free diets on muscle glycogen content and rates of degradation and resynthesis were discerned—increasing glycogen content increased work capacity. Thus, the role of insulin was established in the synthesis of muscle glycogen (Bergström, 1975).

Conclusion

It is difficult to project true human needs above the general noise level of expediency dictated largely by political and cultural processes. Thus, potentialities for progress grounded in research are frequently either overlooked or bypassed. The insights engendered by creativity and the quickened journey to knowledge should be brought to the fore, rather than buried under the cacophony of vested, and frequently biased, interests. To increase our understanding of the acute effects of exercise and the role of regular exercise on lifestyle, health, and susceptibility to disease and mortality, we need to appreciate the promise and importance of the methods of science and the credibility of verifiable findings.

The role of the investigator interested in exercise has become accepted within the scientific community. Nevertheless, the element of competition within this community remains an important aspect, for without acceptable credentials garnered through basic science training and rigorous adherence to the scientific method, the impact of effort expended is reduced. We have progressed beyond devotion to skill and games concepts to a philosophy of life embodying the idea that human beings are made to be active and should be studied as such.

An effort must be made to extend support for basic work in exercise-related science. Too frequently, support for such research has come only indirectly from disease-oriented granting agencies. Those organizations, primarily responsible for the management of physical activities and athletics, have failed to adequately support underlying science. Instead, their resources have been devoted to promotional, organizational, and other activities, but not research. Fortunately, as science progresses, so will exercise science progress, largely because of a heightened interest among both the scientific community and the general public.

The documented "track record" of the pioneers in exercise physiology is exemplary, but the possibilities for future meaningful research are extensive. A variety of research opportunities are pointed out in the chapter prepared by Faulkner and White. Over and above, the opportunities they discuss are the issues of research training, environment, support, and academic interaction. The investigator's role extends to one of collaboration with physical educators, for it is the latter who interprets and sells the product: exercise. The scope of physical educators has expanded immensely to include not only students, but other teachers, coaches, parents, preschoolers, and the aged—virtually all subgroups of our population. If there is one overall goal for this collaboration, it is grounded in the belief that human beings have become capable of improving the quality of their lives and should intelligently use the resources available to do so. To this end, continued quality research is essential.

References

Bergström J. Muscle electrolytes in man. *Scandinavian Journal of Clinical and Laboratory Investigations,* 1962, **14**. (Suppl. 68)

Bergström, J. Percutaneous needle biopsy of skeletal muscle in physiological and clinical research. *Scandinavian Journal of Clinical and Laboratory Investigations,* 1975, **35**, 609-616.

Brotherhood, J.R. A philosophy of applied physiology and physical recreation. *Australian Journal of Sports Medicine,* 1978, **10**, 93-95.

Cohen, L. & Rothshield, H. The bandwagons of medicine. *Perspectives in Biology & Medicine,* 1979, **22**, 531-538.

Federation of American Societies for Experimental Biology. Newsletter, FASEB, August 1979, **12**.

Fenn, W.O. *History of the American physiological society: The third quarter century 1937-1962.* Washington, DC: The American Physiological Society, 1963.

Fisler, J.L. & Drenick, E.J. Muscle biopsy needle for the percutaneous excision of large specimens. *Journal of Laboratory and Clinical Medicine,* 1972, **79**, 679-682.

Handler, P. Basic research in the United States. *Science,* 1979, **204**, 474-479.

Henriksson, K.G. "Semi-open" muscle biopsy technique. *Acta Neurologica Scandinavica,* 1979, **59**, 317-323.

President's Council on Physical Fitness and Sports Newsletter. Washington, DC: PCPFS, July 1979.

Chronological Bibliography of Books and Review Articles*

Books

1920. Dreyer, G. *The assessment of physical fitness.* New York: Paul B.

---

*List Arranged Alphabetically by Year of Publication.

Hoeber.

1925. Hill, A.V. *Muscular activity.* Baltimore: Williams and Wilkins Co.

1927. Deutsch, F., Kauf, E., & Warfield, L.M. *Heart and athletics.* St. Louis: C.V. Mosby Co.

1927. Hill, A.V. *Muscular movement in man.* New York: McGraw-Hill.

1928. McCurdy, J.J. *The physiology of exercise* (2nd ed.). Philadelphia: Lea & Fibiger Co.

1931. Bainbridge, F.A. *The physiology of muscular exercise* (3rd ed.). Rewritten by Bock, A.V., & Dill, C.B., London: Longmans, Green and Co.

1933. Haggard, H.W. & Greenberg, L.A. *Diet and physical efficiency.* New Haven: Yale University Press.

1933. Karpovich, P.V. *Physiology of muscular activity.* Philadelphia: W.B. Saunders Co., (With W. Sinning, 7th ed., 1971).

1933. Schneider, E.C. *Physiology of muscular activity.* Philadelphia: W.B. Saunders Co.

1935. Dawson, P.M. *The physiology of physical education.* Baltimore: The Williams and Wilkins Co.

1935. Gould, A.G. & Dye, J.A. *Exercise and its physiology.* New York: A.S. Barnes and Co.

1938. Dill, D.B. *Life, heat and altitude.* Cambridge, MA: Harvard University Press.

1939. Krestovnikoff, A. *Fiziologia sporta. Fizkultura and sport.* Moscow.

1939. McCurdy, J.H. & Larson, L.A. *The physiology of exercise.* Philadelphia: Lea & Febiger.

1948. Morehouse, L.W. & Miller, A.T. *Physiology of exercise.* St. Louis: C.V. Mosby Co.

1950. Clarke, H.H. *The application of measurement in physical education* (2nd Ed.). New York: Prentice-Hall, Inc.

1957. Bogert, L.F. *Nutrition and physical fitness.* Philadelphia: W.B. Saunders Co.

1958. Morehouse, L.E. & Rasch, P.J. *Scientific basis of athletic training.* Philadelphia: W.B. Saunders Co.

1960. Johnson, W.R. (Ed.). *Science and medicine of exercise and sports.* New York: Harper & Row.

1960. Staley, S.C., Cureton, T.K., Huelster, L.J., & Barry, A.J. (Eds.). *Exercise and fitness.* Chicago: Athletic Institute.

1961. Hettinger, T. *Physiology of strength.* Springfield, IL: Charles C. Thomas.

1963. Consolazio, C.F., Johnson, R.E., & Pecora, L.J. *Physiological measurements of metabolic functions in man.* New York: McGraw-

Hill.

1963. Steinhaus, A.H. *Toward an understanding of health and physical education.* Dubuque, IA: Wm. C. Brown Co.

1966. de Vries, H.A. *Physiology of exercise for physical education and athletics.* Aubuque, IA: Wm. C. Brown Co.

1966. Evang, K. & Anderson, K.L. (Eds.). *Physical activity in health and disease.* Baltimore: Williams and Wilkins Co.

1967. Margaria, R. *Exercise at altitude.* New York: Exerpta Medica Foundation.

1967. Ricci, B. *Physiological basis of human performance.* Philadelphia: Lea & Febiger.

1968. Brown, R.C. & Kenyon, G.S. *Classical studies on physical activity.* Englewood Cliffs, NJ: Prentice Hall, Inc.

1968. Cooper, K.H. *Aerobics.* New York: Bantam.

1968. Falls, H.B. (Eds.). *Exercise physiology.* New York: Academic Press.

1968. Jokl, E. & Jokl, P. (Eds.). *Exercise and altitude.* Basel: S. Karger.

1968. Poortmans, J.R. (Ed.). *Biochemistry of exercise.* Baltimore: University Park Press.

1969. Cureton, R.K. *The physiological effects of exercise programs upon adults.* Springfield, IL: Charles C. Thomas.

1969. Franks, B.D. (Ed.). *Exercise and fitness-1969.* Chicago: Athletic Institute.

1969. O'Shea, J.P. *Scientific principles and methods of strength fitness.* Reading: MA: Addison-Wesley.

1969. Shephard, R.J. *Endurance fitness.* Toronto: University of Toronto Press.

1970. Astrand, P.O. & Rodahl, K. *Textbook of work physiology.* New York: McGraw-Hill.

1970. Cooper, K.H. *The new aerobics.* New York: Bantam.

1971. Mathews, D.K. & Fox, E.L. *The physiological basis of physical education and athletics.* Philadelphia: W.B. Saunders.

1971. Pernow, B. & Saltin, B. (Eds.). *Muscle metabolism during exercise.* New York: Plenum Press.

1971. Shephard, R.J. *Frontiers of fitness.* Springfield, IL: Charles C. Thomas.

1971. Simonsen, E. (Ed.). *Physiology of work capacity and fatigue.* Springfield, IL: Charles C. Thomas.

1972. Alexander, J.F., Serfass, R.C., & Tipton, C.M., (Eds.). *Physiology of fitness and exercise.* Chicago: Athletics Institute.

1972. Bar-Or, O. (Ed.). *Pediatric work physiology—Proceedings of the*

Fourth International Symposium. Wingate Post, Israel: Wingate Institute

1972. Jensen, C.R. & Fisher, A.G. *Scientific bases of athletic condition-ing.* Philadelphia: Lea & Febiger.

1972. Morgan, W.P. (Ed.). *Ergogenic aids and muscular performance.* New York: Academic Press.

1972. Shephard, R.J. *Alive man! The physiology of physical activity.* Springfield, IL: Charles C. Thomas.

1973. Horvath, S.M. & Horvath, E.C., *The Harvard Fatigue Laboratory: Its history and contributions.* Englewoods Cliffs, NJ: Prentice-Hall, Inc.

1973. Keul, J. (Ed.). *Limiting factors of physical performance.* Stuttgard: Georg Thieme Publishers.

1973. Naughton, J.P. & Hellerstein, H.K., (Eds.). *Exercise testing and exercise training in coronary heart disease.* New York: Academic Press.

1973. Rarick, G.L. (Ed.). *Physical activity: Human growth and develop-ment.* New York: Academic Press.

1973. Wilmore, J.H. *Exercise and sports sciences reviews* (Vol. 1.). New York: Academic Press.

1974. Behnke, A.R. & Wilmore, J.H. *Evaluation and regulation of body build and composition.* Englewood Cliffs, NJ: Prentice Hall.

1974. Fox, E.L. & Mathews, D.K. *Interval training—Conditioning for sports and general fitness.* Philadelphia: W.B. Saudners.

1974. Johnson, W.R. & Buskirk, E.R. (Eds.). *Science and medicine of exercise and sports* (2nd ed.). New York: Harper and Row.

1974. Wilmore, J.H. *Exercise and sports sciences reviews* (Vol. 2.). New York: Academic Press.

1974. Zohman, L.R. *Medical aspects of exercise testing and training.* New York: International Medical Book Inc.

1975. American College of Sports Medicine. *Guidelines for graded exer-cise testing and exercise prescription.* Philadelphia: Lea & Febiger.

1975. Baumgartner, T.A. & Jackson, A.S. *Measurement for evaluation in physical education.* Boston: Haughton Mifflin Co.

1975. Howald, H. & Poortmans, J.R. (Eds.). *Metabolic adaptation to prolonged physical exercise.* Basel: Birkhauser Verlog.

1975. Sharkey, B.J. *Physiology and physical activity.* New York: Har-per and Row.

1975. Wilmore, J.H. & Keogh, J.F. (Eds.). *Exercise and sports sciences reviews* (Vol. 3). New York: Academic Press.

1976. Edington, D.W. & Edgerton, V.R. *The biology of physical activity.* Boston: Haughton Mifflin Co.

1976. Keogh, J. & Hutton, R.S. (Eds.). *Exercise and sports sciences reviews* (Vol. 4). Santa Barbara: Journal Publishing Affiliates.

1976. Margaria, R. *Biomechanics and energetics of muscular exercise.* Oxford: Clarendon Press.

1976. Simonson, E. & Weiser, P.C. (Eds.). *Psychological aspects and physiological correlates of work and fatigue.* Springfield, IL: Charles C. Thomas.

1977. Amsterdam, E.A., Wilmore, J.H., & DeMaria, A.N. *Exercise in cardiovascular health and disease.* New York: Yorke Medical Books.

1977. Dempsey, J.A. & Reed, C.E. (Eds.). *Muscular exercise and the lung.* Madison, WI: University of Wisconsin Press.

1977. Katch, F. & McArdle, W.D. *Nutrition, weight control and exercise.* Boston: Houghton Mifflin.

1977. Milvy, P. (Ed.). *The marathon.* New York: New York Academy of Science.

1977. Nadel, E.R. (Ed.). *Problems with temperature regulation during exercise.* New York: Academic Press.

1977. Parizkova, J. *Body fat and physical fitness.* The Hague, Netherlands: Martinus Nijhoff.

1977. Wilmore J. *Athletic training and physical fitness: Physiological principles and practices of the conditioning process.* Boston: Allyn and Bacon Inc.

1977. Young, D.R. *Physical performance fitness and diet.* Springfield, IL: Charles C. Thomas.

1978. Hutton, R.S. (Ed.). *Exercise and sports sciences reviews* (Vol. 5.). Santa Barbara: CA: Journal Publishing Affiliates.

1978. Lamb, D.R. *Physiology of exercise; Responses and adaptations.* New York: Macmillan.

1978. Shephard, R.J. *Human physiological work capacity.* New York: Cambridge University Press.

1979. Fox, E.L. *Sports physiology.* Philadelphia: W.B. Saunders Co.

1979. Hutton, R.S. (Ed.). *Exercise and sports sciences reviews* (Vol. 6.). Philadelphia: Franklin Institute Press.

1979. Sharkey, B.J. *Physiology of fitness.* Champaign, IL: Human Kinetics Publishers.

Physiological Reviews

1921. Martin, E.G. Tests of muscular efficiency. *Physiol. Reviews,* 1, 454-475.

1922. Hill, A.V. The mechanism of muscular contraction. *Physiol. Reviews,* 2, 310-341.

1925. Cathcart, E.P. The influence of muscle work on protein metabolism. *Physiol. Reviews,* **5**, 225-243.

1925. Cobb, S. Review on the tonus of skeletal muscle. *Physiol. Reviews,* **5**, 518-550.

1928. Vernon, H.M. Industrial fatigue in relation to atmospheric conditions. *Physiol. Reviews,* **8**, 1-91.

1929. Eggleton, P. The position of phosphorous in the chemical mechanism of muscular contraction. *Physiol. Reviews,* **9**, 432-461.

1929. Richardson, H.B. The respiratory quotient (including: The source of energy used for muscular exertion). *Physiol. Reviews,* **9**, 61-125.

1930. Gasset, H.S. Contractures of skeletal muscle. *Physiol. Reviews* **10**, 35-109.

1931. Milroy, T.H. The present status of the chemistry of skeletal muscular contraction. *Physiol. Reviews,* **11**, 515-548.

1932. Baetjer, A.M. The effect of muscular fatigue upon resistance. *Physiol. Reviews,* **12**, 453-468.

1932. Hill, A.V. The revolution in muscle physiology. *Physiol. Reviews* **12**, 56-67.

1933. Jordan, H.E. The structural changes in striped muscle during contraction. *Physiol. Reviews,* **13**, 301-324.

1933. Steinhaus, A.H. Chronic effects of exercise. *Physiol. Reviews,* **13**, 103-147.

1934. Hinsey, J.C. The innervation of skeletal muscle. *Physiol. Reviews,* **14**, 514-585.

1936. Dill, D.B. The economy of muscular exercise. *Physiol. Reviews,* **16**, 263-291.

1936. Fenn, W.O. Electrolytes in muscle. *Physiol. Reviews,* **16**, 450-487.

1939. Bozler, E. Muscle. *Ann. Rev. Physiol.,* **1**, 217-234.

1939. Dill, C.B. Applied physiology. *Ann. Rev. Physiol,* **1**, 551-576.

1939. Millikan, G.A. Muscle hemoglobin. *Physiol. Reviews,* **19**, 503-523.

1939. Tower, S.S. The reaction of muscle to denervation. *Physiol. Reviews,* **19**, 1-48.

1940. Hellebrandt, A. Exercise. *Ann. Rev. Physiol,* **2**, 411-432.

1941. Fenn, W.O. Muscle. *Ann. Rev. Physiol.,* **3**, 209-232.

1941. Sacks, J. Changing concepts of the chemistry of muscular contraction. *Physiol. Reviews,* **21**, 242-265.

1941. Steinhaus, A.H. Exercise. *Ann. Rev. Physiol,* **3**, 695-716.

1942. Behnke, A. & Stephenson, C. Applied physiology. *Ann. Rev. Physiol,* **4**, 575-598.

1942. Gemmill, C.D. The fuel for muscular exercise. *Physiol. Reviews,*

22, 32-53.

1943. Fischer, E. Muscle. *Ann. Rev. Physiol,* **5,** 133-156.

1944. Comroe, J.H., Jr. The hyperpnea of muscular exercise. *Physiol. Reviews,* **24,** 319-339.

1944. Simonson, E. Industrial physiology. *Ann. Rev. Physiol,* **6,** 543-578.

1945. Johnson, R.E. Applied physiology. *Ann. Rev. Physiol,* **7,** 599-622.

1945. Solant, D.Y. Muscle. *Ann. Rev. Physiol,* **7,** 275-304.

1945. Taylor, C.L. Exercise. *Ann. Rev. Physiol,* **7,** 599-622.

1946. Johnson, R.E. Applied physiology. *Ann. Rev. Physiol,* **8,** 535-558.

1947. Karpovich, P.V. Exercise. *Ann. Rev. Physiol,* **9,** 149-162.

1950. Grodins, F.S. Analysis of factors concerned in regulation of breathing in exercise. *Physiol. Reviews,* **30,** 220-239.

1955. Asmussen, E. & Nielsen, M. Cardiac output during muscular work and its regulation. *Physiol. Reviews,* **35,** 778-800.

1955. Gregg, D.E., Sabiston, D.C., & Theilen, E.O. Changes in left ventricular end-diastolic pressure and stroke work during infusion and following exercise. *Physiol. Reviews,* **35,** 130-136.

1955. Morales, M.F., Botts, J., Blum, J.J., & Hill, T.L. Elementary processes in muscle action: An examination of current concepts. *Physiol. Reviews,* **35,** 475-505.

1955. Passmore, R. & Durnin, J. Human energy expenditure. *Physiol. Reviews,* **35,** 801-824.

1956. Astrand, P.O. Human physical fitness with special reference to sex and age. *Physiol. Reviews,* **36,** 307-335.

1956. Buchtal, F., Svensmark, O., & Rosenfalk, P. Mechanical and chemical events in muscle contraction. *Physiol. Reviews,* **36,** 503-538.

1956. Perry, S.V. Relation between chemical and contractile function and structure of skeletal muscle cell. *Physiol. Reviews,* **36,** 1-76.

1957. Conway, E.J. Nature and significance of concentration relations of potassium and sodium ions in skeletal muscle. *Physiol. Reviews,* **37,** 84-132.

1960. Mayer, J. & Bullen, B. Nutrition and athletic performance. *Physiol. Reviews,* **40,** 369-397.

1967. Bevegard, B.S. & Shepherd, J.T. Regulation of the circulation during exercise in man. *Physiol. Reviews,* **47,** 214-288.

1969. Mommaerts, W.F.H.M. Energetics of muscular contraction. *Physiol. Reviews,* **49,** 427-508.

1973. Weber, A. & Murray, J.M. Molecular control mechanisms in muscle contraction. *Physiol. Reviews,* **53,** 612-673.

1974. Rowell, L.B. Human cardiovascular adjustments to exercise and thermal stress. *Physiol. Reviews,* **51,** 75-159.

1977. Clausen, J.P.   Effect of physical training on cardiovascular adjustments to exercise in man. *Physiol. Reviews,* **57**, 779-815.
1978. Curtin, N.A. & R.C. Woledge. Energy changes and muscular contraction. *Physiol. Reviews,* **58**, 690-761.

Current and Future Topics in Exercise Physiology

6

J.A. Faulkner and T.P. White

Exercise physiology focuses primarily on the effects of physical activity on physiological systems, organs, cells, and subcellular constituents. Normally, exercise physiologists investigate hypotheses regarding the transient effects of selected exercises on metabolic, cardiovascular, ventilatory, and renal variables. Another experimental approach is to characterize adaptive responses to physical conditioning programs. Thus, exercise physiologists are interested in the physiological effects of both acute and chronic exposures to exercise.

Exercise may be separated into sports activities that are primarily aerobic in nature (running, cycling, cross-country skiing, swimming), and those which are largely anaerobic, involving muscular power (sprint running, discus throwing, pole vaulting, weight lifting). Physical activities may be further differentiated by muscle group involvement (finger, arm or leg exercise) or by the predominant type of muscle contraction (isometric or isotonic, concentric or eccentric).

The intensity of physical activity is a function of the speed of contraction and the resistance to the movement. When considering activities of more than 10 minutes duration, the intensity may be represented as a percentage of maximum oxygen consumption ($\dot{V}O_2max$), since energy production occurs primarily through cellular respiration. Different types of exercise elicit different values of $\dot{V}O_2max$, depending upon the muscle mass involved and the degree to which the muscles are conditioned for the task. The best method to physiologically represent the intensity of tasks with high energy requirements and durations of less than two minutes has remained elusive. Intramuscular stores of adenosine triphosphate (ATP) and creatine phosphate (CP) are used and heavy reliance is placed on glycolytic and glycogenolytic energy pathways. Despite our

The authors thank Victor Katch, Steven Segal and John Villanacci for their reviews of the manuscript.

biochemical knowledge of underlying energetic pathways, a valid non-invasive measure of this so-called "anaerobic" power has not been developed. The intensity of activities dependent upon muscle strength may be represented as a percentage of the maximum voluntary isometric contraction (MVC) strength. Although underlying physiological processes can be separated conceptually, most human exercise performances require interaction of these systems. Each system functions simultaneously to a different degree, moment to moment and from muscle fiber to muscle fiber, as dictated by the demands of the activity. Therefore, it is difficult to evaluate human performance physiologically as activities become increasingly complex.

Current Areas of Emphasis

Some current areas of research emphasis in exercise physiology are: (a) substrate utilization during exercise, (b) the kinetics of oxygen uptake, (c) the anaerobic threshold, (d) the efficiency of physical exercise, (e) the factors limiting performance, (f) environmental influences on performance, (g) the mechanisms of muscle weakness and fatigue, (h) the physiological adaptations to conditioning programs, and (i) the role of endurance conditioning in the prevention of and rehabilitation from disease.

Because exercise physiology is a cross-disciplinary science, these areas are not mutually exclusive. Each area is amplified below, including an overview of the current state of knowledge and comments on directions for future research. Also, throughout the chapter, representative references pertaining to each topic have been selected; however, the bibliography is not intended to be comprehensive.

Substrate Utilization During Exercise

The substrates (lipid, carbohydrates, and amino acids) used by skeletal muscle and other tissues during exercise are either located in the tissue itself (endogenous substrates), or are supplied to the tissue by the systemic circulation (exogenous substrates). These substrates catabolize to maintain a physiological concentration of ATP, the only energy source used for muscle contraction. Oxidative metabolism is the major pathway of energy flow at rest and during steady-rate submaximal exercise. Under these conditions, cell respiration fulfills metabolic demands, and the major substrates are lipids; carbohydrates are used at a lesser rate. If the exercise requires more energy than cell respiration can provide, glycolysis is accelerated and the use of carbohydrates is increased. This occurs at the onset of exercise, in supramaximal exercise, or in prolonged exercise where the metabolic demand exceeds the oxidative energetic capability.

Studies of the role of skeletal muscle glycogen (storage form of glucose) during physical exercise indicate that the quantity of skeletal muscle glycogen is a limiting factor in the ability to perform endurance exercise (Bergström, 1967; Hermansen, Hultman, & Saltin, 1967; Hultman, 1967; Saltin & Karlsson, 1971). A diet high in carbohydrates following an exercise-instigated depletion of skeletal muscle glycogen results, within several days, in muscle glycogen concentrations three-fold greater than the control values (Hultman, 1967; Hultman & Bergström, 1967). It is not known whether such an exercise-diet regimen increases the glycogen concentration and enhances the endurance performance of highly conditioned athletes. Mirkin (1973) has questioned the use of such regimens since some individuals on high-carbohydrate diets show ECG changes. Despite efforts to resolve the issue (Conlee, Hickson, Winder, Hagberg, & Holloszy, 1978), the mechanism of excess glycogen synthesis is yet unknown.

Ahlborg, Felig, Hagenfeldt, and Hendler (1974) published a comprehensive study on splanchnic and leg metabolism of glucose, free fatty acids (FFA) and amino acids during prolonged exercise in humans (4 hours at 30% $\dot{V}O_2$max). Their data support the conclusions that: (a) exogenous substrates (blood glucose and FFA) account for the major portion of leg muscle metabolism, with the relative contribution of FFA increasing progressively; (b) blood glucose levels fall because liver glucose output fails to keep up with elevated glucose utilization by exercising skeletal muscle; and (c) a large portion of liver glycogen is mobilized, and the formation of new glucose (gluconeogenesis) is augmented. Limited information is available on the role of gluconeogenesis during exercises of varying intensities and durations and on its adaptation to chronic exercise.

The traditional view is that when caloric supply is adequate, carbohydrates and lipids catabolize to meet metabolic demands (Astrand & Rodahl, 1977), and amino acids are not used. These views are based largely upon studies which observed insignificant alterations in urinary nitrogen excretion during exercise (Gontzea, Sutzescu, & Dumitrache, 1974). While net deamination of amino acids during exercise apparently does not occur, evidence suggests that particular amino acids are involved in energy flux during exercise. In rat skeletal muscles, transaminase activity is high (Scrutton & Utter, 1968) and glutamate-pyruvate transaminase activity increases in response to endurance training (Molé, Baldwin, Terjung, & Holloszy, 1973). Moreover, isolated skeletal muscle preparations can oxidize selected amino acids during exercise (Dohm, Askew, Beecher, Brown, Hecker, Klain, & Puenter, 1977; White, 1977). Ahlborg et al. (1974) demonstrated significant participation of the "glucose-alanine cycle" (Felig & Wahren, 1971) in metabolic adjustments to prolonged exercise. There is still need for research on the quantitative role of amino acids in exercise of various intensities and durations.

Kinetics of Oxygen Uptake

The time course of the total body $\dot{V}O_2$ response to increases in power output reflects a summation of cardiovascular and metabolic events, including the magnitude and time course of increased cardiac output, increased capillary surface area, peripheral blood flow distribution, oxidative capacity of recruited muscle fibers, and the ability to maintain adequate venous return and central blood volume. As such, the type of physical activity in terms of muscle mass involvement and type of contraction will profoundly influence the kinetics of $\dot{V}O_2$. Many studies have focused on the kinetics of $\dot{V}O_2$ from rest to initial steady-rate values durin during submaximal exercise (Cerretelli, Di Prampero, Pendergast, Rennie, & Shindell, 1977; Hagberg, Carlson, & Nagle, 1978; Hickson, Bomze, & Holloszy, 1978; Karlsson, 1971), while others have investigated the mechanism of continued increase in $\dot{V}O_2$ during prolonged submaximal exercise (Hagberg, Mullin, & Nagle, 1978). Whipp and Wasserman (1972) studied nonconditioned subjects and found that the steady-rate value of $\dot{V}O_2$ was reached exponentially within 3 minutes at low exercise intensities (less than 100 watts·min^{-1}), but at higher exercise intensities, a second slower exponential component became evident and steady-rate values were reached by 6 minutes. Research reports have appeared differentiating the precise halftime and fulltime response to different relative and absolute exercise intensities (Hagberg et al., 1978; Hickson et al., 1978) the more rapid response in physically conditioned individuals compared to controls (Hickson et al., 1978) and differences between arm and leg exercise (Cerretelli et al., 1977). Several investigators refer to the hypoxic status of skeletal muscle and the relative contribution of anaerobiosis during initial exercise. In light of the number of intervening variables between cellular metabolism and measurement at the mouth, the interpretation of such inferences requires caution. An exercising human is not the most appropriate model for studying skeletal muscle metabolism during nonsteady-rate conditions. Nevertheless, oxygen uptake kinetics do provide an index of integrated cardiovascular and metabolic function. Further research in the area using asymptomatic people, as well as people with known heart disease or muscle weakness, could enhance the usefulness of $\dot{V}O_2$ kinetic data as a diagnostic tool.

$\dot{V}O_2$ continues to increase after the initial 2-6 minute transient period of exercise when external work levels exceed 60% of $\dot{V}O_2$max. Despite earlier claims (Henry, 1951) that this constant increase in oxidative metabolism was for removal of lactate from the blood, recent evidence by Hagberg et al. (1978) attributes portions of this increase to the effect of temperature on muscle metabolism per se (Q-10 effect) and on ventilation (slight hyperventilation), thus increasing the O_2 requirement. Future research should focus on the mechanism of the slow rise in $\dot{V}O_2$ during steady-rate exercise and establish if there are differences between diverse populations (e.g., conditioned or nonconditioned asymptomatic subjects, and patients with heart and muscle diseases).

The Anaerobic Threshold

The anaerobic threshold (AT) was defined by Wasserman and co-workers (1973) as the level of exercise of $\dot{V}O_2$ just below that at which metabolic acidosis and the concomitant alterations in gas exchange occur. As exercise intensity is increased incrementally, the AT can be identified by the occurence of a nonlinear increase in ventilation and CO_2 production, an increase in end-tidal O_2 without a corresponding decrease in end-tidal CO_2, and an increase in the respiratory exchange ratio. Few would debate the existence of alterations in ventilatory gas exchange characterizing the concept of AT. As with values for $\dot{V}O_2$max, there appears to be a specific AT for different activities, such as arm cranking, leg cycling, and treadmill walking (Davis, Kurtz, Vodak, Vodak, & Wilmore, 1976). During these activities, the AT occurs at different relative values of $\dot{V}O_2$max (46-64%). Endurance conditioning of previously sedentary men increases the AT by 44% of the absolute $\dot{V}O_2$ and by 15% of the relative $\dot{V}O_2$ (Davis, Frank, Whipp, & Wasserman,1979). More data are required to document the role of absolute and relative ATs in endurance performance, the influence of frequency, intensity and duration of physical conditioning upon alterations of the AT, and the usefulness of the AT as a diagnostic tool in various disease states.

There has been considerable debate questioning whether the AT is a threshold of anaerobiosis in exercising skeletal muscle fibers, or whether other alterations which occur during incremental exercise explain the alterations in gas exchange. The observation that increases in circulating concentrations of lactate approximately coincide with alterations in gas exchange has led to the concept of the AT as representative of the onset of anaerobiosis (Davis et al., 1976; Wasserman et al., 1973). The critical question is whether significant hypoxia occurs in skeletal muscle contracting under physiological conditions. Jöbsis and Stainsby (1968) evaluated the steady-rate oxidation-reduction relationship of mitochondrial nicotinamide adenine dinucleotide in contracting dog skeletal muscle. Although they found no indication of tissue hypoxia, they did observe that lactate concentrations increased in the effluent blood. Venous PO_2 did not fall below the critical oxygen tension required for mitocondrial activity (Stainsby, 1966). This evidence does not rule out the possibility that selected motor units become hypoxic to some degree during submaximal exercise. As compared to those in a nonconditioned state, physically conditioned individuals have a smaller increase in blood and muscle lactate concentrations in response to the same relative or absolute submaximal exercise (Saltin & Karlsson, 1971). Moreover, the oxidative capacity of skeletal muscle increases with endurance training (Holloszy & Booth, 1976). If the difference in lactate between conditioned and nonconditioned subjects could be ascribed to tissue hypoxia, then conditioned subjects should have a higher $\dot{V}O_2$ than nonconditioned subjects at a given submaximal exercise intensity. However, the data do not support this argument (Saltin & Karlsson, 1971). A critical assessment of the effects of circulating catecholamines, the distribution of cardiac output away from the liver and kidney removing lactate from the blood, and the recruitment of more glycolytic motor units need to be investigated as possible mechanisms explaining the concept of anaerobic threshold.

Efficiency of Physical Exercise

Efficiency expresses the ratio of work accomplished to energy expended. Most studies have investigated submaximal exercise intensities to ensure that the measured $\dot{V}O_2$ reflects the totality of energy expenditure. The choice of a baseline correction substantially alters efficiency ratios. Gaesser and Brooks (1975) found that at an exercise intensity of 65 watts·min^{-1} on a bicycle ergometer (60 rpm), average efficiencies ranged from 17-27%, depending on the baseline correction used: gross efficiency (no baseline correction), work efficiency (unloaded cycling baseline), or net efficiency (resting metabolism baseline). Delta efficiency was defined as the ratio of increment in energy cost to the increment in exercise intensity, thus it provided a floating base-line. The similarity between delta efficiencies and theoretical muscle efficiencies calculated from thermodynamic assumptions (Gaesser & Brooks, 1975; Whipp & Wasserman, 1969) has been used as a rationale for the propriety of delta efficiency calculations. Additional work is required to establish that this coincidence of values is not fortuitous. Efficiency measured at the mouth represents the metabolic summation of concentric, eccentric, and isometric contractions of individual skeletal muscles with contractions initiated at different fiber lengths. These variables have been shown to effect the energetics of isolated dog muscle during exercise (Stainsby, 1976; Stainsby & Barclay, 1976). Moreover, measured efficiencies are altered by storage and utilization of elastic energy (Cavagna, 1977) and exhibit variable effects depending on type of activity. Estimates of whole body efficiencies determined in ergometry and with sophisticated goniometric and computer techniques agree with values obtained by indirect calorimetry (Zarrugh & Radcliffe, 1979).

Interest has also been focused on energy expenditure during eccentric contractions of the muscle as opposed to concentric contractions. During eccentric exercise, fewer motor units are recruited and the VO_2 is less than during concentric exercise at a given power output (Bigland-Ritchie & Woods, 1974). In spite of work with isolated muscle, the mechanism which differentiates energy output for eccentric and concentric contractions remains unknown.

Valid measures of heavy exercise efficiency when anaerobic glycolysis and glycogenolysis play a significant role in energy production have, for the most part, remained elusive. Earlier studies have reported "anaerobic" efficiencies in the 10-12% range, but such work can be criticized for methodological and theoretical reasons. Biochemically, one would predict anaerobic glycolysis to be more efficient than aerobic glycolysis (Lehninger, 1975). Gladden and Welch (1978) empirically established a $\dot{V}O_2$ equivalent of circulating blood lactate concentrations and found no difference between aerobic and anaerobic efficiencies.

Another unresolved issue involves the metabolic basis of postexercise oxygen uptake. Oxygen uptake remains elevated above resting values during recovery from exercise largely as a function of the intensity and duration of exercise. Since no external work is being performed during this time, it is inappropriate to include recovery $\dot{V}O_2$ in determinations of efficiency. However, recovery $\dot{V}O_2$ may indeed be considered as part of the total metabolic cost of activity. It is apparent that the totality of elevated postexercise metabolism cannot be ascribed to anaerobic energy production occurring at the onset of exercise (Stainsby & Barclay, 1970). Investigations are required to clearly identify the mechanism of the elevated metabolism during recovery from exercise and to determine its relevance to the calculations of physical activity efficiency (see chapter 7).

Factors Limiting Performance

To understand mechanisms involved in the regulation and limitations of whole body responses to exercise is a difficult task, but it is one that has captured the interest of exercise physiologists for years. The response of an intact organism to exercise reflects the integration of a multitude of cellular events in different physiological systems. As a consequence, research must be incorporated from several fields in order to appreciate our present state of knowledge.

Increased energy requirements in a muscle cell alter the adenine nucleotide ratios, and thereby stimulate cellular respiration. There is a linear relationship between blood flow and $\dot{V}O_2$ in an isolated muscle or an intact organism. In isolated muscle, the $\dot{V}O_2$ during maximal exercise can be varied by alterations in the delivery of O_2 (Barclay & Stainsby, 1975). Moreover, the oxidative capacity of whole muscle homogenates is much greater than the predicted $\dot{V}O_2$max of the muscle *in situ* (Gollnick, Armstrong, Saltin, Saubert, Sembrowich, & Shephard, 1973; Gollnick, Armstrong, Piehl, Saltin, & Saubert, 1972). These data suggest the oxidative capacity of muscle is not a limitation to $\dot{V}O_2$max. The relative contributions of the pumping capacity of the heart, the total blood volume, and the local control of skeletal muscle fiber blood flow in limiting O_2 delivery and consumption are not clear at this time. Research needs to focus on the relative importance of local and central control mechanisms (neural, humoral, and metabolic) during exercise-induced alterations in metabolism and on the adaptation of these controls to chronic endurance activity.

Descriptive research characterizing the physiological profiles of endurance athletes has focused on measurements of $\dot{V}O_2$max (Costill & Fox, 1969; Hanson, 1973; Magel & Faulkner, 1967). It is apparent that a relatively high $\dot{V}O_2$max is one characteristic separating elite endurance athletes quantitatively from sedentary and moderately active individuals. However, $\dot{V}O_2$max itself is not adequate for the prediction of performance among elite athletes (Costill, Fink, & Pollock, 1976). Furthermore, with conditioning, maximum performance may increase significantly without changing the $\dot{V}O_2$max (Faulkner, 1970). These data indicate that other physiological, biomechanical, and psychological variables may influence maximum endurance performance. The anaerobic power, the duration that a given percentage of $\dot{V}O_2$max can be maintained, joint mobility, genetic predisposition, muscular strength, the efficiency with which a task is performed, and psychological factors such as aggressiveness and the will to win are among those variables deserving attention.

Although the concept of "anaerobic" power has been used in exercise physiology, the precise definition and measurement of this concept is not clear. Biochemically, there are specific energy transducing processes which produce ATP and do not require O_2 (i.e., "anaerobic"). The rate and magnitude of these processes may be considered biochemically in terms of enzyme kinetics and concentrations, as well as the availability of substrates and co-factors. Even during activities requiring high-power output, these metabolic processes are not used exclusively as activity duration is prolonged. Cellular respiration is stimulated and supports an increasing proportion of the energy transductions. Because of the complexity of these interrelationships, no quantitative physiological measure of anaerobic power has been developed. Despite claims to the contrary (Astrand &Rodahl, 1977), blood lactate concentrations cannot be used as the sole quantitative index of anaerobic metabolism; lactate is in a dynamic turnover state during exercise with skeletal muscle producing and using lactate simultaneously (Issekutz, Issekutz, & Shaw, 1976; White, 1977). Future research should develop a physiologic measure for anaerobic metabolic capacity, determine its relevance to sport activities, and study its adaptation to selected conditioning protocols.

For exercise physiologists, the focus of attention on muscular strength is directed to the force that a group of muscles can exert on an external object. Studies of mammalian skeletal muscles *in vitro* and *in situ* indicate that 20-30 Newtons of force are generated for each square centimeter of muscle fiber cross-sectional area (Close, 1972). It is not possible to estimate the cross-sectional area in humans of the functional skeletal muscle fiber because of complex fiber angles and the contribution of more than one muscle to the expression of strength. Strength determinations are further complicated in humans by the lever systems through which the force is generated. Neural factors may also attenuate the expression of muscular strength, shown by the rapid increase in maximal voluntary contraction strength (MVC) unaccompanied by fiber hypertrophy at the beginning of training (Rasch & Morehouse, 1957). Merton (1954) concluded that a maximal voluntary contraction of the adductor pollicus muscle in the hand produced the same maximal tension as elicited by stimulation of the motor nerve. In contrast, data by Sugai, Worsley, and Payne (1975) indicate a greater tension was elicited with electrical stimulation than during voluntary contraction. Individuals with the greatest muscle strength have the longest absolute endurance time, but muscles with greater strength maintain a given proportion of MVC strength for a shorter endurance time than weaker muscles. The effect of strength training on MVC strength and endurance is not well understood; moreover, the role of specific strengths in sport activities needs careful evaluation.

Environmental Influences on Performance

There has been a long interest in the study of the effect of temperature, humidity, wind velocity, terrain, hypoxia, and hyperoxia on human physical performance. In most cases, these environmental factors attenuate physical performance to varying degrees, depending on the intensity, duration and type of activity. The mechanisms altering performance in different environments are only partially understood.

A number of studies have investigated the effect of heat (Dill, Nelson, & Yosef, 1973) and cold (Buskirk, 1978) on physical performance. Although the exact interaction between temperature and performance is not clear, extremes of ambient temperature have been reported to impair endurance activity. Edwards, Harris, Hultman, Kaijser, Koh, and Nordesjo (1972) have demonstrated an optimal muscle temperature range of 30-33°C for a static hold at a given percentage of MVC. These data contrast with human rectal temperatures as high as 42°C following 2-mile runs in hot environments (Faulkner, 1979). Muscle temperature in maximum exercise is usually several degrees centigrade higher than rectal temperature. Since maximum performance was not affected, the optimal muscle temperature for dynamic exercise is higher than for static; however, more definitive studies are needed in this area. Muscle performance capabilities appear to be much more limited by cold (Faulkner, White, & Markley, 1980). This is consistent with Arrhenius plots for a variety of oxidative enzymes which show large Q-10 values. Contractile properties of isolated skeletal muscle, such as contraction time, relaxation time and maximum velocity of shortening, are also slowed considerably by low temperatures. Additional research is required to understand the effect of ambient temperature on performance. One major experimental problem is that muscle temperature may vary widely during exercise, even though ambient temperature is held constant.

The energetics of performance are altered by both wind and terrain. The effect of wind velocity on performance has been studied in detail by Pugh et al. (1976). During walking or running against the wind, the energy cost of performance increases as the square of the wind velocity. Ramaswamy, Dua, Raizada, Dimri, Viswanathan, Madhaviah, and Srivastava (1966) found a linear increase in energy expenditure with the foot depression depth in snow up to a depth of 40 cm. The energy cost of uphill walking or running has been evaluated successfully by assessing the horizontal and vertical components separately (Donovan & Brooks, 1977).

The effect of hypoxia on performance has been investigated both at different altitudes in a natural environment and in hypobaric chambers

(Goddard, 1966). The effect of these environments on respiration, circulation, acid-base balance, and renal function are well described at rest and in exercise. An area of continuing controversy is the hypothesis that adaptation following conditioning at altitude is physiologically superior to conditioning at sea level (Balke, Daniels, & Faulkner, 1967). Also, it is yet unknown if patients with coronary artery disease are at greater risk at altitude than at sea level, and if not, whether cardiac preventive and rehabilitative programs are more effective at altitude (Balke, 1978). Sufficient data are not available to answer either of these questions.

There has been a long and continuing interest in the effect of breathing high oxygen mixtures (60 to 100% O_2) on performance since Bannister's (1954) early observation that performance was enhanced with high oxygen mixtures. Wilson et al. (1975) have studied the problem extensively and have confirmed the initial observations that high oxygen mixtures enhance endurance performance, but the mechanism responsible for enhancement has not been resolved.

Mechanisms of Muscle Weakness and Muscle Fatigue

Muscle weakness and muscle fatigue are different entities from a physiological and clinical viewpoint. Muscle weakness is the failure of a rested muscle or muscle group to generate the required or expected force (Edwards, 1972). Muscle fatigue is the failure of a muscle or a group of muscles to maintain the required or expected force during a sustained voluntary maximal isometric contraction, or with repeated isometric or isotonic contractions (Merton, 1954).

Muscle weakness may reflect an unwillingness or inability of the subject to make a maximum voluntary contraction. Motivational artifacts may be avoided by electrical stimulation of the motor nerve or by direct stimulation of the muscle (Edwards, 1967). Weakness in the presence of a maximum contraction may be due to atrophy of skeletal muscle fibers, a failure of some motor units to be activated, an asynchrony in motor unit recruitment, or various combinations of these factors. Atrophy of skeletal muscle fibers may result from either disuse or disease, whereas impaired activation of motor units may be a consequence of failure in neuromuscular transmission or defective propagation of the action potential (Edwards, 1979). Research should continue to study the mechanisms involved in muscle weakness and to assess the role of various treatment interventions, including physical activity, in attenuating these symptoms.

Muscle fatigue is an extremely complex phenomenon. ATP is the immediate source of energy for muscle contraction. When ATP concentration is depleted, a skeletal muscle fiber ceases to generate active tension (Cain & Davies, 1962). However, *in vivo* ATP concentrations are not decreased significantly when fatigue is clearly evident (Dawson, Gadian, & Wilkie, 1977). The causes of fatigue are still unknown and appear to vary depending on type of physical activity involved (Simonson, 1971). The degree of fatigue-associated impairment in skeletal muscle with high power output correlates with a decrease in the concentration of muscle glycogen (Bergström et al., 1967; Hermansen et al., 1967; Hultman, 1967; Saltin & Karlsson, 1971) and an increase in the concentration of blood and muscle lactate (Asmussen, 1950; Karlsson & Saltin, 1970). However, fatigue after prolonged exercise occurs with low blood and muscle lactate concentrations (Karlsson, 1971). Total body fatigue is even more difficult to evaluate than isolated muscle fatigue. Motivational factors, central nervous system fatigue, and changes in total body chemistry or electrolyte balances may be factors contributing separately or in concert. Future research will require innovative approaches to advance our knowledge of fatigue processes.

Physiological Adaptations to Conditioning Programs

Cardiopulmonary endurance conditioning results from participation in activities like running, swimming, cross-country skiing, and bicycling, which involve large muscle masses contracting against relatively low resistance (less than 30% MVC) for long durations several times per week. General minimum criteria for inducing physiological changes have been identified; however, there is little definitive data on the optimal conditioning program for a given individual of a specified initial physiological status. The recommendation of the American College of Sports Medicine (*Medicine and Science in Sports*, 1978) for "healthy adults" is exercise 3-5 days a week at an intensity of 50-80% of $\dot{V}O_2$max for a continuous duration of 15-60 min. The rate and magnitude of change in $\dot{V}O_2$max are dependent on the intensity, duration, and frequency of the conditioning sessions. The improvement in $\dot{V}O_2$max, which usually ranges from 5-25%, is influenced by the initial $\dot{V}O_2$max level, alterations in the mass of body fat, and the increase in oxidative capacity of skeletal muscles used in the activity. Data do not exist to quantitatively relate these variables, yet this relation is fundamentally important for those involved in implementing physical conditioning programs.

Researchers must remain mindful that $\dot{V}O_2$max is not the sole criteria governing physical performance. The effects of physical conditioning on "anaerobic" threshold, muscular strength, efficiency, body fat composition, joint flexibility, and psychological factors appear to be important components which should be considered and evaluated in applied psychological research. Conditioning studies are difficult to implement because of the attrition or failure of subjects to comply with the specifics of the conditioning program. Consequently, the majority of studies on humans have terminated after 8 weeks. Hickson, Bomze, and Holloszy (1977) indicated that significant changes in $\dot{V}O_2$max may occur with programs lasting longer than 8 weeks. This reassessment of both the rate of change of $\dot{V}O_2$max with time and the eventual magnitude of change is in need of further documentation.

Considerable information is available on enzymatic and morphological adaptations which allow increases in aerobic capacity to occur (for references, see Holloszy & Booth, 1976). The majority of this research was done with animals. Future research of this nature should focus on the quantitative contributions of nontraditional energy sources, such as amino acids, supporting exercise in nonconditioned and conditioned mammals, and the role of glycolysis and glycogenolysis in supporting lipid oxidation during endurance exercise.

The effect of strength conditioning on MVC strength and endurance is not well understood. The degree of hypertrophy in response to strength conditioning as observed in humans (e.g., football players and body builders) and animals clearly indicates that physiological adaptations are invoked. Most studies of strength conditioning have not been well controlled. Also, it is difficult to separate change in the expression of muscular strength due to alterations in neural disinhibition (Ikai & Steinhaus, 1961) and those due to intrinsic skeletal muscle adaptation. Recent studies of strength conditioning with cats (Gonyea & Bonde-Petersen, 1978) may clarify some of the physiological mechanisms involved. Future research needs to focus on the mechanism of selective hypertrophy of specific muscle fiber types, the collection of definitive data on the role of fiber splitting and hyperplasia, and investigations of the optimal stimulus and molecular mechanism of enhanced protein turnover. The neural aspects of recruitment, inhibition and disinhibition of motor units during voluntary contraction and their adaptation to chronic exercise need to be evaluated. Researchers must remain aware of the hazards of methodological artifacts (Armstrong, Marum, Saubert, & Tullson, 1979). Understanding the physiological mechanisms involved in the adaptation to strength conditioning may have important clinical implications for the rehabilitation of persons who suffer from muscle weakness and fatigue.

The Role of Endurance Conditioning in Prevention
of and Rehabilitation from Disease

Most investigations of physically active and inactive occupation groups (Fox & Skinner, 1964) and leisure groups (Morris, Adams, & Chava, 1973) indicate a two-fold higher incidence of mortality in the inactive populations because of coronary artery disease. Autopsy examinations of persons killed in accidents also support the premise that physically active people have a lower incidence of coronary artery disease than inactive people. In spite of consistent evidence that increased physical activity is associated with a decreased incidence of coronary heart disease, most studies are biased by a self-selection of persons into the physically inactive and active groups. Furthermore, the intensity, duration, and frequency of the physical activity in most population studies has been defined on occupational classifications. The result is considerable variability among subjects within a given physical activity classification. Attempts have been made to initiate prospective studies in which subjects are randomly assigned to the physically inactive and active groups (Taylor, 1973). Unfortunately, evaluations of these studies have been hampered by subjects' lack of adherence to the prescribed exercise intensities in the physically active and inactive groups.

Light activity was once considered adequate to provide protection from coronary artery disease, but moderate activity was credited with even greater protection (Fox & Skinner, 1964). There is now evidence that vigorous physical activity, of approximately seven times the resting metabolism, is necessary to decrease to risk of coronary heart disease (Paffenbarger & Hale, 1975). The recency of a physically inactive lifestyle (Kahn, 1963) and the effects of ischemic injury to the myocardium (Rose, Hamilton, & Keen, 1977) are factors that may further complicate the association between physical activity and the incidence of coronary artery disease. In spite of extravagant claims by some enthusiasts, no exercise program, regardless of intensity and duration, provides immunity from coronary artery disease (Opie, 1975).

Recent epidemiologic studies have found that children in teen and preteen years have indicators of coronary risk factors (Boyer, 1974). The role of physical exercise in modifying this profile requires systematic and well-controlled research. Eliciting the cooperation of clinicians in studies of appropriate patient populations is a significant problem needing to be overcome.

Much remains to be done in the design and implementation of studies of high-risk subjects suffering from cardiopulmonary abnormalities. Recent evidence suggests that the metabolic and cardiovascular responses to graded exercise might differ significantly in patient populations compared to asymptomatic populations (Faulkner, 1978). The interactions of these differences, coupled with the difficulties in selecting optimal intensities, durations, and frequencies for conditioning, make this a difficult although rewarding field for research.

Future Prospects

There are innumerable problems to be investigated in each of the major areas described. Many problems have remained unsolved for years, partially because of technical and methodological reasons. Also, the practice of some exercise physiologists of investigating trivial aspects of the major issues or reinvestigating minor aspects of problems essentially solved is another factor in the present lack of answers. This has been particularly true, for example, with studies in the area of $\dot{V}O_2$max and physical performance. There have been significant contributions, but once methods are established, exercise physiologists must ensure they are applied to a significant problem area. It is not appropriate to develop or learn a method and then seek a problem to which it can be applied. Exercise physiologists must put considerable effort into the formulation of testable hypotheses to strive for an understanding of mechanisms. This kind of effort will clarify the factors which regulate, facilitate, and limit our ability to exercise in health and disease.

Significant problems in exercise physiology could be more effectively pursued if an accumulative method of inductive inference, termed "Strong Inference" by Platt (1964), were systematically taught and used. In essence, strong inference consists of (a) development of alternative testable hypotheses; (b) devising and performing critical experiments(s) which, based on the outcome, will exclude one or more of the hypotheses; and (c) recycling the procedure by making subhypotheses or sequential hypotheses to refine the remaining possibilities. Platt likens the process to climbing a tree; as the tree branches, the experimental outcome dictates the logical branch to take by rejecting one of the alternative hypotheses. The researcher then proceeds up the "tree" from choice to choice until the problem is solved.

There appear to be other reasons for the apparent failure of many exercise physiologists to design and implement significant investigations. Compared to their colleagues in physiology or biochemistry, many graduate students in exercise physiology have had less exposure to basic science courses, less time in their program devoted to research, and much less emphasis on postdoctoral training before obtaining a faculty position. The result is that young faculty members in exercise physiology are often at a disadvantage in competition for research grants, in the general conduct of research programs, and ultimately in the quality of research publications.

Graduate curricula in exercise physiology should rely on other disciplines within the university for selected quantitative courses in anatomy, biology, biochemistry, physiology, physics, mathematics, and nutrition. It is a task of exercise physiology programs to extract from these basic curricula the knowledge relevant to understanding exercise as a science. Furthermore, coalescing knowledge should occur in courses, and most importantly, in research laboratories.

Obtaining post doctoral research experience of two to three years duration appears critical for optimal development of exercise physiologists. Potential post doctoral scholars are well advised to select a research setting other than where they earn a Ph.D. The choice is critical: the major criteria should be a currently productive and well-funded laboratory with a senior scientist who has a favorable international or national reputation. Graduate students should think of possible locations by the end of their first year and initiate inquiries when no less than two years remain before earning their Ph.D. There are several possibilities of funding. A few investigators will have institutional funds which they can award to scholars at their own discretion. A more frequent approach is to work with a scientist and third-party funding, (e.g., the National Institutes of Health, Muscular Dystrophy Association, American Heart Association, and a State Heart Association).

Exercise physiology is an exciting and challenging field. The prospects for future research are extremely promising for imaginative, properly trained, and insightful scientists.

References

Ahlborg, G., Felig, P., Hagenfeldt, L., Hendler, R., & Wahren, J. Substrate turnover during prolonged exercise in man. *Journal of Clinical Investigations,* 1974, **54**, 1080-1090.

American College of Sports Medicine: Position statement on the recommended quantity and quality of exercise for developing and maintaining fitness in healthy adults. *Medicine and Science in Sports*, 1978, **10**, VII-X.

Armstrong, R.B., Marum, P., Tullson, P., & Saubert IV, C.W. Acute hypertrophic response of skeletal muscle to removal of synergists. *Journal of Applied Physiology: Respiration, Environmental and Exercise*

Physiology, 1979, **46**, 835-842.

Asmussen, E. Pyruvate and lactate content of the blood during and after muscular work. *Acta Physiologica Scandinavica,* 1950, **20**, 125-132.

Astrand, P.O. & Rodahl, K. *Textbook of work physiology.* McGraw-Hill: New York, 1977.

Balke, B. Altitude and cold: The cardiac patient. In M.L. Pollock & S.H. Schmidt (Eds.), *Heart disease and rehabilitation.* Boston, MA: Houghton-Mifflin Co., 1978.

Balke, B., Daniels, J.T., & Faulkner, J.A. Training for maximum performance at altitude. In R. Margaria (Ed.), *Symposium proceedings on exercise at altitude.* Amsterdam, The Netherlands: Excerpta Medica, 1967.

Bannister, R.G. & Cunningham, D.J.C. The effects on the respiration and performance during exercise of adding oxygen to the inspired air. *Journal of Physiology,* 1954, **125**, 118-137.

Barclay, J.K. & Stainsby, W.N. The role of blood flow in limiting maximal metabolic rate in muscle. *Medicine and Science in Sports,* 1975, **7**, 116-119.

Bergstrom, J., Hermansen, L., Hultman, E., & Saltin, B. Diet, muscle glycogen and physical performance. *Acta Physiologica Scandinavica,* 1967, **71**, 140-150.

Bigland-Ritchie, B. & Woods, J.J. Integrated EMG and oxygen uptake during dynamic contractions of human muscles. *Journal of Applied Physiology,* 1974, **36**, 475-479.

Boyer, J.L. Coronary heart disease as a pediatric problem. *American Journal of Cardiology,* 1974, **33**, 784-786.

Buse, M.G., Biggers, J.F., Friderici, K.H., & Buse, J.F. Oxidation of branched chain amino acids by isolated hearts and diaphragms of the rat. *Journal of Biological Chemistry,* 1972, **247**, 8085-8096.

Buskirk, E.R. Cold stress: A selective review. In L.J. Falinsbee et al., (Eds.), *Environmental stress: Individual human adaptations.* New York: Academic Press, 1978.

Cain, D.F. & Davies, R.E. Breakdown of adenosine triphosphate during a single contraction of working muscle. *Biochemical and Biophysical Research Communications,* 1962, **8**, 361-366.

Cavagna, G.A. Storage and utilization of elastic energy in skeletal muscle. In R. Hutton (Ed.), *Exercise and sports science reviews* (Vol. 5). Santa Barbara, CA: Journal Publishing Affiliates, 1977.

Cerretelli, P., Shindell, D., Pendergast, D.P., DiPrampero, P.E., & Rennie, D.W. Oxygen uptake transients at the onset and offset of arm and leg work. *Respiration Physiology,* 1977, **30**, 81-97.

Close, R.I. Dynamic properties of mammalian skeletal muscles. *Physiological Reviews*, 1972, **52**, 129-197.

Conlee, R.K., Hickson, R.C., Winder, W.W., Hagberg, J.M., & Holloszy, J.O. Regulation of glycogen resynthesis in muscles of rats following exercise. *American Journal of Physiology*, 1978, **235**, R145-R150.

Costill, D.L., Fink, W.J., Pollock, M.L. Muscle fiber composition and enzyme activities of elite distance runners. *Medicine and Science in Sports*, 1976, **8**, 96-100.

Costill, D.L. & Fox, E.L. Energetics of marathon running. *Medicine and Science in Sports*, 1969, **1**, 81-86.

Davis, J.A., Frank, M.H., Whipp, B.J., & Wasserman, K. Anaerobic theshold alterations caused by endurance training in middle-aged men. *Journal of Applied Physiology:Respiration, Environmental and Exercise Physiology*, 1979, **46**, 1039-1046.

Davis, J.A., Vodak, P., Wilmore, J.H., Vodak, J., & Kurtz, P. Anaerobic threshold and maximal aerobic power for three modes of exercise. *Journal of Applied Physiology*, 1976, **41**, 544-550.

Dawson, M.J., Gadian, D.G., & Wilkie, D.R. Contraction and recovery of living muscles studies by ^{31}P nuclear magnetic resonance. *Journal of Physiology*, 1977, **267**, 703-735.

Dill, D.B., Yousef, M.K., & Nelson, J.D. Responses of men and women to two-hour walks in desert heat. *Journal of Applied Physiology*, 1973, **35**, 231-235.

Dohm, G.L., Hecker, A.L., Brown, W.E., Klain, G.J., Puente, F.R., Askew, E.W., & Beecher, G.R. Adaptation of protein metabolism to endurance training. *Biochemical Journal*, 1977, **164**, 705-708.

Donovan, C.M., & Brooks, G.A. Muscular efficiency during steady rate exercise II. Effects of walking speed and work rate. *Journal of Applied Physiology:Respiration, Environmental and Exercise Physiology*, 1977, **43**, 431-439.

Edwards, R.H.T. Physiological and metabolic studies of the contractile machinery of human muscle in health and disease. *Physics in Medicine and Biology*, 1979, **24**, 237-249.

Edwards, R.H.T., Harris, R.C., Hultman, E., Kaijser, L., Koh, D., & Nordesjo, L-O. Effect of temperature on muscle energy metabolism and endurance during successive isometric contractions, sustained to fatigue, of the quadriceps muscle in man. *Journal of Physiology*, 1972, **220**, 335-352.

Faulkner, J.A. Muscle fatigue. In E.J. Briskey, R.G. Cassens, & B.B. Marsh (Eds.), *The physiology and biochemistry of muscle as a food*, (Vol. 2), Madison, WI: University of Wisconsin Press, 1970.

Faulkner, J.A. Cardiac rehabilitation: Major concerns in basic physiology. In M.L. Pollock & S.H. Schmidt (Eds.), *Heart disease and rehabilitation.* Boston, MA: Houghton-Mifflin, 1978.

Faulkner, J.A. Heat and contractile properties of skeletal muscle. In M.K. Yousef & S.M. Horvath (Eds.), *Life, heat and altitude.* Springfield, IL: Charles C. Thomas, 1979.

Faulkner, J.A., White, T.P., & Markley, J.M. The 1979 Canadian ski marathon: A natural experiment in hypothermia. In F.J. Nagle & H.J. Montoye (Eds.), *Exercise in health and disease-Balke symposium.* Springfield, IL: Charles C. Thomas, 1980.

Felig, P. & Wahren, J. Amino acid metabolism in exercising man. *Journal of Clinical Investigation,* 1971, **50**, 2703-2714.

Fox, S.M. III, & Skinner, J.S., Physical activity and cardiovascular health. *American Journal of Cardiology,* 1964, **14**, 731-746.

Gaesser, G.A. & Brooks, G.A. Muscular efficiency during steady-rate exercise: effects of speed and work rate. *Journal of Applied Physiology,* 1975, **38**, 1132-1139.

Gladden, L.B. & Welch, H. Efficiency of anaerobic work. *Journal of Applied Physiology:Respiration, Environmental and Exercise Physiology,* 1978, **44**, 564-570.

Goddard, R.F., (Ed.). *The effects of altitude on physical performance.* Albuquerque, NM: The Athletic Institute, 1966.

Goldberg, A.L. & Odessey, R. Oxidation of amino acids by diaphragms from fed and fasted rats. *American Journal of Physiology,* 1972, **223**, 1384-1391.

Gollnick, P.D., Armstrong, R.B., Saltin, B., Saubert IV, C.W., Sembrowich, W.L., & Shephard, R.E. Effect of training on enzyme activities and fiber composition of human skeletal muscle. *Journal of Applied Physiology,* 1973, **34**, 107-111.

Gollnick, P.D., Armstrong, R.B., Saubert IV, C.W., Piehl, K., & Saltin, B. Enzyme activity and fiber composition in skeletal muscle of untrained and trained men. *Journal of Applied Physiology,* 1972, **33**, 312-319.

Gontzea, I., Sutzescu, P., & Dumitrache, S. The influence of muscular activity on nitrogen balance and on the need of man for protein. *Nutrition Reports International,* 1974, **10**, 35-43.

Gonyea, W. & Bonde-Petersen, F. Alterations in muscle contractile properties and fiber composition after weight-lifting exercise in cats. *Experimental Neurology,* 1978, **59**, 75-84.

Hagberg, J.M., Mullin, J.P., & Nagle, F.J. Oxygen consumption during constant-load exercise. *Journal of Applied Physiology:Respiration,*

Environmental and Exercise Physiology, 1978, **45**, 381-384.

Hagberg, J.M., Nagle, F.J., & Carlson, J.L. Transient O_2 uptake response at the onset of exercise. *Journal of Applied Physiology: Respiration, Environmental and Exercise Physiology,* 1978, **44**, 90-92.

Hanson, J.S. Maximal exercise performance in members of the U.S. Nordic Ski Team. *Journal of Applied Physiology,* 1973, **35**, 592-595.

Henry, F.M. Aerobic oxygen consumption and alactic debt in muscular work. *Journal of Applied Physiology,* 1951, **3**, 427-438.

Hermansen, L., Hultman, E., & Saltin, B. Muscle glycogen during prolonged severe exercise. *Acta Physiologica Scandinavica,* 1967, **71**, 129-139.

Hickson, R.C., Bomze, H.A., & Holloszy, J.O. Linear increase in aerobic power induced by a strenuous program of endurance exercise. *Journal of Applied Physiology: Respiration, Environmental and Exercise Physiology,* 1977, **42**, 372-376.

Hickson, R.C., Bomze, H.A., & Holloszy, J.O. Faster adjustment of O_2 uptake to the energy requirement of exercise in the trained state. *Journal of Applied Physiology : Environmental and Exercise Physiology,* 1978, **44**, 877-881.

Holloszy, J.O. & Booth, F.W. Biochemical adaptations to endurance exercise in muscle. *Annual Reviews of Physiology,* 1976, **38**, 273-291.

Hultman, E. Physiological role of muscle glycogen in man, with special reference to exercise. *Circulation Research,* 1967, Suppl. I, I 99-I 114.

Hultman, E. & Bergstrom, J. Muscle glycogen synthesis in relation to diet studied in normal subjects. *Acta Medica Scandinavica,* 1967, **182**, 109-117.

Ikai, M. & Steinhaus, A.H. Some factors modifying the expression of strength. *Journal of Applied Physiology,* 1961, **16**, 157-163.

Issekutz, B.J., Shaw, W.A.S., & Issekutz, A.C. Lactate metabolism in resting and exercising dogs. *Journal of Applied Physiology,* 1976, **40**, 312-319.

Jobsis, F.F. & Stainsby, W.N. Oxidation of NADH during contractions of circulated mammalian skeletal muscle. *Respiration Physiology,* 1968, **4**, 292-300.

Kahn, H. The relationship of reported coronary heart disease mortality due to physical activity of work. *American Journal of Public Health,* 1963, **53**, 1058-1067.

Karlsson, J. Lactate and phosphagen concentrations in working muscle of man. *Acta Physiologica Scandinavica,* 1971, Suppl. 358, 7-72.

Karlsson, J. & Saltin, B. Lactate, ATP and CP in working muscles during exercise in man. *Journal of Applied Physiology,* 1970, **29**, 598-

602.

Lehninger, A.L. *Biochemistry* (2nd ed.). New York: Worth Publishers, 1975.

Magel, J.R. & Faulkner, J.A. Maximum oxygen uptakes of college swimmers. *Journal of Applied Physiology,* 1967, **22,** 929-938.

Merton, P.A. Voluntary strength and fatigue. *Journal of Physiology,* 1954, **123,** 553-564.

Mirkin, G. Carbohydrate loading: a dangerous practice. *Journal of the American Medical Association,* 1973, **223,** 1511-1512.

Molé, P.A., Baldwin, K.M., Terjung, R.L., & Holloszy, J.O. Enzymatic pathways of pyruvate metabolism in skeletal muscle: adaptations to exercise. *American Journal of Physiology,* 1973, **224,** 50-54.

Morris, J.N., Adams, C., & Chave, S.P.W. Vigorous exercise in leisure-time and the incidence of coronary heart disease. *Lancet,* 1973, **1,** 333-339.

Opie, L.H. Sudden death and sport. *Lancet,* 1975, **1,** 263-266.

Paffenbarger, R.S. & Hale, W.E. Work activity and coronary heart mortality. *New England Journal of Medicine,* 1975, **292,** 545-550.

Platt, J.R. Strong inference. *Science,* 1964, **146,** 347-352.

Pugh, L.G.C.E. The influence of wind resistance in running and walking and the mechanical efficiency of work against horizontal or vertical forces. *Journal of Physiology,* 1976, **213,** 255-276.

Ramaswamy, G.L. Dua, Raizada, W.V., Dimri, G.P., Viswanathan, K.R., Madhaviah, J., & Srivastava, T.N. Effect of looseness of snow on energy expenditure in marching on snow covered ground. *Journal of Applied Physiology,* 1966, **21,** 1747-1749.

Rasch, P.J. & Morehouse, L.E. Effect of static and dynamic exercise on muscular strength and hypertrophy. *Journal of Applied Physiology,* 1957, **11,** 29-34.

Rose, G., Hamilton, P.J.S., & Keen, H. Myocardial ischemia, risk factors and death from coronary heart disease. *Lancet,* 1977, **1,** 105-109.

Saltin, B. & Karlsson, J. Muscle glycogen utilization during work of different intensities. In B. Pernow & B. Saltin (Eds.), *Muscle metabolism during exercise.* New York: Plenum Press, 1971.

Scrutton, M.C. & Utter, M.F. The regulation of glycolysis and gluconeogenesis in animal tissues. *Annual Reviews of Biochemistry,* 1968, **37,** 249-302.

Simonson, G. *Physiology of work capacity and fatigue.* Springfield, IL: Charles C. Thomas, 1971.

Stainsby, W.N. Some critical oxygen tensions and their physiological importance. In *Cardiovascular and Respiratory Effects of Hypoxia, International Symposium.* New York, NY: Karger, Basel, 1966.

Stainsby, W.N. Oxygen uptake for negative work, stretching contractions by *in situ* dog skeletal muscle. *American Journal of Physiology,* 1976, **230**, 1013-1017.

Stainsby, W.N. & Barclay, J. Exercise metabolism: O_2 deficit, steady level O_2 uptake and O_2 uptake for recovery. *Medicine and Science in Sports* 1970, **2**, 177-181.

Stainsby, W.N. & Barclay, J.K. Effect of initial length on relations between oxygen uptake and load in dog muscle. *American Journal of Physiolog* 1976, **230**, 1008-1012.

Sugai, N., Worsley, R., & Payne, J.P. Tetanic force development of adductor pollicis muscle in anesthetized man. *Journal of Applied Physiology,* 1975, **39**, 714-717.

Taylor, H.L., Buskirk, E.R., & Remington, R.D. Exercise in controlled trials of the prevention of coronary heart disease. *Federation Proceedings,* 1973, **32**, 1623-1627.

Wasserman, K., Whipp, B.J., Koyal, S.N., & Beaver, W.L. Anaerobic threshold and respiratory gas exchange during exercise. *Journal of Applied Physiology,* 1973, **35**, 236-243.

Whipp, B.J. & Wasserman, K. Efficiency of muscular work. *Journal of Applied Physiology,* 1969, **26**, 644-648.

Whipp, B.J. & Wasserman, K. Oxygen uptake kinetics for various intensities of constant-load work. *Journal of Applied Physiology,* 1972, **33**, 351-356.

White, T.P. *The influence of metabolic rate upon the metabolism of lactic acid and the oxidation of glucose, alanine and leucine.* Unpublished doctoral dissertation, University of California, Berkeley, 1977.

Wilson, B.A., Welch, H.G., & Liles, J.N. Effects of hyperoxic gas mixtures on energy metabolism during prolonged work. *Journal of Applied Physiology,* 1975, **39**, 267-271.

Zarrugh, M.Y. & Radcliffe, C.W. Computer generation of human gait kinematics. *Journal of Biomechanics,* 1979, **12**, 99-111.

The Physiological Bases of Elevated Postexercise Oxygen Consumption

7 G.A. Brooks

Studies of lactic acid metabolism and the relationship between lactic acid[1] and the extra O_2 consumed during recovery from exercise can be traced to the beginnings of modern physiology. These problems have held the attention of individuals interested in both basic and applied aspects of research. Investigators in the areas of muscle energetics and biochemistry have studied lactic acid metabolism in detail. Lactic acid metabolism during exercise and recovery has also been of interest to zoologists who have endeavored to determine how exercise capability and metabolic function have effected territorial dominance, survival, and ecological impact of various species. Clinically, the point at which lactic acid starts to accumulate in the blood during a graded exercise test has been used to study and classify the severity of coronary artery disease.

Investigations into lactic acid formation and removal, and the relationships among these processes and recovery from hard exercise, have also occupied the interest of many physical education researchers interested in the factors limiting human exercise performance. Indeed, mechanisms of lactic acid metabolism and "O_2 debt" may constitute the major body of research developed by exercise physiologists in departments of physical education. Students interested in this topic will gain several insights into physical education research. For instance, this chapter describes how applied research grew out of earlier basic research, and the reader can

Research supported by DHEW Grand NIH AM19577.

[1]Lactic acid is a by-product of the rapid breakdown of glucose (a sugar) and glycogen (a stored carbohydrate). At a physiological pH, a lactic acid molecule will disassociate a proton (H+) and leave a lactate ion ($C_3H_5O_3$-). Although they are not precisely the same thing, the terms lactic acid and lactate are used interchangably for convenience.

get a feel for how technical advances have allowed understanding of a long studied phenomenon to progress.

Questions of lactic acid metabolism and the O_2 debt are long standing. Recently, our view of how these processes are related has changed. In all likelihood, future research will continue to expand our understanding of lactic acid metabolism during recovery from exercise. Knowledge of the basic physiology should result in improvement in exercise training and recovery procedures.

Basic Terminology

In response to a sudden (step function) increase in exercise work rate, such as during the transition from rest to a constant exercise work load, the rate of O_2 consumption ($\dot{V}O_2$) increases from a low level, to a new, higher level. In the case of submaximal exercise, this increase in $\dot{V}O_2$ is proportional to the exercise work load (see Figure 1A). In the case of maximal exercise, the O_2 consumption reaches its highest possible value ($\dot{V}O_2$ max) (see Figure 1B). During the transition from rest to exercise in untrained subjects, it takes approximately 30 seconds for $\dot{V}O_2$ to achieve half of its ultimate response. The half-response time can be somewhat reduced by training. In submaximal, steady-rate exercise (see Figure 1A), the difference between the steady-rate $\dot{V}O_2$ and the actual $\dot{V}O_2$ is the "O_2 deficit." In maximal exercise (see Figure 1B), the O_2 deficit is larger than that in submaximal exercise, but the O_2 deficit cannot be estimated with certainty in maximal exercise as there is no precise value for the O_2 requirement as exists for steady-rate, submaximal exercise. After exercise, O_2 consumption returns to resting levels in a curvilinear, exponential fashion (see Figure 2A). When plotted using semi-log coordinates, the postexercise $\dot{V}O_2$ curve after easy exercise has only one, initial fast component (see Figure 2B). After moderate intensity, and hard exercise, the fast curve component is followed by a second, slow curve component (see Figure 2C). In cases such as this (see Figure 2), semi-log plots are useful because variables which change at constant rates are revealed as straight lines on the graph. The extra O_2 consumed above resting values after exercise was termed the "O_2 debt" by Hill and associates (Hill & Lupton, 1923; Hill, Long, & Lupton, 1924a). The "O_2 debt" after exercise (see Figure 2A) is therefore described in terms of its volume and curve kinetics of exponential decay. The elevated postexercise O_2 consumption (EPOC) is still generally referred to as the "O_2 debt."

In reading classical papers (Hill & Lupton, 1923; Hill et al., 1924a; Hill et al., 1924b; Hill et al., 1924c; Margaria, Edwards, & Dill, 1933),

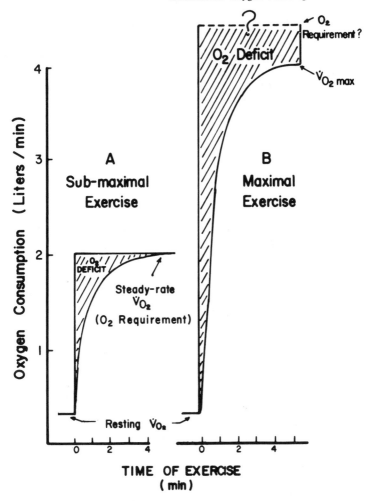

Figure 1. Oxygen consumption ($\dot{V}O_2$) before and during continuous bouts of steady-rate submaximal, and maximal exercise. In submaximal exercise (A), the O_2 deficit can be estimated as the difference between the steady-rate $\dot{V}O_2$ and the actual $\dot{V}O_2$ prior to attainment of the steady-rate $\dot{V}O_2$. In maximal exercise, (B) the O_2 deficit cannot be estimated with certainty for lack of a precise value of the O_2 requirement.

and contemporary textbook descriptions on the subject (Åstrand & Rodahl, 1970; Lehninger, 1970), it appears that the elevated O_2 consumption after exercise has a simple explanation. It is commonly believed that the energy cost of converting the lactic acid formed during

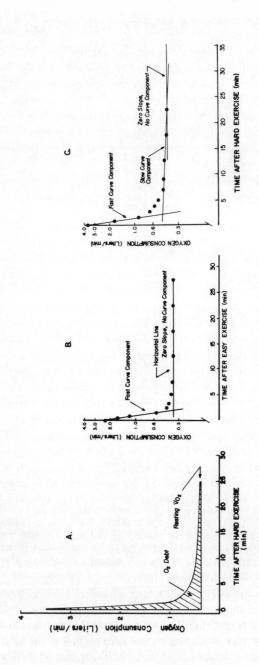

Figure 2. Oxygen consumption ($\dot{V}O_2$) after a period of exercise requiring a constant work output. In part (A), plotted on linear coordinates, the "O_2 debt" is the area under the postexercise $\dot{V}O_2$ curve above the resting $\dot{V}O_2$ baseline. In part (B), $\dot{V}O_2$ after easy exercise is plotted on semi-log coordinates. Note one postexercise $\dot{V}O_2$ curve component after easy exercise (B), and two components after hard exercise (C).

exercise to glycogen is largely responsible for the elevated O_2 consumption observed in recovery.

However, rather than a simple explanation of the "O_2 debt" involving the elevation of lactic acid to glycogen, I hypothesize that the reasons for an elevated rate of postexercise O_2 consumption are complex. Physical exercise results in profound alterations in body homeostasis. The changes in tissue temperatures, hormones, ions and metabolite levels which occur during exercise persist during the recovery period. These factors affect O_2 consumption during recovery and are responsible for the phenomenon known as the "O_2 debt."

The Classical Research

In 1923 and 1924, A.V. Hill and colleagues attempted to unify the results of experiments on isolated muscles with results obtained on intact humans. Figure 3 summarizes some of the observations considered by these early investigators. Hill (1913) expanded his earlier finding using the thermopile on isolated frog muscles stimulated to contract at 0°C to include a component of the heat release called the "recovery heat" which is at least equal to that liberated during contraction itself. In contrast to the initial heat release during a contraction, which was completely independent of the presence of O_2, only very small amounts of recovery heat were observed in the absence of O_2. Since Fletcher and Hopkins (1907) had previously shown that lactate formation was independent of the presence of O_2, but the presence of O_2 was requisite for the disappearance of lactate, "the natural conclusion was that the energy of contraction was derived from the breakdown of some precursor to lactate—a process accompanied by the production of heat and not requiring oxygen; while recovery was associated with the oxidation of lactate—a process also accompanied by the production of heat but dependent on the presence of O_2"(Harris, 1969, p. 381). Also, Hill (1914) determined that the recovery heat was equivalent to the heat of combustion (i.e., the enthalpy) of only a minor fraction (1/5 to 1/6) of the lactate formed during contractions (see Figure 3). Hill, therefore, suggested that only part of the lactate was oxidized during recovery, the rest being resynthesized to its precursor.

Subsequent to Hill (1913, 1914), Otto Meyerhof (1920a, 1920b, 1920c) determined that the precursor of lactate was glycogen. Additionally, Meyerhof found that the O_2 consumed during frog muscle recovery from stimulation was only equivalent to 1/3 of the lactate which disappeared in recovery, and that the heat given off during re-

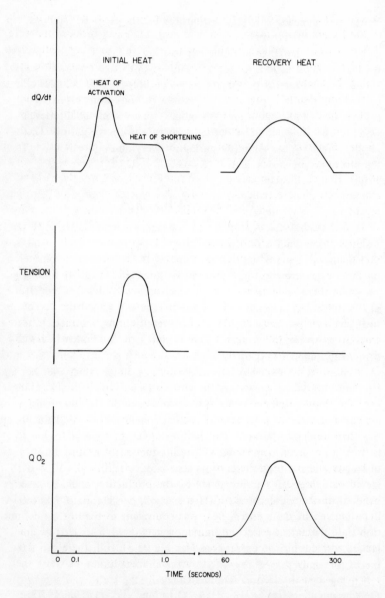

Figure 3. Schematic depiction of the heat production (dQ/dt), tension development, and O_2 consumption (QO_2) in isolated amphibian muscle twitching at $0°C$, adopted from Hill (1913, 1914) and Mommaerts (1969). The recovery heat happens to equal the enthalpy of 1/5 of the lactate formed during the twitch.

covery was also approximately equal to the heat of combustion of 1/3 of the lactate disappearing. So even though the exact proportions were different from the results of Hill's work, Meyerhof also concluded that a minor fraction of the lactate was oxidized during recovery, thus providing the energy for the resynthesis of the remainder to glycogen.

It is important to note parenthetically here the existence of an important species difference between the frog and the human. That is, frog muscle is capable of converting lactic acid to glycogen (Meyerhof, 1920a). Mammalian skeletal muscle is, however, not capable of performing this process at rates of quantitative importance (Scrutton & Utter, 1968). Rather, in mammals the liver and kidney perform the tasks of making new glucose (gluconeogenesis). The glucose formed in these gut organs which is released into the circulation provides the precursor for skeletal muscle glycogen restitution.

Since the classic work of Benedict and Cathcart (1913), it was known that the basal O_2 consumption of a human remained elevated for as much as a day after exercise. Hill and Lupton (1923) reported that in moderate steady-rate exercise the oxygen uptake gradually rises until 2 or 3 minutes it equals the oxygen requirements, the recovery oxygen in this case is simply equal to the initial lag in the oxygen intake. In severe exercise, however, the oxygen intake cannot match the oxygen requirement, and a large oxygen debt is incurred which is paid off in recovery. In attempting to explain the observation of an increased rate of O_2 consumption after exercise in the human, Hill et al., (1924a) used the finding that the concentration of lactate in the blood was increased as a result of exercise, but that it decreased in recovery. It was therefore appropriate to conclude that in the whole body, just as in isolated muscle, the recovery O_2 was associated with the oxidation of lactate and the resynthesis of glycogen. Since Hill et al. (1924b) observed that the postexercise oxygen consumption curve could be described by two exponential components (for example, see Figure 2C), it was hypothesized that the initial, fast component was due to the oxidation of lactate within the exercised muscle, and that the second, slow component was due to the oxidation of lactate that had diffused out of the muscle and escaped elsewhere via the circulation.

Through the 1920s and early 1930s, while the lactic acid theory of EPOC was still widely accepted, the lactic acid theory of muscle contraction fell into disfavor (Mommaerts, 1969). In their experiments, Margaria et al. (1933) observed that most of the "O_2 debt" was over before arterial lactate level started to decline. Therefore, Margaria et al. proposed that the "O_2 debt" consisted of fast "alactacid" as well as slow "lactacid" components. In this terminology, "alactacid" meant not having to do with lactic acid. The EPOC observed during recovery was thought not only to represent the reconversion of lactate to glycogen, (i.e., lactacid O_2 debt), but also to be attributable to the re-esterification of phosphagen (ATP and creatine phosphate; i.e., the "alactacid" O_2 debt).

Perhaps some of the most significant of all work on the so-called "O_2 debt" was published by Ole Bang (1936). The insight Bang was able to bring to the postexercise O_2 consumption phenomena was made possible by monitoring blood lactate during, not just after, exercise and by varying the duration and intensity of exercise. During prolonged bicycle exercise, Bang observed that the concentration of blood lactate reached a maximum in five to ten minutes and then declined again even though exercise continued. After prolonged exercise then, there was the finding of an "O_2 debt" to be paid in the absence of an elevated lactate concentration. On the other hand, using exercise bouts lasting only a few minutes, Bang found that the concentration of lactic acid in the blood reached a maximum after exercise had ended, and depending on the intensity of the exercise, remained elevated long after the oxygen intake had returned to initial preexercise baseline levels. The results of these experiments on short exercise tasks, as with the results on the prolonged exercise tasks, could not be reconciled with the idea that the metabolism of lactate determined oxygen consumption after exercise.

In spite of Bang's work, general belief in the lactic acid basis of O_2 debt has continued. As noted above, Hill et al. (1924b) had observed that the postexercise oxygen consumption curve consisted of two components. Margaria et al. (1933) corroborated the result that both the fast and slow portions of the O_2 debt declined exponentially. Subsequent work by Henry, and Henry and De Moor (Henry, 1951; Henry & De Moor, 1950; Henry & De Moor, 1956), which precisely described the shapes of the two postexercise O_2 consumption exponentials, supported the hypothesis that the two curve components measured separate "alactacid" and "lactacid" debts. As noted by Harris (1969), however, the decline in O_2 consumption after exercise in these experiments was at no time shown to coincide with any physiological entity, even blood lactate. It now appears that some experiments, in which the shapes of the fast (alactacid) and slow (lactacid) curve components were carefully described, were below the threshold for lactate accumulation in the blood (Wasserman & McIlroy, 1964). Therefore, the shape of the "lactacid" curve was described when there should not have been a "lactacid O_2 debt."

Other Experimental Approaches

Since the classical work of the 1920s and 1930s, several approaches have been taken to improve understanding of the phenomena of elevated postexercise O_2 consumption. Utilizing dog preparations, Alpert and workers in his laboratory (Alpert, 1965; Alpert & Root, 1954; Kayne & Alpert, 1964) were particularly involved in studying the role of lactic acid as determining the "O_2 debt." Kayne and Alpert observed that functionally eviscerated dogs had O_2 debts of the same magnitude as control animals whose circulation to the gut was intact. Since gluconeogenesis, with lactate as the carbon source, does not take place to any appreciable extent in skeletal muscle but occurs primarily in the liver and kidney (Scrutton & Utter, 1968), the bulk of the O_2 debts in these experiments must have been of "alactacid" origin. Alpert and Root also observed that infusion of lactate did not produce an O_2 debt. These findings challenged the existence of a "lactacid O_2 debt" component. Furthermore, Alpert and Root disputed the proposition that the "O_2 deficit" could be used to estimate the anaerobic metabolism that occurred during contractions. As described earlier, the "O_2 deficit" can be defined as the difference between the quantity of oxygen required by a tissue or an organism and that which is consumed by it. Classically, O_2 debts have been produced during the transition from rest to exercise (see Figure 1). An O_2 deficit can also be produced in animals by reducing the cardiac output or by causing the animals to breathe gases deficient in O_2. By means of these later two techniques, Alpert and Root demonstrated that the magnitude of O_2 debt was not necessarily equal to, or even correlated with, the magnitude of the preceding O_2 deficit. Investigators had generally assumed that the deficit in aerobic energy production during the initial period of adjustment to exercise was met by the expenditure of anaerobic energy stores. The expenditure of anerobic energy credits during the deficit period was thought to result in the O_2 debt.

From this perspective it seems unfortunate that Alpert and his associates moved on to study other problems and did not continue research on postexercise metabolism. The number of animals they studied was not large, and they reported extremely variable data. This later result may have been due to the lack of control of work ($W = F \times D$) during the tetanic contractions of the dog preparations. Alpert and his associates (Alpert, 1965; Alpert & Root, 1954; Kayne & Alpert, 1964) produced results inconsistent with classical "O_2 debt" theory, but they did not continue to the next step, to produce results that would explain the EPOC.

Oxygen debts and lactate metabolism have also been studied with dogs *in situ* by Welch and Stainsby (1967). Taking the maximum O_2 debt observed in these experiments to be 200 ml O_2/g muscle, and assuming that 20 kg of a 70 kg man would be working at its maximal rate during exhaustive exercise, Welch and Stainsby proposed that the maximum O_2 debt of a human should be only 4 liters of O_2. This quantity does not compare with the twenty or more liter O_2 debts observed in humans (J. Karlsson, personal communication). Therefore, it would appear that more than just tissues active during exercise are involved in determining postexercise O_2 consumption.

Brooks, Brauner and Cassens (1973) have used radioactive tracers to study the metabolism of lactic acid after exercise. After exhausting exercise and injection with [L-^{14}C] -lactate, approximately 75% of the labeled carbon infused appeared as [14]CO_2 during the immediate postexercise period. It was concluded, therefore, that the primary fate of lactic acid after exercise is toward oxidation, not glycogen synthesis. While this experiment showed that the fate of lactate ultimately is oxidation, the experiment was too simple to elaborate upon the various metabolic pathways taken by the lactate. Also noted in these experiments was the lower initial rate of labeled [14]CO_2 production in exercised compared to nonexercised control animals. While this difference is explainable in part to isotope dilution in a far greater lactate pool, and in part to postexercise CO_2 retention in exercised animals, the data leave 15-25% of the isotope to be accounted for. Increased lactate carbon recycling via various metabolic pathways including glucose synthesis have been discussed as possible explanations (Brooks et al., 1973). However, in the temporary absence of experiments to precisely determine the pathways of lactate metabolism after exercise, the possibility must be left open that 15 to 25% of the lactate present at the end of exercise may go for glycogen or glucose replenishment. While lactate conversion to glycogen in muscle does not appear to be significant, it may be that a large portion of the lactate not oxidized is taken up by the liver and kidney, converted to glucose, and released into the circulation. This glucose derived from lactate may be taken up by heart tissues for instance and converted to glycogen after exercise. Additionally, the incorporation of lactate carbon into amino acids (e.g., alanine, glutamine, glutamate) and tissue protein must be considered as possible destinies of nonoxidized lactate.

In their report, Brooks et al. (1973) observed little glycogen repletion in muscle and liver immediately after exhausting exercise by rats. Muscle biopsy studies on humans reveal similar results. Figure 4 is redrawn from Hultman (1967) and describes muscle glycogen after prolonged exhausting

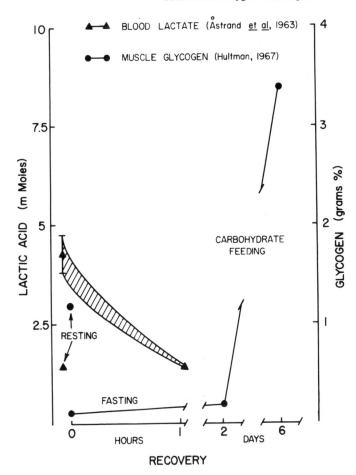

Figure 4. Muscle glycogen after prolonged exhausting exercise in man (from Hultman, 1967). Also depicted is blood lactic acid concentration after prolonged exercise in man [from Åstrand et al. (1963)]. In the shaded area, the assumption has been made that the removal of lactate following prolonged exercise approximates the time course after maximal exercise.

exercise in man. In these studies, it is apparent that glycogen synthesis after exercise depletion depends on carbohydrate feeding. Unfortunately, muscle lactate levels were not reported by Hultman. However, also depicted in Figure 4 is blood lactate concentration immediately after prolonged exercise reported by Åstrand, Hallback, Hedman, and Saltin (1963). In the shaded area representing the removal of blood lactate after exercise, the

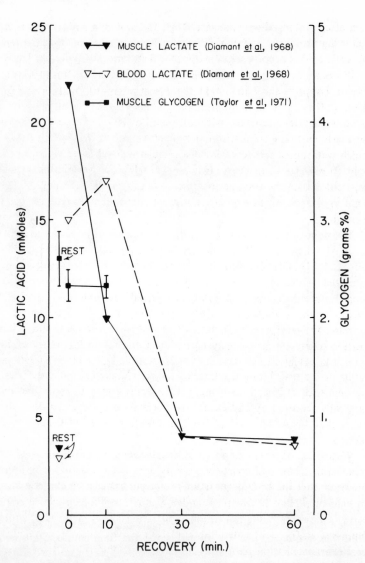

Figure 5. Muscle and blood lactic acid after maximal exercise in man [from Diamant et al. (1968)]. As in Figure 4, there is no indication of glycogen replenishment during the period of lactate removal.

assumption has been made that the removal of lactate after prolonged exercise follows the same approximate time course as it does after maximal exercise. As with the data on glycogen synthesis and lactate metabolism after prolonged exercise in the rat, the available data on humans following prolonged exercise allows the same conclusion—that the removal of lactic acid is accomplished without a restoration of glycogen levels.

In Figure 5, compiled from Diamant, Karlsson and Saltin (1968) and Taylor, Lappage, and Lao (1971), there is an attempt to make a case for the hypothesis that in humans after maximal exercise, as after prolonged exercise, lactate is removed without quantitatively significant glycogen replenishment. The comparison in Figure 5 is limited by Taylor's data, which were unconcerned with EPOC, and which followed glycogen for only 10 minutes of recovery. However, no glycogen replenishment was apparent during the time period when, on the basis of the data of Diamant et al., one might expect removal of approximately half the lactate formed.

The publication of data on lactate concentration in human muscle after maximal exercise allows another important observation to be made. Hill et al. (1924b) observed that the postexercise O_2 consumption curve consisted of two components. On the basis of their observations of arterial lactate, Margaria et al. (1933) suggested that only the slow EPOC curve compnent was associated with the removal of lactic acid after exercise. However, results such as those in Figure 5 indicate that a large portion of muscle lactate may be removed during the fast phase of EPOC via direct oxidation and vascular convection, and that blood lactate may return to normal during the time of the slow curve component. Thus, the sequence of events involving lactate removal may be more like those originally reported by Hill et al. (1924b), but what has changed is the belief that lactate removal, glycogen restoration, and EPOC are causally related.

With these observations in mind, it is possible to ask if the oxidative removal of lactic acid constitutes an O_2 debt. This question may imply however, that the body is an incinerator and that lactic acid is waste. In light of present biochemical understanding, it is impossible to conceive of how the oxidation of one substrate, such as lactic acid, could represent an O_2 debt unless the oxidation were selectively uncoupled, or disassociated from phosphorylation (the making of ATP). At present there exists no evidence that a mechanism such as the selective uncoupling of oxidative-phosphorylation occurs for lactic acid. It would be difficult to conceive of how such a mechanism could operate without the coupling of other pyridine nucleotide linked substrates, such as pyruvate, being affected also. Recent work (Brooks, 1971a, 1971b, 1971c) suggests that the efficiency of coupling between oxidation and phosphorylation (ATP/O) may be diminished by as much as 20% at the end of prolonged exercise resulting in hyperthermia (elevated body temperatures). However, this effect would apply to the oxidation of all substrates, not lactate in particular. Under such conditions, a greater than normal quantity of O_2 is consumed for the oxidation of given quantities of all substrates. Since the concentration of lactic acid can be greatly elevated after exercise, its oxidation probably represents a mass action effect. The oxidation of lactic acid in preference to some other substrate to supply ATP, therefore, involves *no extra* O_2 consumption, and should not be labeled a "debt."

The Contemporary Case for the "Lactacid O_2 Debt"

Perhaps the strongest argument in favor on the concept of a lactic acid component contributing to the magnitude of EPOC is that of Åstrand and Rodahl (1970). This position, which is based on observations made during maximal leg and arm ergometer work, proceeds as follows. By knowing the work load and the duration of exercise, and by assuming a constant mechanical efficiency of 22.5%, one can calculate the energy cost of a particular exercise bout in calories. In some instances, by Åstrand and Rodahl's estimate, this cost may amount to as much as 150 Kcal. To estimate the aerobic component supporting such work tasks, the O_2 stores in the body at the beginning of exercise are added to the O_2 uptake during exercise. This may measure 22 to 23 liters of O_2, or by conversion, a figure in the neighborhood of 114 Kcal. The equivalent of 36 Kcal. then must be supported by anaerobic processes. If one then assumes all available phosphagen to have been hydrolyzed in muscle during exercise, a subtraction of 6 to 7 Kcal. can be made, leaving approximately 30 Kcal. to have been supported by anaerobic glycolysis. Again, using Åstrand and Rodahl calculations, this would correspond to the formation of approximately 100g of lactic acid. Since the oxidation of this quantity of lactate after exercise would require an enormous quantity of O_2, far more than that observed as the "O_2 debt," Åstrand and Rodahl conclude that the main course of lactic acid after exercise must be back to glycogen. This conclusion is supported by the observation that the respiratory exchange ratio (R) drops below 1.0 shortly into recovery. Although allowances must be made for CO_2 retention by the blood bicarbonate system after exercise as compensation for hyperventilation during exercise, it would appear that some substrate other than lactate, such as fat, is being oxidized during the recovery period.

In attempting to reconcile the positions taken by proponents and opponents of the lactic theory of O_2 debt on this issue, it becomes obvious that the estimate of a body lactate content of 100g to be metabolized after exercise is at the root of the divergent conclusions. Taking the data of Karlsson (1971), who measured muscle and blood lactate after maximal exercise, it is obvious that no more than 40g of lactate is present in the body at the conclusion of maximal exercise. Similarly, Karlsson (personal communication) has determined that maximal exercise produces O_2 debts as great as 24 liters. Taking the figures of 40g of lactic acid and 24 liter O_2 debt, it is very possible then to account for: (a) rephosphorylation of ADP and creatine, (b) oxidation of 70 to 100% of the lactate present at the end of exercise, and (c) an overall respiratory exchange ratio of less than unity.

These values of EPOC at present under discussion (i.e., values in excess of 20 liters) were obtained on fairly large, and highly trained males after maximal efforts. Ordinarily, with less capable subjects, smaller EPOC volumes are reported after exercise. In these cases, the lactate pool size would coincidentally also be substantially less than 40 grams, and the observed EPOC would be adequate to explain an oxidative removal of the lactic acid.

At this time it is interesting to speculate on the 250% divergence between estimates of lactate formed as the result of anaerobic glycolysis in exercise, and the quantity of lactate actually found in the tissues after exercise. One possibility is that the lactate, if formed, constitutes the majority of the lactate-pyruvate pool, and consequently, probability may favor oxidation of lactate during exercise (Depocas, Minaire, & Charonnet, 1969; Drury & Wick, 1956). A second possibility is that Åstrand and Rodahl's (1970) calculations neglect the contribution of the enzyme myokinase. This component is undoubtedly small, but it merits consideration. A third possibility is that much of the lactate under discussion is not formed. This would imply that the assumption of a constant mechanical efficiency of 22.5%, or other assumptions used to calculate the O_2 deficit in nonsteady-state exercise situations are not valid. And finally, the discrepancy may indicate that the process of energy transduction in muscle is different than at present conceived.

Towards a Contemporary Interpretation

With displacement of the classical theory of "O_2 debt," the concept is emerging that the explanation of EPOC may be found at the level of mitochondria. Although control of mitochondrial respiration *in vitro* is relatively well understood at this time, few studies have been attempted on the workings of mitrochondria after exercise. Given the present level of understanding of mitrochondrial energetics, and some knowledge of the disturbances to homeostasis caused by exercise, it is profitable now to speculate on mechanisms responsible for EPOC.

Catecholamines have long been recognized as possessing O_2 wasting effects (Harris, 1969). Recently, Barnard and Foss (1963) and Cain (1971) presented data suggesting that there is a component to EPOC which is attributable to the effects of elevated concentrations of catecholamines. These experiments on dogs which used the β-blocking agent propanolol, indicated a decrease in EPOC of 35 to 43% following infusion of the blocking agent. Although these studies do not allow consideration of the secondary effects of drug infusion, it is not beyond reason that the effects of catecholamines on EPOC are in the range quoted. Catecholamines probably elevate mitochondrial respiration indirectly by stimulating energy-requiring processes in the cell.

Recently, based on the effects of elevated temperatures on mitochondrial respiration *in vitro,* it was hypothesized that increased tissue temperatures after exercise were involved in determining EPOC (Brooks et al., 1971a). On the basis of thermodynamic principles (i.e., the Q_{10} effect, and the second law of thermodynamics) it must be that with increasing temperatures (up to the point of thermal damage), there is an increase in the rate of O_2 consumption and an eventual decline in mitochondrial energy-trapping efficiency. A mitochondrion and a mechanical model for oxidative phosphorylation are diagrammed in Figure 6. It must be emphasized that the process of oxidation (O_2 consumption) and phosphorylation (ATP production) are separate (Chance & Williams, 1956). Ordinarily, the two processes are linked in that oxidation provides the energy for phosphorylation. Here the linkage is simplistically diagrammed as a mechanical gear linkage, an analogous situation to the automobile. The engine can run full speed, consume oxygen, and utilize fuel, but unless the transmission and differential are in good operating order, nothing meaningful will happen in terms of rotation of the driving wheels. Recently, it was demonstrated (Brooks et al., 1971a) that elevated temperatures of the magnitude experienced in heavy exercise have the effect of loosening the coupling or linkage between oxidation and phosphorylation. Since the beginning of the twentieth century, when Dubois (1921) thoroughly studied basal metabolic rate (BMR), it has been known that the BMR is increased in humans during fever about 13% per °C increase in body temperature. Elevated tissue temperatures in humans after exercise have been demonstrated to be associated with EPOC (Claremont, Nagle, Reddan, & Brooks, 1975).

Beyond the direct effects of temperature on stimulating cellular res-

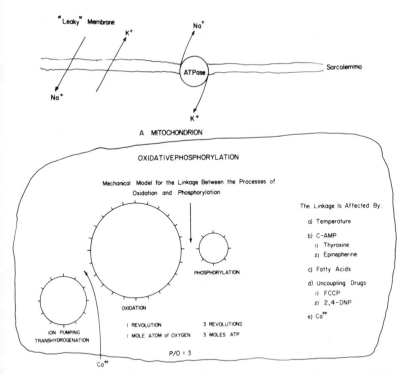

Figure 6. A mitochondrion with the coupling mechanism between oxidation and phosphorylation depicted as a mechanical linkage. Substances suspected to affect the coupling between oxidation and phosphorylation during the postexercise period are indicated. In addition, the hormones which have O_2 wasting effects are depicted as stimulating Na^+/K^+-ATP pump activity at the cell membrane.

piration, temperature may also indirectly elevate O_2 consumption in the intact individual. Although ventilatory and cardiac costs during recovery have been investigated and found to be minor (Welch, Faulkner, Barclay, & Brooks, 1970), it seems only reasonable that exercise tasks which result in significant elevations in muscle and core temperatures should be accompanied by an increased O_2 cost of breathing and cardiac function.

Throughout the biosphere, phenomena occur which are mechanistically related to EPOC. Metabolic diseases are known to exist as a result of aberrant mitochondrial function. Extremely high rates of basal O_2 consumption in certain individuals have been traced to the loosening of coupling between mitochondrial O_2 consumption and phosphorylation. Usually O_2 consumption is linked to phosphorylation, and O_2 consumption is inhibited when ATP levels are high. This loosening of coupling is much like that which occurs in normal individuals after exercise when tissue temperatures are elevated. Another, more common metabolic disease is hyperthyroidism. Individuals who are hyperthyroid are often thin and consume extraordinary quantities of food and oxygen. They are in a perpetual state of "O_2 debt." In the past, the substance 2,4-dinitrophenol (DNP) has been used to treat obesity and hypothyroidism. Since the effect of the drug is to loosen the coupling between oxidation and phosphorylation, the effect of DNP treatment is to increase O_2 consumption and the utilization of substrates, which in this instance will include body fat.

One very interesting physiological phenomenon, not generally familiar to students interested in exercise, is the phenomenon of nonshivering thermogenesis in certain animals. When placed in cold environments most mammals will shiver to develop adequate body heat. After a week or 10 days, some species such as the rat, however, will stop shivering yet continue to generate adequate heat to maintain internal temperature. The animal's basal metabolic rate will be up 2 to 3 times. There are several theories about how the rat accomplishes this. One theory is that oxidation is uncoupled from phosphorylation (Smith & Hoijer, 1962). The sites of this uncoupling may be skeletal muscle as well as brown fat deposits in the body core. Brown fat deposits in hibernating animals have a similar capability, and in this instance, the brown fat functions to maintain an adequate temperature around the hibernating animal's vital organs. Here, the specific agent which uncouples oxidation from phosphorylation may be a fatty acid (Hittelman, Lindberg, & Cannon, 1969). Although this phenomenon has not been studied in relation to postexercise metabolism, it is possible that the lipolysis and release of fatty acids which occurs during exercise has some effect on O_2 consumption after exercise. It has been long recognized that, somehow, hibernating animals maintain adequate heat, but it is not beyond conjecture that the same mechanism participates in the EPOC.

Another theory on the mechanism of nonshivering thermogenesis is that the hormone norepinepherine directly, or indirectly, causes cell membranes to become more permeable to sodium ion (Na^+) and potassium ion (K^+) (Horowitz, 1978). In order to compensate for the ion leaks, the cell membrane Na^+/K^+ pump activity is increased. This pump requires an energy input in the form of ATP. Increased ATP demands for the pump are met by mitochondrial oxidative phosphorylation. Consequently, O_2 consumption is increased. Recently, it has also been found that thyroid hormone and glucocorticoids can contribute to Na^+/K^+ pump activity

(Horowitz, 1979) (see Figure 6). Since exercise affects both Na+ and K+ balance and hormone levels, these factors probably serve to elevate O_2 consumption after exercise.

Another effect which has been studied in some detail, but unfortunately not in relation to postexercise metabolism is the effect of calcium ion (Ca^{++}) on mitochondrial respiration (see Figure 6). Carafoli and Lehninger (1971) have shown that (Ca^{++}) has similar effects on mitochondria isolated from all tissues on all animals studied. The effect of calcium ion is to increase oxygen consumption in two ways. First, mitochondria have a great affinity for calcium ions. Mitochondria, given the chance, will sequester Ca^{++} at a great rate. This process requires energy which is reflected in an increased rate of O_2 consumption. This O_2 consumption is not associated with ATP generation. Second, increased amounts of Ca^{++} within mitochondria ultimately affect the mechanism linking oxidation and phosphorylation. Again, the result is an increased rate of O_2 consumption.

During each muscle contraction of exercise, Ca^{++} is liberated from the sarcoplasmic reticulum. In heart, as well as skeletal muscle, some of this Ca^{++} is probably taken up by mitochondria. The mechanism by which mitochondria, during recovery, dispose of the Ca^{++} accumulated during exercise is at present not understood. However, it is likely that Ca^{++} accumulated by mitochondria during exercise affects mitochondrial respiration during exercise as well as recovery.

Selection of a Term

Throughout this discussion, the descriptive term "elevated postexercise O_2 consumption" has been used as has the classical term, "O_2 debt." Since it is evident that there exists at present no complete explanation of postexercise metabolic phenomena, it may be advantageous to substitute another term for the "O_2 debt." While other investigators (Harris, 1969; Stainsby & Barclay, 1970) join in the conclusion that a name change is due, there exists some disagreement as to the term to select. An alternative was suggested by Stainsby and Barclay who used the term "recovery O_2." A disadvantage of this term is that is does not completely escape the implication of a mechanism or explanation. It is now probable that two factors responsible for significant parts of the elevated postexercise O_2 consumption (i.e., the calorigenic effects of catecholamines and temperature) occur during recovery from exercise, but are not obligatory and necessary for recovery. Therefore, the purely descriptive term of "elevated postexercise O_2 consumption" is probably most appropriate.

References

Alpert, N.R. Lactate production and removal and the regulation of metabolism. *Annals of the New York Academy of Science,* 1965, **119**, 995-1012.

Alpert N.R.,& Root, N.S. Relationship between excess respiratory metabolism and utilization of intravenously infused sodium racemic lactate and sodium L-(+)-lactate. *American Journal of Physiology,* 1954, **177**, 455-462.

Åstrand, P., Hallback, I., Hedman, R., & Saltin, B. Blood lactates after prolonged severe exercise. *Journal of Applied Physiology,* 1963, **18**, 619-622.

Åstrand, P.O., & Rodahl, K. *Textbook of work physiology.* New York: McGraw-Hill, 1970.

Bang, O. The lactate content of the blood during and after muscular exercise in man. *Skandinavian Archives of Physiology,* 1936, **74** (Suppl. 10), 49-82.

Barnard, R.J., & Foss, M.L. Oxygen debt: effect of beta adrenergic blockage on the lacticacid and alactacid components. *Journal of Applied Physiology,* 1969, **27**, 813-816.

Benedict, F., & Cathcart, E.P. *Muscular Work.* Washington: Carnegie Institution of Washington (Publication 187), 1913.

Brooks, G.A., Brauner, K.E., & Cassens, R.G. Glycogen synthesis and metabolism of lactic acid after exercise. *American Journal of Physiolog* 1973, **224**, 1162-1166.

Brooks, G.A., Hittelman, K.J., Faulkner, J.A., & Beyer, R.E. Temperature skeletal muscle mitochondrial functions, and oxygen debt. *American Journal of Physiology,* 1971, **220**, 1053-1059. (a)

Brooks, G.A., Hittelman, K.J., Faulkner, J.A., & Beyer, R.E. Temperature liver mitochondrial respiratory functions, and oxygen debt. *Medicine and Science in Sports,* 1971, **2**, 71-74. (b)

Brooks, G.A., Hittelman, K.J. Faulkner, J.A., & Beyer, R.E. Tissue temperatures and whole-animal oxygen consumption after exercise. *American Journal of Physiology,* 1971, **221**, 427-431. (c)

Cain, S.M. Exercise O_2 debts and dogs at ground level and at altitude with and without β-block. *Journal of Applied Physiology,* 1971, **30**, 830-843.

Carafoli, E., & Lehninger, A.L. A survey of the interaction of calcium ions with mitochondria from different species. *Biochemical Journal,* 1971, **122**, 681-690.

Chance, B., & Williams, C.R. The respiratory chain and oxidative phosphorylation. In *Advances in Enzymology* (Vol. 17). New York: Interscience, 1956.

Claremont, A.D., Nagle, F., Reddan, W.D., & Brooks, G.A. Comparison of metabolic, temperature, heart rate and ventilatory responses to exercise at extreme ambient temperatures (0°C and 35°C). *Medicine and Science in Sports*, 1975, 7, 150-154.

Depocas, F., Minaire, Y., & Charonnet, J. Rate of formation and oxidation of lactic acid in dogs at rest and during moderate exercise. *Canadian Journal of Physiology and Pharmacology*, 1969, 47, 603-610.

Diamant, B., Karlsson, J., & Saltin, B. Muscle tissue lactate after maximal exercise in man. *Acta Physiologica Scandinavica*, 1968, 72, 383-384.

Drury, D.R., & Wick, A.N. Metabolism of lactic acid in the intact rabbit. *Journal of Physiology*, 1956, 184, 304-308.

DuBois, E.F. The basal metabolism in fever. *Journal of the American Medical Association*, 1921, 77, 352-355.

Fletcher, W.M., & Hopkins, F.G. Lactic acid in amphibian muscle. *Journal of Physiology*, 1907, 35, 247-309.

Harris, P. Lactic acid and the phlogiston debt. *Cardiovasular Research*, 1969, 3, 381-390.

Henry, F.M. Aerobic oxygen consumption and alactic debt in muscular work. *Journal of Applied Physiology*, 1951, 3, 427-438.

Henry, F.M., & DeMoor, J.C. Metabolic efficiency of exercise in relation to work load at constant speed. *Journal of Applied Physiology*, 1950, 2, 481-487.

Henry, F.M., & DeMoor, J.C. Lactic and alactic oxygen consumption in moderate exercise of graded intensity. *Journal of Applied Physiology*, 1956, 8, 608-614.

Hill, A.V. The energy degraded in recovery processes of stimulated muscles. *Journal of Physiology*, 1913, 46, 28-80.

Hill, A.V. The oxidative removal of lactic acid. *Journal of Physiology*, 1914, 48, x-xi.

Hill, A.V. & Lupton, H. Muscular exercise, lactic acid and the supply and utilization of oxygen. *Quarterly Journal of Medicine*, 1923, 16, 135-171.

Hill, A.V., Long, C.N.H, & Lupton, H. Muscular exercise, lactic acid and the supply and utilization of oxygen (Pt. I-III). *Proceedings of the Royal Society of London, Series B*, 1924, 475. (a)

Hill, A.V., Long, C.N.H., & Lupton, H. Muscular exercise, lactic acid, and the supply and utilization of oxygen (Pt. IV-VI). *Proceedings of the Royal*

Society of London, Series B, 1924, **97**, 84-138. (b)

Hill, A.V., Long, C.N.H., & Lupton, H. Muscular exercise, lactic acid, and the supply and utilization of oxygen (Pt. VII-VIII). *Proceedings of the Royal Society of London, Series B,* 1924, **97**, 155-176. (c)

Hittelman, K.J., Lindberg, O., & Cannon, B. Oxidative phosphorylation and compartmentation of fatty acid metabolism in brown fat mitochondria. *European Journal of Biochemistry,* 1969, **11**, 183-192.

Horwitz, B.A. Neurohumoral regulation of nonshivering thermogenesis in mammals. In L.C.H. Wang & J.W. Hudson (Eds.), *Strategies in cold: Natural torpidity and thermogenesis.* New York: Academic Press, 1978.

Horwitz, B.A. Metabolic aspects of thermogenesis: Neural and hormone control. *Federation Proceedings,* 1979, **38**, 2147-2149.

Hultman, E. Physiological role of muscle glycogen in man, with special reference to exercise. In *Physiology of muscular exercise.* New York: American Heart Association, 1967. (Monograph 15)

Karlsson, J. Lactate and phosphagen concentrations in working muscle of man. *Acta Physiologica Scandinavica* (Suppl. 358), 1971.

Kayne, H.L., & Alpert, N.R. Oxygen consumption following exercise in the anesthetized dog. *American Journal of Physiology,* 1964, **206**, 51-56.

Lehninger, A.L. *Biochemistry.* New York: Worth, 1970.

Margaria, R., Edwards, H.T., & Dill, D.B. Possible mechanisms of contracting and paying oxygen debt and the role of lactic acid in muscular contraction. *American Journal of Physiology,* 1933, **106**, 689-715.

Meyerhof, O. Die Energiewandlungen im Muskel I. Uber die Beiziehungen der Milchsaure Warmebildung und Arbeitstung des Muskels in der Anaerbiose. *Archiv fuer die Gesamte physiologie des Menschen und der Tiere,* 1920, **182**, 232-284. (a)

Meyerhof, O. Die Energiewandlungen im Muskel. II Des Schichsal der Milchsaure in der Erholungs periode des Muskels. *Archiv fuer die Gesamte physiologie des Menschen und der Tiere,* 1920, **182**, 284-317. (b)

Meyerhof. O. Die Energiewandlungen im Muskel. III. Kohlenhydrat- und Milchsaureumsatz im Froschmuskel. *Archiv fuer die Gesamte physiologie des Menschen und der Tiere,* 1920, **185**, 11-32. (c)

Scrutton, M.C., & Utter, M.F. The regulation of glycolysis and gluconeogenesis in animal tissues. *Annual Review of Biochemistry,* 1968, **37**, 269-302.

Smith, R.E., & Hoijer, D.J. Metabolism and cellular function in cold acclimation. *Physiological Review,* 1962, **42**, 60-142.

Stainsby, W.N., & Barclay, J.K. Exercise metabolism: O_2 deficit, steady level O_2 uptake in recovery. *Medicine and Science in Sports*, 1970, **2**, 177-186.

Taylor, A.W., Lappage, R., & Lao, S. Skeletal muscle glycogen stores after submaximal and maximal work. *Medicine and Science in Sports*, 1971, **3**, 75-78.

Wasserman, K., & McIlroy, M.B. Detecting the threshold of anaerobic metabolism. *American Journal of Cardiology*, 1964, **14**, 844-852.

Welch, H.G., Faulkner, J.A., Barclay, J.K., & Brooks, G.A. Ventilatory response during recovery from muscular work and its relation with O_2 debt. *Medicine and Science in Sports*, 1970, **2**, 15-19.

Welch, H.G., & Stainsby, W.N. Oxygen debt in contracting dog skeletal muscle *in situ*. *Respiration Physiology*, 1967, **3**, 229-242.

PART-6

PART 3

Biomechanics of Sport

The term "Biomechanics" is described and defined by Ronald Zernicke in the following chapter (Chapter 8). As will be elaborated in his chapter, biomechanics refers to that aspect of the physical education discipline which describes structure and motion of the human body by means of the methods of mechanics. The terms "biomechanics" and "kinesiology" are usually synonomous, kinesiology being perhaps the older term and biomechanics the term now in vogue. Biomechanics is the preferred term in disciplinary departments which are called "Department of Kinesiology." Departments of physical education use either of the above terms to identify those aspects of the discipline which employ mechanics to understand structure and motion. Regardless of the term (biomechanics will be used here), this is an aspect of the physical education discipline which is undergoing a phenomenal growth.

As is described in Chapter 8, and also in Chapter 9 by Peter Cavanagh and Richard Hinrichs, the burgeoning of activity in biomechanics is due to a number of factors, the main one being an advance in technology. It was not too long ago that competence in kinesiology required some knowledge of anatomy, Newtonian physics, and planar cinematography. In some instances also, the ability to record an electromyograph (EMG), and the signals from a joint displacement transducer, allowed an investigator to infer something about muscle contraction. Mainly, however, free body (stick figure) diagrams were used to describe human of motion. In the contemporary field, it is possible to find laboratories where films produced in two and three dimensional cinematography are subjected to rigorous digital analysis. In some laboratories force and joint displacement transducers are used in conjunction with computers to obtain, store, reduce, and interpret data. Subjects can be "wired" to, or perform with, instruments wired to a computer which analyzes the movement while it is taking place. Occasionally, measurement of the kinetics of motion are accompanied by simultaneous readings of EMG and determinations of respiratory gases. Together, these technological advances allow for mathematical modeling of movement patterns. These models can have great predictive and theoretical value.

Remarkable advances in technology have been made by engineers and scientists in a variety of disciplines related to biomechanics. The technology has been taken and applied to study sports biomechanics by physical educators. These investigators have addressed a whole series of questions in biomechanics. Interest has existed in analyzing skilled movement patterns, in describing the efficiency of motion, in analyzing the forces on tissues during activity, in identifying potentially injurious situations, in designing equipment to minimize the possibility of injury, and in designing prosthetic devices for the handicapped.

The effects that advances in technology have had on the body of knowledge related to biomechanics are similar to the effects of technology on other specializations in the physical education discipline (e.g., exercise physiology) and on research in many disciplines. In science, when ideas are shared among scientists, the validity of those ideas can be tested by many researchers under a variety of conditions. Frequently, when the results of research are critically evaluated, the science takes a quantum step forward, as in the recent history of biomechanics.

Recent advances in biomechanics in the USA, Europe, and Japan have resulted in the formation of several new scholarly societies. These societies publish journals dealing with biomechanics and hold meetings where the papers presented frequently are assembled into published volumes. The circulation of technically sophisticated journals and volumes on biomechanics has served to promote interest on the subject still further.

The field of biomechanics may be emerging as a distinct discipline. The interdisciplinary, as well as cross-disciplinary interest in biomechanics, the institution of new scholarly societies, the emergence of the term biomechanics in preference to kinesiology, and the publication of journals and books on biomechanics follow a pattern by which many disciplines have emerged. Biomechanics benefits greatly from its descriptive and identifiable name as well as a common methodology. This trend for emerging interest in biomechanics doubtlessly shall continue strongly for a time. Whether biomechanics evolves into a discrete discipline probably will depend upon how well departments from which investigators interested in human biomechanics come support research on problems related to biomechanics. Most likely, students of biomechanics shall continue to hold positions in traditional college and university departments, and the biomechanics societies shall continue to exist as scholarly outlets for research on the subject.

The Emergence of Human Biomechanics

8 *R.F. Zernicke*

    Significant scientific developments related to mechanics, muscle physiology, and anatomy have occurred over a period of centuries; yet, only in the 1970s (Nelson, 1971, 1973) has biomechanics research in physical education, sport, recreation, and dance developed past childhood. Less than 20 years ago, Dempster (1961) was still imploring students and researchers in the "science of human movement" to discard the "armchair approach" for an approach based on rigorous and proven analytical/experimental techniques. Although the methods and principles of mechanics were effectively applied for analyses of the moving human musculoskeletal system in fields like physical and rehabilitation medicine and industrial engineering, equal intensity of application was lacking in the discipline of physical education. Why?

    From a historical perspective, this recent era of dramatic growth in biomechanics research in contrast with the preceding era, may be attributed to at least two factors: (a) the development of a community of biomechanists within the discipline of physical education, and the effective interaction between biomechanists from different fields; and (b) the widespread adoption and application of mechanics' tools and techniques to human movement analyses. In the following paragraphs, these two notions will be examined in light of the general history of human movement analyses and scientific discoveries in related disciplines. This examination is not exhaustive, however, for several well-written and well-documented reviews of the history of the study of human biomechanics and kinesiology have already been published (e.g., Atwater, 1980; Contini & Drillis, 1954; Cooper, 1977; Cooper & Glassow, 1976; Evans, 1971; Fung, 1968; Hirt, 1955; Rasch, 1958; Rasch & Burke, 1978). Therefore, the historical elements which are presented here serve to amplify and clarify my selection of the scientific community and analytical/experimental tools as the pivotal factors in the emergence of human biomechanics in physical education.

Biomechanics/Kinesiology

Woven into history exposition are comments on the usefulness of the semantic split between the terms "biomechanics" and "kinesiology." In the "human movement sciences," there are no absolutely accepted definitions for the two terms (Atwater, 1980; Burke, 1977; Dillman & Sears, 1977; Gregor & Zernicke, 1977; Hay, 1978; Locke, 1965, 1967; Luttgens & Zernicke, 1977; Ulrich & Nixon, 1972). In fact, many scientists when asked to define biomechanist or kinesiologist would probably prefer to paraphase Supreme Court Justice Stewart, and say, "I don't know that I can define one, but I know one when I see one."

Nevertheless, global definitions of biomechanics which have appeared in recent years have achieved a great deal of congruity. For example: (a) "Biomechanics is anything directly or indirectly pertaining to the effects of forces upon the form or motion of organic bodies or tissues" (Evans, 1971, p. 3); (b) "Biomechanics is the study of the structure and function of biological systems by means of the methods of mechanics" (Hatze, 1974, p. 189); and (c) "Biomechanics is the science which investigates the effect of internal and external forces on human and animal bodies in movement and rest" (Contini, 1963, p. 16).

Applying these definitions to human movement results in a trilevel, biomechanical characterization of the human—from external forces, to internal forces, to the internal effects of the forces. Regarding the first-level characterization, the motion and position of the multilinked human body are influenced by external forces like ground reaction and by gravitational acceleration. The internal generation of force for motion or for maintaining body segment position is directly related to skeletal muscles; thus, the second level of biomechanical analysis comprises functional kinetics of muscle. The third level of biomechanics characterization includes the assessment of the structural and functional changes in body tissues which are a result of the external and internal forces. The trilevel biomechanical characterization seeks to answer the questions: (a) How does the environment influence or modify movement? (b) How is movement of the body generated? (c) How do movement kinetics influence the very structure of the body tissues, such as bone, tendon, and ligament?

Kinesiology, on the other hand has not achieved the same unanimity of definition as biomechanics. Beyond a fundamental Greek to English translation as the "study of movement," from the roots "kinein" or "to move," and "logos" meaning "to discourse" (Atwater, 1980; Rasch, 1958; Rasch & Burke, 1978), there is still little agreement about what constitutes kinesiology. In a historical context, kinesiology has taken on meanings ranging from body mechanics to the study of movement in an academic and scholarly discipline. A careful study of the historical background and genesis of each of the terms may provide a logical basis for differentiating between them.

A Historical Milieu

Intuitively, the study of movement began with human movement; Drillis (1963) stated that the fundamental principles of mechanics have been applied empirically to human movements since tools were first used. Scientific thinking with its inductive and deductive reasoning, however, has generally been ascribed to the ancient Greeks (Hirt, 1955; Singer, 1959). Hippocrates (460-370 B.C.) was a pioneer in the use of rational scientific thought in the practice of medicine, but it was Aristotle (384-322 B.C.) who set to writing the first descriptions of human and animal movements. Aristotle's observations and thoughts about the interrelations between "physics" or "description of the universe" and living things (Fung, 1968) were recorded in the *Treatise on Parts of Animals, Movements of Animals,* and *Progression of Animals* (Aristotle, trans. 1927). In the treatises, Aristotle formulated elemental ideas including the role of external reaction forces in walking, pushing, and jumping, and the interplay between segmental rotation and translation in bipedal locomotion. Aristotle's scientific ideas have prompted several authors of historical accounts (for example, Atwater, 1980; Braun, 1941; Cooper & Glassow, 1976; Hirt, 1955; Locke; 1967; Robinson, 1943) to name him "Father of Kinesiology," in that he was the first to study movement in a scholarly and systematic fashion.

During the more than 1500 years between the death of Aristotle and the birth of the Renaissance, only two people are usually cited as having made significant contributions to the study of human movement: Archimedes (287-212 B.C.) and Claudius Galen (131-210 A.D.). The formulations of the Greek mathematician Archimedes—*On the Equilibrium of Planes* and *On Floating Bodies*—established basic principles in mechanics (Health, 1897); whereas Galen was the dominating influence in the early study of anatomy and muscle function. Hirt (1955) noted that Galen's anatomical and myological studies remained the final and complete authority in medical science throughout the Middle Ages—nearly 1300 years.

Leonardo da Vinci was born in 1452, a year that serves as a milestone in the history of science. Before his death in 1519, da Vinci distinguished himself as one of the most prolific, imaginative, and inventive scientists ever. His artistic genius, evident in his anatomical studies (Hopstock, 1921), was also demonstrated effectively in his many mechanical drawings and engineering sketches. Yet Bronowski (1978) stated, rather startlingly, that da Vinci failed to make any impact on science at that time; the reason—he had no colleagues. There were colleagues in art, such as Michelangelo and Raphael, and ". . . they undoubtedly had an influence which produced more and better paintings that we should otherwise have. . . ." (Bronowski, 1978, p. 123). But no scientific society existed at that time, and even da Vinci's brilliant mind could not work and effect scientific changes in isolation. His studies, however, planted the seed for renewed interest in science.

With da Vinci's seminal contributions during the Renaissance, science began to reawaken and revitalize. Italy was the center for the growth of science during that period and produced scientists such as Andreas Vesalius (1514-1564), Galileo Galilei (1564-1642), and Giovanni Alphonso Borelli (1608-1679). Vesalius, in 1543, published his monumental book of anatomy: *De Humani Corporis Fabrica* (The Fabric of the Human Body). Saunders and O'Malley (1950) considered this prodigious text as the greatest single contribution to medical sciences. The paintings and drawings of the human form and musculoskeletal structures accurately portrayed the dynamic lines of the moving human body. Vesalius, as well as da Vinci, was able to illustrate the functional significance of body structures, and therefore, to provide the anatomical basis for the study of the living human body. Although more recent studies (e.g., Braus, 1954) may be more accurate in anatomical detail, the aesthetic quality and inherent vitality of da Vinci's and Vesalius's creations remain unparalleled.

During this period of scientific revitalization, it was the astronomer and mathematician Galileo who was the first to use the modern "scientific method." He posed hypotheses which could be experimentally tested and either refuted or accepted. In his 1636 edition of *Two New Sciences,* Galileo was the first to refer to a science of "mechanics" (Singer, 1959) and to give mathematical precision and expression to mechanical events (Hirt, 1955). After studying medicine at Pisa, Galileo turned his primary attention to the mathematical and physical sciences. However, throughout his life, even in the midst of his central role in the maelstrom revolving about the Ptolemaic versus Copernican view of the cosmos, Galileo conducted basic experiments to quantify the function of biological systems by means of his newly developed methods of mechanics. For example, he used his discovery of the constancy of a pendulum swing to quantify the human heart rate. It is interesting to note that Galileo was still lecturing at Padua when William Harvey (1578-1658) was matriculating there. Galileo was able to exert a greater influence on science than da Vinci because a scientific community was then beginning to form. For example, one of Galileo's pupils was the Italian physician Borelli. An eminent mathematician and astronomer in his own right, Borelli was also a friend and colleague of Galileo, and their interactions undoubtedly influenced Borelli as he formulated his classic mechanical analyses of the musculo-skeletal system. The work, *De Motu Animalium* (The Motion of Animals), in 1680 (1685), distinguished Borelli as the progenitor of modern bio-mechanics (Steindler, 1935) and the founder and developer of that branch of physiology characterizing musculoskeletal motion with mechanical methods (Cooper & Glassow, 1976; Hirt, 1955; Skarstrom, 1909). Borelli produced qualitative, graphical solutions to the mechanics of muscle-bone levers, the static equilibration of muscle moments and opposing forces, and body center of gravity locations. Dempster (1961) noted that Borelli's approach to body statics was sound, even though he had no quantitative information about many of the factors involved. Although Borelli's general influence on the development of the study of human movement was considerable (Foster, 1901), he preceded the genesis and maturation of a branch of physics which would have allowed him to deal quantitatively with problems of body *motion*. He needed the fundamentals of dynamics in a Newtonian world view.

On the whole, Bronowski (1978) noted that science "took off" about 300 years ago. Not only were profound works of scientific reasoning being published, such as Newton's *Principia* (1686), but also it was during the 17th century that effective scientific communication began to emerge. Rather than transmitting scientific experiments and results through personal letters between scientists, the first scientific journals appeared simultaneously in England and France; the growth of science began to accelerate.

Between the 1686 appearance of Newton's (1642-1727) *Principia Mathematica Philosophiae Naturalis (Mathematical Principles of Natural Philosophy)* (Cajori, 1946/1729) and the 1788 publication of Lagrange's *Analytical Mechanics* (Serret, 1888-1889), rigid body mechanics became a mature science. Dempster (1961) highlighted several scientific principles pertinent to the analysis of body motion which were formulated during that epoch: the dynamics of particles and rigid bodies, moment of inertia, d'Alembert's principle of dynamic equilibrium (d'Alembert, 1758), and the application of analytical geometry to mechanics to convincingly demonstrate the interrelationships between mass, inertia, velocity, and acceleration. Even the most elementary methods of dynamics, however, were not applied to human movement analyses until the Weber brothers (Ernst 1795-1878, Whilhelm 1804-1891, and Eduard 1806-1871) published their classic studies of muscle dynamics and bipedal locomotion: *Die Mechanik der menschlichen Gehwerkzeuge (Mechanics of Human Gait)* (Weber &

Weber, 1836).

In the more than 100 year interim between the biomechanical treatises of Borelli and the Webers, an "anatomico-physiological" influence
was paramount in the study of human movement. Key discoveries about
the effects of electricity on skeletal muscle by Luigi Galvani (1737-1798),
and about the innate contractility of muscle by Albrecht von Haller (1708-
1777) had a stimulating effect on muscle physiology research (Basmajian,
1962). During the same period, the modern concept of structure as the
basis of function—form follows function—was established, primarily
through the work of the French anatomist, M. Francoise Xavier Bichat
(1771-1802) (Thayer, 1903).

It was during this century between Borelli and the Webers when a
strong and pervasive anatomico-physiological foundation was laid for
several professional fields associated with the assessment of normal and
pathological human movement including: physical education, physical
and occupational therapies, physical and rehabilitation medicine, and
orthopaedics. Hirt (1955) emphasized that it was during the "Age of
Enlightenment" when the French philosopher, Jean Jacques Rousseau
(1712-1778), encouraged a "return to nature," with an emphasis on
physical activity for the development of the whole person. Nicholas
Andre (1658-1742), who first used the word "orthopaedics," meaning
"straight child," proposed that through exercise, childhood musculoskeletal deformities could be prevented or corrected. The Swedish physical
educator, Per Hendrik Ling (1776-1839) pioneered the anatomico-physiological approach to physical education in his country in 1801. In Germany
it was Frederick Jahn (1776-1850) who generated a similarly based physical education curriculum in 1842. With the influx of Europeans to the
United States at the beginning of the 19th century, the Swedish and German anatomico-physiological bases of physical education became firmly
ingrained in the academic and professional physical education curricula.

Qualitative observation was appropriate for some anatomico-physiological analyses of the human body, but it was not effective
for the assessment of the quantitative dynamics of human movement. Deficiencies in motion-recording methods and experimental tools reinforced
an observational approach to movement analyses; before the principles of
dynamics could be applied in a quantitative manner to human and animal
motion analyses, accurate discretization of space-time parameters was necessary. Cinematography provided such a recording method.

The enigmatic and eccentric Eadweard Muybridge (1831-1904), an
English expatriot, was an eminent "still" photographer before he began
his "electro-photographic investigations" in the United States (Haas,

1976). He developed a new photographic technique for "capturing" human and animal motion, and this technique led him into the extensive work documented in the 11 volumes of *Animal Locomotion* (Muybridge, 1957) and in *The Human Figure in Motion* (Muybridge, 1955). The earliest (1872) technique that Muybridge used was a series of 24 cameras each spaced one foot apart from the next; this set-up, in which each individual exposure time was estimated to be 0.2 milliseconds, was used for the initial studies of horse locomotion. In 1881, Muybridge and the Frenchman Etienne Jules Marey (1830-1904) collaborated in Paris. The collaboration resulted in Muybridge substituting multiple apparatus for a single apparatus that produced one plate which recorded the multiple images of the moving human or animal form (Haas, 1976).

Fung (1968) stated that ". . . every scientific advance in history was heralded by a new tool. . . ," and the development of the photographic techniques by Muybridge and Marey led to the pioneering studies in human body dynamics by the Germans, Christian Wilhelm Braune (1831-1892) and Otto Fischer (1861-1917). Their work (Braune, 1889; Fischer, 1895-1904), incorporated elements of Newtonian rigid body mechanics while using photographic recording of the body segmental positions during a known time-frame. Their estimates of body segment parameters (e.g., center of mass, moments of inertia, and percent mass), remained the authoritative values until Dempster's (Note 1) definitive work.

Concommitant advances were being made in electro-physiology during the latter portion of the 19th century. Emil DuBois-Reymond (1818-1896) laid the foundations of electrophysiology; he concerned himself with "medical physics" or the anatomico-physiological basis of movement (Dempster, 1961). *The Physiology of Motion*, which Guillaume B.A. Duchenne (1806-1875) published in 1865 (trans. 1959) classically detailed the potential actions of human superficial muscles; he effected the contractions of the muscles with faradic stimulation of skin overlying the muscles. The next effective stage in the electrophysiological aspects of human motion analyses was made possible by the development of another experimenal tool: the electromyogram (EMG). H. Piper, a German, presented the physiological bases of EMG in 1910-1912; it was the Englishman, E.D. Adrian (1925), however, who inspired English-speaking scientists to begin studies of normal and pathological skeletal muscle function with EMG.

The dawning of the 20th century revealed rather interesting comparisons between the United States and Eurasia in the state of the art of human movement studies. In the United States, a didactic approach was all-important; "gymnastic" and orthopaedic exercise programs, based on the foundations laid by Andre, Ling, and Jahn, formed the elemental components of the study of human movement. The books, *The Special Kinesiology of Educational Gymnastics* (Posse, 1890), and *Gymnastic Kinesiology* (Skarstrom, 1909), respectively written by Posse and Skarstrom, typified the approach adopted in the United States at the turn of the century. Their application of the term "kinesiology" to the analysis of muscles and movements in physical education set a precedent for one of the definitions of the term still used today.

In contrast to the United States, Eurasian researchers added practical education to the significant basic research in biomechanics and muscle dynamics burgeoning simultaneously in several countries. In France, Jules Amar (1920) published his classic study of human movement efficiency, *The Human Motor*. Nicholai Bernstein was directing the creative research in movement at the Central Institute of Work in Moscow. Bernstein (1926) was probably one of the first authors, if not the first, to use specifically the word "biomechanics"; it was a decade later that the term first appeared in the English literature (Gratz, 1936). The Russian ergonomic studies and investigations in locomotion were unique in their integrative approach to the study of coordinated human motion and its regulation. In England, Archibald V. Hill (for example, see Hill, 1927, 1970) and his associates were not only unraveling the intricacies of muscle contractile mechanics, but were also applying these results to such topics as the energetics of sprint running.

Atwater (1980) recently prepared an excellent historical-chronological examination of the growth of human movement study in the United States. She highlighted the research efforts of Ruth B. Glassow (1932), Thomas K. Cureton (1932), and Charles H. McCloy (1937), in physical education during the 1930s. The kinematic studies by these and other researchers did not have the impact they could have had if a large community of human movement scientists had existed in the United States at that time.

It was in the 1930s when Arthur Steindler's classic text (1935) was published. His text became a standard reference for the qualitative assessment of the structure, movements, and muscular actions of the human body, and after its publication, physical education did not gravitate to quantitative biomechanics for over twenty years. Indeed, from 1940-1960, seven new kinesiology textbooks appeared in physical education (Atwater, 1980), and each, in somewhat modified formats, dealt with the same three fundamental elements presented in Steindler's book. In physical education, rigorous application of the principles of statics and dynamics to human motion analyses had not yet reached fruition. However, in the related fields of physical medicine and physiology, rather sophisticated research was being conducted in human movement by such researchers as Basmajian (1962), Elftman (1939a, 1939b), Fenn (1930a, 1930b), and Inman, Saunders, and Abbott (1944).

Recent Developments

The last two decades have seen significant growth and maturation of biomechanics in physical education. It has been within this period that an effective and vigorous research community of biomechanists emerged; Atwater (1980) noted that the important national and international scholarly societies in biomechanics developed just in the past ten years. Additionally, the biomechanists emerging from physical education and movement studies programs are now more uniformly knowledgeable in physical, mathematical, and biological sciences, and thus, they can freely and effectively interact with biomechanists from disciplines like engineering, ergonomics, and orthopaedics. The biomechanists of these interactive disciplines are able to exchange knowledge and ideas, and also to make competitive scientific efforts—an indication of a viable scientific community (Hagstrom, 1965; Mahoney, 1979).

Not only have experimental tools, such as cinematography, electromyography, and ergometry (Cavagna, 1975) opened new chapters in human motion analysis, but more recently, the rigorous tools of mechanics and mathematical modeling have also revealed themselves as powerful analytical elements in modern biomechanics. In the relatively brief period of two decades, the field of human movement biomechanics emerged from infancy to where the state of the art includes mathematical models at the cutting edge of science (for example, Hatze, 1976). The quality and the quantity of published research in biomechanics has increased and should continue to increase in future decades.

Conclusion

Leonardo da Vinci once said that ". . .to understand motion is to understand nature. . . ." (Dempster, 1961, p. 131). The application of the principles and methods of mechanics quantitatively enhance the study of movement and kinesiology. Today's biomechanist enjoys the benefits of deep scientific roots, powerful analytical and exerimental tools, and effective scientific and intellectual stimulation from colleagues. In such a context, the maturation of human movement biomechanics should be rapid, and the subsequent scientific discoveries—exciting.

Reference Note

1. Dempster, W.T. *Space requirements of the seated operator; geometrical, kinematic and mechanical aspects of the body with special reference to the limbs.* (WADC Technical Report No. 55-159). Wright-Patterson Air Force Base: Ohio, 1955.

References

Adrian, E.D. Interpretation of the electromyogram. *Lancet,* 1925, **2**, pp. 1229-1233; 1283-1286.

Amar, J. *The human motor.* New York: E.P. Dutton, 1920.

Aristotle. *Progression of animals.* (E.S. Forster, trans.) Cambridge: Harvard University Press, 1937.

Atwater, A.E. Kinesiology/biomechanics: perspectives and trends. *Research Quarterly,* 1980, **51**, 193-218.

Basmajian, J.V. *Muscles alive: their functions revealed by electromyography.* Baltimore: Williams & Wilkins, 1962.

Bernstein, N. *General biomechanics* (Part 1). Moscow: Central Institute of Work, 1926. (In Russian)

Borelli, G.A. *De motu animalium.* Editio Altera Correctior emendatior. Lugduni Nin Batavis, J. de Vivie, C. Boutesteyn, D. a Gaebuck, & P. Vander Aa, 1685. (Later edition).

Braun, G.L. Kinesiology: from Aristotle to the twentieth century. *Research Quarterly,* 1941, **12**, 163-173.

Braune, C.W., & Fischer, O. Ueber den schwerpunkt des menschlichen koerpers mit ruecksicht auf die ausruestung des deutschen infanteristen. *Abhandlungen der Mathematische-physischen Classe der Königl. Sachischen Gesellschaft der Wissenschaften,* 1889, **15**, 561-572.

Braus, H. *Anatomie des Menschen* (Vol. 1). Berlin: Springer-Verlag, 1954.

Bronowski, J. *The origins of knowledge and imagination.* New Haven: Yale University Press, 1978.

Burke, R.K. The future of kinesiology at the undergraduate level. In J.C. Dillman & R.G. Sears (Eds.), *Proceedings. Kinesiology: A national conference on teaching.* Urbana-Champaign: University of Illinois, 1977.

Cajori, F. (Ed.). *Sir Issac Newton's mathematical principles of natural philosophy and his system of the world.* (A. Mottee, trans.). Berkeley: University of California Press, 1946. (Originally published, 1729.)

Cavagna, G.A. Force platforms as ergometers. *Journal of Applied Physiology,* 1975, **39**, 174-179.

Contini, R. Preface. *Human Factors,* 1963, **5**, 423-425.

Contini, R., & Drillis, R. Biomechanics. *Applied Mechanics Review,* 1954, **7**, 49-52.

Cooper, J.M. The historical development of kinesiology with emphasis on concepts and people. In C.J. Dillman & R.G. Sears (Eds.), *Proceedings. Kinesiology: A national conference on teaching.* Urbana-Champaign: University of Illinois, 1977.

Cooper, J.M., & Glassow, R.B. *Kinesiology.* St. Louis: C.V. Mosby, 1976.

Cureton, T.K.. Physics applied to physical education. *Journal of Health, Physical Education and Recreation,* 1932, **3**, 23-25.

d'Alembert, J.L. *Traite de dynamique.* Paris: David, 1758.

Dempster, W.T. Free body diagrams as an approach to the mechanics of human posture and motion. In F.G. Evans (Ed.), *Biomechanical studies of the musculo-skeletal system.* Springfield, IL: C.C. Thomas, 1961.

Dillman, C.J., & Sears, R.G. (Eds.). *Proceedings. Kinesiology: A national conference on teaching.* Urbana-Champaign: University of Illinois, 1977.

Drillis, R. Folk norms and biomechanics. *Human Factors,* 1963, **5**, 427-442.

Duchenne, G.B.A. *Physiology of motion.* (E.B. Kaplan, Ed. and trans.). Philadelphia: W.B. Saunders, 1959.

Elftman, H. Forces and energy changes in the leg during walking. *American Journal of Physiology,* 1939, **125**, 339-356. (a)

Elftman, H. The function of muscles in locomotion. *American Journal of Physiology,* 1939, **125**, 357-366. (b)

Evans, F.G. Biomechanical implications of anatomy. In J.M. Cooper (Ed.), *Selected topics on biomechanics.* Chicago: Athletic Institute, 1971.

Fenn, W.O. Frictional and kinetic factors in the work of sprint running. *American Journal of Physiology,* 1930, **92**, 582-611. (a)

Fenn, W.O. Work against gravity and work due to velocity changes in running. *American Journal of Physiology,* 1930, **93**, 433-462. (b)

Fischer, O. Der gang des menschen. *Abhandlungen der Mathematische-physischen Class der Königl. Sachischen Gesellschaft der Wissenschaften,* 1895-1904, **21**, 151; **25**, 1; **26**, 87, 471; **28**, 321, 353.

Foster, M. *Lectures on the history of physiology during the sixteenth, seventeenth, and eighteenth centuries.* Cambridge: Cambridge University Press, 1901.

Fung, Y.C. Biomechanics—its scope, history, and some problems of continuum mechanics in physiology. *Applied Mechanics Review,* 1968,

21, 1-20.

Glassow, R.B. *Fundamentals of physical education.* Philadelphia: Lea & Febiger, 1932.

Gratz, C.M. New method of studying physical disabilities. *Archives of Physical Therapy and X-ray Radiation,* 1936, **17**, 145-150.

Gregor, R.J., & Zernicke, R.F. Kinesiology as a life science: An undergraduate curriculum. In C.J. Dillman & R.G. Sears (Eds.), *Proceedings. Kinesiology: A national conference on teaching.* Urbana-Champaign: University of Illinois, 1977.

Haas, R.B. *Muybridge, man in motion.* Berkeley: University of California Press, 1976.

Hagstrom, W.O. *The scientific community.* New York: Basic Books, 1965.

Hatze, H. The meaning of the term 'Biomechanics.' *Journal of Biomechanics,* 1974, **7**, 189-190.

Hatze, H. The complete optimization of a human motion. *Mathematical Biosciences,* 1976, **28**, 99-135.

Hay, J.G. The biomechanics of sports techniques. Englewood Cliffs, NJ: Prentice-Hall, 1978.

Health, T.L. (Ed.). *The works of Archimedes.* Cambridge: Cambridge University Press, 1897.

Hill, A.V. *Muscular movement in man.* New York: McGraw-Hill, 1927.

Hill, A.V. *First and last experiments in muscle mechanics.* London: Cambridge University Press, 1970.

Hirt, S. What is kinesiology? A historical review. *Physical Therapy Reviews,* 1955, **35**, 419-426.

Hopstock, H. Leonardo as anatomist. (E.A. Fleming, trans.) In C. Singer (Ed.), *Studies in the history and method of science* (Vol. 2). Oxford: Clarenden Press, 1921.

Inman, V.T., Saunders, J.B.DeC., & Abbott, L.C. Observations on the function of the shoulder joint. *Journal of Bone and Joint Surgery,* 1944, **26**, 1-30.

Locke, L.F. Kinesiology and the profession. *Journal of Health, Physical Education and Recreation,* 1965, **36**, 69-71.

Locke, L.F. Kinesiology: A word or a discipline? *Journal of Health, Physical Education and Recreation,* 1967, **38**, 50.

Luttgens, K., & Zernicke, R.F. Structure and organization of kinesiology/biomechanics content at undergraduate level. In C.J. Dillman & R.G. Sears (Eds.), *Proceedings. Kinesiology: A national conference on teaching.* Urbana-Champaign: University of Illinois, 1977.

Mahoney, M.J. Psychology of the scientist: an evaluative review. *Social*

Studies of Science, 1979, **9**, 349-375.

Marey, E.J. *Mouvement.* Paris: B. Masson, 1894.

McCloy, C.H. The organization and teaching of apparatus work and tumbling. *Journal of Physical Education,* April 1937, 60-62.

Muybridge, E. *The human figure in motion.* New York: Dover, 1955.

Muybridge, E. *Animals in motion.* New York: Dover, 1957.

Nelson, R.C. Biomechanics of sport: An overview. In J.M. Cooper (Ed.), *Selected Topics on Biomechanics.* Chicago: Athletic Institute, 1971.

Nelson, R.C. Biomechanics of sport: Emerging discipline. In S. Cerquiglini, A. Venerando, & J. Wartenweiler (Eds.), *Biomechanics III.* Baltimore: University Park Press, 1973.

Posse, N. *The special kinesiology of educational gymnastics.* Boston: Lothrop, Lee & Shepard, 1890.

Rasch, P.J. Notes toward a history of kinesiology (Parts 1, 2, & 3). *Journal of the American Osteopathic Association,* 1958, **57**, 572-574; 641-644; 713-715.

Rasch, P.J., & Burke, R.K. *Kinesiology and applied anatomy: The science of human movement.* Philadelphia: Lea & Febiger, 1978.

Robinson, V. *The story of medicine.* New York: Doubleday, 1943.

Saunders, J.B.DeC., & O'Malley, C.D. (Eds.). *The illustrations from the works of Andreas Vesalius.* Cleveland: World Publishing, 1950.

Serret, M.J.-A. *Oevres de Lagrange* (Vols. 11 & 12). Paris: Guther-Villars, 1888-1889.

Singer, C. (Ed.). *A short history of scientific ideas to 1900.* New York: Oxford University Press, 1959.

Skarstrom, W. *Gymnastic kinesiology.* Springfield, MA: F.A. Bassette, 1909.

Steindler, A. *Mechanics of normal and pathological locomotion in man.* Springfield, IL: C.C. Thomas, 1935.

Thayer, W.S. Bichat. *Johns Hopkins Hospital Bulletin,* 1903, **14**, 197-210.

Ulrich, C., & Nixon, J.E. *Tones of theory.* Washington, DC: AAHPER Press, 1972.

Weber, W., & Weber, E. *Die mechanick der menschlichen gehwerkzeuge (Mechanics of Human Gait).* Goettingen: Dieterichschen Buchbandlung, 1836.

Biomechanics of Sport: The State of the Art

9

P.R. Cavanagh and R. Hinrichs

In the last decade, the discipline of sport biomechanics has grown from an exercise in the filming of sports activities to an applied science with a powerful array of measurement techniques which is beginning to provide explanations for previously unsolved questions in human motion. The simple descriptive approach, characteristics of early work, has been superceded by attempts to explain the mechanisms underlying movement.

Biomechanics has not been the source of these new techniques and concepts. Rather, a realization that existing ideas in other disciplines have a ready application to the study of the human body in motion has occurred. The rapid growth of science and technology in the 1970s left many solutions in search of a problem. This situation was the antithesis of sport biomechanics which consisted of many problems in search of a solution.

The rapid growth of biomechanics both in size and in substance can be noted by several landmarks. Today, almost a dozen flourishing graduate programs in biomechanics are invariably able to place their graduates. Graduate students specializing in biomechanics within physical education now receive training in the relevant branches of physical science and mathematics as well as biology and physical education. New professional societies have emerged, such as the International Society of Biomechanics (founded in 1973) and the American Society of Biomechanics (founded in 1977). The number of papers on the biomechanics of sport in a variety of professional journals has increased dramatically.

All these developments have afforded added respectability to biomechanics, which is now considered a valid field of study in itself. Previously, occasional papers that could be classified as biomechanics appeared in engineering and physics journals written by scientists for whom the study of sport was a spare time avocation rather than a profession.

A growing realization that biomechanics provides the potential for improvement of both sports techniques and sports equipment has also occurred. The US Olympic Committee now includes biomechanics as part of its effort in sports medicine and has a biomechanics laboratory at the permanent Olympic training center. Manufacturers of such diverse products as tennis rackets and running shoes have used a biomechanical approach to make improvements in design. In some cases, such as the pole vault, the improvement in equipment has led directly to changes in technique and improvements in performance (Hay, 1978).

To acquaint students with the state of the art in biomechanics, we have chosen a number of topics which together represent the core elements of the discipline. Many of these topics cover measurement techniques which are essential tools in biomechanics research, and applications of these techniques are also included. An individual pursuing an advanced degree in biomechanics will want a good working knowledge in all of these areas. Graduate students in other specialties of physical education will benefit from an awareness of the scope of the field of biomechanics.

The Measurement of Motion

The development of accurate methods to measure the position of parts of the body during motion in space has been a prime objective of biomechanics research. The actual motion is sometimes of interest in its own right. Frequently, however, the information is used to aid in achieving the ultimate goal of understanding the forces creating and resulting from the motion. The usual vehicle for obtaining this information is high-speed cinematography and subsequent film analysis (Miller & Nelson, 1973). In this process, points of interest on the body are converted into pairs of (x, y) coordinates in a process known as film digitization. Each frame of film is analyzed successively to provide a set of discrete data points describing the motion of part of the body in space. Recently several optoelectronic methods such as SELSPOT AND POLGON (Mitchelson, 1976; Oberg, 1974) have become available to obtain similar information to that derived from film digitization.[1] These new methods can provide results immediately without the delays involved in the tedious process of frame-by-frame analysis. Unfortunately, film is still the most accurate method of locating body landmarks in space, and it has the added advan-

---

[1]"Optoelectronic" is an adjective combining the two words "optical" and "electronic." It is used here in reference to methods of recording movement which involve both optics and electronics. Recording from a television camera onto videotape or monitoring the motion of moving light sources can both be described as optoelectronic methods of recording movement.

tage of providing a permanent record of the movement. The remainder of the present discussion will consider cinematographic methods because they are still most widely used.

A major criticism of much of the early and indeed present work in biomechanics is that movements which are actually three-dimensional are frequently analyzed as if they occurred in a single plane. Because one camera is sufficient for a two-dimensional analysis, the motivation to make the planar assumption is understandable. This does not, however, make the assumption tenable when one considers activities such as the hammer throw, a twisting dive, or a high jump.

Viable techniques of locating the coordinates of landmarks on the body in three-dimensional space are now readily available. Although many different techniques have been devised for this purpose, at least two cameras must be used for all the methods. The most widely used method, the Direct Linear Transformation (DLT), had been available for some time in the area of close range photogrammetry (Abdel-Aziz & Karara, 1971) before it was applied to cinematography (Shapiro, 1978). The great advantage of the DLT is that the cameras do not have to be aligned in any predetermined manner and their orientations do not have to be known. Before actual data is collected, the experimental space must be calibrated to allow a relationship to be established between the image of a point in the field of view and its actual location. The calibration procedure involves filming targets with known locations (control points) and solving for a series of constants which define the locations, orientations, and optical properties of the cameras. The control points are then removed, and the subject performs in the same field of view.

Simultaneous views of each point of interest must be available in a *minimum* of two cameras to reconstruct the three-dimensional coordinates of that point. Surprising accuracy can be obtained with these techniques. Points on the body can be located in three dimensions to within a few millimeters under normal laboratory conditions. This is considerably better accuracy than can be obtained by the various optoelectronic techniques mentioned earlier.

Errors in Data Collection

All measurements are only estimates of the variable being studied, and cinematography is no exception. The data are in discrete rather than continuous form, and the digitized values contain components of both the true variable and error from various sources. If the error is random rather than systematic, a number of techniques can reduce the effects of this "noise" on the desired "signal." These methods are sometimes called "filtering" or "smoothing" of data, and they are important in biomechanics because it is frequently necessary to calculate the accelerations of points on the body to estimate force. To achieve this, the process of double differentiation is used to generate first velocity and then acceleration from displacement data; this procedure is extremely sensitive to the presence of noise. The digital filter[2] (Winter, Sidwall, & Hobson, 1974) and the cubic spline[3] (Soudan & Dierckx, 1979) techniques have been shown to be the most effective for application to data in biomechanics.

Kinematic Analysis

The branch of mechanics dealing with the motion of objects without regard to the forces causing the motion is called kinematics. To illustrate how data collected from cinematography can be used to gain insight into human movement, some examples from the kinematic studies of locomotion are considered.

Walking and running are almost ideal activities for biomechanical study because they are cyclic in nature and well learned by almost everyone. The contact of the foot with the ground and the subsequent flight phase are quite reproducible in a given subject at a given speed. Also, the variety of speeds at which the movements can be performed offers the opportunity to examine, under controlled experimental conditions, steady increases in the ranges of joint motion and changes in forces and pressure distributions under the foot. We will return to this subject later.

Because walking and running are the epitome of well-coordinated movements, a kinematic description of body segments during locomotion should emphasize this coordination as well as the cyclic nature of the activity. The technique developed by Grieve (Cavanagh & Grieve, 1973; Grieve, 1969) presents the angular motion of two adjacent joints or segments plotted one against the other, and fulfills the requirements mentioned above to a much greater degree than simply plotting the angles as functions of time.

Thigh-knee diagrams for walking and running are shown in Figure 1.

---

[2]"Digital Filter" refers to a numerical method of treating a set of discrete data points in a manner analagous to passing a continuous signal through an electronic network. In biomechanics, the filter is usually designed to eliminate high frequency noise.

[3]"Cubic Spline" refers to a numerical method of piecewise curve fitting to a set of discrete data points. It is frequently used as a method of smoothing or filtering.

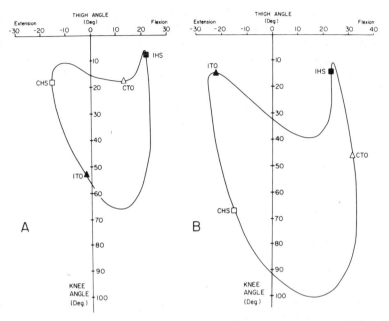

Figure 1. Thigh-knee diagrams from walking and running at different speeds: (A) slow walking (approx. 1 m/s); (B) fast running (approx. 5.6 m/s).

Both diagrams start in the top right hand corner at ipsilateral heel-strike (IHS) and proceed in a counterclockwise direction. ITO stands for ipsilateral toe-off, CHS stands for contralateral heel-strike, and CTO stands for contralateral toe-off. A downward movement of the graph indicates knee flexion and upward movement knee extension. Side-to-side migrations of the curves indicate that hip flexion (to the right) or hip extension (to the left) is underway. Diagonal lines imply that movements at both joints are occurring simultaneously.

Note that the shape and size of the diagrams differ between the two locomotor activities.

The shapes of the diagrams show clear differences in both size and form, indicating different ranges of motion and coordination respectively. For example, the appearance of knee flexion as a cushioning mechanism immediately following footstrike is more apparent in running. An interesting feature of the curves is that they can be appreciated on the basis of shape alone, although they do contain exact numerical information if it is required.

Analyzing energy levels of parts of the body, which is a further application of kinematics, provides further insight into human movement. An object can have mechanical energy due to its position in space (potential energy) and due to its motion (kinetic energy). Each form of energy can be transformed into the other, and energy can also be transferred between parts of the body.

The total energy, E, of a body part or segment moving in a plane can be represented by the summation of three terms: the potential energy and the kinetic energies of translation and rotation. Symbolically,

$$E = mgh + \frac{1}{2} mv^2 + \frac{1}{2} I\omega^2$$

where

   m is the mass of the segment.
   g is the acceleration due to gravity.
   h is the height of the segment above a datum.
   v is the linear velocity of the segment.
   I is a segmental moment of inertia.
   ω is the angular velocity of the segment.

The quantities h, v, and ω can be calculated from cinematographic data, g is a constant, and the quantities m and I are known as inertial properties of the segment (body segment parameters) and will be discussed shortly.

Winter (1979a) and his associates have extended the pioneering work of early investigators such as Fenn (1930) and Elftmann (1939) by presenting a complete description of the changes in kinetic and potential energies of the body and its segments. The example in Figure 2 shows the partitioning of the total energy of the leg during the swing phase of walking. Winter pointed out errors in earlier work (Cavagna, Saibene, & Margaria, 1963) which considered only the motion of the body center of mass and ignored the energy required to change the orientations and velocities of the individual body parts relative to an external reference frame.

One reason for interest in the topic of energy levels of body segments is that it provided a link with physiological estimates of energy cost (Kanko, Ito, Fuchimoto, & Toyooka, 1981). Changes in the energy levels of all parts of the body can be calculated from film analysis. By comparing mechanical and metabolic energy estimates, one can make a tentative statement about the efficiency of running. The connection, however, is an extremely complex one, complicated by such phenomena as the different energy costs of positive and negative work (Asmussen, 1952), energy exchange between segments, and the possible utilization of stored elastic energy (Cavagna, 1978). These problems have led various authors to pro-

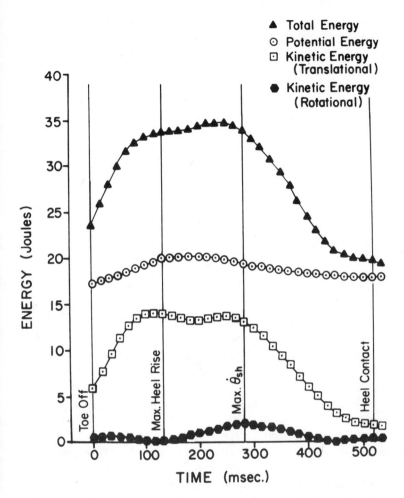

Figure 2. The instantaneous energy components of the shank (foot and leg) during the swing phase of walking. (Redrawn, with permission, from A.O. Quanbury, D.A. Winter, and G.D. Reimer, *Journal of Human Movement Studies,* 1975, 1, 59-67.)

pose that running is anywhere from 25-50% efficient (Norman, Sharratt, Pezzack, & Noble, 1976).

Body Segment Parameters

The points of interest in cinematography are frequently anatomical landmarks which define the endpoints of specific body segments. These segments are usually considered to be rigid and connected to each other at frictionless joints. This simplification is a first order model of the true situation and is used because classical rigid body mechanics can then be employed to estimate the forces and torques within the system.

Even the simplest segments such as a thigh or forearm could actually be better described as "flexible rods from which deformable fluid bags are suspended at unknown positions. . ." (Pheasant, Note 1). As Pheasant has pointed out, the mathematics required to deal with such a system would be extremely complex, hence the longevity of the rigid body assumption.

For the purposes of analysis, the basic parameters needed for each segment of the body are mass, center of mass location, and moments of inertia. The latter parameter is the rotational equivalent of mass and characterizes the resistance of the segment to changes in its angular motion.

Traditionally, these have been obtained by using information from cadavers to estimate values in particular living subjects (Dempster, Note 2). Such an application might be that the mass of the thigh is estimated as 10% of total body mass. This is known as an indirect method and is clearly susceptible to many sources of error. It assumes that all people have the same body proportions and that these proportions are the same as the aged and emaciated cadavers used in the original study (Dempster, Note 2). Clauser, McConville, and Young (Note 3) attempted to overcome these limitations by providing equations which would yield personalized estimates of body segment parameters from anthropometric measurements made on the subjects themselves. These investigators provided equations for the prediction of segmental mass, volume, and center of mass based on data obtained from the measurement and dissection of 13 cadavers of an average age of 49 years. The major limitation of the Clauser study is the absence of data on segmental moments in inertia.

The only publication of note that presents experimental data on segmental moments of inertia is that of Chandler, Clauser, McConville, Reynolds, and Young (Note 4). In this study, moments of inertia about three specific axes (called principal axes) for all 14 segments from each of six cadavers were experimentally determined. Although a large number of anthropometric measures were taken on the cadavers, no attempt was made to use these data as predictors of segmental inertias. Considering the overwhelming importance of moments of inertia in dynamic calculations, it is unfortunate that so few investigators have addressed themselves to this problem.

Ideally, it would be possible to measure body segment parameters directly on each subject used in an experiment. An approach to this ideal situation has been made through a procedure called gamma scanning. This method, originally validated on animal tissue by Brooks and Jacobs (1975) is now in use in the Soviet Union on human subjects (Zatsiorski, Note 5). A collimated beam of gamma radiation (approximately 4 cm by 2 cm) is directed through the human tissue onto a detector. The absorption of the gamma rays is related to the mass of the tissue between source and detector. By scanning the whole body under computer control in a stepwise manner, a composite picture of mass and mass distribution can be obtained. The procedure is said to involve minimal radiation dosage ($\leqslant$ 10 mrad) and has been shown through validation on cadaveric tissue to yield accuracies of 3% for mass and 10% for moments of inertia.

Because this technique is not widely available, a viable alternative is the use of indirect predictive methods based on gamma scanning or other methods. Zatsiorski and his colleagues have used the gamma scanner to determine the body segment parameters of 100 young male athletes. They have also performed extensive anthropometric measurements on the same subjects. This has allowed predictive equations to be generated in which the body segment parameters of an individual comparable to the test population can be estimated from measurements taken on that person's body.

A major limitation of all published work on body segment parameters is the dearth of information on women and children. Future application of Computerized Axial Tomography (CAT) scanning (Huang, Suarez, Toridis, Khozeimeh, & Ovenshire, 1980) may yield a new and important means of obtaining direct personalized estimates of body segment parameters.

Kinetic Analysis

Once suitable methods have been used to quantify the motion and estimate the inertial properties of parts of the body, the techniques of mechanics can be applied to estimate the forces involved in human motion. This area is known as kinetics.

In biomechanics, forces are frequently characterized as internal or external. Forces from the environment such as those arising from contact, gravity, and air resistance are termed external. Internal forces include such things as muscle and ligamentous forces and the contact forces between adjacent bones.

External Forces

A typical problem involves the calculation of unknown forces when

SPACE DIAGRAM   FREE BODY DIAGRAM

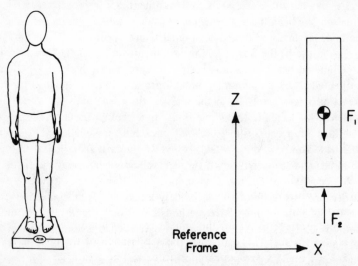

Figure 3. A simple free body diagram (FBD, right) representing the situation shown in the space diagram (left), where a person is standing on a weighing machine.

In the FBD, the body is treated as a rigid mass with weight F_1 and the ground reaction force F_2 is shown acting in the opposite direction to the weight.

The reference frame indicates the conventions for positive forces in the X and Z directions. See text for further details.

other forces and movement parameters are known. A free body diagram (FBD) is commonly used to formulate equations of motion needed for the solution of unknown quantities. In this diagram, all external forces must be indicated.

A simple example of a free body diagram for a person standing still on a bathroom scale is shown in Figure 3. Only two forces act in this situation, F_1, the force of gravity tending to pull the body down, and the ground reaction force, F_2, tending to push the body upwards. Newton's Second Law states that the net force F, acting on an object is equal to the product of the mass of the object and its acceleration ($F = ma$).

In this case, no acceleration occurs because the person is standing still, and therefore, a and hence ($m \cdot a$) equals zero. Also, the net force, F, is equal to ($F_2 - F_1$) with the conventions of positive upwards being defined according to the reference frame shown in Figure 3.

Newton's Second Law applied to this situation yields the following relationship:

$$F_2 - F_1 = 0$$

Therefore:

$$F_2 = F_1$$

In words, rather than symbols, this calculation has told us that the person's body weight, which is unknown in this example, is exactly equal to the ground reaction force during stationary standing. This fact is used every day to determine the body weight using a conventional bathroom scale.

Let us continue this example a little further and assume that instead of standing still, the person begins to move rapidly up and down. The scale will continue to record the ground reaction force which will no longer be constant. This is because the acceleration of the body is no longer zero, and the ground reaction force will be greater or less than body weight depending upon the direction of the acceleration. Referring to Figure 3, F_1 remains constant while F_2 fluctuates. To accelerate upwards, F_2 must be greater than body weight. To accelerate downwards, F_2 must be smaller than body weight. A good example of the latter case is "unweighting" in skiing where the skier wants to reduce the force under the skis to make turning possible. This is achieved by a downward acceleration of the body.

The ground reaction forces during dynamic activities can be measured quite accurately using a force platform, which is a widely used tool in biomechanics research. The force platform acts like a sophisticated bathroom scale which follows rapid fluctuations in the ground reaction force, and measures not only the vertical component, but the side-to-side and front-to-back forces acting in the ground plane (shear forces) as well.

Figure 4 shows the vertical component of ground reaction force measured in our laboratory by a force platform during ground contact in distance running. The curve shows that the force rises to a peak of three times the subject's body weight during the contact phase. The peak force is greater than body weight because the body is being accelerated upwards in preparation for the flight phase.

The force platform also allows information on the effective point of force application, known as center of pressure, to be measured. Figure 5 shows the path of the center of pressure relative to the outline of a right foot for speeds of walking and running between 3 and 10 miles per hour.

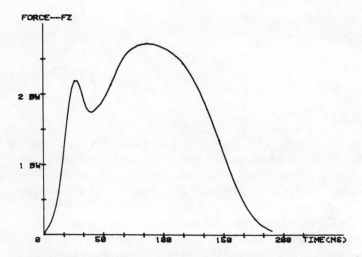

Figure 4. The vertical component of ground reaction force during the contact phase of distance running. Notice that the force rises to approximately three times body weight approximately one tenth of a second (100 milliseconds) after contact.

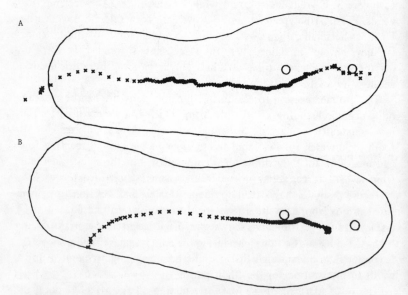

Figure 5. Center of pressure patterns from the same subject walking at 3 mph (A) and running at 10 mph (B). Readers should imagine they are looking down on top of a right foot. The crosses indicate the location of the center of pressure at 2 millisecond intervals.

Figure 6. The pressure distribution under the foot during mid support in walking. The height of the surface above the foot outline indicates the magnitude of the pressure at that location.

The crosses in the diagrams represent the center of the total pressure distribution, but this should not be interpreted as meaning the absence of pressure in other areas of the shoe. This is reinforced by a more detailed presentation of the pressure distribution at one instant under the walking foot shown in Figure 6. The center of pressure at this time would be between the two peaks of forefoot and rearfoot pressure. Such analyses as center of pressure and pressure distribution are useful for a clearer understanding of the mechanics of locomotion, in the design of footwear, and in the evaluation of pathological locomotor patterns.

Internal Forces

An important aspect of biomechanics is to provide an insight into how injuries occur with the eventual goal of reducing their incidence. For this purpose, the important forces are the ones internal to the body such as those in muscle, ligament, and between the bones at a joint. In such cases, direct measurement is usually out of the question (except for animal studies), and simplified FBDs are constructed in an attempt to estimate some of these forces. In this case the system described by the FBD consists only of a part of the body. Next, we will discuss an example where the objective is to determine the force between the bones of the ankle joint (talocrural joint) during running.

Figure 7 shows one instant in time from the contact phase in running.

SPACE DIAGRAM   FREE BODY DIAGRAM

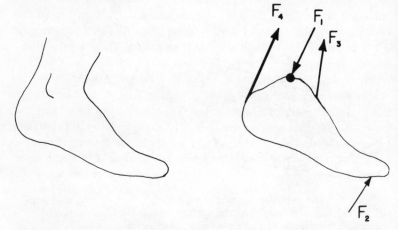

Figure 7. A space diagram and FBD of the foot during ground contact. F_1 is the joint force at the talo-crural joint, F_3 and F_4 are the dorsi and plantar flexor muscle forces respectively. F_2 is the ground reaction force. The weight of the foot has been ignored in this example because it is negligible. See text for further details.

Starting with the realistic situation of the foot striking the force platform, progressive simplifications are made. First, only two muscles, one plantar flexor and one dorsiflexor are considered, and many structures such as the ligaments at the joint and other muscles are ignored in this simple example. Next, because the foot is the segment of interest, its contact with the leg and the ground have been replaced and represented by forces.

The ankle is assumed to be a smooth pin joint, with a single center of rotation, so the force between the bones of the leg and foot is shown as F_1 acting downwards at the joint center. The ground reaction force, F_2, acts upwards on the foot.

The remaining forces which complete this simple FBD are those representing the two muscles shown as F_3 and F_4. As the running cycle progresses, all of the forces shown will change their magnitude and direction and the ground reaction force F_2 will also change its effective point of application.

The reader should have already realized that the many assumptions and simplifications made to obtain the FBD have removed us some distance from biological reality. It may therefore come as a surprise that even this simple model cannot lead to a solution of the unknown forces F_1, F_3, and F_4 without making some further assumptions. The magnitudes and directions of the three unknown forces give a total of six unknowns. A standard analysis using Newton's Second Law for both translation and rotation will yield only three equations. There are therefore two alternatives. The forces can be estimated by optimization techniques which allow more variables than equations (Seireg & Arvikar, 1975), or further simplifications can be made (Stauffer, Chao, & Brewster, 1977). Both approaches have been attempted. The results have shown that the joint force F_1 reaches values between 5-12 times body weight (BW) during various locomotor activities. These are enormous forces compared to the peak ground reaction force of 3 BW. The reason for the large forces is that the muscles crossing the joint exert a compressive component as they contract to support and propel the body. Similar calculations reveal that forces exerted by the muscles are also considerable in relation to the loads that the body can lift. This is because of the unfavorable leverage that most muscles have.

Because muscle forces are by far the largest influence on joint forces, it would be of great experimental significance if muscle force in living subjects could be directly measured or estimated. Although the electrical activity of skeletal muscles can be rather easily detected using electromyography (EMG), numerous barriers prevent the use of EMG as an estimator of muscle force (Winter, 1979b). The fact that muscle force for a given level of activation is a function of both length (and consequently joint angle) and velocity means that any predictions of force from EMG which does not take these and other factors such as elastic storage into account is doomed to failure except under extremely limited conditions. Although several promising attempts to provide a comprehensive model of the EMG-Force relationship have been made (de Luca, 1973; Hof & van den Berg, 1978), there is little likelihood that EMG will be useful for the generalized prediction of muscle force in the near future. Electromyography is, however, a valuable tool for obtaining insight into the patterning of muscle activity during movement (Pedotti, 1977) and for understanding certain neurophysiological mechanisms such as muscle fatigue (Stevens & Taylor, 1972).

Once estimates are obtained for forces acting on the various tissues of the body, they can be compared with data from direct experiments on the mechanical properties of tissue (Yamada, 1970). Certain situations may be predicted to cause forces equal to or greater than those required to injure tissues. This approach also offers the possibility of predicting the effect of such surgical procedures as tendon transfer on the function of a certain joint (Close, 1973).

All of the kinetic examples discussed so far have been two-dimensional in nature. The shift from considering the dynamics of rigid body motion in two dimensions to a true three-dimensional analysis involves mathematical techniques of considerably greater complexity. For example, where we had used only a single moment of inertia of a segment in two dimensions, we must now use the inertia tensor, which contains six independent elements describing the inertial properties of the segment in three dimensions. One of the few 3-D kinetic studies in the literature is that of Aleshinsky and Zatsiorsky (1978) who present a method for calculating three components of net force and torque at the major joints of the body that future researchers may emulate. A three-dimensional study of the fosbury flop style of high jumping has also been accomplished (Dapena, 1980). This is clearly an activity which could not be satisfactorily understood by a two-dimensional analysis.

Modeling and Simulation

A frequently employed alternative to performing experiments on human subjects is known as modeling. This involves the creation of a set of mathematical relationships which can be used to predict the behavior of an actual situation. For example, the distance traveled by a discus can be estimated from a knowledge of the physical structure of the discus, the take-off conditions (velocity, spin and orientation, etc.), and flight conditions (wind speed, climatic factors, etc.). This approach has a number of advantages which sometimes outweigh the disadvantages created by the oversimplification inherent in most models.

Once the model is established and validated, a range of values can be tried for critical variables and the effect on final outcome can be predicted. This approach is known as simulation. With the model of the discus throw mentioned above, it would be a relatively simple matter to simulate the effects of increased spin or inclination of the discus and predict the effect on the distance thrown without needing any direct experimentation to reach the conclusions. This kind of simulation has obvious applications in coaching where technical questions asked by an athlete can be given quantitative answers.

The human body is much more difficult to model than the discus because it cannot reasonably be represented by a single rigid mass. Kane and Scher (1970) modeled the body as three rigid segments to study the effects of arm and leg movements on the reorientation of the trunk of an astronaut when no external forces were available to create an acceleration.

Hatze (1976) developed a mathematical model of the lower extremity which incorporated the mechanical properties of muscles and their attachments on the skeleton together with other body segment parameters. He used the model to predict the optimum pattern of segmental motion which would allow a simple kicking task to be performed in minimum time. Using the output from the model to instruct the subject, an improvement in performance was achieved after the subject had apparently reached a plateau on his own self-paced learning curve. If these results can be demonstrated on a larger population, they will have far-reaching effects. Athletes might receive quite specific instructions on the modification of technique which a model predicts would improve their performance. It may be, however, that many elite athletes are already operating under optimal conditions through a long learning process which might be described as "self-optimization."

Sports Equipment

Almost all sports involve the use of some equipment which interacts with the athlete in the performance of a skill. This may vary from a tennis racket, to an artifical surface, to a piece of protective equipment such as a football helmet or a running shoe. Although in the past, the design of such equipment was the province of artistic designers, this area has become an increasing focus of biomechanics research.

Frequently the stimulus for research has been injury prevention. For example, early studies with humans, primates, and cadavers established a level of tolerance for impacts to the head which, if exceeded, would lead to head injury (Guardjian, Roberts, & Thomas, 1966). A measure called the severity index (SI) was formulated to characterize the intensity of the impact (Gadd, 1967). Thorough scientific testing of football helmets (Calvano & Berger, 1979; Hodgson, 1975) has led to improvements in helmet design in which the SI has been reduced for a given impact on the helmet. This attention has undoubtedly resulted in fewer injuries in football.

Similar improvements have occurred in footwear for running as a result of the increased scientific scrutiny. Basic studies in the mechanics of running (Cavanagh & Lafortune, 1980) have generated design criteria in terms of the location and magnitude of forces applied to the shoe during running. The application of such studies to the design and testing of footwear have increased the level of awareness of both manufacturers and consumers to the point that people now realize biomechanics has an important part to play.

Beside making sport safer, a motivating factor in the study of sports equipment is the improvement of performance. Several examples demonstrate how mechanical factors in equipment design can affect performance. The fiberglass pole for valuting, the Held javelin, the elliptical chain wheel in cycling, the carbon fiber tennis racket, and the inflatible landing pit in high jumping have all facilitated improved performance. Several of these innovations resulted from intuitions rather than research, but new ideas today are increasingly the product of a biomechanics research program rather than a moment's insight on the part of an athlete, coach, or inventor.

Conclusion

Although we have considered sport biomechanics in this chapter as a free-standing discipline, it is important that its relationship to the other academic areas of physical education not be overlooked. The link with exercise physiology is perhaps one of the more obvious. In many cases, the criterion of improved "efficiency of movement," which is frequently a stated goal of biomechanical analysis, can be directly measured in terms of steady-rate (steady-state) oxygen uptake. A quantitative perspective on growth and development can be readily obtained by describing patterns of movement in biomechanical terms. The techniques of biomechanics also allow pathological movement patterns to be characterized and the effectiveness of various treatment programs to be evaluated. Learning profiles and strategies can also be quantified at a level of complexity which is beyond a simple tabulation of performance outcome. Increasingly, the techniques of biomechanics research are providing a framework on which interdisciplinary projects can be built.

The discipline of sport biomechanics is still, however, in its infancy. Much effort is still devoted toward attempts at understanding how skilled athletes perform the way they do. This is just the first stage in a process which should eventually lead to improvements in technique based on well-formulated research. So far only isolated movements from a few sports have been subjected to intensive study, and it would be premature to claim that far-reaching improvements in performance can routinely result from biomechanical analysis. In the area of injury prevention, biomechanics is also at a somewhat primitive stage. The etiology of many sports injuries are still at a level of subtlety which is below the threshold of either measurement or model. The future, however, is one of challenge and opportunity. Progress is now so rapid that a review of this article in 1990 may reveal that the state of the art in 1980 was, at best, embryonic.

Reference Notes

1. Pheasant, S. Personal communication, September 1976.
2. Dempster, W.T. *Space requirements of the seated operator.* (WADC Technical Report No. 55-159.) Wright-Patterson Air Force Base, Ohio, 1955. (AD-087-892)
3. Clauser, C.E., McConville, J.T., & Young, J.W. *Weight, volume, and center of mass segments of the human body.* (AMRL Technical Report No. 69-70.) Wright-Patterson Air Force Base, OH, 1969. (AD-710-622).
4. Chandler, R.R., Clauser, C.E., McConville, J.R., Reynolds, H.M., & Young, J.W. *Investigation of inertial properties of the human body.* (AMRL Technical Report No. 74-137.) Wright-Patterson Air Force Base, Ohio, 1975. (AD-A016-485)
5. Zatsiorski, V.M. Personal communication, November 1979.

References

Abdel-Aziz, Y.I., & Karara, H.M. Direct linear transformation from comparator coordinates into object-space coordinates in close-range photogrammetry. *Proceedings of ASP/UI Symposium on Close-range Photogrammetry,* 1979, pp. 1-18.

Aleshinsky, S.Y., & Zatsiorsky, V.M. Human locomotion in space analyzed biomechanically through a milti-link chain model. *Journal of Biomechanics,* 1978, **11,** 101-108.

Asmussen, E. Positive and negative muscular work. *Acta Physiologica Scandinavica,* 1952, **28,** 364-382.

Brooks, C.B., & Jacobs, A.M. The gamma scanning technique for inertial anthropometric measurement. *Medicine and Science in Sports,* 1975, **7,** 290-294.

Calvano, N.J., & Berger, R.E. Effects of selected test variables on the evaluation of football helmet performance. *Medicine and Science in Sports,* 1979, **11,** 293-301.

Cavagna, G.M. Storage and utilization of elastic energy in skeletal muscle. In R.S. Hutton (Ed.), *Exercise and sport sciences reviews* (Vol. 5). Santa Barbara, CA: Journal Publishing Affiliates, 1978.

Cavagna, G.A., Saibene, F.P., & Margaria, R. External work in walking. *Journal of Applied Physiology,* 1963, **18,** 1-9.

Cavanagh, P.R., & Grieve, D.W. The graphical display of angular movement of the body. *British Journal of Sports Medicine,* 1973, **7,** 129-133.

Cavanagh, P.R., & Lafortune, M.A. Ground reaction forces in distance running. *Journal of Biomechanics,* 1980, **13,** 397-406.

Close, J.R. *Functional anatomy of the extremities.* Springfield, IL: Charles C. Thomas, 1973.

Dapena, J. Mechanics of rotation in the fosbury flop. *Medicine and Science in Sports and Exercise,* 1980, **12**, 45-53.

de Luca, C.J., & Forrest, W.J. Force analysis of individual muscles acting simultaneously on shoulder joint during isometric abduction. *Journal of Biomechanics,* 1973, **6**, 385-393.

Elftman, H. Forces and energy changes in the leg during walking. *American Journal of Physiology,* 1939, **125**, 339-356.

Fenn, W.O. Work against gravity and work due to velocity changes in running. *American Journal of Physiology,* 1930, **93**, 433-462.

Gadd, C.W. Use of a weighted-impulse criterion for estimating injury hazard. *Proceedings of Tenth Stapp Car Crash Conference,* 1967, pp. 164-174.

Grieve, D.W. The assessment of gait. *Physiotheraphy* (UK), 1969, pp. 452-460.

Guardjian, E.S., Roberts, V.L., & Thomas, L.M. Tolerance curves of acceleration and intracranial pressure and protective index in experimental head injury. *Journal of Trauma,* 1966, **6**, 600-604.

Hatze, H. The complete optimization of a human motion. *Mathematical Biosciences,* 1976, **28**, 99-135.

Hay, J.G. *The Biomechanics of sports techniques.* Englewood Cliffs, NJ: Prentice-Hall, 1978.

Hodgson, V.R. National operating committee on standards for athletic equipment football helmet certification program. *Medicine and Science in Sports,* 1975, **7**, 225-232.

Hof, A.L., & van den Berg, J.W. EMG to force processing under dynamic conditions. In E. Asmussen & K. Jorgensen (Eds.), *Biomechanics VI-A.* Baltimore: University Park Press, 1978.

Huang, H.K., Suarez, F., Toridis, T.G., Khozeimeh, K., & Ovenshire, L. Utilization of CT scans as input to finite element analysis. *Proceedings of the International Conference on Finite Elements in Biomechanics,* Tucson, AZ, 1980, pp. 797-816.

Kane, T.R., & Scher, M.P. Human self rotation by means of limb movements. *Journal of Biomechanics,* 1970, **3**, 39-49.

Kaneko, M., Ito, A., Fuchimoto, T., & Toyooka, J. Mechanical work and efficiency of young distance runners during level running. In A. Morecki, K. Fidelus, K. Kedsior, & A. Wit (Eds.), *Biomechanics VII-B.* Baltimore: University Park Press, 1981.

Klopsteg, P.E., & Wilson, P.D. (Eds.). *Human limbs and their substitutes.* New York: Hafner, 1968.

Miller, D.I., & Nelson, R.C. *Biomechanics of sport.* Philadelphia: Lea & Febiger, 1973.

Mitchelson, D.L. Recording of movement without photography. In D.W. Grieve, D.I. Miller, D.L. Mitchelson, J.P. Paul, & A.J. Smith (Eds.), *Techniques for the analysis of human movement.* Princeton, NJ: Princeton Book Company, 1976.

Norman, R.W., Sharratt, M.R., Pezzack, J.C., & Noble, E.G. Reexamination of the mechanical efficiency of horizontal treadmill running. In P.V. Komi (Ed.), *Biomechanics V-B.* Baltimore: University Park Press, 1976.

Oberg, K. Mathematical modelling of human gait: An application of the SELSPOT System. In R.C. Nelson & C.A. Morehouse (Eds.), *Biomechics IV.* Baltimore: University Park Press, 1974.

Pedotti, A. A study of motor coordination and neuromuscular activities in human locomotion. *Biological Cybernetics,* 1977, **26**, 53-62.

Seireg, A., & Arvikar, R.J. The prediction of muscular load sharing and joint forces in the lower extremities during walking. *Journal of Biomechanics,* 1975, **8**, 89 -102.

Shapiro, R. Direct linear transformation method for three-dimensional cinematography. *Research Quarterly,* 1978, **49**, 197-205.

Soudan, K., & Dierckx, P. Calculation of derivatives and fourier coefficients of human motion data while using spline functions. *Journal of Biomechanics,* 1979, **12**, 21-26.

Stauffer, R.N., Chao, E.Y., & Brewster, R.C. Force and motion analysis of the normal, diseased and prosthetic ankle joint. *Clinical Orthopaedics,* 1977, **122**, 189-196.

Stevens, J.A., & Taylor, A. Fatigue of maintained voluntary muscle contraction in man. *Journal of Physiology* (London), 1972, **220**, 1-18.

Winter, D.A. Calculation and interpretation of mechanical energy of movement. In R.S. Hutton (Ed.), *Exercise and sport sciences reviews* (Vol. 6). Philadelphia: Franklin Institute Press, 1979. (a)

Winter, D.A. *Biomechanics of human movement.* New York: Wiley, 1979. (b)

Winter, D.A., Sidwall, H.G., & Hobson, D.A. Measurement and reduction of noise in kinematics of locomotion. *Journal of Biomechanics,* 1974, **7**, 157-159.

Yamada, H. *Strength of Biological Materials,* F.G. Evans (Ed.). Baltimore: Williams and Wilkens, 1970.

PART 4

Motor Development

This section on development contains four chapters; there is one chapter each on the emergence and current status study on human growth and motor development, and there are two additional chapters related to development. In a book honoring Professor G. Lawrence Rarick, it is appropriate that the number of chapters concerning development be the most numerous in this section of the volume. The influence of G.L. Rarick is clearly felt in this section. In addition to his chapter, two other chapters have been written by former students, and the fourth chapter has been written by a university colleague.

Studies on human growth and development and the various factors, such as exercise, which affect it are of importance to many disciplines. In particular, the influence of exercise on development of various tissues (muscle, bone, and adipose), and coordinated neural function are central interests in physical education. Just as several aspects of the school curriculum are intended to enhance the intellectual growth of children, physical education activities are intended to enhance the physical and motoric growth and development of children. Indeed, this role of physical education in promoting development may be one of the most universally accepted roles of physical education in the school curriculum. The favorable effects of exercise on growth and development may also be one of the most defensible reasons for having physical education in the curriculum

So strong and universal is the interest in studying the factors which influence growth and development, that it is inescapable that this aspect of physical education be interdisciplinary. The following chapters reflect the interdisciplinary effects of study on human growth and development. In Chapter 10, Dr. Rarick describes some of the contributions to our knowledge of human development which come from such diverse fields as developmental anatomy, developmental physiology, and developmental psychology. Chapter 11, by Robert Malina, relies heavily upon contributions supplied by physical anthropologists, exercise physiologists, and biochemists. Chapter 11 is an excellent example of how information supplied by workers in various disciplines can be unified to describe a particular process.

Chapter 12, by Jack Keogh, emphasizes a cross-disciplinary approach to understanding the development of human movement patterns. In Keogh's view, the complexities of understanding human movement are such that understanding the development of the processes of movement requires the contributions of researchers trained in "exercise, skill, and behavior." From Dr. Keogh's perspective, the importance of specialized training in anatomy, exercise physiology, exercise biochemistry, motor learning, sport psychology, and sport sociology becomes important. The "scientific migration" of which Dr. Keogh writes is the ever-increasing trend of scientists from diverse fields to contribute to the understanding of the development of human movement patterns. The integration of knowledge supplied by diverse disciplines, as well as subareas of particular disciplines, represents a truly cross-disciplinary approach to studying human motor development.

The following chapters present several different aspects of study on human motor development. In Chapter 10, Dr. Rarick presents information on the chronological or maturational development of motor skills. In Chapter 11, Dr. Malina is more concerned with describing physical growth and development. Although these two investigators have addressed different aspects of human development, they share a common approach to to studying the subject; both are concerned with the outcomes of growth and development. This is to say that these investigators have chronicled the course of psychomotor skills and physical development. In Chapter 12, Dr. Keogh presents a very different approach to the study of motor development. In fact, Keogh goes so far as to use a different term: "movement development." As opposed to the classical approach of charting the course of growth and the development of physique and motor skills, Dr. Keogh is concerned with the development of those neural mechanisms which determine motor performance. This approach attempts to ask "how" performance is accomplished, rather than "what" performance is accomplished.

The ontogenic changes in human physique and movement patterns described by Rarick and Malina share a common approach with studies in related fields (e.g., developmental anatomy, physical anthropology). The genesis of the approach taken by Keogh is cognitive psychology, a field in which interest has burgeoned in the last several decades. In the model of motor performance presented by Keogh (Figure 1, Chapter 12), the child is presented as active in relation to the environment.

Evaluation of theories of information processing and the accomplishment of motor tasks, then, depend heavily upon the techniques developed for study in the area of psychomotor performance research usually termed "motor learning."

Chapter 13, the fourth component of this section of the volume, is by Dr. Geoff Broadhead who describes the emergence and current status of work in the field of "adapted physical education." Not only is there a solid research base which supports the proposition that physical activity can benefit the intellectual as well as motor performance of normal and atypical students, but it has also become law that participation in physical education activities not be denied to handicapped individuals. The importance of civil rights statutes (Public Laws 93-112 and 94-142) and the ways in which they are implemented cannot be overemphasized. These laws shall significantly impact physical education programs across the nation. The law mandates that prior to placement in physical education classes, each handicapped student's individualized education program (IEP) must be developed and written down. Immediate as well as long-range goals need to be defined, and assessments of progress need to be made intermittently. Physical education in American schools is about to change rapidly.

An immediate question regarding evaluation of students and their assignment to physical education classes is: "Who is to evaluate students, and by what standards are the students to be evaluated?" It is obvious that the Public Laws demand increased knowledge in the area of motor development by physical education practitioners. If each student is to be evaluated, and an individualized physical education program is to be designed for him or her, then a perceptual-cognitive framework for movement evaluation, as well as a detailed knowledge of the ontological patterns, and variability of change in physique and movement patterns will be required of physical educators. As described by Dr. Broadhead, the possibilities for advancement in adapted physical education mandated by the civil rights laws hold great prospects for advancement in physical education. With any sort of compliance with the law, adapted physical education programs shall rapidly become equal or superior to regular programs. Ultimately, the public laws regarding physical education for the handicapped may, therefore, positively effect physical education as a whole.

The Emergence of the Study of Human Motor Development

10 *G.L. Rarick*

Motor development is a specialized field of inquiry concerned with studying the origins and development of motor behavior in humans. By some it has been defined as the study of the ontogenetic changes in human movement. Investigations in such diverse fields as developmental anatomy, developmental physiology, and developmental psychology have produced much of our early and current knowledge of motor development. These disciplines focused on the development of very young animals and humans as the basis for drawing inferences about the growth of the nervous system and its control over the organisms's developing motor capabilities.

Among the early investigators, Coghill (1929) had perhaps the greatest influence in laying the foundation for the study of motor development with his research on behavioral development of the *Amblystoma* salamander. Shortly after the turn of the century, he began to chart the growth and development of the *Amblystoma's* nervous system and demonstrated, in a series of detailed studies, the close relationship between the growth of the neural mechanisms underlying the animal's initial movements and its subsequent movement sequences. His observations showed that the initial limb movements are an integral part of the animal's total response mechanism, and that independence or individuation of limb action occurs only in later development. Thus, as the limbs appear, their movements become integrated into the whiplike swimming motion of the *Amblystoma,* a movement characteristic of the early development of many higher animals. According to Coghill, such movements follow a cephalocaudal progression; that is, the forelimbs gradually gain autonomy, followed later by movements of the hind limbs. Both movements are essentially a coordinated extension of the time-motion relationship needed in swimming. Coghill concluded that as the *Amblystoma* first begins to walk, its trunk movement is basically a slow swimming motion which becomes less prominent as the walk

assumes the characteristics of land locomotion. Coghill's work provided the impetus for other investigations on the relationship between
the growth of the nervous system and movement in animals, and also
influenced the views on early behavioral development of humans.

It is only in the past 30 to 40 years that investigators in physical
education have begun systematic research on the motor development
of children and adolescents. It is the purpose of this chapter to discuss the development and current knowledge of human motor development, particularly attending to those sources which have contributed
most to our understanding.

Methodological Approaches in Motor Development Investigations

Investigations in human motor development have used primarily two
methodological approaches. One method uses data coming from
samples of children categorized according to age and sex. This approach,
known as the cross-sectional method, has supplied extensive information
on age norms for a wide range of motor activities and has provided performance guidelines for evaluating children's motor proficiency. A second
approach, the longitudinal method, has been used to secure data on the
same children over relatively long periods of time for observing and recording changes in performance characteristics during development.

The longitudinal method is the preferred approach because it enables
the investigator to examine the broad range of differences among children in their rates of physical and behavioral development as well as
their individual responses to varying environmental conditions. This method is not without its problems, however, for substantial family mobility
makes it difficult to maintain complete groups of children over long term
periods. Also, frequent dropouts can distort the characteristics of the
sample and may materially affect the findings. Decisions regarding the
frequency of observations present another problem for those using the
longitudinal methods particularly during the critical periods of rapid
growth: infancy and adolescence. At these stages, the risk of missing the
impact of significant developmental changes becomes great. Fortunately,
most longitudinal studies have recognized this problem and planned accordingly.

Essentially two kinds of measurement procedures have been employed
in motor development research. The most frequently used is performance
data based on scores from motor performance tests, such as measures of
strength, power, balance, flexibility, running, jumping, and throwing.

Such scores are sometime labeled "product data," since the measurements quantify the overall performance with relevant and logical scores. The second type of measurement examines skill execution in detail, typically by using high speed photography as the skill is performed. This approach, when employed in longitudinal investigations, is known as developmental kinesiology.

Genetic and Maturational
Factors in Motor Development

The developmental potential of all life forms is preset by heredity, although the extent to which the potential is realized may be materially affected by environmental forces. As Weiss (1949) has pointed out, the environment is incapable of creating patterns of growth and development for which the organism was not already predisposed. No nutrient or chemical agent is able to force cells or tissues to perform any function other than that originally planned by nature. Consistent with this principle is the fact that each organism in its own growth and development passes through well-defined structural and functional stages characteristic of the species, modifiable only in degree by environmental forces—not in essential detail. Even though there may be substantial individual differences, each organism within a species moves through the same developmental stages in the same sequence and on approximately the same time schedule.

Origin and Early Patterns of Motor Behavior

Behavior originates at the moment of the first neuromuscular response. This phenomenon has been characterized by Gesell (1946) as the "ontogentic zero." Information on the origin and early stages of human motor development has come from observations of fetuses taken from their mothers for medical reasons. The earliest movement responses in the fetus appear during the eighth week of prenatal life. At this time tactile and electrical stimulation bring about diffuse movements which are organized and controlled at the spinal cord level. By the fourteenth week, stimulation of the skin produces reasonably well-organized but generalized responses, such as flexion of both arms, and opening and closing of the mouth with simultaneous retraction of the head (Minkowski, 1922). By the sixteenth week, the fetus has developed diagonal reflexes; that is, stimulation of one foot results in movements of the arm on the opposite side of the body. Such responses are sometimes considered precursors of the "trotting reflex," a basic movement pattern used in crawling and walking. Some authorities believe these early motor responses have the characteristics and basic neuro-controls common to all vertebrates in their early development. However, Carmichael (1946) believed that such a parallel is hazardous and an overgeneralization, that real differences in the development of these behaviors do exist.

At birth, many simple motor responses of the neonate are reasonably well coordinated. For example, holding a newborn infant upright with the feet resting on a supporting surface elicits stepping movements. Momentarily changing the neonate's body position activates postural reflexes; placing the infant in a prone position while applying pressure to the feet will initiate creeping movements. The result of this pressure is alternate movement of the arms combined with vigorous thrusting of one or both feet with simultaneous side to side bending of the body. Likewise, the grasping reflex is firmly established at birth; therefore, a newborn will hold a rod with sufficient strength to support the body weight for several seconds.

All of the above responses are controlled at the subcortical level of the brain and retained until approximately the end of the fourth month; retention for longer periods of time may indicate central nervous system dysfunction. Thus, the motor patterns present at birth, sometimes considered phyletic in character, are organized at the subcortical level and gradually suppressed as the motor area of the cortex assumes dominance.

Among the more dramatic indications that intrinsic factors play a major role in shaping human motor development is the orderly sequence of events in postural and locomotor development. The gradual and well-regulated progression of those primary motor abilities which precede creeping, crawling, standing, and walking are nicely illustrated by Shirley's (1933) observations. The cephalocaudal sequence of motor development is clearly evident in human development: motor control is first established in the region of the head and neck, passes next to the upper trunk and arms, and then to the lower trunk and inferior extremities.

The cephalocaudal sequence lies within the general framework of developmental change proposed by McGraw (1939) in which the first two years of life are divided into four periods, each representing a progressive reduction in subcortical control produced by the increasing dominance of the motor cortex. The first four months of postnatal life are characterized by reduction in rhythmic movements and a gradual loss of the reflex responses present at birth. The second period, that of the fourth through the ninth month, shows a development of voluntary movements in the upper spinal region and a reduction of unilateral movements in the pelvis and lower extremities. The third period, extending through the fourteenth month, is characterized by increased control over the lower body and inferior extremities; the final ten months (fourth period) is typified by development of the association centers of the brain which give rise to symbolic and language expression.

The development of manual coordination and prehension skills also follows well-defined and orderly developmental changes. The first evidence of budding prehension skills can be observed at approximately the twentieth week of postnatal life when the infant reaches out simultaneously with both hands, often without making contact with the object. Between weeks 24 and 34, the infant attempts to "corral" small objects using a palmar grasp in a scooping motion. The infant does not routinely and effectively use the pincer movement (thumb against forefinger) until nearly the end of the first year. Thus, both gross and fine movement patterns follow well-defined developmental sequences during infancy.

Maturational Readiness

While the early years of life reveal orderly sequences in the development of structural and behavioral traits, there are nevertheless well-defined differences among infants in the ages at which these phenomena occur. Such differences are attributed to variations among children in their rates of anatomical, physiological, and neurological maturation.

Maturation is regarded as a function of an organism's intrinsic regulatory mechanisms. These regulatory mechanisms, however, are sensitive to a wide range of environmental forces; therefore, the rate of maturation is influenced by such factors as diet, injury, disease, and use. While structure sets the limits of function, use does in turn have its effect upon structure and thus plays a significant role in affecting maturational status.

The impact of maturational status on the performance and development of motor skills early in life has received considerable attention over the years. One of the most frequently cited studies of the role of maturation and training in the acquisition of motor skills is the classic investigation of McGraw (1935) on the twins, Jimmy and Johnny. Johnny, the less mature of the twins, was given special training in a variety of motor activities from 21 days old until he was 20 months old, whereas no special training was given to Jimmy at this time. In comparing the performance capabilities of the twins at the conclusion of the experiment, it was determined that special exercise in no way altered the early age of extinction of the subcortical responses nor materially accelerated the developmental trends of such phylogenetic activities as crawling and walking. However, with activities of a more specialized character, marked changes were brought about through training. For example, the trained twin roller skated shortly after he was able to walk, and by fourteen months, he was highly proficient at skating. While roller skating is a complicated skill, it required locomotor movement patterns with which the child was already familiar. In a similar manner, the trained twin rapidly developed skill in climbing incline boards, beginning while in the creeping stage. It should be noted that in both roller skating and climbing, the child was using basic movement patterns upon which he easily added the more advanced elements involved in the new activities. The possibility that early training might affect aspects of motor development not directly included in the training program was also investigated. While the sequences leading up to walking occurred at approximately the same time for the two infants, the trained twin appeared to move more gracefully and maintained better carriage during the early stages of walking. These differences in movement were still noticeable at six years of age.

Studies on both animals and humans have presented evidence which shows that critical periods are reached in the development of the organism when physical and behavioral characteristics are most susceptible to modification. As living beings mature, the accompanying growth changes produce a higher degree of organization of bodily functions, thus equipping them to cope more effectively with increasingly complex environmental situations. Recognition of these findings has focused attention on the concept of maturational readiness and its impact on educational programs. The evidence clearly indicates that maturation and learning are inseparable during the developmental period, although the relative influence of maturation may be greater in the acquisition of certain skills whereas learning may predominate in others.

The futility of forcing children to acquire motor skills at an early age was the focus of many early studies. For example, Gesell and Thompson (1929) trained one of a pair of identical twins in block handling and climbing activities over a period of six weeks beginning at 46 weeks of age. At the end of the six week period, conditions were made as similar as possible for both twins. The control twin during the first three weeks made greater progress than had been made by the experimental child during the preceeding six weeks of special training. Similarly, Hicks (1931), in his study of 2½ to 6½ year old children, found that the children given experimental practice in hitting a moving target gained no more in this skill than a matched group given general practice involving elements of this skill.

Dennis (1940) showed that acquisition of certain skills is not materially delayed by deprivation of opportunity prior to the age the skill would normally develop. He demonstrated that the cradle-binding practice used by the Hopi and Navajo Indians which restricted physical activity for the first 6 to 12 months of life (except for approximately 1 hour each day) had little, if any effect on walking age.

Maturational Factors and the Development of Basic Motor Skills

Numerous investigations have proven the importance of maturation in the acquisition of motor skills well beyond the period of infancy. For example, the evolution of the behavioral changes seen in the development of the standing long jump is nicely illustrated by the work of Hellebrandt, Rarick, Glassow and Carns (1961) (see Figure 1). The investigators believed that jumping per se is a phylogenetic skill: its primary set is present at birth and awaits central nervous system maturation to unfold the total pattern response. As the skill becomes established, the sequence and timing of muscle action also becomes essentially involuntary. Thus, the investigators proposed that this skill does not develop by the synthesis of movement fragments, but rather by the expanding pattern of central nervous system integration which results from the growth and development of the controlling mechanisms.

Over 40 years ago, Wilde (1938) described the sequential stages in the development of a mature overarm throwing pattern. Using cinematography, she reported that the earliest and least mature pattern of this skill appears at two to three years of age and it is characterized by arm and trunk movements in the anteroposterior plane with no foot displacement. In the second stage (ages 3½ to 5 years), there is an introduction of arm and body movement in the horizontal plane without transfer of weight and without the forward step. Stage three (5 to 6 years) introduces a forward step during execution of the throw, but the step is ipsilateral with respect to the throwing arm; therefore, there is little trunk rotation or transfer of body weight. The throw at this stage has both anteroposterior and horizontal features, but it lacks power because of limited rotation of the trunk and little adduction of the throwing arm. The fourth and mature stage appears at approximately 6½ years of age in boys. This stage is characterized by well-established opposition of limb movement with transfer of weight as well as trunk rotation, horizontal arm adduction, and elbow extension. These clearly defined age-related sequences strongly suggest that the development of the overarm throw is controlled by maturational processes and is not solely a function

Figure 1. Transition from an infantile to a relatively mature pattern of performance of the standing long jump (age 37-43 months).

Row 1. John performing the standing long jump at 37 months of age.

Row. 2. Full-blown "winging" at 41 months. The poise is that of a bird soaring in flight.

Rows 3 and 4. Transition from infantile to a more mature arm positioning during a jump from a two-footed takeoff by John at 43 months of age. The first attempt to bring the arms forward during the propulsive phase of the jump was disastrous (Row 3); the second was successful (Row 4).

(From Hellebrandt, Rarick, Glassow and Carns, 1961. Reprinted by permission of American Journal of Physical Medicine).

of practice. These findings are supported by Dusenberry's (1952) research which found that specific short-term throwing practice accomplished little prior to five years of age, but achieved a great deal during the fifth and sixth years with the same amount of practice.

Running, generally considered a natural activity, is not established into an adult pattern until the fifth or sixth year. Prior to this age, there

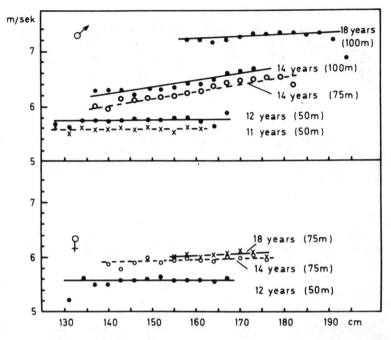

Figure 2. Maximal running speed in relation to body height for girls and boys of different ages; almost 100,000 subjects are included in the statistics. (From Asmussen, 1957. Reprinted by permission of Tidskrift Legemsovelser.)

is a gradual but well-defined increase in length and frequency of the stride which coincides with the child's leg strength and balance capabilities. With advancing age, the relative rise of the center of gravity during the run lessens with each stride, the pelvic rotation increases as the propulsive force in leg extension becomes greater and the arm action becomes stronger and more uniform.

While there is generally a linear trend for age-related running speed in both sexes from six years of age to puberty, there is also evidence that subtle maturational processes are at work. For example, Asmussen and Heebøll- Nielsen (1955) showed that performance of physical activities primarily dependent on elements of strength and power is more highly related to chronological age than to indices of body size. When data on running speed were plotted against chronological age and stature, age played a much greater role in accounting for performance differences than did height (see Figure 2). As will be noted, age per se added much more to running velocity for boys and girls than did height, with the exception of the 14-year-old boys affected by the adolescent growth spurt. The investigators concluded that age causes a maturation of neuro-mechanisms, and perhaps qualitative changes in muscle tissue, each of which enables individuals to coordinate and utilize their neuromuscular mechanisms with increasing skill and power.

Differential Effects of Age, Sex, and Maturity

Chronological age has been and continues to be the most widespread measure of children's maturational state. It provides a standard time referent within which developmental changes can be evaluated. The rationale for using chronological age to measure maturity is that age produces well-defined developmental changes, providing a convenient means of grouping children of similar physical and mental abilities. However, it is widely recognized that chronological age is far from a satisfactory method of determining maturational levels. Chronological age, in fact, is only a measure of how long an individual has lived. As such, it is a highly confounded measure because age carries with it the effects of innate and environmental influences which may vary widely among individuals. While chronological age is still widely used for classification purposes, problems with its use during periods of rapid developmental change, as in adolescence, are well known and will be discussed in the following sections.

Numerous investigations have shown that muscular strength and proficiency in gross motor skills improve with advancing chronological age during the school years. For example, performance of the basic skills of running, jumping, and throwing increase linearly with age in middle childhood (ages 5 to 11 years); boys on the average show superior performance to girls at all age levels. With the onset of puberty, girls' performance at approximately 12 to 13 years of age levels off, whereas that of boys continues to increase up to and beyond 17 years of age. Other measures of gross motor performance show similar age and sex trends. Only in the case of balance-type tasks and measures of fine motor control do girls on the average show equal or superior performance to boys.

Similar, but perhaps more dramatic evidence of the role of chronological age and sex on developmental changes may be seen when body weight and muscular strength of the sexes are plotted against chronological age. There is a strikingly close parallel of growth in weight and strength of boys ranging from 9 to 19 years old, whereas in girls, growth in strength ceases on the average at approximately age 13 and increases in weight

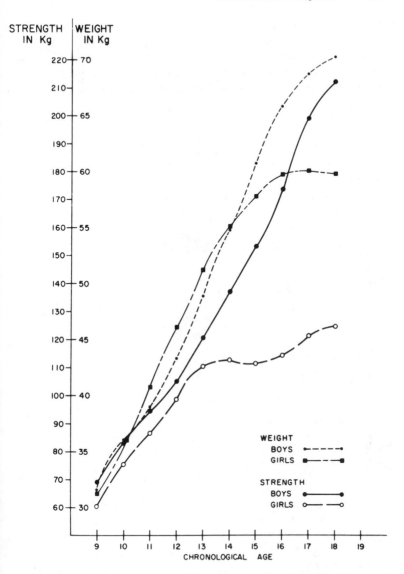

Figure 3. Annual growth in weight and muscular strength of boys and girls, ages 9-18 years.

level off at about 16 years of age (see Figure 3). As is the case in motor performance, the onset of sexual maturity in females does not have a positive influence on strength development. It is well known that the onset of pu-

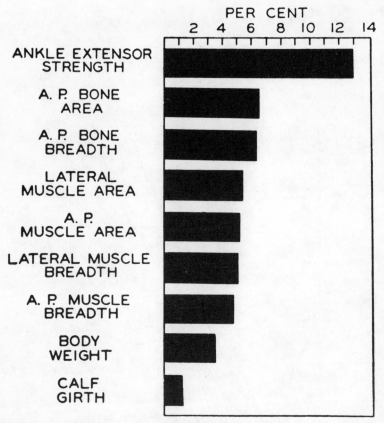

Figure 4. Percentage superiority of 7-year-old males to 7-year-old females in ankle extension strength and in measures of muscle and bone tissue, body weight, and calf girth. (From Rarick and Thompson, 1956. Reprinted by permission of the American Association for Health, Physical Education, Recreation and Dance.)

berty in boys carries with it an increase in testosterone production with an accompanying increase in muscle mass. However, adolescence in the female brings about little if any increased production of androgens, and therefore, no increase in muscularity.

Reasons for the long recognized differences in strength and motor performance of the sexes in adolescence are primarily biological, although cultural factors certainly cannot be ignored. It is well known that males from childhood through adolescence are heavier boned and more muscular than females, whereas females have relatively more adipose tissue (Reynolds, 1944; Stuart & Dwinell, 1942). These differences become exaggerated in adolescence, although there are rather clearly defined metabolic and functional differences in the childhood years. For example, Garn and Clark (1953) showed that when the sexes were equated on the basis of muscle mass, the basal metabolic rate in boys was greater than that in girls, indicating a higher concentration of active tissues in males. Research of Rarick and Thompson (1956) offers further support for these findings. They demonstrated that, as early as age seven, boys have more strength than girls when proper allowances are made for differences in muscle mass (see Figure 4). It may be that the differences at this age level reflect, in part, the impact of cultural influences on the role models for the sexes; that is, strength and power are more highly valued and more sought after by males than females even at this early age.

It is in adolescence that maturational and sex factors become most evident. These factors are brought into clear focus by findings from Jones' (1949) research in which strength data were obtained semi-annually on the same group of boys and girls from 11 through 17 years of age. When the strength data (right grip) of early and late maturing boys and girls were plotted against chronological age, the impact of maturational status on strength development was clearly evident. Maturational status in the boys was evaluated in terms of skeletal age (development of the bones of the hand, wrist, and knee), and in girls as menarcheal age. In the boys, the difference in means between the early and late maturers was greatest at age 15, being more than two standard deviations (see Figure 5). It is interesting that the age of maximum strength difference in males was coincident with age differences in the creatine-creatinine ratio, an index which is frequently used as a chemical "puberty indicator" in males. In the girls, the strength differences between early and late maturers was less dramatic than in the boys, yet the role of menarche as the precipitating agent was clearly evident. Also, it should be pointed out that when I used body weight data on this sample of boys and girls and plotted age-weight curves of the early and late maturers, differences in the weight between the two groups were of approximately the same magnitude as the differences in strength recorded by Jones. Thus, the strength difference Jones obtained seems to be largely a reflection of differences in body size; this finding is not surprising, for it has long been recognized that size and strength are related, and that early maturity is accompanied by accelerated physical growth. However, as Jones' data indicate there is at least a 6-month lag before the early maturing male's strength is commensurate with his body size.

As indicated above, the onset of puberty carries with it a surge in

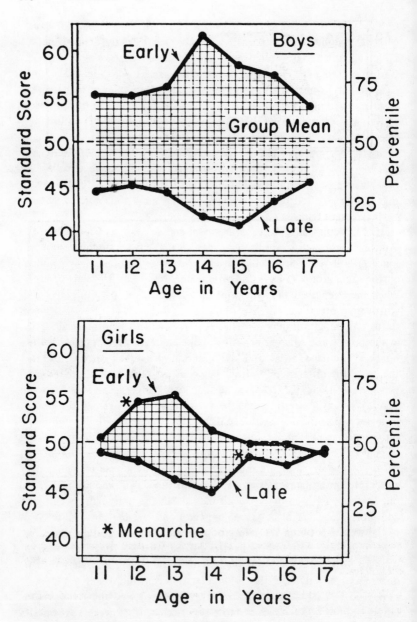

Figure 5. Growth curve scores (right grip) for early and late maturing boys and girls expressed in standard scores (*M*=50, *SD*=10). (From Jones, 1949. Reprinted by permission of the University of California Press.)

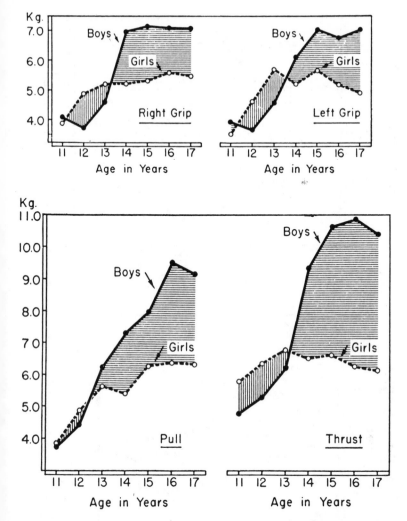

Figure 6. Age-based variability of grip and shoulder girdle strength of adolescent males and females as reflected by standard deviations of grip strength, and standard deviations of pulling and thrusting isometric muscular force.

both body size and strength, but the age at which puberty occurs varies widely in both sexes. Thus, in early adolescence, there is great variability in muscular strength. Age differences in the occurrence of the adolescent growth spurt, with the accompanying differences in strength, mean that the variability in body size and strength becomes greatly exaggerated in

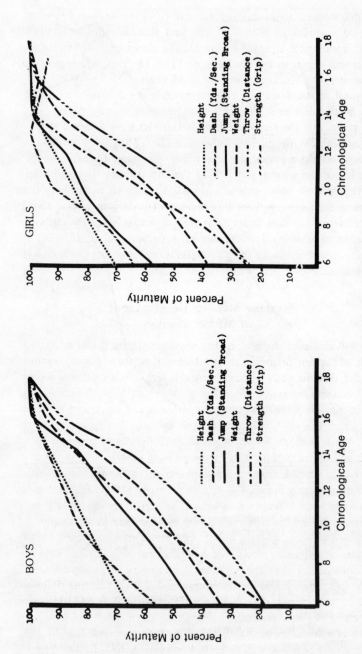

Figure 7. Percent of mature status (18 years of age) in measures of physical growth, strength, and motor performance of children 6-18 years.

early adolescence. Jones (1949) effectively demonstrated this when he plotted standard deviations of grip and shoulder muscle strength against chronological age (see Figure 6). The increases in variability of girls' strength occurs in the age range of 11 to 13 years, and that of boys approximately 2 years later, from 13 to 15 years.

A procedure occasionally used in comparing the development of different growth variables is plotting by chronological age the percent of mature status that the respective growth variables have achieved at a given age using data from cross-sectional studies. Thus, as shown in Figure 7, boys on the average have achieved by six years of age 67% of the stature, 1/3 of the weight, and 19% of the grip strength they will have at age 18. On most traits, girls at a given age are closer to maturity than are boys, and on some performance measures (running speed and strength) their achievement at ages under 18 is greater than at maturity. Although this method of assessing development has little practical significance, it does bring into sharp focus the role maturational rate plays in the physical growth and motor performance of the sexes.

Physique and the Development of Motor Abilities

Few will challenge the notion that physique affects the muscular strength and motor performance of athletes. It is, for example, common knowledge that the body build of weight lifters differs markedly from that of distance runners, and that the physiques of football linemen and basketball players show little similarity. What is not so evident is the extent to which this relationship varies with age, sex, and type of physical activity. What, then, do we know about the influence of physique on strength and motor performance in the growing years?

There is some evidence that physique-associated factors may affect motor behavior early in life. For example, Shirley (1933) reported that muscular and small-boned infants walk at an earlier age than heavy infants. Similarly, large muscle mass in the leg is associated with early standing and walking, whereas infants with small muscles acquire these capacities later (Garn, 1963). Although there is only limited data on the influence of physique on motor development of young children, evidence indicates a higher energy output and a more vigorous childhood in children with sturdy body build contrasted with obese and extremely slender children (Walker, 1962).

In the childhood years, the relationship of physique to strength and motor proficiency is not well defined. Considering that ultimate body

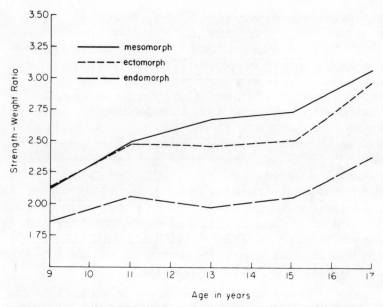

Figure 8. Longitudinal strength-weight ratios of adolescent males grouped by physique categories (strength scores: sum of right and left grip, pull, and thrust). (From Rarick, 1973. Reprinted by permission of Academic Press.)

size and rate of physical growth are regulated by genetic factors, and that physique is important in accounting for individual strength differences, there is reason to believe that body build and strength have more than a chance relationship during the growing years. In children of linear frame (late maturers), there is a preponderance of endochondral bone formation resulting in accentuation of the linear component of growth and the formation of long slender bones. In children of mesomorphic build (early maturers), bone formation is predominantly appositional, resulting in heavier and shorter bones, and relatively more muscle mass. The evidence reveals that when strength-weight ratios of males with mesomorphic, ectomorphic, and endomorphic body builds are plotted against chronological age (see Figure 8), the mesomorphic individual is, in later childhood and in adolescence, stronger per unit of weight than the ectomorph and endomorph. Notice that although the differences are negligible in the age level of 9 to 11 years when comparing the mesomorphic and ectomorphic groups; thereafter the superiority of the mesomorph is clearly evident. Jones (1949) demonstrated the importance of physique to strength when he found that 75 percent of the variance in strength of adolescent

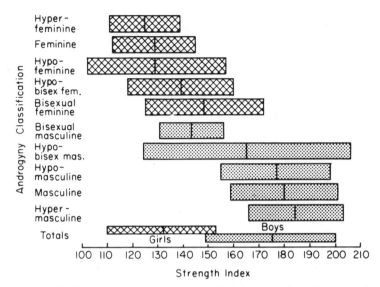

Figure 9. Strength index scores according to somatic androgeny classification (strength scores: sum of right and left grip, pull, and thrust). (From Bayley, 1951. Reprinted by permission, *Child Development*, 1951.)

males was attributable to the proper weighting of five factors: height, weight, mesomorphy, endomorphy, and ectomorphy.

Bayley's (1951) research shows that body build is important in accounting for individual differences in strength within and between the sexes. She collected static muscular strength data on adolescent boys and girls grouped into somatic androgeny classifications—a scale based on masculinity and femininity morphological characteristics. As noted in Figure 9, mean strength per pound of body weight for the boys was substantially greater than that for girls and similarly greater in all androgeny classifications with the exception of the bisexual feminine and bisexual masculine categories. Also, as one moves from the hyperfeminine category to the hypermasculine category, strength per pound of body weight becomes progressively greater. Such data strongly suggest that body build as reflected by somatic androgeny scores is an important factor in accounting for individual strength differences both within and between the sexes.

Ethnic and Cultural Factors
in Motor Development

Investigations of the influence of ethnic origin and background on the motor development of children in this country have, for the most part, compared motor performance data of blacks and whites. These studies used samples of children within well-defined age categories including infants, children, and adolescents and employed a wide range of motor tasks for the data source. Most studies agree that in infancy, black children are slightly advanced over white children in the accomplishment of common motor tasks (Bayley, 1965; Knobloch & Pasamanick, 1953; Williams & Scott, 1953). The superiority of black children in the first two or three years of life, however, becomes less evident in the latter part of early childhood. It has been proposed by Bayley (1965) that black infants may, by nature, be motorically more precocious than whites, although there is no concrete evidence in support of this. Black infants are, however, slightly advanced in such physical maturity indicators as age of dentition and appearance of the bony ossification centers. Whether the performance differences noted at this early age can be attributed to biological factors or to differences in child rearing practices must await further study.

Reports of the comparative motor performance of school-age black and white children generally show an overall superiority of black boys and girls. Again, the reason for this trend is not apparent from the data. In activities like running and jumping, where body weight must be propelled, Malina's (1968) findings suggest that such differences may be attributable to the lesser quantity of adipose tissue in black boys and girls. Malina reported that the skinfold thickness (log transformation) at all ages from 6 to 13 years, was, on the average, greater in whites of both sexes than in blacks. Cultural factors play a significant role in motor performance levels of children as was shown by the results of the AAHPER Physical Fitness Test. The test was given to American and British children and adolescents, and the average performance of the British males exceeded that of American males on all test items except for distance throwing, an activity seldom used in British sports (Campbell & Pohndorf, 1961).

Stability and Change in Motor Abilities

One of the most intriguing questions in our field and one that can be answered only from longitudinal data is the predictability of the motor proficiency levels in children over relatively long periods of time. Many studies have been made on the prediction of such physical attributes as height and weight, and although the prediction of stature over time can be done with reasonable accuracy, the same is not true

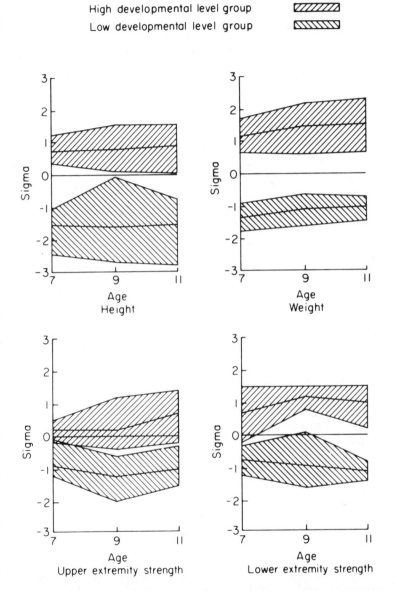

Figure 10. Mean and range of standard scores measuring strength and physical growth of physically mature and immature boys plotted over a period of 5 years. (From Rarick, 1973. Reprinted by permission of Academic Press.)

for the prediction of body weight. Weight is susceptible to many environmental influences and tends to fluctuate over time, whereas growth in height is strictly additive (one does not have periods of height loss during the growing years) and controlled to a considerable extent by genetic factors.

Motor proficiency, as it true of most behavioral phenomena, is influenced by use as well as by variations in maturational rates, and thus is not highly predictable over long periods of time. Strength, on the other hand, being more closely associated with body structure, tends to be more predictable than tasks depending largely on neuromuscular coordination. Data taken from the Wisconsin Growth Study (Rarick, 1973) illustrate the long term relationship between measures of strength and body size where composite measures of upper body strength and lower body strength of children with contrasting developmental levels are plotted against age (see Figure 10). Where extremes of maturity levels were used to predict growth of a variable such as strength, the prediction was reasonably good—particularly during childhood when the growth tempo is reasonably constant. However, in the same study, when longitudinal motor performance data were obtained for predictive purposes on such fundamental skills as running, jumping, and throwing, predictions were relatively poor. For example, between-year correlations, ages 7 to 17 years for males on jumping, running, and throwing performance were .60, .18, and .29 respectively, and for females of the same age, the correlations were .50, .56, and .13 (Rarick & Smoll, 1967). With between-age correlations of this magnitude, it is evident that the chances for relatively good performers at age 7 to be among the best at 17 is not very likely. On the other hand, the one or two exceptional performers may retain relatively high positions over several years. Making predictions relative to physical growth or motor performance is most hazardous during early adolescence, for at this time, the age at which the growth spurt occurs varies widely among children.

Intellectual Factors

It is widely recognized that there is a low correlation between motor performance test scores and measures of intelligence for normal children and adolescents. In other words, normal intelligence, IQ range of 90 to 130, as measured by standard intelligence tests, is of little value in differentiating between skilled and unskilled performers. However, the motor performance capabilities of the mentally retarded are decidedly substand-

Table 1

**Magnitude of the Differences between Normal and
EMR Children (Ages 6-9 Years) in Components of Motor
Performance Expressed in Standard Deviation Units**

Component	Females	Males
Muscular strength and power	-2.10	-1.18
Gross limb-eye coordination	-1.31	- .64
Fine visual motor coordination	-1.94	-1.13
Balance	-1.90	- .91
Leg power and coordination	-1.89	- .95
Average of the five motor performance components (standard deviation units)	-1.83	- .96

ard, and the greater the retardation, the poorer the motor performance.

The lag in motor development of the mentally retarded is noted early in life when such motor functions as sitting, creeping, crawling, standing, and walking are considerably delayed. Among school-age children, those who are moderately retarded (IQ's 50-70), are on the average two to four years behind intellectually normal children in motor skill development; with advancing age the difference becomes greater. The magnitude of the motor deficiency across the broad spectrum of motor abilities is evident when motor test scores of the retarded are expressed in standard deviation units using data on intellectually normal children of the same age for comparative purposes (unpublished observation). Thus, the average of the standard deviation units of some 39 motor performance tests grouped according to five components of motor performance placed the retarded girls 1.83 standard deviation units below the mean of intellectually normal girls (see Table 1). The same procedure placed the retarded boys .96 standard deviation units below those of normal intelligence. Thus, the average performance of the retarded girls would be expected to be exceeded by 95% of normal girls, and the mean performance of the retarded boys by 87% of normal boys.

One reason for the lower test scores is that retarded males and females on the average have substantially more body fat than their intellectually normal counterparts, a factor that adversely affects their gross motor performance. The excess body fat of the retarded would seem to be primarily due to lack of physical activity since no well-defined metabolic deficiencies have been identified in populations of mentally retarded children.

The poor motor performance of the retarded, while in part related to inadequate motor opportunities, is primarily a function of their limited learning capability. Research findings to date indicate that with the mildly retarded, problems of motor learning are largely those of comprehending and attending to the specific requirements of the task, rather than to execution once the task requirements are clearly understood. With proper instructional help and with practice under nonstressful conditions, the motor performance level of many mildly retarded boys and girls can approximate that of intellectually normal children of the same age level.

Conclusion

Many advances have been made in our knowledge of human motor development, yet many important questions remain unanswered. For example, little is known about the influence of maturation on motor skill development beyond infancy and childhood. We speak of the importance of maturational readiness in skill learning, yet we know very little about the physiological or psychological factors affecting the development of motor abilities in school-age children. Research is needed to clarify the nature of the maturational process itself and its effect upon skill acquisition in the growing years. For example, are there identifiable maturational factors of readiness that underlie the basic controls for motor learning which are themselves influenced by motor activities? If so, what are they and how are they affected by early motor experiences?

Little is now known about children's information processing mechanisms and how these change with age. Nor is much known about the ways in which children use sensory cues in learning gross motor skills. Future research will focus on developmental changes in the foregoing as well as the strategies children use in solving motor problems.

The following are a few additional questions which undoubtedly will be seriously researched in the near future:

1. What role does heredity play in the development of motor skills in childhood and adolescence? Are certain classes of motor abilities especially dominated by genetic factors?

2. Are sex differences in the motor skills of children less prominent today than formerly? Are such differences largely a function of biological or cultural forces?

3. What are the long-range physical and psychological effects of organized competitive sports programs on the growth and development of children and adolescents? To what extent have such effects been

minimized by sports-enthusiastic adults and exaggerated by those opposed to these programs?

4. What are the effects of instructional physical education programs as now conducted in the schools upon the health, physical fitness, and motor skill development of children?

5. Why do most children become less physically active as they grow older?

These and many other questions need to be researched if we are serious about advancing our understanding of the motor development of children.

References

Asmussen, E. & Heebøll-Nielson, K.A. Dimensional analysis of physical performance and growth in boys. *Journal of Applied Physiology,* 1955, **6**, 585-592.

Bayley, N. Some psychological correlates of somatic androgeny. *Child Development,* 1951, **22**, 47-60.

Bayley, N. Comparisons of mental and motor test scores for ages 1-15 months by sex, birth order, race, geographical location, and education of parents. *Child Development,* 1965, **36**, 379-411.

Campbell, W.R. & Pohndorf, R.H. Physical fitness of British and United States children. In L.A. Larson (Ed.), *Health and fitness in the modern world*. Chicago: The Athletic Institute, 1961.

Carmichael, L. The onset and early development of behavior. In L. Carmichael (Ed.), *Manual of child psychology*. New York: Wiley, 1946.

Coghill, G.E. *Anatomy and the problem of behavior.* New York: Cambridge University Press, 1929.

Dennis, W. Does culture appreciably affect patterns of infant behavior? *Journal of Social Psychology,* 1940, **12**, 305-317.

Dusenberry, L. A study of the effects of training in ball throwing by children ages three to seven. *Research Quarterly,* 1952, **23**, 9-14.

Garn, S. Human biology and research in body composition II. Body Composition. *Annals of the New York Academy of Science,* 1963, **110**, 429-446.

Garn, S. & Clark, L.C. Sex differences in metabolic rate. *Child Development,* 1953, **24**, 215-224.

Gesell, A. The ontogenesis of infant behavior. In L. Carmichael (Ed.), *Manual of child psychology*. New York: Wiley, 1946.

Gesell, A. & Thompson, H. Learning and growth in identical twins. *Genetic Psychology Monographs,* 1929, **6**, 1-124.

Hellebrandt, F.A., Rarick, G.L., Glassow, R., & Carns, M.L. Physiological analysis of basic motor skills. *American Journal of Physical Medicine* 1961, **40**, 14-25.

Hicks, J.A. The acquisition of motor skills in young children I. A study of the effects of practice in throwing at a moving target. *Child Development,* 1931, **2**, 156-158.

Jones, H. *Motor performance and growth.* Berkeley: University of California Press, 1949.

Knobloch, H. & Pasamanick, B. Further observations on the behavioral development of Negro children. *Journal of Genetic Psychology,* 1953, **83**, 137-157.

Malina, R.M. *Growth, maturation, and performance of Philadelphia Negro and white elementary school children.* Unpublished doctoral dissertation, University of Pennsylvania, 1968.

McGraw, M.B. *Growth: A study of Johnny and Jimmy.* New York: Appleton-Century, 1935.

McGraw, M.B. Behavior of the newborn infant and early neuro-muscular development. *Research Publications, Association for Research in Nervous and Mental Disease,* 1939, **19**, 244-246.

Minkowski, M. Ueber fruhzeitige bewegungen. Reflexe und musckulare reaktionen beim menschlichen fotue und ihre beziehungen zum fotalen neven und muskelsystem. *Schweizerische Medizinische Woschenscheift,* 1922, **52**, 721-724; 751-755.

Rarick, G.L. Stability and change in motor abilities. In G.L. Rarick (Ed.), *Physical activity: Human growth and development.* New York: Academic Press, 1973.

Rarick, G.L. & Smoll, F.L. Stability of growth in strength and motor performance from childhood to adolescence. *Human Biology,* 1967, **39**, 295-306.

Rarick, G.L. & Thompson, J.J. Roentgenographic measures of leg muscle size and ankle extensor strength of 7 year old children. *Research Quarterly,* 1956, **27**, 321-332.

Reynolds, E.L. Differential tissue growth in the leg during childhood. *Child Development,* 1944, **15**, 181-205.

Shirley, M.M. *The first two years. A study of twenty-five babies. Postural and locomotor development* (Vol. 1). Minneapolis: University of Minnesota Press, 1933.

Stuart, H.C. & Dwinell, P.H. The growth of bone, muscle, and overlying tissue in children 6 to 10 years of age as revealed by studies of roentgenograms of the leg area. *Child Development,* 1942, **13**, 195-213.

Walker, R.N. Body build and behavior in young children I. Body build and nursery school teachers' ratings. *Monographs of the Society for*

Research in Child Development, 1962, **27**(3), 1-92.

Weiss, P.   Differential growth. In A.K. Parpat (Ed.), *The chemistry and physiology of growth.* Princeton: Princeton University Press, 1949.

Wilde, M.R. The behavior pattern of throwing and some observations concerning its course of development in children. *Research Quarterly,* 1938, **9**,   20-24.

Williams, J.R. & Scott, R.B. Growth and development of Negro infants IV. Motor development and its relationship to child rearing practices in two groups of Negro infants. *Child Development,* 1953, **24**, 103-121.

Growth, Maturation, and Human Performance

11 *R.M. Malina*

The processes of growth and maturation are two of the dominant activities during the first 20 years of life. Other activities in this period include, for example, neuromuscular maturation and motor development, cognitive development, the development of social competence, and so on. Prenatal growth and maturation are important as are changes into and during adulthood. The focus of this presentation, however, is growth and maturation during childhood and adolescence.

Growth and maturation are biological processes. We do not, however, ordinarily study the processes per se. Rather, we observe or measure the outcomes of the underlying processes (e.g., size attained or level of skeletal maturation). Since growth and maturation have a time framework, and outcomes are measured over time, the study of growth and maturation focuses on change, that is, changes in number, kind and position of cells, changes in size, shape, and composition. The study of change in turn implies velocity or the rate at which size is attained.

The study of growth during childhood and adolescence has generally concerned age changes and sex differences in size, body proportions, physique, and body composition. The study of biological maturation has been somewhat variable, focusing largely on skeletal and sexual maturation and the attainment of adult stature. Needless to say, other indicators or outcomes of growth and maturation have been used, such as dental maturation, or growth of specific tissues, organs and systems.

The study of growth and maturation during childhood and adolescence has also included physical performance to some extent. Physical performance is a general concept comprised of three interrelated components: motor or movement skills, organic or physical fitness (the processes of energy production and work output), and muscular strength. Other components like flexibility can perhaps be added, but the three suggested components of physical performance are often used in studies of children and youth. Physical activities are the substrate of physical performance, and regular physical activity is often considered essential to normal growth and maturation.

Overview of Postnatal Growth,
Maturation, and Performance

The pattern of postnatal growth has been described in considerable detail. Observations are largely based on cross-sectional data, and in many cases, longitudinal data treated in a cross-sectional manner. Observations of height and weight are most abundant and cover the postnatal period from birth to adulthood. Hence, most generalizations on postnatal growth are based on height and weight. Data for proportions and body composition are less complete, but provide a reasonable indication of changes in these parameters of growth during the postnatal period (Falkner & Tanner, 1978a, 1978b, 1979; Malina, 1969a. 1975a; Tanner, 1962, 1978).

Maturation implies progress towards maturity, which of course varies with each criterion. Skeletal and sexual maturation have been used most often. The former spans the entire growth period, while the latter is limited to adolescence. Estimates of skeletal maturation can be made from several available methods using either the hand-wrist (Greulich & Pyle, 1959; Tanner, Whitehouse, Marshall, Healy, & Goldstein; 1975), or the knee (Roche, Wainer, & Thissen, 1975). The knee is more suitable for children under 6 years of age, while the hand-wrist area by itself or in combination with the knee can be used at later ages (Roche, 1980).

Sexual maturation is more difficult to assess. Presently available criteria include the age of menarche and breast development in females, genital development in males, and pubic hair development in both sexes (Malina, 1978; Marshall & Tanner, 1969, 1970; Tanner, 1962). Secondary sex characteristics are, however, outward signs of neuroendocrine changes which have been in progress for some time prior to the appearance of menarch or stages of breast, genital, and pubic hair development. Note, however, that the development of the breasts, genitals, and pubic hair is a continuous process, and thus, the stages are somewhat arbitrary. Ages of sexual maturation levels in a number of populations are summarized elsewhere (Eveleth, 1976; Malina, 1978).

The pattern of development in physical performance is largely based on cross-sectional data, although several longitudinal studies are available (Carron & Bailey, 1974; Clarke, 1971; Espenschade, 1940; Jones, 1949; Rarick & Smoll; 1967). Motor performance is ordinarily viewed in terms of the development of basic or fundamental movement patterns and skills, and then in terms of the skill performance outcomes. Organic fitness is considered in terms of aerobic capacity, while muscular strength is ordinarily viewed in the context of static measures.

Growth, maturation, and performance are interrelated, and the pattern of interrelationships has received considerable attention (Malina, 1975, 1980b). Most of the early efforts evaluating the relationships utilized simple correlational procedures. The use of newer analytic methods, especially multivariate models, has added to the understanding of the interrelationships.

The measurement of shape, and more specifically shape change during growth, needs further refinement. The biochemical framework based upon indirect estimates of body composition, is derived from a small number of adult cadavers; this framework needs further evaluation on its applicability to children and youth. There is also a need for new, noninvasive methods of studying children and youth. Advances in technology, for example, serum analyses of hormonal levels, biopsy techniques, and so on, have moved far ahead and are perhaps closer to the processes of growth, maturation, and performance than ever. However, they are in most instances not readily applicable to large-scale studies outside the clinical and/or laboratory context.

Factors Influencing
Growth and Maturation

A variety of factors underlie the expression of growth and maturation in an individual. In addition to the more obvious regulating factors of a genetic, endocrine, and nutritional nature, there are other actual or potential growth influencing factors, the operation and function of which are not completely understood. These include infectious and parasitic diseases, climate, physical activity, season of the year, and various factors related to the sociocultural milieu, for example, socioeconomic status, psychosocial stress, family size.

The integrated nature of growth and maturational processes is maintained by the interaction of genes, hormones, nutrients, and the individual's environment. This complex interaction regulates an individual's growth, maturation, and in general, its physical and physiological metamorphosis. An individual's genotype can be representative of potential for growth and maturity. Whether a child attains or is delayed in reaching this potential depends on the environment in which he or she is reared. In a growth study, the child comes to us in phenotypic form, (i.e., a product of his or her genotype and environments). The partitioning of genotypic and environmental sources of variation in growth and maturation is obviously important to the understanding of these processes and their outcomes.

Endocrine secretions are basically regulatory and have an important function in growth and maturation. Some growth, however, will occur in the absence of growth-promoting hormones, emphasizing the organism's inherent tendency to grow. The hormones are essential for the full expression of the intrinsic, genetically determined growth and maturation patterns of tissues and systems, and ultimately, of the individual. The nervous system in turn is intimately involved in regulating endocrine secretions. Since the nervous system also mediates our interactions with the external environments, there are many sources for potential variation.

Interacting with an individual's genotype and endocrine secretions is the nutritional state. The many nutrient requirements can be viewed as necessary for growth, maintenance, and repair. The nutritional requirements for physical activity, like calories especially, are additional. Although much attention is given to the nutrient requirements for growth and maturation, little is actually known of the nutrient and energy costs. What we have today are at best estimates (Bergmann & Bergmann, 1979).

Factors Influencing Physical Performance

Physical performance is in part related to age, size, physique, body composition, and maturity status. Evidence suggests that excess body weight and fat have negative effects, especially on performance of tasks involving movement of the entire body; however, body size has positive effects on muscular strength. Correlations of body weight, mesomorphy, and lean body mass with strength are not appreciably different. The magnitude of relationships of size, physique, composition, and maturity status with physical performance, however, is generally low and at best moderate. As such, they are limited in predictive utility. Further, the effects of these growth and maturity parameters on performance are more apparent at the extremes of the physique composition, and maturity continuum (Malina, 1975b; Malina & Rarick, 1973).

The complex interrelationships among growth, maturation, and performance suggest a significant role for other factors in determining performance levels. These include, for example, sex, ethnicity, rearing practices, birth order, social class, nutritional status, training, and practice to mention several (Malina, 1973, 1974, 1980a). Genetic factors in performance are undoubtedly important, but require further elucidation

(Bouchard, 1978; Malina, 1980a).

There are other factors affecting growth, maturation, and performance, either directly or indirectly, which are more difficult to quantify. One of these—physical activity—merits consideration, as it is generally suggested that regular activity has a beneficial influence on the developing organism.

Physical activity has no apparent effects on stature, although prolonged unilateral activity may influence specific bone lengths. Prolonged training favorably influences body weight regulation, the ratio of leanness to fatness, skeletal mineralization, muscle size and metabolism, and cardiorespiratory function. The changes associated with physical activity are a function of the intensity and duration of training, and some changes are specific to the type of training. The persistence of some observed changes is apparently dependent upon continued regular physical activity. Regular activity during childhood and adolescence may be significant in determining the quantity of bone mineral, fat and muscle tissues, and aerobic function in adulthood. More active individuals generally show less fatness and greater functional capacity at all ages, and this may function to alleviate aging-associated changes (Malina, 1969b, 1979c; Rarick, 1960, 1974).

Just how much physical activity is necessary during the growing years is not known with certainty. Individual variation is great. A certain level of physical exercise ia apparently necessary to support normal growth, maintain the integrity of osseous and muscular tissues, regulate fatness, and maintain aerobic fitness. Just what the minimum level is or should be, and what effects more regular and extended training programs may have on the growth and functional development of the young child and adolescent, remain to be determined. There is also a need to develop methods of monitoring and quantifying the amount and intensity of physical activity in children and youth.

Selected Developments and Directions

Although much is known about growth, maturation, and performance, understanding these developments is far from complete. This applies to the processes underlying growth, maturation, and performance, as well as their outcomes and changes. Selected developments in the study of these areas follow. They are not the only developments in the area, but serve to illustrate some directions of research.

Analytic Methods

The development of new analytic methods has permitted better description and interpretation of postnatal growth. Results of two analytic methods will be mentioned—curve fitting of longitudinal data and path analysis.

Fitting curves to individual growth records enables a maximum amount of information about an individual child's growth to be extracted; individual curves can, of course, also be compared and contrasted. Further, when fitted growth curve parameters are available for a large number of children, mean parameters and variation around them are a convenient way of summarizing a large amount of data for comparison of growth patterns between sexes or between populations (Thissen, Bock, Wainer, & Roche, 1976). Thus, fitting curves provides a convenient means of characterizing individual or group differences in a growth pattern.

The aim of fitting growth curves is threefold (Israelsohn, 1960): (a) the curve should provide a good statistical fit, that is, adequate within levels of measurement error; (b) its functional expression should be reasonably simple, and (c) the curve should have relatively few constants which can be interpreted biologically. The biological significance of the constants is most important to the understanding of human growth.

Fitting curves to the human growth process is a complex task. The pattern begins at conception and continues through adolescence; therefore, a single curve does not fit the entire span. As a result, the growth period is generally divided into different stages. Most endeavors at curve fitting have partitioned postnatal growth into prepubertal and adolescent periods (Marubini, 1978).

Using a double logistic model, Thissen et al. (1976) compared the prepubertal and adolescent components of statural growth (recumbent length) in children from four American longitudinal studies (Berkeley, Denver, Fels, Harvard), while Tanner, Whitehouse, Marubini, and Resele (1976) fitted a single logistic model to the stature of children from the Harpenden study. Before summarizing results of these analyses, it should be noted that the fitted parameters cannot be directly compared; they are more appropriately considered as best estimates.

Observations based on the five studies imply that prepubertal growth is the major contributor to adult sex differences in stature. On the average, the pre-pubertal component is greater in boys than girls, while the pubertal component and the peak height velocity during the adolescent growth spurt are only slightly greater in boys. Boys are only slightly longer than girls at birth, and thus become taller than girls through a prolonged period of prepubertal growth. Since the male adolescent spurt or peak height velocity occurs about two years later than in females, boys apparently experience about two more years of prepubertal growth.

In the five serial studies of children with European ancestry, the overall impression of the comparison of statural growth parameters was that the mean growth curves were similar rather than different (Malina, 1978).

The double logistic model has been fitted to the statural growth of Guatemalan and European children living in Guatemala (Johnston, Wainer, Thissen, & MacVean, 1976), while the single logistic model has been fitted to individual growth curves for sitting height, estimated leg length, biacromial breadth, and bicristal breadth from the Harpenden growth study (Tanner et al., 1976). Rarick, Wainer, Thissen, and Seefeldt (1975) applied the double logistic model to the statural growth of children with Down's syndrome, a condition characterized by growth failure. The model fit the Down's data well, but comparisons with normal children showed significant differences in all six parameters, i.e., three prepubertal and three adolescent). Thus, the growth curve for stature in normal and Down's children differs in degree, not in form.

Familial correlations (e.g., parent-child, sibling-sibling) are commonly used to estimate the contributions of genetic and environmental factors in quantitative traits. A major problem in the correlation approach is the difficulty in controlling for common familial environmental factors. The use of multivariate models have enhanced estimates of variance due to genetic and environmental sources.

Relative to the study of growth, a basic question deals with the partitioning of variance in quantitative traits. What proportion of the variance around the population phenotypic mean for a given trait can be imputed to environmental and genetic causes? The basic model states that the total phenotypic variance for a given trait is equal to the sum of genetic variance, environmental variance, genotype and environment covariation, genotype-environment interaction, and error.

Path analysis is a multivariate method used to quantify relationships between related variables (Li, 1975). A path diagram depicts the relationship among variables in a schematic form, and the direction of the flow in the model can be easily determined. Multivariate methods are then applied (e.g., multiple regression analyses) and tested for accuracy of fit. Notice that path analysis is not a genetic method and does not yield conventional genetic estimates. This multivariate method, however, can be used advantageously to test for the presence of a genetic effect under various hypotheses.

Bouchard, Demirjian, and Malina (in press), for example, estimated with path analysis procedures the quantitative biological contribution of parents to observed variation in several anthropometric dimensions of their offspring. A simplified linear causal model described the relationships within and between generations in the presence of indices of socioeconomic factors as indicators of a common familial environment. The path model was also fitted to the data under fluctuating conditions of assortative mating and socioeconomic effects. The lowest mean narrow heritability value was obtained for the triceps skinfold (.03), whereas the highest was obtained for stature (.65). Comparisons of parent-child data in this analysis strongly suggest that the latter value is often spuriously inflated by the contribution of common familial conditions. Heritability estimates for measurements sensitive to environmental stresses, such as soft tissue variables for fatness and muscularity, appear to be more influenced by common familial environmental conditions than are skeletal dimensions.

Biopsy Procedures

Biopsy procedures enable scientists to sample body tissues from living subjects, and thus allow a more detailed study of the tissues. The technique, however, is "blind"; it assumes that the sample taken is representative of the tissue as a whole. Nevertheless, results of studies utilizing biopsy procedures have added significantly to our understanding of the growth of muscle and fat tissues, and are relevant to those concerned with the influence of physical activity on growth.

Growth of muscle tissue after the first few months of postnatal life is characterized by constancy in number of muscle fibers, an increase in fiber size, and a considerable increase in number of muscle nuclei (Malina, 1978; Montgomery, 1962). The latter type of growth has received considerable focus recently. Cheek and his colleagues (see Cheek, 1968, 1974) used estimates of the number of muscle nuclei to assess muscle growth in a small sample of normal children.

The number of nuclei in developing muscles was estimated from measurements of DNA. Since DNA per nucleus is relatively constant at 6.2 pg/diploid nucleus, total number of nuclei in a muscle tissue sample is estimated by dividing the total DNA in the tissue by 6.2. Using DNA content of a gluteal muscle tissue sample to index the nuclear or "cell" number, and the ratio of protein to DNA to derive "muscle cell size", Cheek (1968, 1974) showed an increase in nuclear number or DNA, and an increase in amounts of protein or cell mass per nucleus or per unit DNA during growth. Assuming that the gluteal biopsy sample is representative of body musculature in general, and using creatinine excretion per day as an estimate of total muscle mass in the body, Cheek and colleagues generalized nuclear number and cell-size estimates to total

muscle mass in growing children. Their estimates suggest that from infancy through adolescence, boys increase 14-fold in muscle nuclear number, whereas girls increase only 10-fold.

Males increase in muscle nuclear number especially prior to two years
of age and after nine years of age; the latter comprises the adolescent
spurt in muscle mass. Prior to the adolescent spurt, sex differences in
estimated nuclear numbers are not obvious. On the other hand, increase
in estimated "cell size," or protein per nucleus or per unit of DNA is
only two-fold for boys and girls. Cheek's (1974) data indicate larger
protein/DNA ratios in girls at an earlier age, implying accelerated growth
of "muscle cell size" in females. Males eventually catch up in muscle tissue, and may eventually surpass females. Indeed, it would be interesting
to hypothesize a relationship between the male adolescent spurt in strength,
elevated testosterone levels, enzymatic changes in muscle tissue, and the
doubling of muscle nuclear number during adolescence.

Changes in muscle tissue with regular physical activity or training are
well documented (Malina, 1979c; Rarick, 1974). It is difficult, however,
to partition training-induced changes from normal growth in children and
youth. It is perhaps significant that studies of the DNA content in muscle
of growing animals undergoing regular training indicate a significant rise
in DNA content above that expected from normal growth. This would
suggest that training during growth may be a significant factor influencing
nuclear number and determining adult levels of DNA in muscle tissue
(Bailey, Bell, & Howarth, 1973; Buchanan & Pritchard, 1970; Hubbard,
Smoake, Mather, Linduska, & Bowers, 1974).

Also meriting consideration are the functional implications of muscle
tissue changes with training. Such muscle changes include, for example,
enhanced oxidative enzyme activity (Holloszy, 1967). This heightened
enzyme activity is a mechanism by which muscle tissue adapts to the
chronic overload from vigorous physical activity. Most of the observations,
however, are based on experimental animals; there is only limited information on humans, especially children and youth.

Results of the three studies using human subjects, two on adults
(Gollnick, Armstrong, Saltin, Saubert, Sembrowich, & Shepherd, 1973;
Thorstensson, 1976) and one on young boys (Eriksson, 1972), indicate
that the distribution of skeletal muscle fiber types is probably not altered by training—either endurance or strength. This would suggest that
genetic factors are of primary significance in muscle fiber distribution.
Indeed, monozygous twins are quite similar in their skeletal muscle fiber
composition, while dizygous twins are quite variable in fiber composition
(Komi, Vittasalo, Havu, Thorstensson, Sjodin, & Karlsson, 1977; Sjodin,

1976). However, the relative area of muscle composed of fast- or slow-twitch fibers may change in response to training.

In muscle enzyme activity, monozygous and dizygous twin pairs show similar variation; that is, the former show as much variation as the latter (Howald, 1976; Komi et al., 1976; Sjodin, 1976). However, these observations may reflect training differences. While one member of a monozygous twin pair (n = 7 pairs) participated in a 23-week endurance training program, the other maintained usual activity. Howald noted significant increases in selected extra- and intra-mitochondrial enzymes. Succinatedehydrogenase (intra) and hexokinase (extra) activities, for example, increased by 28% and 17% with training in one member of the monozygous twin pair compared to the other. Although genetic factors are important in muscle tissue fiber composition, these results emphasize the significance of physical training on the functional capacity of muscle tissue.

There is much current emphasis on adipose tissue cellularity during growth. Adipose cell growth may result from increases in fat cell number or size. Estimates of fat cell (adipocyte) development in children, however, are not consistent across several studies, probably reflecting methodological and site differences in estimating adipose cell size and number. There is in general an increase in adipose cell number from one-year old until adulthood (Brooks, 1972; Hager, Sjostrom, Arvidsson, Bjorntorp, & Smith, 1977; Knittle, 1972, 1978).

A question that merits consideration is the potential of regular physical activity programs, initiated during early childhood, to influence the development of adipose tissue cellularity. Some experimental evidence suggests that training introduced very early in life of rats (preweaning) effectively reduced the rate of fat cell accumulation, producing a significant reduction in fat cells and body fat later in life (Oscai, Babirak, McGarr, & Spirakis, 1974; Oscai, Spirakis, Wolff, & Beck, 1972). On the other hand, endurance running in rats, begun after seven weeks of age, had no effect on adipose cell number, but significantly reduced adipose cell size (Askew & Hecker, 1976; Booth, Booth, & Taylor, 1974). These experimental observations suggest an important role for regular physical activity initiated very early in life in regulating fat cell number and size.

One can inquire, therefore, as to a possible implication of these findings for fat cell development in humans. If applicable, up to what age can cell numbers be influenced by activity programs, if at all? A smaller fat cell size is associated with physical training in adult humans (Bjorntorp, Grimby, Sanne, Sjostrom, Tibblin, & Wilhelmsen, 1972). Some observations suggest a coupling between fat cell size and multiplication.

Multiplication of adipocytes occurs when the cells are filled with lipid to a size comparable to that of young adults (Hager et al., 1977). This coupling may simply be a coincidence, or it may be biologically meaningful. If would be interesting to speculate a possibly significant role for regular training. Since physical training can reduce adipose cell size (Askew & Hecker, 1976; Booth et al., 1974; Oscai et al., 1974), and in light of the suggested coupling of size and multiplication, a reduced cell size may delay or inhibit adipocyte proliferation.

Aerobic Power: Genetic and Training Effects

Definitions of organic or physical fitness vary considerably, but most agree that aerobic power (maximal oxygen uptake) is a sensitive index. During childhood, aerobic power (1/min) increases with age in both sexes. However, when body size is accounted for (i.e., ml/min/kg body weight), observations on children in Canada and the United States indicate little or no increase in aerobic power from age 8 to age 14.

On the other hand, children exposed to regular endurance-type training programs show different age-associated trends in aerobic power, but the degree of improvement in aerobic power per unit body weight is variable. Summarizing six studies of 6 to 15-year-old children in different age groups, Mocellin (1975) reported relative changes ranging from -2% to +14%, with only a small increase (+1 to +4%) in six of the 10 reported changes.

The role of hereditary factors in maximal aerobic power during childhood adds another dimension to the training and growth differences. Data from twins suggest that genetics are the principal determinant of variability in maximal aerobic power and aerobic capacity among individuals who have lived under similar environmental conditions (Holmer & Astrand, 1972; Howald, 1976; Klissouras, 1971, 1972; Klissouras, Pirnay, & Petit, 1973; Komi & Karlsson, 1979; Komi, Klissouras & Karvinen, 1973; Leitch, 1976). Training, of course, is an environmental factor. In this regard, the co-twin control method provides a powerful approach for evaluating growth and possible activity effects. Given a pair of monozygotic twins with differing environmental factors (i.e., regular physical activity), a comparison of the twins will provide a measure of the net effect of the environmental factor, all things, including heredity, being equal. This method has been used in early motor development studies, and only more recently for work capacity.

Thus, using monozygotic twin pairs, Weber, Kartodihardjo, and Klissouras (1976) studied the effects of physical training on one member of the pair, while the other served as a control. Twelve pairs of identical twin boys were studied, four pairs at each of three age levels, 10, 13, and 16 years. The trained members of each twin pair experienced a 10-week endurance program, while the untrained member went through normal daily routines and regularly scheduled physical education classes. The twins did not differ in functional measures prior to the training program. After 10 weeks, the trained 10 and 16-year-old twins improved significantly in maximal oxygen uptake (1/min), compared to their untrained counterparts (23.5% and 20.5% respectively in the trained twins compared to 11.8% and 3.2% respectively in the untrained twins). In contrast, both the trained and untrained 13-year-old twins improved commensurately (14.2% for the trained and 15.9% for the untrained twins). Based on these observations, Weber et al. suggested that the ". . . old hypothesis that more might be gained by introducing extra exercise at a time when the growth impulse is the strongest is not longer tenable." Notice, however, that the untrained twins did in fact participate in regular physical education classes.

Using young adult ($\overline{x}$ age 18, range 15-25 years) monozygotic twin pairs (n = 7 pairs), Howald (1976) studied the effects of endurance training on one member of the pair, while the other served as a control. Maximum ergometric performance (10.1%) and maximal oxygen uptake (15.4%) increased significantly in the trained twins compared to the untrained twins. When comparing monozygotic and dizygotic twins, Howald noted that if three pairs of twins with contrasting activity experiences (i.e., environmental differences) were retained in the comparison of maximal oxygen uptake in monozygotic and dizygotic twins, the resulting intrapair variance was not different. However, deleting the three pairs to meet the assumption of environmental influence comparability resulted in a significant difference between monozygous and dizygous twins in a maximal oxygen uptake (Howald, 1976). Thus, as in muscle tissue studies, genetic factors may limit oxygen uptake, but regular physical training exerts a significant influence.

Critical Weight Hypothesis

Within the past ten years of growth- and maturity-related research, no concept has spurred as much debate as the proposed association between the attainment of a critical body weight and the timing of menarche. Frisch and Revelle (1969, 1970, 1971) hypothesized a direct relationship between attaining a specific body weight during the adolescent growth spurt and menarche. They initially proposed that attaining a certain critical weight alters the metabolic rate. This affects the hypothalamic-ovarian feedback loop, which in turn reduces the sensitivity of the hypothalamus to circulating estrogens. As a result, gonadotrophic and gonadal hormones are at sufficiently high levels in circulation to induce the maturation of the ovaries and uterus, resulting in menarche. The critical body weight was estimated at 47 to 48 kg.

The critical weight hypothesis was subsequently altered (Frisch, 1974, 1976; Frisch & McArthur, 1974; Frisch, Revelle, & Cook, 1973) to incorporate body composition estimates. Total body water, lean body weight, and body fat were estimated from height and weight. The revised hypothesis suggests that critical weight is a critical body composition of relative fatness (22-24%): "A minimal fatness level of about 17% of body weight is apparently necessary for the onset of menstrual cycles. A minimal fatness level of about 22% fat of body weight is apparently necessary to maintain regular ovulatory cycles, normally established in American girls by ages 16-18 years" (Frisch, 1976, p. 353).

The critical weight or fatness hypothesis has spurred much debate. Evidence suggested that the critical weight was an artifact resulting from the failure to consider the interrelationship of age, weight, and height at menarche. At a constant height, the correlation between weight and age at menarche was negative (-0.26), so that girls who menstruate earlier tend to be heavier than those menstruating later (Johnston, Malina, & Galbraith, 1971). Other data indicated an increase in mean weight at menarche with increasing age at menarche ($r = 0.23$) (Billewicz, Fellowes, & Hytten, 1976). Such results are contrary to a relatively constant critical weight at menarche.

In a summary of weight-at-menarche data from 11 samples, Johnston, Roche, Schell, and Wettenhall (1975) noted a range of 71.4 kg (25.9 to 97.3) across the samples, and a range of 28.0 to 54.6 kg within samples. Partial correlation analysis of age, weight, and height at menarche, also showed that among girls of the same stature, those reaching menarche earlier tended to be heavier.

If a certain level of weight is critical for menarche, there should be a reduction in body weight variation at the time of menarche. However, the body weight distribution of girls who had not attained menarche and those who had attained menarche at specific ages showed similar variations at all ages (Billewicz et al., 1976). And, in a subsample of 20 girls weighing 48 kg or more between 10.5 and 11 years of age, Billewicz et al. (1976, p. 55) observed that ". . . two reached menarche between 11 and 11.5 years, six between 11.5 and 12.0 years and eleven did not start to menstruate although 1-1.5 years had elapsed since they attained the critical weight." In their sample of girls who had already started to menstruate, only 41% did so at weights of 48 ± 5 kg.

The revision of the critical weight hypothesis to include total body water and fat is confounded by the use of derived rather than measured estimates of body composition. Using the equation of Mellits and Cheek (1970), total body water is estimated as a linear function of height and weight. The equation was based on 45 females, 6 to 31 years of age. Less than one-half of the subjects were in the age range appropriate for an analysis of body composition at menarche, and their menarcheal status was not known (Billewicz et al., 1976). In applying the equation to their data, Frisch and colleagues apparently overlooked the error term, or random deviation from the regression line in the equation. As a result, the variance of estimated total body water at menarche was reduced relative to the variation in weight at menarche. The reduction of variation when using estimated total body water at menarche is a function of arithmetic procedures arising from the failure to consider the error term of the prediction equation (Billewicz et al., 1976; Johnston et al., 1975; Reeves, 1979).

Since skinfolds provide reasonably accurate estimates of body fatness, they also have been related to the timing of menarche. If a certain level of fatness is critical in determining menarche, fat measurements should exhibit reduced variability at menarche. In one study, subscapular skinfold thicknesses appeared to increase with age among premenarcheal girls, but remained rather stable at menarche. At all ages, girls who attained menarche had thicker subscapular skinfolds (Billewicz et al., 1976) Other evidence indicated increased variation (Cameron, 1976). Variation in skinfolds in the same girls was slightly higher at menarche (9.7%) than at premenarcheal (9.6%) and postmenarcheal (9.3%) times. The results of these two studies thus do not support a critical role for body fatness at menarche, as measured by skinfolds.

The hypothesis of a critical weight or fatness at menarche is not disproved by the criticisms reviewed in the preceding discussion. However, the data do not support the specificity of weight or fatness as the critical variable for menarche. Rather, changes in weight and body composition during puberty are a ". . . manifestation of the process of maturation without either of them having a level which could be called critical" (Billewicz et al., 1976, p. 58).

Continuation of "Traditional" Approaches

Growth and maturation processes are ecosensitive, (i.e., sensitive to the environments in which children are reared). As such, the growth status of children serves as a good indicator of the health and nutritional status of a community. Thus, there is a need to monitor children's growth in the more or less traditional manner of measuring stature and weight.

The sensitivity of growth and maturation is especially apparent in the secular trend (Malina, 1979a, 1979b; Roche, 1979; Van Wieringen, 1978). The tendency towards larger body size and earlier maturation has occurred primarily in the United States, and in European and Japanese populations, although it has apparently ceased in parts of all three (Malina, 1976b). This secular trend is not universal; it has not occurred in most of Africa and Latin America, and there appears to have been a reversal in India. Implications of such observations for the study of growth and maturation are apparent. Relatively simple measures of growth and maturation serve as indicators of health and nutritional status of a population.

Postnatal Effects of Prenatal Activity

There is concern for the persistence of exercise-induced changes in body composition and functional measures produced during the growing years. Available information indicates that continued activity is necessary to maintain the positive changes. Equally important is the age of initiation into regular activity or training programs. (Malina, 1979c; Rarick, 1974). Recent experimental evidence suggests there are beneficial and persistent effects of mild exercise during pregnancy on the microstructure of neonatal and adult heart muscle of rats (Bonner et al., 1978; Parizkova, 1975, 1978). Thus, there appears to be some persistence of prenatal activity effects on heart microstructure postnatally.

Conclusion

Growth, maturation, and performance are continuous processes that are reasonably regular and predictable. Nevertheless, there is also individual variation, and many factors can influence the expression of these processes. Much of our information of growth, maturation, and performance is based on outcomes of the underlying processes. Thus, we observe or measure the outcomes and changes in the outcomes.

There is no need to abandon older and more traditional approaches to the study of growth, maturation, and performance. Some of the newer developments serve to complement the older methods, and are moving us closer to understanding the underlying processes.

References

Askew, E.W., & Hecker, A.L. Adipose tissue cell size and lipolysis in the rat: response to exercise intensity and food restriction. *Journal of Nutrition,* 1976, **106**, 1351-1360.

Bailey, D.A., Bell, R.D., & Howarth, R.E. The effect of exercise on DNA and protein synthesis in skeletal muscle of growing rats. *Growth,* 1973, **37**, 323-331.

Bergmann, R.L., & Bergmann, K.E. Nutrition and growth in infancy. In F. Falkner & J.M. Tanner (Eds.), *Human growth: Neurobiology and nutrition* (Vol. 3). New York: Plenum, 1979.

Billewicz, W.Z., Fellowes, H.M., & Hytten, C.A. Comments on the critical metabolic-mass and the age of menarche. *Annals of Human Biology,* 1976, **3**, 51-59.

Bjorntorp, P., Grimby, G., Sanne, H., Sjostrom, L., Tibblin, G., & Wilhelmsen, L. Adipose tissue fat cell size in relation to metabolism in weight-stable, physically active men. *Hormone and Metabolic Research,* 1972, **4**, 178-182.

Bonner, H.W., Buffington, C.K., Newman, J.J., Farrar, R.P., & Acosta, D. Contractile activity of neonatal heart cells in culture derived from offspring of exercised pregnant rats. *European Journal of Applied Physiology,* 1978, **39**, 1-6.

Booth, M.A., Booth, M.J., & Taylor, A.W. Rat fat cell size and number with exercise training, detraining and weight loss. *Federation Proceedings,* 1974, **33**, 1959-1963.

Bouchard, C. Genetics, growth and physical activity. In F. Landry & W.A.R. Orban (Eds.), *Physical activity and human well-being.* Miami, FL: Symposia Specialists, 1978.

Bouchard, C., Demirjian, A., & Malina, R.M. Path analysis of family resemblance in physique. *Studies in Physical Anthropology,* in press.

Brooks, C.G.D. Evidence for a sensitive period in adipose-cell replication in man. *Lancet,* 1972, **2**, 624-627.

Buchanan, T.A.S., & Pritchard, J.J. DNA content of tibialis anterior of male and female white rats measured from birth to 50 weeks. *Journal of Anatomy,* 1970, **107**, 185.

Cameron, N. Weight and skinfold variation at menarche and critical body weight hypothesis. *Annals of Human Biology,* 1976, **3**, 279-282.

Carron, A.V., & Bailey, D.A. Strength development in boys from 10 through 16 years. *Monographs of the Society for Research in Child Development,* 1974, **39**(4).

Cheek, D.B. *Human Growth.* Philadelphia: Lea and Febiger, 1968.

Cheek, D.B. Body composition, hormones, nutrition, and adolescent growth. In M.M. Grumbach, G.D. Grave, & F.E. Mayer (Eds.), *Control of the onset of puberty.* New York: Wiley, 1974.

Clarke, H.H. *Physical and motor tests in the Medford boy's growth study.* Englewood Cliffs, NJ: Prentice-Hall, 1971.

Eriksson, B.O. Physical training, oxygen supply and muscle metabolism in 11-13 year old boys. *Acta Physiologica Scandinavica,* 1972, (Suppl. 384).

Espenschade, A. Motor performance in adolescence. *Monographs of the Society for Research in Child Development,* 1940, **5**(1).

Eveleth, P.B., & Tanner, J.M. *Worldwide variation in human growth.* Cambridge, England: Cambridge University Press, 1976.

Falkner, F., & Tanner, J.M. (Eds.). *Human growth: Principles and prenatal growth* (Vol. 1). New York: Plenum, 1978. (a)

Falkner, F., & Tanner, J.M. (Eds.). *Human growth: Postnatal growth* (Vol. 2). New York: Plenum, 1978. (b)

Falkner, F., & Tanner, J.M. (Eds.). *Human growth: Neurobiology and nutrition* (Vol. 3). New York: Plenum, 1979.

Frisch, R.E. Critical weight at menarche, initiation of the adolescent growth spurt, and control of puberty. In M.M. Grumbach, G.D. Grave, & F.E. Mayer (Eds.), *Control of the onset of puberty.* New York: Wiley, 1974.

Frisch, R.E. Fatness of girls from menarche to age 18 years, with a nomogram. *Human Biology,* 1976, **48**, 353-359.

Frisch, R.E., & McArthur, J.W. Menstrual cycles: fatness as a determinant of minimum weight for height necessary for their maintenance or onset. *Science,* 1974, **185**, 949-951.

Frisch, R.E., & Revelle, R. The height and weight of adolescent boys and girls at the time of peak velocity of growth in height and weight: longitudinal data. *Human Biology,* 1969, **41**, 536-559.

Frisch, R.E., & Revelle, R. Height and weight at menarche and a hypothesis of critical body weight and adolescent events. *Science,* 1970, **169**, 397-399.

Frisch, R.E., & Revelle, R. Height and weight at menarche and a hypothesis of menarche. *Archives of Disease in Children,* 1971, **46**, 695-701.

Frisch, R.E., Revelle, R., & Cook, S. Components of weight at menarche and the initiation of the adolescent growth spurt in girls: estimated total water, lean body weight and fat. *Human Biology,* 1973, **45**, 469-483.

Gollnick, P.D., Armstrong, R.B., Saltin, B., Saubert, C.W., Sembrowich, W.L., & Shepherd, R.E. Effect of training on enzyme activity and fiber composition of human skeletal muscle. *Journal of Applied Physiology,* 1973, **34**, 107-111.

Greulich, W.W., & Pyle, S.I. *Radiographic atlas of skeletal development of the hand and wrist* (2nd ed.). Palo Alto, CA: Stanford University Press, 1959.

Hager, A., Sjostrom, L., Arvidsson, B., Bjorntorp, P., & Smith, U. Body fat and adipose tissue cellularity in infants: a longitudinal study. *Metabolism: Clinical and Experimental* 1977, **26**, 607-614.

Holloszy, J.O. Biochemical adaptations in muscle: effects of exercise on mitrochondrial oxygen uptake and respiratory enzyme activity in skeletal muscle. *Journal of Biological Chemistry*, 1967, **242**, 2278-2282.

Holmer, I., & Åstrand, P.-O. Swimming training and maximal oxygen uptake. *Journal of Applied Physiology*, 1972, **33**, 510-513.

Howald, H. Ultrastructure and biochemical function of skeletal muscle in twins. *Annals of Human Biology*, 1976, **3**, 455-462.

Hubbard, R.W., Smoake, J.A., Mather, W.T., Linduska, J.D., & Bowers, W.S. The effects of growth and endurance training on the protein and DNA content of rat soleus, plantaris, and gastrocnemius muscles. *Growth*, 1974, **38**, 171-185.

Israelsohn, W.J. Description and modes of analysis of human growth. In J.M. Tanner (Ed.), *Human Growth*. Oxford: Pergamon Press, 1960.

Johnston, F.E., Malina, R.M., & Galbraith, M.A. Height, weight and age at menarche and the "critical weight" hypothesis. *Science*, 1971, **174**, 1148.

Johnston, F.E., Roche, A.F., Schell, L.M., & Wettenhall, N.B., Critical weight at menarche: critique of a hypothesis. *American Journal of Diseases of Children*, 1975, **129**, 19-23.

Johnston, F.E., Wainer, H., Thissen, D., & MacVean, R. Hereditary and environmental determinants of growth in height in a longitudinal sample of children and youth of Guatemalan and European ancestry. *American Journal of Physical Anthropology*, 1976, **44**, 469-475.

Jones, H.E. *Motor performance and growth*. Berkeley: University of California Press, 1949.

Klissouras, V. Heritability of adaptive variation. *Journal of Applied Physiology*, 1971, **31**, 338-344.

Klissouras, V. Genetic limit of functional adaptability. *Internationale Zeitschrift Für Angewandte Physiologie*, 1972, **30**, 85-94.

Klissouras, V., Pirnay, F., & Petit, J.-M. Adaptation to maximal effort: genetics and age. *Journal of Applied Physiology*, 1973, **35**, 288-293.

Knittle, J.L. Obesity in childhood: A problem in adipose tissue cellular development. *Journal of Pediatrics*, 1972, **81**, 1048-1059.

Knittle, J.L. Adipose tissue development in man. In F. Falkner &

J.M. Tanner (Eds.), *Human growth: Postnatal growth* (Vol. 2). New York: Plenum, 1978.

Komi, P.V., & Karlsson, J. Physical performance, skeletal muscle enzyme activities, and fibre types in monozygous and dizygous twins of both sexes. *Acta Physiologica Scandinavica,* 1979, (Suppl. 462).

Komi, P.V., Klissouras, V., & Karvinen, E. Genetic variation in neuromuscular performance. *Internationale Zeitschrift Für Angewandte Physiologie,* 1973, **31,** 289-304.

Komi, P.V., Vittasalo, J.H.T., Havu, M., Thorstensson, A., Sjodin, B., & Karlsson, J. Skeletal muscle fibres and muscle enzyme activities in monozygous and dizygous twins of both sexes. *Acta Physiologica Scandinavica,* 1977, **100,** 385-392.

Leitch, A.G. Chemical control of breathing in identical twin athletes. *Annals of Human Biology,* 1976, **3,** 447-454.

Li, C.C. *Path analysis: A primer.* California: Boxwood Press, 1975.

Malina, R.M. The quantification of fat, muscle and bone in man. *Clinical Orthopaedics,* 1969, **65,** 9-38. (a)

Malina, R.M. Exercise as an influence upon growth. *Clinical Pediatrics,* 1969, **8,** 16-26. (b)

Malina, R.M. Ethnic and cultural factors in the development of motor abilities and strength in American children. In G.L. Rarick (Ed.), *Physical activity: Human growth and development.* New York: Academic Press, 1973.

Malina, R.M. Motor development: determinants and the need to consider them. In M.G. Wade & R. Martens (Eds.), *Psychology of motor behavior and sport.* Urbana, IL: Human Kinetics, 1974.

Malina, R.M. *Growth and development: The first twenty years in man.* Minneapolis: Burgess, 1975. (a)

Malina, R.M. Anthropometric correlates of strength and motor performance. *Exercise and Sport Sciences Reviews,* 1975, **3,** 249-274. (b)

Malina, R.M. Adolescent growth and maturation: selected aspects of current research. *Yearbook of Physical Anthropology,* 1978, **21,** 63-94.

Malina, R.M. Growth of muscle tissue and muscle mass. In F. Falkner & J.M. Tanner, (Eds.), *Human growth: Postnatal growth* (Vol. 2). New York, Plenum, 1978.

Malina, R.M. Secular changes in size and maturity: causes and effects. *Monographs of the Society for Research in Child Development,* 1979, **44**(3-4), 59-102. (a)

Malina, R.M. Secular changes in growth, maturation, and physical performance. *Exercise and Sport Sciences Reviews,* 1979, **6,** 203-255. (b)

Malina, R.M. The effects of exercise on specific tissues, dimensions, and functions during growth. *Studies in Physical Anthropology,* 1979, **5**, 21-52. (c)

Malina, R.M. Biosocial correlates of motor development during infancy and early childhood. In L.S. Greene & F.E. Johnston (Eds.), *Social and biological predictors of nutritional status, physical growth and behavioral development.* New York: Academic Press, 1980. (a)

Malina, R.M. Growth, strength, and physical performance. In G.A. Stull (Ed.), *Encyclopedia of physical education, fitness and sports: Training, environment, nutrition, and fitness* (Vol. 2). Salt Lake City, UT: Brighton, 1980. (b)

Malina, R.M., & Rarick, G.L. Growth, physique,and motor performance. In G.L. Rarick (Ed.), *Physical activity: Human growth and development.* New York: Academic Press, 1973.

Marshall, W.A., & Tanner, J.M. Variations in pattern of pubertal changes in girls. *Archives of Disease in Childhood,* 1969, **44**, 291-303.

Marshall, W.A., & Tanner, J.M. Variations in the pattern of pubertal changes in boys. *Archives of Disease in Childhood,* 1970, **45**, 13-23.

Marubini, E. The mathematical handling of long-term longitudinal data. In F. Falkner & J.M. Tanner (Eds.), *Human growth: Principles and prenatal growth* (Vol. 1). New York: Plenum, 1978.

Mellits, E.D., & Cheek, D.B. The assessment of body water and fatness from infancy to adulthood. *Monographs of the Society for Research in Child Development,* 1970, **35**(7), 12-26.

Mocellin, R. Jugend und sport. *Medizinische klinik,* 1975, **70**, 1443-1457.

Montgomery, R.D. Growth of human straited muscle. *Nature,* 1962, **195**, 194-195.

Oscai, L.B., Babirak, S.P., McGarr, J.A., & Spirakis, C.N. Effect of exercise on adipose tissue cellularity. *Federation Proceedings,* 1974, **33**, 1956-1958.

Oscai, L.B., Spirakis, C.N., Wolff, C.A., & Beck, R.J. Effects of exercise and of food restriction on adipose tissue cellularity. *Journal of Lipid Research,* 1972, **13**, 588-592.

Parizkova, J. Impact of daily work-load during pregnancy on the microstructure of the rat heart in male offspring. *European Journal of Applied Physiology,* 1975, **34**, 323-326.

Parizkova, J. The impact of daily work load during pregnancy and/or postnatal life on the heart microstructure of rat male offspring. *Basic Research in Cardiology,* 1978, **73**, 433-441.

Rarick, G.L. Exercise and growth. In W.R. Johnson (Ed.), *Science and medicine of exercise and sports.* New York: Harper, 1960.

Rarick, G.L. Exercise and growth. In W.R. Johnson & E.R. Buskirk (Eds.), *Science and medicine of exercise and sports* (2nd ed.). New York: Harper & Row, 1974.

Rarick, G.L., & Smoll, F.L. Stability of growth in strength and motor performance from childhood to adolescence. *Human Biology,* 1967, **39**, 295-306.

Rarick, G.L., Wainer, H., Thissen, D., & Seefeldt, V. A double logistic comparison of growth patterns of normal children and children with Down's syndrome. *Annals of Human Biology,* 1975, **2**, 339-346.

Reeves, J. Estimating fatness. *Science,* 1979, **204**, 881.

Roche, A.F. Secular trends in stature, weight, and maturation. *Monographs of the Society for Research in Child Development,* 1979, **44** (3-4), 3-27.

Roche, A.F. Measurement of skeletal maturation. In F.E. Johnston, A.F. Roche, & C. Sussanne (Eds.), *Methodologies for analyzing human growth and development.* New York: Plenum, 1980.

Roche, A.F., Wainer, H., & Thissen, D. *Skeletal maturity: The knee joint as a biological indicator.* New York: Plenum, 1975.

Sjodin, B. Lactate dehydrogenase in human skeletal muscle. *Acta Physiologica Scandinavica,* 1976, (Suppl. 436).

Tanner, J.M. *Growth at adolescence* (2nd ed.). Oxford: Blackwell, 1962

Tanner, J.M. *Fetus into Man: Physical growth from conception to maturity.* Cambridge, MA: Harvard University Press, 1978.

Tanner, J.M., Whitehouse, R.H., Marshall, W.A., Healy, M.J., & Goldstein, H. *Assessment of skeletal maturity and prediction of adult height.* New York: Academic Press, 1975.

Tanner, J.M., Whitehouse, R.H., Marubini, E., & Resele, L.F. The adolescent growth spurt of boys and girls of the Harpenden growth study. *Annals of Human Biology,* 1976, **3**, 109-126.

Thissen, D., Bock, R.D., Wainer, H., & Roche, A.F. Individual growth in stature: A comparison of four growth studies in the USA. *Annals of Human Biology,* 1976, **3**, 529-542.

Thorstensson, A. Muscle strength, fibre types and enzyme activities in man. *Acta Physiologica Scandinavica,* 1976, (Suppl. 443).

Van Wieringen, J.C. Secular growth changes. In F. Falkner & J.M. Tanner (Eds.), *Human growth: Postnatal growth* (Vol. 2). New York: Plenum, 1978.

Weber, G., Kartodihardjo, W., & Klissouras, V. Growth and physical training with reference to heredity. *Journal of Applied Physiology,* 1976, **40**, 211-215.

A Movement Development Framework and a Perceptual-Cognitive Perspective

12 *J. Keogh*

Movement development, as an area of study, has been limited primarily to establishing a normative sense of the general flow of movement development. Very little is known about movement development beyond the general and obvious fact that individuals improve in movement performance from infancy through adolescence. We now appear ready to expand and focus our views on what is movement development and what are important issues and questions in studying movement development. A movement development framework will be presented as a basis for considering how we need to expand our sense of what is movement development. A perceptual-cognitive perspective of movement skill development, as an emerging research direction, then will be elaborated to illustrate an increased depth of focus in studying movement skill development.

Movement Development Framework

A framework is presented in Figure 1 to identify major outcomes and determinants of human movement. The framework becomes developmental by viewing the outcomes and determinants in terms of their progressive and directional change from less mature to more mature states. The flow of movement development can be traced as changes in movement fitness, movement skills and movement behaviors which are the observable outcomes we seek to understand. Fitness, skill and behavior interact to limit or enhance each other. Changes in skill and fitness depend to a considerable extent on the type and amount of movement activity in which an individual engages. Fitness and skill levels will affect behavior in a movement situation; behavior will affect extent of involvement and level of achievement.

The primary determinants of fitness, skill and behavior development are the maturation of the physiological and neuromuscular systems and the development of perceptual-cognitive and personal-social functioning of the individual. Environmental demands and constraints are assumed

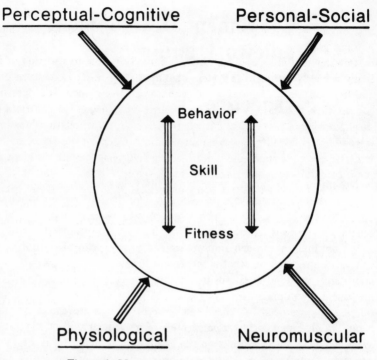

Perceptual-Cognitive   **Personal-Social**

Behavior

Skill

Fitness

Physiological   **Neuromuscular**

Figure 1. Movement development framework.

as integral parts of these systems and functionings. Physiological and neuromuscular maturation are the primary determinants of early movement development. Perceptual-cognitive and personal-social development are placed higher in Figure 1 to indicate their role in extending movement development, particularly skill and behavior, toward more complex levels of performance and involvement. Perceptual-cognitive mechanisms provide executive control of the neuromuscular system with some direct influence on personal-social functioning and movement behavior. Personal-social functioning mediates or influences perceptual-cognitive mechanisms, thus indirectly affecting movement skill development, while directly affecting movement behavior development.

If the general sense of the framework in Figure 1 is accepted, it follows that developmental issues and questions need to be pursued in all aspects of human movement, whether one is concerned with fitness, skill or behavior. Our research efforts in studying human movement, however, have been limited primarily to mature or more fully developed individuals in terms of how they achieve high level or maximal performance. Movement development has seldom been studied except in the context of describing changes in movement skills as related to age, sex and physical growth.

Development is focused on how one initially is able to function or initially achieves control of a system or output, then what is achieved next and how are the many changes accomplished. Development is a dynamic process such that change in one component may change the contribution of another component, thus changing the lawfulness of relationships or introducing new and higher level mechanisms in the system. Also, outcome expectancies or goals of the individual may change to create different and more complex movement problems to be solved.

We need to recognize that development is not an area of study except in relation to a particular aspect of movement, such as fitness, skill or behavior. A researcher first must understand fitness or skill or behavior, then must learn to approach them from a developmental point of view. This means that a new group of researchers, coming from their primary training in exercise, skill and behavior, are needed to expand the study of movement development. There are indications that a scientific migration to study movement development is in progress, as will be illustrated later.

As an additional comment, movement behavior development requires some elaboration in that movement behavior generally is not included as a movement outcome. Movement behavior is used here as a general term to identify personal-social behaviors and feelings (e.g., effort, enjoyment, confidence, cooperation, competition) which are a natural part of participation in movement activities. Not only are these behaviors and feelings developed in relation to movement situations, but these behaviors and feelings serve to enhance or limit movement performance. If a child enjoys movement and seeks involvement in movement situations, opportunities for movement fitness and skill development will be increased and participation will be perceived as positive. The opposite will be true if a child does not enjoy movement.

Griffin and Keogh (in press) recently proposed a model for movement confidence, which is a feeling about skill difficulties and movement dangers in a movement situation, as an approach to studying one aspect of movement behavior development. Movement confidence is proposed both as a consequence or outcome and as a mediator to influence movement performance and behavior. The orientation of the model is developmental in terms of how movement confidence is developed and how movement confidence affects movement skill development.

Another promising approach in studying movement behavior development is the research on youth sports programs, particularly as summarized in two publications (Magill, Ash, & Smoll, 1978; Smoll & Smith, 1978). The thrust of this work is to understand competitive and related behaviors in movement situations, with little attention to movement skill development. The focus is on higher levels of performance and more intense participation, but developmental models of personal-social development are used. As an example, Scanlan (in Magill et al., 1978; Smoll & Smith, 1978) proposes a developmental basis for understanding competition in terms of development of social evaluation and other personal-social factors.

Movement Skill Development:
A Perceptual-Cognitive Perspective

The development of movement skills by an individual is a complex and dynamic process that can be characterized as the progressive achievement of movement control, both of movements-for-self and movements-with-others (Keogh, 1978). Newborns have limited control of their neuromuscular system and have not yet developed basic movement patterns to provide adequate body control in terms of postural control, locomotion and manipulation. The basic control of ones own body, or movements-for-self, develops in a rather predictable sequence in children throughout the world, although individual quality and rate may vary (Kopp, 1979). A more complicated movement problem for the developing child is to achieve movement control in relation to others (objects and people), particularly when self and others are moving. Movement-with-others involves extensive processing of external information and complicated planning in relation to others along the lines of what Poulton (1957) identifies as an open task.

The level of perceptual and cognitive development would seem to be an important determinant of the development of movement control, particularly when moving-with-others. Perceptual-cognitive functioning is the processing of sensory information to make decisions, which in our case is solving movement problems. The general concern is the information processing of the mover to learn how the mover perceives a situation or makes meaning from existing or imagined information, and how the mover operates on the perceived meaning to produce and regulate movement action plans. The developmental concern is to understand how the mover achieves increased sophistication in organization, execution and refinement of movement action plans (Keogh, 1977).

Connolly (1970) convened a symposium in 1968 to discuss the perceptual and cognitive mechanisms of movement skill development as an alternative to the more descriptive and normative approaches. Only fragmented efforts have been made to pursue the issues identified in this landmark symposium (see reviews by Wade, 1976, and Keogh, 1977), but a number of researchers in motor learning and motor control have started to explore developmental issues, as shown by their participation in a recent movement development symposium organized by Clark and Kelso (in press). These researchers are concerned with information-processing functions in what can be identified as a perceptual-cognitive approach to motor learning and motor control. They are now extending their interests in mature performers to include developmental issues.

A number of general issues and ideas have been proposed in terms of how movement skill development might be understood from a perceptual-cognitive perspective. The summary by Keogh (1977) provides the basis for the present discussion, particularly in terms of an historical overview and a set of proposed research directions. The characteristics listed by Bruner (1973) and refined by Hogan and Hogan (1975) are useful for conceptualizing what is involved in movement skill. The three characteristics of sequencing, timing and modularization identify important movement problems to be solved as an individual develops. Connolly (1973) notes that we also should consider what are processing and organizing constraints. He emphasizes in a positive vein that movement skill development depends upon increased performance capabilities of sensory-motor systems, functional integrity of subroutines, and richness of motor syntax. The recent reviews of movement development and information processing by Sugden and Connell (1979) and Thomas (1980) direct our attention to memory and other processing systems, and levels of processing. Movement skill development in these and similar perspectives depends upon the development and functioning of perceptual-cognitive mechanisms which organize action.

Movement skill development will be reviewed in relation to two aspects of perceptual-cognitive development. The first aspect is processing skills in that development in the rate, kind, and quality of information processing may contribute substantially to the development of many movement skills. The second aspect is the role of vision, a primary sensory modality which appears to contribute differently to movement control as development progresses. Although interrelated in the overall functioning of the perceptual-cognitive system, processing skills and processing modalities (vision) are reviewed separately because the conceptual sophistication and experimental evidence to consider their interactions are currently lacking. One set of studies will be examined in detail for both processing skills and vision. A number of additional studies will be presented briefly to suggest promising directions for future research. The reviews are further limited by excluding movement skill development in infancy and early childhood, as well as abnormal movement skill development.

Processing Skills

Children do not perform as well as adults on a number of movement tasks that require processing of environmental and movement information. In laboratory tests of this nature, children have slower reaction times (Noble, Baker, & Jones, 1964) and movement times (Salmoni & Pascoe, 1978), are less able to coincide or time their movements in relation to the path of a moving object (Dorfman, 1977) or an external rhythm (Smoll, 1974), and are less accurate when positioning a limb (Thomas & Bender, 1977) or pushing an object (Whiting & Cockerill, 1972). Experience may be important in that children may not accurately recognize and organize some information. Children also may process information in less efficient ways, thus requiring more time and possibly producing less effective movement solutions. These two interactive concerns of (a) processing speed and time, and (b) processing operations will be used as general topics in reviewing processing skills and movement skill development.

It should be noted that information processing often is conceived in a computer analogy as a hardware structure controlled by software operations. A developmental issue is whether differences in child-adult processing are related more to changes in structure or operations. The issue likely cannot be resolved definitively because the answer probably is a combination of structure and operations. Evidence and inference for both sides of the issue will be noted to illustrate some of the complexity of the issue. A possibility is that development of structure is more critical early in life whereas development of operations is more important as movement tasks demand more complex processing.

Processing Speed and Time

Processing speed or rate is calculated as the amount of information processed in a particular time. Processing capacity, an elusive concept suggesting total volume or maximum functioning, often is used interchangeably with processing rate, which leads to ambiguous and conflicting interpretations about child-adult differences in speed of processing. Processing rate and capacity have been studied in many different ways to consider rate and capacity as a function of changes in stimulus conditions and response demands (Wickens, 1974). A general expectation is that children improve steadily in their speed of processing information, which means that children process less information than adults during the same time interval. An important consideration discussed later is whether children can process the same information if given more time.

Information load for an individual is calculated as units or bits of information to be processed. Processing time is measured as reaction time if the information is needed to initiate a movement and as movement time if the information is needed to control the movement. Reaction time is a function of uncertainty related to the number of stimuli and response choices to be identified, selected, and organized before a movement is initiated. Uncertainty and reaction time can be reduced by anticipating or predicting the order of stimuli and responses. Such anticipations occur in terms of sequential dependencies, that B follows A, and probabilities of occurrence, that A occurs 1 time in 5 and B occurs 4 times in 5. Movement time is a function of movement amplitude and movement accuracy in that variation in amplitude and accuracy demands will change the information load related to control of the movement. Different kinds of information are needed to initiate and control a movement.

Movement time for adults has been determined by Fitts (1954) to vary linearly with the logarithm of an index of difficulty calculated as $\log_2 (2A/W)$, where A is movement amplitude and W is target width. Fitts Law of $MT = a + b \log_2 (2A/W)$ has most often been tested in the serial or repeated movement task of reciprocal tapping. A person starts with a pointer resting on one target, then moves the pointer to tap a second target, and continues to tap back and forth between the two targets for a designated time period. Changes in amplitude and width will affect information load and movement speed, except it is possible to counterbalance the changes in amplitude and width to maintain the same information load. Information load or index of difficulty would be two information bits if A is 8cm and W is 4 cm $[\log_2 (2 \times 8/4)]$. The reduction of A to 4cm and W to 2 cm will keep the index of difficulty unchanged as 2 information bits. But changing A back to 8cm and maintaining W at 2cm could increase the index of difficulty to 3 information bits $[\log_2 (2 \times 8/2)]$. Fitts Law has been found to hold with other tasks, including discrete movements involving only one movement from the starting point to a single target while varing amplitude and width.

The general finding for movement speed of older children performing reciprocal tapping tasks and single, discrete movements is similar to adults (Kerr, 1975; Salmoni & Pascoe, 1978; Sudgen, 1980; Wallace, Newell, & Wade, 1978) as illustrated in Figure 2. Movement time of adults increases linearly in relation to increases in the index of difficulty. Move-

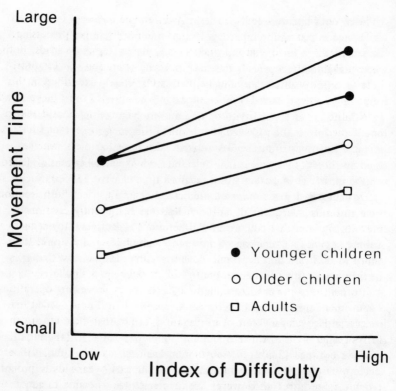

Figure 2. The general relationship of movement time and index of difficulty for different age groups, illustrating the similarity in rate of change for adults and older children as contrasted with the variability of of results reported for younger children.

ment times for older children are larger (slower movement speed), although sometimes approaching adult movement speed. The change in relation to increases in the index of difficulty is linear for older children and the slope of their regression line is similar to adults in that the lines are parallel.

Younger children have larger movement times, as might be expected, but the slope of their regression line does not always match the slope of older children and adults. Salmoni and Pascore (1978) found that the slope of the regression line was steeper on a reciprocal tapping task, whereas Kerr (1975) and Sugden (1980) found a slope similar to older children and adults. Additionally, Wallace, Newell, and Wade (1978) and Sugden (1980) reported a steeper slope for younger children on a discrete movement ask. A difference in slopes indicates a difference in processing capacities in that a relatively larger processing time is required for one group to process higher information loads. Both structural limitations and deficits in processing operations could contribute to capacity differences but neither can be clearly identified in this research paradigm. The difference in study findings also must be resolved.

As noted earlier, reaction time and movement time are considered to be affected by different kinds of information. Reaction time of adults is affected by uncertainty about stimulus and response choices, whereas their movement time generally is not affected by such uncertainties. Based on the results of an earlier study by Bogaritz and Witte (1966), Wickens (1974) suggested that sequential predictability might affect both reaction time and movement time of children. Kerr (1979) recently confirmed previous findings that adults and children were not affected by sequential predictability. Kerr suggests that, although children are slower than adults in both reaction time and movement time, the relative similarity of their response to sequential predictability indicates a similarity in motor control processes, presumably a similarity in processing operations.

Another way to think of processing capacity is the time needed to process a particular amount of information, rather than how much can be processed in a particular amount of time. Surwillo (1977), using differences between simple reaction time and choice reaction time, estimated that 5-year-olds take nearly three times as long as 17-year-olds to process one bit of information. However, children might not be able to adequately process a particular kind of information, regardless of the time available, thus indicating a limitation in the required processing operations.

Newell (1976) recognized this issue with adults when discussing knowledge of results (KR) as information to be processed. He noted that the time period after KR is provided (post-KR time interval) may be too short, thus not providing sufficient processing time between trials. Gallagher and Thomas (1980) subsequently reported that 7-year-olds performed as accurately as 11-year-olds on a ballistic movement task, but the performance of 7-year-olds deteriorated markedly and progressively when the post-KR time interval was shortened from 12 seconds to 6 seconds to 3 seconds. If children can perform adequately when given sufficient time, they demonstrate the capacity to process although not at a rapid rate. Such findings argue for deficiencies in processing operations, rather than in the structures of the processing system.

Another consideration is that the same general information might be provided in ways which are different quantitatively or qualitatively and at different levels of precision. Knowing that a movement is "short" or "long" may have different meaning and utility than "4 cm short" or "4 cm long." Adults generally improve more rapidly and to a higher level when given more precise KR (Newell, 1976), recognizing that an optimum level of precision probably exists in that very precise KR might be difficult to process and use. Newell and Kennedy (1978) found some support for optimum precision level of KR varying with age to indicate that children may not be able to process and use even moderately precise information. We need to consider that more precise information could be misleading and disruptive.

Processing Operations

Another line of research has been focused more directly on processing operations rather than on processing speed and time. The emphasis is on how information is processed in various perceptual-cognitive systems, particularly memory as a major storage and processing system. Memory has been studied extensively, although somewhat narrowly, in relation to adult motor performance and learning, but almost not at all with children and movement skill development.

Memory functions both to store and retrieve information. Additionally, memory or some related system must organize and reorganize information, both as it is received and after it is in store. Similar systems exist to make response decisions and organize movement plans and commands. An individual probably learns relationships, rules, or schemas (Fowler, 1975; Gentile & Nacson, 1976; Schmidt, 1975) that serve as general guidelines in processing information and formulating movement plans

and commands. The various processing systems are viewed as controlled by decision or control processes identified as strategies, ways of organizing and operating the systems to process information (Atkinson & Shiffrin, 1968). Strategies might include rehearsal, labeling, grouping, and similar means of organizing information. More elaborate strategies are proposed as means of organizing information into identifiable and interrelated packages, thus providing for more complex information usage as illustrated in the studies of memory for movement sequence (Foellinger & Trabasso, 1977; Zaichkowsky, 1974).

A basic strategy suggested as a control process is rehearsal of information to better retain information in short-term memory. Rehearsal can be interrupted if an intervening or interpolated task is performed, thus occupying processing space during the intertrial time allocated for rehearsal. Using this general paradigm, Sugden (1978) found that 6-year-olds were not spontaneously rehearsing on a linear positioning task in that their performance did not decrease when an interpolated task was performed during the intertrial interval. Older boys, ages 9 and 12, performed better than 6-year-olds when not doing an interpolated task, but the mean error of older boys increased significantly when involved in an interpolated task. These findings parallel the developmental trend in verbal learning tasks, that younger children do not spontaneously rehearse information as much as older children. These findings support the explanation of a lack of development in processing operations.

Strategies also need to be considered in terms of how an individual organizes movement to solve a movement problem. The observation of movement production provides a record of developmental changes in movement organization from which we can infer strategies used to organize movement. Connolly and Elliott (Connolly & Elliott, 1972; Elliott & Connolly, 1974) made some careful observations of hand movements with interesting suggestions on development and use of movement strategies. When controlling a tilting platform to move a marble to particular locations, children used quick alternating hand movements as a strategy to limit runaway movements of the marble. Children also had to use a second strategy of keeping the marble moving to avoid a stop situation which requires use of considerable force to overcome inertia. We now need to study how children develop movement strategies, such as alternation and continuity, and how such strategies can be used differentially within the information processing requirements of each movement situation. Brown (1975) further argues that we need to determine whether the strategy can be used when needed. This will require a change in our research paradigms to include direct intervention to teach strategies and their use, then evaluate which strategies a child can produce and which can be used.

Role of Vision

Although vision is a sensory modality of obvious importance to a moving person, the functioning of vision in movement skill development has not been well-defined. The primary role of vision is to gather information external to the mover. Such information is particularly useful when an individual is moving in relation to others (objects and persons) in the environment. Increased visual-perceptual development of an individual is needed as the movement environment and movement control become more complex. Vision also is recognized as playing an additional role in terms of controlling body movements, including postural adjustments (Butterworth & Hicks, 1977; Lee & Lishman, 1975). Whatever may be the role or function of vision, we also need to consider what is the need for vision in that less visual input may be needed as individuals develop and other sensory modalities may be used in place of vision.

Visual-Perceptual Development

Children at the end of the first year of life have a well developed visual system in terms of acuity, depth perception, and similar characteristics that enable them to "see" static or nonmoving objects. Children at this age are less well developed in terms of visual-perceptual development, which involves differentiating and assembling visual input to organize different meanings or perception from what they see, as well as seeing and perceiving movement. Visual-perceptual development involves recognition of different features or cues (e.g., color and shape) to identify and classify objects, as well as perceptual organization (e.g., whole-part and figure-ground rearrangements of a visual display). Visual-perceptual development also involves perception of movement in terms of tracking moving objects and predicting locations and flight paths in space. The summary by Williams (1973) provides an orderly review of visual-perceptual development from the perspective of a person interested in movement skill development.

A special comment needs to be inserted here to note that perceptual-motor theories and programs, which have been prominent in recent years, do not provide thinking and research appropriate to this discussion. The thrust of these theories and programs has been on moving to learn, that movement contributes to perceptual development (usually visual-perceptual development) and leads to improved academic skills. Very little attention has been given to learning to move, how visual-perceptual development contributes to movement skill development (Keogh, 1978). Research on perceptual-motor theories and programs is equivocal and generally of poor quality (Meyers & Hammill, 1976), but the important point is that the interest has been focused on how movement affects perception, not on how perception affects movement.

Psychologists have studied recognition and organization aspects of visual-perceptual development more extensively than they have studied perception of movement. The reverse seems to be true in studying movement skill development, recognizing that movement research has not been extensive in either direction. The discussion here will be limited to coincidence timing, a basic and pervasive visual-perceptual movement skill developed in early school years.

A study reported by Williams (1973) illustrates the developmental progression and importance of coincidence timing in the skill of catching. Children standing under a canopy watched a ball projected toward them. The ball disappeared from sight when blocked from view by the canopy and landed silently in a net above the canopy. Children, seeing only the initial part of the flight path, were to move to the place where the ball would have landed. Younger children (ages 6,7,8) moved quickly in the direction of the flight path but their mean estimate of the landing spot was 22 ft. (6.7 m) beyond the projected landing point. The mean estimation errors for older children (ages 9,10,11) was less than three feet. An interesting observation by Williams was that 9-year-olds were accurate but quite slow in making their judgments. They could use the limited flight information if given enough time to process. She also noticed the transition of 10- and 11-year-olds to quick and accurate judgments. Although not required to catch the ball, children demonstrated a developmental sequence in terms of mastery of various aspects of coincidence timing. Younger children recognized the flight path direction, but could not predict the landing spot; preschool children might not predict the direction. Middle-age children knew direction and landing spot if given time; older children knew both without hesitation.

Dorfman (1977) reported some laboratory data on coincidence timing. He used the task of moving a slide to control a cursor dot horizontally on an oscilloscope to intercept the movement of a target dot travelling vertically, similar to an electronic or TV-screen game. As expected, performance during initial trials improved from age 6 to age 19. During later trials, the target dot was masked or blacked out after 90 msec, which left 610 msec to intercept the unseen dot traveling in a predictable path at a constant rate. All age groups decreased in performance, but the size and proportion of loss was greater for younger children.

Similar findings have been reported in a set of studies of rhythmic ability in which individuals moved an arm to a location at a specified rate (Smoll, 1974a, 1974b, 1975; Thomas & Moon, 1976). Both spatial and temporal accuracy were less for younger children. The problem remains to get beyond the descriptive finding that younger children have difficulty in coordinating their movements to match or coincide with movements of others. We probably should extend our research in two quite different but interactive directions. We need to build some general frameworks and models to organize our thinking, a point to be discussed in the concluding comments. An example of a general framework is the diagram by Stubbs (1976) of information flow in coordinating hand movements with vision. Also, we need to focus within these frameworks on specific components, such as eye-head movements (Sharp & Whiting,

1975), visual search strategies (Bard & Fleury, 1976; Haywood, 1977), and speed-direction cues (Ridenour, 1974, 1977).

Need for Vision

A general finding is that children need more vision than adults to establish and maintain an adequate level of performance. An interrelated finding is that vision may be disruptive under certain conditions. The disruptive effect is more pronounced for children, including the observation that children, perhaps beginning learners as well, may choose to use vision even when it is disruptive and limiting.

Establish Performance. The decrement in children's performance when vision is limited is illustrated in the coincidence timing study of Dorfman (1977) and the study of Whiting and Cockerill (1978). Children and adults in the Whiting and Cockerill study pushed a trolley car up an inclined plane, either with the track in view or with a screen to conceal the track. The performance of younger children declined markedly when the screen was used, even though the screen was lifted before each trial to provide a view of the track and KR was given at the end of each trial.

A similar apparatus was used by Carter and Keogh and by Keogh, Burton, and Carter (Note 1, Note 2), except a tunnel was used to cover the track. The tunnel and track were marked in matching colorbands to enable a subject to "see" the track rather than having the track concealed by a screen. Three different experiments (I, II, III) were conducted in the two studies to manipulate vision and KR in various combinations. Summary findings are presented in Figure 3. Performance levels were ordered by age, as expected, with adults more able and younger children often less able than older children.

Children generally needed more vision to establish an appropriate performance level during practice trials, as illustrated by the left-hand dots and squares of each line in Figure 3. When the tunnel was in place during practice trials and verbal KR was provided (II-C), children had markedly poorer performance compared to the performance of children in the open condition (I-C). As a further test of need for visual information, boys and adults were tested in the closed (tunnel) condition with verbal KR, but the tunnel also was lifted to show where the car stopped, thus providing endpoint (visual) KR (III-A-2 and III-C-2). Boys in the tunnel condition (III-C-2) performed as well as boys in the open condition (III-C-1), with 6-year-old boys having higher error scores in both conditions than 8- and 10-year-old boys. Adults had the same mean score in both the open and closed condition (III-A-1, III-A-2, II-A), thus providing

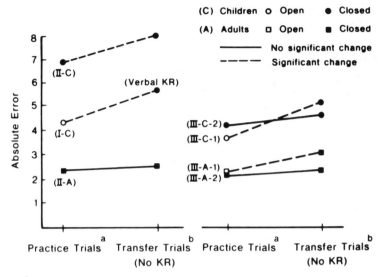

Figure 3. Mean absolute error in pushing a toy truck to a constant target in relation to visual conditions and KR for Experiments I, II, and III.

something of a baseline for adult performance in this task.

Boys established an appropriate performance level with limited (end-point) vision (III-C-2), but they needed more vision than adults and perhaps other assistance as well. Boys who practiced with limited vision (III-C-2) performed better than boys and girls who practiced in the closed condition (II-C). The task was changed in several ways that might have contributed to the improved performance of boys in Experiment III. Subjects in Experiments I and II pushed a block (mounted in a housing) as a means of pushing the truck, whereas subjects in Experiment III pushed the truck while holding it. Holding the truck might provide more body information to use when vision is not available. Pushing a block was selected initially to have force output as a simple and kines-thetically limited response, which may limit response sensitivity when vision is not available.

Subjects in Experiment II also had to listen to white noise which might be disruptive to children, a point discussed later in terms of attention. The track in Experiment III was padded to eliminate most of the truck-track noise. Subjects did not appear to be using noise cues.

The major consideration, in terms of need for vision, is the value of the endpoint (visual) KR to boys in Experiment III. Why would visual KR be useful when verbal KR was provided, granted that verbal KR did not seem useful with children in Experiment II? Visual (endpoint) KR was redundant information, particularly because the experimenter always pointed to the colorband where the truck stopped when telling a subject where the truck stopped.

If children need visual (endpoint) KR, we have identified another child-adult difference in that visual information has been shown as unnecessary for adults when provided verbal KR. The change in performance between the children in Experiments II and III is so striking that major developmental considerations may be involved. Also, experimenters must be cautioned that manipulation of visual conditions may produce qualitatively different pertubations in the motor control systems of children and adults, thus producing unexpected, perhaps unrecognized, and usually undesired results in a controlled experiment.

Maintain Performance. Mixed results for maintaining performance were obtained when children and adults transferred to different feedback and KR conditions. Both children and adults maintained performance on transfer when they practiced on a closed condition with no verbal KR. The practice-transfer result of the group in Experiment II using the tunnel is not relevant because they did not establish an adequate performance level to test their ability to maintain performance. Children and adults did not maintain performance when practicing in an open condition and transferring to a closed condition, a finding consistent with adults on lever positioning tasks (Adams, Gopher, & Lintern, 1977). Children practicing in the open condition could not maintain performance in the closed condition, even when provided with verbal KR.

An important finding is the similarity between children and adults in maintaining performance. Both decreased performance at a similar rate when transferring from open to closed. However, both maintained performance when practicing and transferring in the closed condition with no change in visual conditions. As qualifications, children needed additional visual input in practicing the closed condition (end-point KR) whereas adults in the same condition might maintain performance if provided verbal KR.

Vision may be disruptive in some situations, particularly when using attention or processing space that might be better used to process other information (Thomas & Stratton, 1977). Adults have been reported as attending to visual information when the visual information was not necessary; performance on the movement tasks was poorer in some visual conditions (Posner, Nessen, & Klein, 1976; Smyth, 1977). A related attentional consideration is the improvement in performance by directing attention to pertinent task demands. Subjects practicing in the closed condition were asked on each trial to estimate where the truck stopped before they were provided KR. It is possible that the performance estimate served to direct their attention to their kinesthetic sensations of how much force they just produced, which is the primary information available and needed during the transfer condition with no KR (Hogan & Yanowitz, 1978). If so, the inability of children using the tunnel in Experiment II to establish an appropriate level of performance during practice trials is an even more striking finding, because they also were asked for a performance estimate before receiving verbal KR.

Children and adults commonly watch their own body movements when first performing a new movement task. We look at our feet when first skiing instead of looking ahead to map the terrain and locate other people. We seem to need vision to cope with the basic problem of controlling our body movements, while putting aside the problems to be encountered once in motion. McCracken (1973) found that younger boys persisted in watching each circle as they alternated tapping between two circles, even when the circles were increased in size. Older boys soon learned to watch one circle and occasionally look at the other circle to check their performance. Looking at each circle serves to yoke the eyes to the hand movement which markedly limits the speed of the hand movement. The less mature and less experienced mover may need to use vision to monitor body movements, although using vision may limit or disrupt performance.

habit lag?

Conclusion

Several additional considerations need comment. First, children tend to be more variable in movement performance, thus limiting many of our experimental design and analysis approaches. However, we should recognize that children's variability is important and needs to be studied. Eckert and Eichorn (1977) suggest that changes in relative intraindividual variability may be a useful developmental measure. Second, careful thought must be given to the processing demands of each movement situation, because we use responses to a movement situation to infer processing operations. The work of Temple and Williams (1977) illustrates the concern for movement processing demands in relation to processing skills of children. A taxonomy is needed to conceptualize movement skill in an information processing framework.

Also needed are some general models of movement skill development to provide organization and direction for our research efforts. Many kinds of models are needed both to provide optional and competing arguments and to cover smaller and larger portions of the total problem. Wade (1976) suggests that we begin by using adult models of movement performance and learning, then adapt these models as needed. We also need to look at developmental models of perceptual-cognitive functioning to determine how such models might be useful for studying movement organization and control. Eventually, we must deal with change, how an individual develops from one way of solving movement problems to another way, whatever may be the nature of the change and the change agents. Our larger models of movement skill development may be quite radically different from our adult models, including the addition of a change dimension.

Schema theory, as proposed by Schmidt (1975) to explain adult skill learning, has been tested recently with children. Schemas are learned relationships among movement response specifications and movement outcomes such that a mover can plan and evaluate movement production, including the generation of novel or previously unpracticed movements. Throwing bean bags of different weights to varying target distances should enable the thrower to establish a schema or relationship for force needed to propel an unpracticed weight to an unpracticed distance. The recent tests of schema with children have been primarily to take advantage of children as more naive subjects in searching for the existance of schema and variables hypothesized to strengthen schema (Kelso & Norman, 1978; Kerr & Booth, 1978; Moxley, 1979). Children seem able to generate novel movements, presumably using schemas dependent upon amount and variability of practice. We now need to study how schema functions, both in adults and children, and to determine if schema functions differently in adults and children.

The neo-Piagetian model, which includes the concept of mental space or central computing space, also has been used recently in studying movement skill development (Sugden & Connell, 1979; Thomas, 1980). Structural and functional forms of mental space represent the maximum number of Piagetian schemes or patterns of behavior children can organize in a single act and the tendency to use available mental space, particularly the type of information used. The model is elaborated in various ways to trace the flow of information and the development of many components and operations.

Gerson and Thomas (1977) contrasted schema theory and the neo-Piagetian model in an interesting analysis of children's performance on a curvilinear repositioning task, and included comments and interpretations representing an information-processing perspective. Their paper deserves careful reading as perhaps the first major effort to identify a general model, even though a hybrid, for use in studying movement skill development. Also useful to read in this context is the recent paper of Connolly (1977) who discussed schema theory in relation to some of his ideas on movement skill development.

The development of processing functions is a central issue, both to learn how information is processed and how movement plans and commands are organized. Children seem to need more information and more time to process. They also seem to need more visual information and to use vision even when visual information is disruptive and limiting. We have a descriptive sense of children's information and time needs, but we have only fragmented experimental information available for us to process in seeking answers to our research questions. Educational implications cannot be very precise, but general guidelines are to analyze carefully the processing demands of a movement situation and arrange the educational setting to provide sufficient information and time.

Reference Notes

1. Carter, M.C. & Keogh, J.F. *A preliminary analysis of children's ability to detect and correct movement errors.* Paper presented at the International Congress in Physical Education, Trois Rivieres, Canada, June 1979.
2. Keogh, J.F., Burton, A.W., & Carter, M.C. *Vision and error detection in control of movement force: A developmental problem and an experimental caution.* Paper presented at the International Congress in Physical Education, Trois Rivieres, Canada, June 1979.

References

Adams, J.A., Gopher, D., & Lintern, G. Effects of visual and proprioceptive feedback on motor learning. *Journal of Motor Behavior*, 1977, **9** 11-22.

Atkinson, R.C. & Shiffrin, R.M. Human memory: A proposed system and its control processes. In K.W. Spence & J.T. Spence (Eds.), *The psychology of learning and motivation* (Vol. 2). New York: Academic Press, 1968.

Bard, C. & Fleury, M. Analysis of visual search activity during sport problem situations. *Journal of Human Movement Studies,* 1976, **3**, 214-222.

Bogaritz, R.S. & Witte, K.L. On the locus of stimulus familiarity effect in young children. *Journal of Experimental Child Psychology,* 1966, **4**, 317-331.

Brown, A.L. The development of memory: Knowing, knowing about knowing, knowing how to know. In H.W. Reese (Ed.), *Advances in child development and bahavior* (Vol. 10). New York: Academic Press, 1975.

Bruner, J.S. Organization of early skilled action. *Child Development,* 1973, **44**, 1-11.

Butterworth, G. & Hicks, L. Visual proprioception and postural stability in infancy: A developmental study. *Perception,* 1977, **6**, 255-262.

Clark, J.E. & Kelso, J.A.S. (Eds.). *The development of movement control and coordination.* New York: Wiley, in press.

Connolly, K. (Ed.). *Mechanisms of motor skill development.* New York: Academic Press, 1970.

Connolly, K. Factors influencing the learning of manual skills by young children. In R.A. Hinde & J. Stevenson-Hinde (Eds.), *Constraints on learning.* New York: Academic Press, 1973.

Connolly, K. The nature of motor skill development. *Journal of Human Movement Studies,* 1977, **3**, 128-143.

Connolly, K. & Elliott, J. The evolution and ontogeny of hand function. In N.B. Jones (Ed.), *Ethological studies of child behavior.* Cambridge, England: Cambridge University Press, 1972.

Dorfman, P.W. Timing and anticipation: A developmental perspective. *Journal of Motor Behavior,* 1977, **9**, 67-79.

Eckert, H.M. & Eichorn, D.H. Developmental variability in reaction time. *Child Development,* 1977, **48**, 452-458.

Elliott, J.M. & Connolly, K.J. Hierarchical structure in skill development. In K.J. Connolly & J.S. Bruner (Eds.), *The growth of competence.* New York: Academic Press, 1974.

Fitts, P.M. The information capacity of the human motor system in controlling the amplitude of movement. *Journal of Experimental Psychology,* 1954, **47**, 381-391.

Foellinger, D.B. & Trabasso, T. Seeing, hearing, and doing: A developmental study of memory for actions. *Child Development,* 1977, **48**, 1482-1489.

Fowler, W. The role of cognitive learning in motor development. In G.E. Uhlig & M. Krantz (Eds.), *Psychomotor development in preschool handicapped children.* Milwaukee: Vazquez Associates, 1975.

Gallagher, J.D. & Thomas, J.R. Effects of varying post-KR intervals upon children's motor performance. *Journal of Motor Behavior,* 1980, **12**, 41-46.

Gentile, A.M. & Nacson, J. Organization processes in motor control. In J.F. Keogh & R.S. Hutton (Eds.), *Exercise and sport sciences reviews* (Vol. 4). Santa Barbara, CA: Journal Publishing Affiliates, 1976.

Gerson, R.F. & Thomas, J.R. Schema theory and practice variability within a neo-piagetian framework. *Journal of Motor Behavior,* 1977, **9**, 127-134.

Griffin, N.S. & Keogh, J.F. A model for movement confidence. In J.E. Clark & J.A.S. Kelso (Eds.), *The development of movement control and coordination.* New York: Wiley, in press.

Haywood, K.M. Eye movement during coincidence-anticipation performance. *Journal of Motor Behavior,* 1977, **9**, 313-318.

Hogan, J.C. & Hogan, R. Organization of early skilled action: Some comments. *Child Development* 1975, **46**, 233-236.

Hogan, J.C. & Yanowitz, B.A. The role of verbal estimates of movement error in ballistic skill acquisition. *Journal of Motor Behavior,* 1978, **10**, 133-138.

Kelso, J.A.S. & Norman, P.E. Motor schema formation in children. *Developmental Psychology,* 1978, **14**, 153-156.

Keogh, J.F. The study of movement skill development. *Quest* (Monograph), 1977, **28**, 76-88.

Keogh, J.F. Movement outcomes as conceptual guidelines in the perceptual-motor maze. *Journal of Special Education,* 1978, **12**, 321-330.

Kerr, B. Sequential predictability effects on initiation time and movement time for adults and children. *Journal of Motor Behavior,* 1979, **11**, 71-79.

Kerr, R. Movement control and maturation in elementary-grade children. *Perceptual and Motor Skills,* 1975, **41**, 151-154.

Kerr, R. & Booth, B. Specific and varied practice of motor skill. *Perceptual and Motor Skills,* 1978, **46**, 395-401.

Kopp, C.B. Motor concomitants of early cognitive development. In M. Bornstein & W. Kessen (Eds.), *Psychological development from infancy.* Hillsdale, NJ: Erlbaum, 1979.

Lee, D.N. & Lishman, J.R. Visual proprioceptive control of stance. *Journal of Human Movement Studies,* 1975, **1**, 87-95.

Magill, R.A., Ash, M.J., & Smoll, F.L. (Eds.). *Children in sport: A contemporary anthology.* Champign, IL: Human Kinetics Publishers, 1978.

McCracken, H. *Continuity and discontinuity in boys' eye movement strategies.* Unpublished master's thesis, University of California, Los Angeles, 1973.

Meyers, P.I. & Hammill, D.D. *Methods for learning disorders* (2 nd ed.). New York: Wiley, 1976.

Moxley, S.E. Schema: The variability of practice hypothesis. *Journal of Motor Behavior*, 1979, **11**, 65-70.

Newell, K.M. Knowledge of results and motor learning. J.F. Keogh & R.S. Hutton (Eds.), *Exercise and sport sciences reviews* (Vol. 4). Santa Barbara, CA: Journal Publishing Affiliates, 1976.

Newell, K.M. & Kennedy, J.A. Knowledge of results and children's motor learning. *Developmental Psychology*, 1978, **14**, 531-536.

Noble, C.E., Baker, B.L., & Jones, T.A. Age and sex parameters in psychomotor learning. *Perceptual and Motor Skills* 1964, **19**, 935-945.

Posner, M.I., Nessen, M.J., & Klein, R.M. Visual dominance: An information-processing account of its origins and significance. *Psychological Review*, 1976, **83**, 157-171.

Poulton, E.C. On prediction of skilled movements. *Psychological Bulletin*, 1957, **54**, 467-468.

Ridenour, M. Influence of object size, speed, and direction on the perception of a moving object. *Research Quarterly*, 1974, **45**, 293-301.

Ridenour, M.V. Influence of object size, speed, direction, height, and distance on interception of a moving object. *Research Quarterly*, 1977, **43**, 138-142.

Salmoni, A.W. & Pascoe, C. Fitts' reciprocal tapping task: A developmental study. In G.C. Roberts & K.M. Newell (Eds.), *Psychology of motor behavior and sport*. Champaign, IL: Human Kinetics Publishers, 1978.

Schmidt, R.A. A schema theory of discrete motor learning. *Psychological Review*, 1975, **82**, 225-260.

Sharp, R.H. & Whiting, H.T.A. Information processing and eye movement behavior in a ball catching skill. *Journal of Human Movement Studies*, 1975, **1**, 124-131.

Smoll, F.L. Development of rhythmic ability in response to selected tempos. *Perceptual and Motor Skills*, 1974, **39**, 767-772. (a)

Smoll, F.L. Development of spatial and temporal elements of rhythmic ability. *Journal of Motor Behavior*, 1974, **6**, 53-58. (b)

Smoll, F.L. Variability in development of spatial and temporal elements of rhythmic ability. *Perceptual and Motor Skills*, 1975, **40**, 140.

Smoll, F.L. & Smith, R.E. (Eds.). *Psychological perspectives in youth sports*. New York: Halstead, 1978.

Smyth, M.M. The effect of visual guidance on the acquisition of a simple motor task. *Journal of Motor Behavior*, 1977, **9**, 275-284.

Stubbs, D.F. What the eye tells the hand. *Journal of Motor Behavior*,

1976, **8**, 43-58.

Sugden, D.A. Visual motor short term memory in educationally subnormal boys. *British Journal of Educational Psychology*, 1978, **48**, 330-339.

Sugden, D.A. Movement speed in children. *Journal of Motor Behavior*, 1980, **12**, 125-132.

Sugden, D.A. & Connell, R.A. Information processing in children's motor skills. *Physical Education Review*, 1979, **2**, 123-140.

Surwillo, W.W. Developmental changes in the speed of information processing. *Journal of Psychology*, 1977, **96**, 97-102.

Temple, I.G. & Williams, H.G. Rate and level of learning as functions of information-processing characteristics of the learner and the task. *Journal of Motor Behavior*, 1977, **9**, 179-192.

Thomas, J.R. Acquisition of motor skills: Information processing differences between children and adults. *Research Quarterly*, 1980, **51**, 158-173.

Thomas, J.R. & Bender, P.R. A developmental explanation for children's motor behavior: A neo-piagetian interpretation. *Journal of Motor Behavior*, 1977, **9**, 81-93.

Thomas, J.R. & Moon, D.H. Measuring motor rhythmic ability in children. *Research Quarterly*, 1976, **47**, 20-32.

Thomas, J.R. & Stratton, R.K. Effect of divided attention on children's rhythmic response. *Research Quarterly*, 1977, **48**, 428-435.

Wade, M.G. Developmental motor learning. In J.F. Keogh & R.S. Hutton, (Eds.), *Exercise and sport sciences reviews* (Vol. 4). Santa Barbara, CA: Journal Publishing Affiliates, 1976.

Wallace, S.A., Newell, K.M., & Wade, M.G. Decision and response times as a function of movement difficulty in preschool children. *Child Development*, 1978, **49**, 509-512.

Whiting, H.T.A. & Cockerill, I.M. The development of a simple ballistic skill with and without visual control. *Journal of Motor Behavior*, 1972, **4**, 155-162.

Wickens, C.D. Temporal limits of human information processing: A developmental study. *Psychological Bulletin*, 1974, **81**, 739-755.

Williams, H.G. Perceptual-motor development in children. In C.B. Corbin (Ed.), *A textbook of motor development.* Dubuque, IA: Brown, 1973.

Zaichkowsky, L.D. The development of perceptual motor sequencing ability. *Journal of Motor Behavior*, 1974, **6**, 255-261.

Time Passages in Adapted Physical Education

13

G.D. Broadhead

Although a scholarly approach can be expected in describing and commenting upon most aspects of the discipline of physical education, it may not be possible to do so for adapted physical education. In other areas there is a wealth of quality literature, indicating the amount and nature of the involvement of colleagues to unearth information and explanations about human movement. But the delineation of adapted physical education is as yet unclear, and adapted physical education is still not considered by most people to merit the detailed and academic analysis possible in other topics of this book. However, given a recent upsurge of interest and activity in adapted physical education, it seems reasonable to expect that radical change in this position will occur over the next few years.

It is likely that the rather sluggish development and low level sophistication of adapted physical education, and how seriously it is being studied, is due in large measure to the complexity of the terminology used to describe those who receive adapted physical education. There is perhaps additional confusion when one considers the vastly differing backgrounds presented by professionals and academicians: researchers, teachers, community workers, physicians and the like use terms and concepts with little reference to each other. This variability exists in physical education literature, as it does in literature dealing with atypical behaviors—movement or otherwise. Articles by Kenyon (Note 1, Note 2), Heber (1962), and Armstrong (1976) serve to support such views.

Features of Adapted Physical Education

Adapted physical education, neither a discipline nor yet a describable subdiscipline, is caught in the crossfire of two dynamic areas of interest. But over 25 years or so, a path has steadily been cleared for upgrading the amount, intensity, and quality of the work. A useful starting point is to discuss something of the nature of adapted physical education. Currently available and widely used in universities and colleges in North America and other countries are textbooks which compactly describe adapted physical education concerns. Among many are those by Arnheim, Auxter, and Crowe (1977), Fait (1978), and Winnick (1979). A profitable exercise for students is to compare and contrast the differing notions of adapted physical education elucidated in these as well as other texts (Clarke & Clarke, 1963; Daniels & Davies, 1975; Moran & Kalakian, 1974). However, one definition which may help in examining adapted physical education is that of Sherrill (1976) who considers its major concern is with children who fail. Sherrill stresses the importance of adopting a scientific approach in analyzing movement, so that difficulties can be noted and effectively dealt with while an appropriate self-concept can be retained in the child.

This definition is important because it describes, almost in a nutshell, some of the reasons why the development of adapted physical education has been so slow. For it has clearly been difficult for us to accurately and comprehensively isolate and identify difficulties in the psychomotor domain, bearing in mind that descriptions of the domain have been available for critique only recently; the work of Harrow (1972) is a valuable example of this. Likewise, our understanding of and ability to develop an appropriate and workable pedagogy has been limited by time factors, and because those who rush into print with any type of solution are often subjected to what can be excessive criticism. If problems in adapted physical education cannot be remedied with any surety, then the whole area of study is open to question and debate.

For Sherrill to have commented upon a "preservation of ego-strength," however, brings into focus the increasing acceptance, by colleagues in physical education, of the importance of nonmovement parameters in the whole notion of eliciting and measuring behavior change over time. It should also be noted that what is being described here is an association of circumstances, for the discussion of cause and effect is fraught with problems. Many readers might find it intriguing that Sherrill prefaced her definition with comments on the concept of failure. It would be appropriate for students to read the first few sections of the book, for they provide some stark revelations of the experiences of failure which for many of our children occur daily in both adapted and regular physical education. It seems clear that some of our teachers are unfeeling and inept, providing direction for those responsible for personnel preparation programs.

In considering the idea of failure, it is important to realize that an explicit standard of acceptable behavior or performance must exist. Without it, the size and detailed characteristics of the population which fails depends upon changing views of good or poor scores, approved or non-approved skills and movement patterns, or well-adjusted or maladjusted behaviors. At this point it seems particularly suitable to stress the role of the teachers or researchers who, regardless of quality, skill, care, or knowledge, also help to determine our clientele. While it is not appropriate to "gloat over the failings of our own clay " (Cooke, 1973), a discussion about standards allows for learning and professional maturing to occur.

Many thousands of colleagues spend a considerable amount of time developing, assessing, and scoring aspects of our physical education curriculum. But making decisions which cause types or levels of performance to be at risk or not and which place children into one or another education environment is of critical importance; it is a responsibility not to be shirked.

A Traditional Route to Adapted Physical Education

I describe two routes into adapted physical education: First is the physical education route, which suggests that adapted physical education is part of regular physical education, being an added portion for a few students. It is not easy to trace the evolution of this type of adapted physical education, and indeed there has not been sufficient depth of study using suitable methodology in the literature for an accurate and exhausive picture to be presented.

But if adapted physical education is a part of regular physical education, then its current position can be accounted for by at least some of the same forces and influences which have shaped regular physical education. Thus, the work of the French philosopher, Rousseau, is remembered for its belief that natural exercise, play, and organized games were as important to an educational philosophy as were academic subjects (Rousseau, 1885/1962). Itard (1801/1962) used a medical and educational regimen of systemmatic observation and treatment (diagnosis and prescription) in the daily lives of low functioning individuals. His student Seguin (1866/1907) developed in France a form of sensory-motor training which had a profound influence on thought and practice for a number of years. Indeed, these influences may well have provided Gutsmuths (see Leonard, 1947; Van Dalen & Bennett, 1971) with ideas for producing, in 18th and 19th century Germany, a type of physical education which was largely outdoors, based upon anatomical and physiological principles, and practised on self-devised apparatus. Another major, relevant thrust came from Scandinavia, with Ling in particular, where a system of corrective gymnastics based on a thorough knowledge of both the structure and function of the body was developed. This system could well be considered to be the precursor of present techniques of adapted physical education (Leonard, 1947; Weston, 1962). Better known in this country are well-documented developments in this area associated with Sargent, Hetherington, Rathbone, Daniels, and others (Fait, 1978; Leonard, 1947; Van Dalen & Bennett, 1971; Weston, 1962).

The English have also influenced adapted physical education in the last century as well as this one with major team sports and games developed largely in the elitist private schools, supposedly bringing about the building of good character (McAdam, 1962). However, it should not be forgotten that the massive change in physical education thought and practice was brought about by the introduction of the educational gymnastics or basic movement approach to programming in the elementary schools. Remarkably this development can be partially attributed to the British Government Board of Education with its variety of advisory documents (British Government Board of Education, 1933, 1953; British Government Department of Education and Science, 1972.) The range and benefits of these activities expanded the content of physical education, but at the same time, they also expanded the range of experiences of failure in some children. Above all has been the work of Rudolf Laban (1948) in England, with a movement system emphasizing the components of time, space, force, and flow.

What message is there to be culled for those in adapted physical education as a part of regular physical education? Perhaps it is the insight it provides for those who see in our textual materials references to activity as being adaptive, corrective, developmental, rehabilitative, remedial, therapeutic and so on; adapted physical education clearly has its problems of terminology too. It would be a useful simulation exercise for students to imagine a situation where something is being adapted, where something is therapeutic or rehabilitative or, of course, where someone is being educated. What is in a name? Are these words or concepts synonomous? Can we just brush away these difficulties by assigning to them the usual semantic difference?

Adapted physical education in the form being described, provides mostly for children with orthopedic, crippling, postural, and respiratory types of conditions, a feature which can be quite clearly seen from examining many textbooks (if the amount of space devoted to these conditions is a valid criterion). This type of adapted physical education exists in many of today's schools. But is is easy to forecast that it will diminish in focus and in size in the near future, particularly because of the interrelatedness of adapted and regular physical education. For example, one could point to the improvements which have occurred in the training and education of our physical education teachers. In addition, the tendency to separate safety, health, athletics, and coaching from physical education has been increased, enabling the inclusion of a greater depth of anatomy, physiology, and learning courses to be in an undergraduate curricula. Likewise, there has been the move to provide students with the skills to cope with a wider range of within-class problems as well as an understanding of within-child performance variability.

In some states, improved pupil-teacher ratios in the public schools and the existence of helpful equipment has been developed. And the thrust to provide improved physical education at the preschool and elementary school stages is also a potent force in helping to transform the physical education situation and to increase the number of children who can benefit from and cope with regular physical activity.

The New Adapted Physical Education

The second route to adapted physical education has stolen the limelight. It has got us all sprinting, for in this adapted physical education one cannot afford to jog. It may have been Odgen Nash who said of a similar situation that it has "got us galloping away in all directions." This second route is the special education way into adapted physical education, and like the first described route, is also concerned with failure; however, it places special emphasis on failure, for to be in adapted physical education via special education is in many ways to be placed outside the confines of regular education.

Hence, two pieces of education legislation appear of immediate relevance (U.S. Congress, 1973, 1975). First is the Rehabilitation Act of 1973 (Public Law 93-112), as amended in 1974 (Public Law 93-516), although its rules and regulations were only finalized in 1977 (U.S. Office of Education, 1977a). Section 504 states that "no otherwise qualified handicapped person shall on the basis of handicap, be excluded participation in, be denied the benefits of, or otherwise be subjected to discrimination under any program or which receives or benefits from Federal financial assistance" (paragraph 84.4 [a]). Although there has been widespread publicity given to the importance of providing physical access and facilities, the availability of programs may well prove to be a problem to tax us all in the future.

The second public law is P.L. 94-142 (The Education for All Handicapped Children Act, 1975), although its rules and regulations are also very recent (U.S. Office of Education, 1977b).

Some of the ramifications of this law and its interpretations at the state level will be discussed in more detail later (and should also be topics for detailed discussion with students undergoing training courses in adapted physical education). But it is necessary here to point out that children whose assessed impairment is of educational significance, are considered handicapped if they meet the criteria for one of the categories of handicap specified in the Regulations (U.S. Office of Education, 1977b). These categories, or groups of complex symptoms are: deaf, deaf-blind, hard of hearing, mentally retarded, multihandicapped, orthopedically impaired, other health impaired, seriously emotionally disturbed, specific learning disabled, speech impaired, and visually handicapped. What can be immediately noted are the psychological-medical terms and concepts inherent in the categories, and the obvious lack of education terminology being employed.

According to the Public Law, each child identified as handicapped must receive direct special education services and may warrant supportive, related services as well. Physical education is the only curriculum area specifically named in the legal definition of special education (U.S. Office of Education, 1977b, paragraph 121a.14). All handicapped children must have physical education, but the significant question concerns the type of program which suits each child's unique needs. This may be the regular arrangements his or her nonhandicapped peers receive or an adapted program considered necessary because of the many weaknesses in an assessed profile of motor abilities, skills, and patterns. A third type of program is a likely necessity for some handicapped students. Because the motor profile contains both marked weaknesses and relative strengths, this program combines elements of both regular and adapted physical education.

Current Forces and the Future

This civil rights legislation for handicapped children provides them with a new deal. But just what brought about the need to provide physical education for all handicapped children, even if it is not provided for all regular children (Martin, 1977), is an issue which all students of adapted physical education should be acquainted with. A brief glimpse of a number of research studies shows why adapted physical educators are currently so energetic in developing and exercising their professional expertise. These studies indicate significant evolutionary developments and contemporary issues, as well as indicators for future action. Such literature represents the life and spirit of those who work in adapted physical education (Dobie, 1944).

Currently, the most significant study published in this area is the research of James Oliver (1958). With a thought-provoking title, "The Effect of Physical Conditioning Exercises and Activities on the Mental Characteristics of Educationally Sub-normal Boys," the study included an experimental and a control group of mildly mentally retarded boys (using U.S. terminology). The experimental group was provided with almost three hours of physical education each day for ten weeks, while the control group had its usual physical education program which was composed of two indoor gymnasium lessons and a sports lesson each week. A number of tests was administered prior to and at the end of the experimental program. Not unexpectedly, motor performance differences which favored the experimental group were apparent. However, changes in the intelligence of the subjects were of the same order and the same direction. And more subjectively assessed, but showing a similar type of improvement were parameters of social and personality development.

Often overlooked by students of Oliver's work are the results concerning the school achievement of the boys of the experimental group. They received almost 3 hours of physical education instruction each day, and therefore, the number of hours devoted to academic aspects of their total program was substantially decreased during the 10-week period of time. If behavior improvements were to be sought by introducing new curriculum components, then diminished performance might have occurred when the reverse position existed. However, Oliver reported that no such decreases were measured.

The question of why nonmotor behavior change was measured remains a difficulty. In his paper, Oliver specificially indicated that the boys had a feeling of achievement and increased confidence which appeared to accompany their involvement in the experimental program. Their participation in successful activities and their realization that the focus of attention was upon them was a clear reference to the Hawthorne phenomenon (Roethlisberger & Dickson, 1947) which is widely written about, yet seldom adequately incorporated into the experimental research design of studies of this type. This experimental variable and a general understanding that factors and influences over and above programmatic content are powerful need to be studied by those in adapted physical education.

A range of problems can be found in Oliver's work, particularly if the evaluation of his work in the late 1950s is placed under the scrutiny of our present day knowledge and expertise. The study involved only a small number of subjects, no girls, only educable mentally retarded children, no contrasting handicapping condition, and only subjects at the adolescent stage. Likewise, the broad range of physical education activities—remedial, sporting, fitness and so forth—makes it impossible to know which aspect or aspects were associated with the measured behavior changes of the experimental group. Three hours of physical education may be thought unrealistic, an undue upset to the overall curriculum rather than a probable benefit. Other defects in the study are that Oliver used an inappropriate gain-score analysis and that he ignored the influence of Hawthorne phenomenon in his research design. Yet, even with such difficulties, the work was not rejected, but rather it appears to have provoked others to investigate that general research question, and brief comment about three additional studies indicates increased sophistication in this area as a result.

A study by Corder (1966), with a title similar to Oliver's stressed other aspects of the research. Although most of the reported results closely mirrored the earlier work, two differences need comment. First, is the time element; in place of Oliver's 3 hours a day for 10 weeks, Corder substituted 1 hour a day for 4 weeks. This raises the whole question as to the importance of the duration of this or other experiments or of adapted physical education as a whole, for it seems unlikely that such short term magic-pill approaches to eliciting behavior change in children can be supported currently in research of this type. Corder also attempted to control for and measure the Hawthorne influence. Instead of following Oliver and having a control group which did not receive the experimental program as well as a group which received not only the posited advantages of the program content, but also the focus of special attention, Corder included three groups. One group was the control group, while the other two groups both had special programs which differed as to physical education or nonphysical education content. With three groups of educable mentally retarded (EMR) adolescents boys, the experimental or physical education group received a physical fitness program, whereas the other special experimental group was allowed to carry the equipment, measure and time activities, and so forth. Many of the reported results did resemble those of Oliver, but a significant question can be asked about the two special programs. The reason why the results favored the fitness group over the "officials" group may have been due to the uneven quality of the two programs. With the thrust of the research being on physical fitness, it may have been perceived by the "officials" that they were in a position of secondary importance. It is suggested that in research where experimental programs are being contrasted, program quality must be equivalent. Again, the extent to which behavior change can be elicited and assessed with any surety is questionable.

A study by Solomon and Pangle (1967) further developed our understanding of the assessability of behavior change, involving small numbers of adolescent boys in a 7 week, 45 minutes a day program. From this research two points are significant. First, Solomon and Pangle, although reporting results which were similar in some ways to those of Oliver and of Corder, failed to report the differential changes in intelligence test results noted before. However, they also reported that the children were administered tests during a period of routine school district assessment and were administered a large number of psychological tests during the duration of a few days. It is important to stress here the need to obtain data from children under conditions which are most likely to produce maximum performance levels.

The second interesting feature of the research relates to added data collected six weeks after the actual end of the experimental program, when the children were tested again for their physical fitness. Solomon and Pangle (1967) noted some permanence in the score improvements achieved between the pre- and post-testing, and also that no regression occurred resulting in old pre-test performance levels being achieved.

These results raise again an issue which has been dealt with in a number of other studies. For example, Doll (1941), writing about an all-inclusive definition of mental deficiency, believed that permanent behavior change for such people was not possible. But inasmuch as a training program might bring about change, such change wrote Doll, was only likely to exist for the duration of the special training. Additionally, the large amount of research on intervention programming is relevant too, for although it is clear that short term behavior changes have been reported in numerous studies, the permanence of such changes has not been well demonstrated (Smith & Bissel, 1970; Yinger, Ikeda, Laycock, & Cutter, 1977).

Several aspects of this type of research were developed and refined by Broadhead (1968), (also found in Rarick and Broadhead [1968] and Rarick, Dobbins, and Broadhead [1976]). First, the teaching program lasted for over 6 months rather than for a few weeks, and involved girls and boys of two chronological age levels at the elementary school stage. The subjects were almost 500 EMRs and learning disabled children (called minimally brain-injured at the time of the study), and were taught by special education teachers with appropriate in-service training and on-site supervision and guidance. In addition to the traditional type of control group which did not receive any change in its daily curriculum, there were three different special experimental programs: two physical education and one visual arts program. The special instruction took place every day for approximately 35 minutes, which in the light of studies reported earlier, seemed a realistic duration for young children. The following three basic research questions were asked:

1. Do differences exist in the behaviors of classes of children who were included in a specially designed program of either physical education or art (used as a nongross movement program), compared with those who pursued the usual instructional program?

2. Do differences in these behaviors exist between classes of children who were included in the physical education programs, compared with those who were in a visual arts program?

3. Do differences in these behaviors exist between classes of children who participated in a PE program which was highly individualized, compared with those in a more group-oriented program?

By using standardized tests at the beginning and at the end of the experiment, the motor, strength, intellectual, social, and emotional characteristics were evaluated. Data analysis used multivariate and univariate covariance procedures and the following results were reported:

1. Students who took part in any of the three specially designed experimental programs were subject to significantly greater positive changes in movement, intellectual, and emotional behavior than students who were denied the opportunity.

2. Of the three special programs, the PE programs demonstrated a superior role in modifying movement behavior, the art program indicated a superior role in modifying emotional behavior, and both types of programs elicited improvements in the intellectual behavior of the students.

3. The physical education program which was oriented towards the individual rather than the group was more successful in eliciting positive behavior change in the students.

Bearing in mind the brevity of the description of the research, it is believed that the findings of this physical education study are significant. In highlighting not only demonstrated improved movement behavior but also improved behavior in nonmovement parameters, the association (not a causative relationship) of physical education program participation and positive behavior change was impressive. The importance of an individualized approach to providing physical education instruction can be considered paramount in these days of individualized education program (IEP) writing.

Not surprisingly, this type of research has been recently attempted with more severely handicapped children. Such physical education programming is of particular importance in the light of the priorities noted in the 1975 Education Act, and it remains an understandable priority with the United States Department of Education, Office of Special Education. Space prevents elaboration of any such studies but what has been reported are behavior changes not previously thought possible in these children. An unheralded but high quality report by Widdop, Barton, Cleary, Proyer, and Wall (1969) can be forwarded as an outstanding example of such work, and papers by Auxter (1971) and Webb (1969) should also be examined by interested students.

It is important to point to a question which remains still unresolved in the preceding studies, one which hinders adapted physical education specialists from eliciting behavior change in children. The question of the permanence of any gains which occur in direct association with the experimental conditions needs to be examined under stringent research conditions.

Concerning further developments, three sets of forces which may have influenced the passing of the legislative mandates, are worthy of note. First is the development and use of approaches to eliciting behavior change, sometimes called perceptual-motor, visual-motor, or neurophysiological, and so on. Among others, one associates with these approaches, the names of Barsch (1965, 1968), Cratty (1969, 1970, 1971), Delacato (1963, 1966), Doman, Delacato and Doman (1963), Frostig (1970, 1973), Getman (1965), and Kephart (1971). The work of these scholars could be in itself a study of some substance, worthy of specific analysis by students in adapted physical education. All the programs advocated have been both widely discussed and subject to widespread controversy and often destructive criticism. Much of this has undoubtedly been caused by the use of difficult terminology and not always approved experimental procedures. There is much doubt concerning the viability of an approach to effecting improved behaviors in handicapped children when there appear to be difficulties with the experimental procedures. Nevertheless, the literature in adapted physical education is all the richer for these ideas and investigations. Indeed in the current Zeitgeist, those with courage could do well to examine and develop these approaches, for they appear to have a diagnostic and prescriptive methodology, which is now in vogue, considered sensible, and required by our education legislation. It may have been that among professionals there has been unwillingness to see the many possibilities posed by the research cited above.

A second group of studies has provided rather full information on the movement characteristics, both gross and fine, of boys and girls over a range of chronological age and handicapping conditions. These studies, mostly cross-sectional by design, provide much information considered fundamental to an understanding of present-day adapted physical education. Studies by Broadhead (1972, 1974, 1975), Clausen (1966), Hayden (1964), and Rarick and colleagues (1967, 1970, 1976, 1977) have shown that there are marked performance deficits in handicapped children. However, the structure of motor abilities in handicapped and nonhandicapped children is essentially the same (Rarick, Dobbins, & Broadhead, 1976; Rarick & McQuillan, 1977). It is clear that the work of G. Lawrence Rarick has been largely responsible for such advances in our knowledge. A feature of Rarick's work has been the careful planning of the procedures for data collection. The most conducive environment possible helps to ensure valid responses from educationally handicapped children who, by definition, often demonstrate great variability in test performance.

A third influence in obtaining changed legislation has been a number of studies, three of which are mentioned here. The work of Brace (1968), a paper by the Physical Education Association of Great Britain (formerly the Ling Association) (1969), and a report by Rarick, Widdop, and Broadhead (1967), have all indicated that handicapped children seldom have been able to receive the type, quality, and range of physical education programs afforded to children in the regular grades. Pooling the ideas in these reports may have produced a coordinated thrust for a governmental lobby of such influential proportions that an accommodation of the Federal Law resulted. The concerns of individuals working with handicapped children, the wealth of documented research evidence, the influence of professional associations, and perhaps the hand of The Joseph P. Kennedy Jr. Foundation together provided this success.

The importance of the Public Law, and the ways in which it is being implemented cannot be stressed too much. It has clearly overtaken many of the developments which were underway before it was passed and has gone beyond what many have even dreamed of. The demands of the law are such that it can confidently be forecasted that our whole profession will be affected in some way. For the researcher, the personal or ideosyncratic approach to research may have to be replaced, for the Public Law requires a vast range of researchable topics of immediate importance. While an examination of the Federal Law and its state counterpart is necessary for students in adapted physical education, the central focus of the law should be the process which results in children receiving special education (which includes physical education).

Prior to the child's placement, an IEP must be developed and written down. This describes many aspects of the special and maybe the related services (physical therapy, for example) the child is to receive. One view is that since physical education is the only direct service mentioned in the definition of special education, it should be discussed in the IEP development meeting—at least in terms of whether a regular, adapted, or mixed program is required to meet the unique needs of the child in an educational environment which is as free of restrictions as possible. If adapted physical education is suggested, then annual goals or expected attainments, short-term instructional objectives, the frequency and regularity of the program, and appropriate time-lines are to be included. And the IEP must be reviewed and probably revised at least every year (exact details should be examined in the Federal Regulation [(1977b, paragraph 121a.346)].

Long before placement is even discussed, an evaluation of children's psychomotor abilities should be part of the sophisticated individual evaluation completed by the multi-disciplinary process. However, it is unlikely that this occurs for more than a handful of children. Although this type of evaluation program exists in a local Louisiana Parish (District) with the full cooperation of the team leaders, in general the leaders — psychologists or educational consultants—most likely do not see a need for it. Perhaps these people consider it very simple to determine which children have physical education needs outside the compass of the regular program. This is reminiscent of the Supervisor of Special Education in one of the largest school districts in the country, who declared that such an evaluation is unnecessary, as if one could tell just by looking at them. It is apparent that adapted physical education personnel must persuade others—with supportive evidence—of the importance of an evaluation program. There is an immediate need to sensitize regular and special education classroom teachers to looking for and understanding something of movement problems. A checklist approach would be helpful for many teachers.

When one considers the ramifications of the requirements of the PL 94-142 Regulations (U.S. Office of Education 1977b), including the need for nondiscriminating tests validated for specific purposes (paragraph 121a 532), then the research implications are substantial and longterm. The law has set our research priorities in adapted physical education.

Though much more could be written about the Public Law as it affects handicapped children's physical education as well as the need for high quality, large-scale research, one topic is paramount above others: mainstreaming. A common, and mistaken, belief is that the term mainstreaming exists in the Public Law. Children must be educated in an environment which approximates the norm as much as possible; deviations need to be explained, documented, and overcome (U.S. Office of Education [1977b, paragraph 121a.550-551]). Since the vast majority of handicapped children are only mildly affected, it is clear that the focus of this issue lies with ways of integrating the mildly handicapped into the educational milieu of their nonhandicapped peers (Broadhead, 1979). However, to release the restrictive environment of the residential institution, for example, is an aim of enormous consequence to severely handicapped children and also to the profession. This type of research in physical education is scant and only in the early stages of investigation (Stein, 1976). Pilot investigations by Broadhead (Note 1), Rarick (Note 2), and Sherrill (Note 3) are currently examining different facets of providing handicapped children physical education in the least restrictive environment.

There are numerous noncompliant and sometimes bizarre situations occurring throughout the country, but one of great significance and concern to adapted physical educators is the extent to which physical and/or occupational therapists (providers of related services) are being used to teach physical education and assess which children can or should take part in adapted physical education. While this is strictly a situation of noncompliance, it poses difficulties to the physical education profession in its quest to define its role. This is particularly evident when the law presses physical educators to work with children who are younger and more severely handicapped than these professionals have been used to working with.

Whatever the difficulties attached to the compliance issue, the law, by including physical education in its definition of special education, has caused a quickening of effort, a quality of work, and the cooperative working relationship of administrators, educators, and researchers in a happy blend of theory and application. These people must pursuade the few in universities, schools, and offices who delay or avoid the challenge to be concerned and involved.

Conclusion

There are some general messages for the profession: Think, for a moment, of the future likelihood of a physical education plan being drawn up for each regular child before the start of the school year, subject to a midyear and end-of-year assessment. Think of the individual traits of each child being taken into account, lessening the haziness which the umbrella effect causes when groups of children are treated all the same. The Public Law may induce us to tidy up our Professional Act. It demands for handicapped children what is not always provided for regular children; a well-rounded physical education curriculum which is properly evaluated and monitored. Regular physical educators must not lose this opportunity to meet the rights of the majority. They too must follow the sounds of the drum (White, 1979).

Over the years the researcher and the practitioner have had much freedom of action, but the developments which have occurred recently have brought constraints, control, and quality. In this way, adapted physical education and regular physical education may come of age. Colleagues could even treat the study of atypical behavior in children as meriting consideration. Indeed, adapted physical education may already have acquired some new Discipline.

Reference Notes

1. Kenyon, G.S. *Do we really know what we are doing?* Paper presented at the State University of New York, Brockport, November 1967. (Available from Geoffrey Broadhead, Louisiana State University.)
2. Kenyon, G.S. *On the conceptualization of sub-disciplines within an academic discipline dealing with human movement.* Paper presented to the 71st annual meeting of the National College Physical Education Association, Houston, 1968. (Available from Geoffrey Broadhead, Louisiana State University.)
3. Broadhead, G.D. *A restriction-relief paradigm in physical education for handicapped children.* Paper presented at a meeting of the American Alliance for Health, Physical Education, Recreation and Dance, Detroit, April, 1980.
4. Rarick, G.L. *Reverse mainstreaming in physical education: An evaluation.* Paper presented at a meeting of the American Alliance for Health, Physical Education, Recreation and Dance, Detroit, April, 1980.
5. Sherrill, C. *Assessment of an administrative commitment to mainstreaming.* Paper presented at a meeting of the American Alliance for Health, Physical Education, Recreation and Dance, Detroit, April, 1980.

References

Armstrong, J.R. Taxonomies in special education. In L. Mann & D. Sabatino (Eds.), *The Third Review of Special Education.* New York: Grune & Stratton, 1976.

Arnheim, D.D., Auxter, D., & Crowe, W.C. *Principles and methods of adapted physical education and recreation* (3rd ed.). St. Louis, MO: C.V. Mosby, 1977.

Auxter, D. The motor skill development in the profoundly retarded.

Training School Bulletin, 1971, **68**, 5-9.

Barsch, R.W. *A movigenic curriculum.* Madison, WI: Wisconsin State Department of Public Instruction, 1965, (Bulletin No. 25).

Barsch, R.H. *Achieving perceptual-motor efficiency* (Vol. 1). Seattle, WA: Special Child Publications, 1968.

Brace, D.K. Physical education and recreation for mentally retarded pupils in public schools. *Research Quarterly,* 1968, **39**, 779-782.

British Government Board of Education. *A physical training syllabus.* London, England: His Majesty's Stationary Office, 1933.

British Government Ministry of Education. *Planning the programme.* London, England: His Majesty's Stationary Office, 1953.

British Government Department of Education and Science. *Movement: physical education in the primary years.* London, England: Her Majesty's Stationary Office, 1972.

Broadhead, G.D. The role of educational physical activity programs in the modification of selected parameters of the behavior of educable mentally retarded children and minimally brain-injured children of elementary school age (Doctoral dissertation, University of Wisconsin, Madison, 1968). *Dissertation Abstracts,* 1969, **29**, 4305A-4306A. (University Microfilms No. 69-12, 877).

Broadhead, G.D. Gross motor performance in minimally brain-injured children. *Journal of Motor Behavior,* 1972, **4**, 108-111.

Broadhead, G.D. Beam walking in special education. *Rehabilitation Literature,* 1974, **35**, 145-147; 151.

Broadhead, G.D. Factors of gross motor performance in special education. *Journal of Biosocial Science,* 1975, **7**, 57-65.

Broadhead, G.D. Integrating special children in Scotland: A PL 94-142 is needed. *Journal of Special Education,* 1979, **13**, 91-98.

Clarke, H.H., & Clarke, D.H. *Developmental and adapted physical education.* (2nd ed.) Englewood Cliffs, NJ: Prentice-Hall, 1978.

Clausen, J. *Ability structure and subgroups in mental retardation.* London, England: The Macmillan Company, 1966.

Cooke, A. *America.* London, England: The British Broadcasting Corporation, 1973.

Corder, W.O. Effects of physical education on intellectual, physical, and social development in educable mentally retarded boys. *Exceptional Children,* 1966, **32**, 357-364.

Cratty, B.J. *Motor activity and the education of retardates.* Philadelphia, PA: Lea and Febiger, 1969.

Cratty, B.J. *Perceptual and motor development in infants and children.* London, England: The Macmillan Company, 1970.

Cratty, B.J. *Active learning: games to enhance academic abilities.* Englewood Cliffs, NJ: Prentice-Hall, 1971.

Daniels, A.S., & Davis, E.A. *Adapted physical education.* New York: Harper and Row, 1975.

Delacato, C.H. *The diagnosis and treatment of speech and reading problems.* Springfield, IL: Charles C. Thomas, 1963.

Delacato, C.H. (Ed.). *Neurological organization and reading problems.* Springfield, IL: Charles C. Thomas, 1966.

Dobie, J.F. *A Texan in England.* Boston, MA: Little, Brown and Company, 1944.

Doll, E.A. The essentials of an inclusive concept of mental deficiency. *American Journal of Mental Deficiency,* 1941, **46**, 214-219.

Doman, G., Delacato, C.H., & Doman, R. *The Doman-Delacato Development Profile.* Philadelphia, PA: The Institutes for the Achievement of Human Potential, 1963.

Fait, H.F. *Special physical education: adapted, corrective, developmental* (4th ed.). Philadelphia, PA: W.B. Saunders, 1978.

Frostig, M., & Maslow, P. *Movement education: theory and practice.* Chicago: Follett Publishing Company, 1970.

Frostig, M., & Maslow, P. *Learning problems in the classroom.* New York: Grune & Stratton, 1973.

Getman, G.N. The visuomotor complex in the acquisition of learning skills. In J. Hellmuth (Ed.), *Learning disorders* (Vol. 1). Seattle, WA: Special Child Publications, 1965.

Harrow, A.J. *A taxonomy of the psychomotor domain.* New York: David McKay, 1972.

Hayden, F.J. *Physical fitness for the mentally retarded.* Toronto: Toront Association for Retarded Children, 1964.

Heber, R. Mental retardation: concept and classification. In E.P. Trapp & P. Himelstein (Eds.), *Readings on the exceptional child* (1st Ed.). New York: Appleton-Century-Crofts, 1962.

Itard, J. *The wild boy of Aveyron* (translation by G. & M. Humphrey). New York: Appleton-Century-Crofts, 1962. (Originally published, 1801.

Kephart, N.C. *The slow learner in the classroom.* Columbus, OH: Charles E. Merrill, 1971.

Laban, R. *Modern educational dance.* London, England: Macdonald & Evans, 1948.

Leonard, F.E. *A guide to the history of physical education* (3rd ed.). London, England: Henry Kimpton, 1947.

Martin, E.W. Handicapped must get services they need, not just what's available. *Education Daily (Capitol Publications Inc.),* 1977, **10**, 1-3.

McAdam, K.J. The place of physical education in character-training. *Teacher Education (London)*, 1962, **3**, 18-36.

Moran, J.M., & Kalakian, L.H. *Movement experiences for the mentally retarded or emotionally disturbed child.* Minneapolis, MN: Burgess Publishing Co., 1974.

Oliver, J.N. The effect of physical conditioning exercises and activities on the mental characteristics of educationally sub-normal boys. *British Journal of Educational Psychology*, 1958, **28**, 155-165.

P.E. Association of Great Britain. *National Survey of physical education for handicapped children.* London, England: The P.E. Association of Great Britain, 1969.

Rarick, G.L., & Broadhead, G.D. The effects of individualized versus group-oriented physical education programs on selected parameters of the development of educable mentally retarded, and minimally brain-injured children. Madison, Wisconsin: Department of Physical Education, Report to U.S.O.E. (Contract O.E.G.-0-8-071097-1760), and The Joseph P. Kennedy Jr. Foundation, August 31, 1968.

Rarick, G.L., Dobbins, D.A., & Broadhead, G.D. *The motor domain and its correlates in educationally handicapped children.* Englewood Cliffs, NJ: Prentice-Hall, 1976.

Rarick, G.L., Widdop, J.H., & Broadhead, G.D. Environmental factors associated with the motor performance and physical fitness of educable mentally retarded children. University of Wisconsin, Madison: Department of Physical Education, Report to The Joseph P. Kennedy Jr. Foundation, 1967.

Rarick, G.L., Widdop, J.H., & Broadhead, G.D. The physical fitness and motor performance of educable mentally retarded children. *Exceptional Children*, 1970, **36**, 509-519.

Rarick, G.L., & McQuillan, J.P. The factor structure of motor abilities of trainable mentally retarded children: implications for curriculum development. Berkeley, CA:Department of Physical Education, University of California. Report to the U.S.O.E. (Project No. H 23-2544), 1977.

Roethlisberger, F.J., & Dickson, W.J. *Management and the worker.* Cambridge, MA:Harvard University Press, 1947.

Rousseau, J.J. *Emile.* (trans. by B. Foxley). New York: E.P. Dutton, 1962. (Originally published, 1885.)

Seguin, E. *Idiocy and its treatment by the physiological method.* New York: Teachers College Press, Columbia University, 1907. (Originally published, 1866.)

Sherrill, C. *Adapted physical education and recreation: a multi-disciplinary approach.* Dubuque, IA: Wm. C. Brown, 1976.

Smith, M.S., & Bissel, J.S.   Report analysis: the impact of Head Start. *Harvard Educational Review,* 1970, **40**, 51-104.

Solomon, A., & Pangle R.   Demonstrating physical fitness improvement in the EMR. *Exceptional Children,* 1967, **34**, 177-181.

Stein, J.U.   Sense and nonsense about mainstreaming. *Journal of Physical Education and Recreation,* 1976, **47**, 43.

U.S. Congress. *The Rehabilitation Act of 1973* (P.L. 93-112), 1973.

U.S. Congress. *Education for All Handicapped Children Act* (P.L. 94-142), 1975.

U.S. Office of Education.   Non-discrimination on the basis of handicap. *Federal Register Part IV,* 1977, May 4. (a)

U.S. Office of Education. Education of Handicapped Children: Implementation of Part B of the Education of the Handicapped Act. *Federal Register Part II,* 1977, August 23. (b)

Van Dalen, D.B., & Bennett, B.L. *A world history of physical education* (2nd ed.). Englewood Cliffs, NJ: Prentice-Hall, 1971.

Webb, R.C.   Sensory-motor training of the profoundly retarded. *American Journal of Mental Deficiency,* 1969, **74**, 283-295.

Weston, A.   *The making of American physical education.* New York: Appleton-Century-Crofts, 1962.

White, T.H. *In search of history: a personal adventure.* New York: Warner Books, 1979.

Widdop, J.H., Barton, P., Cleary, B., Proyer, V.A., & Wall, A.E.   The effects of two programmes of physical education upon the behavioural and psychological traits of trainable retarded children. Montreal, Canada: McGill University, A report to the Quebec Institute of Research in Education, (Contract No. 68-AS-11-04-01, 1969).

Winnick, J.P. *Early movement experiences and development: habilitation and remediation.* Philadelphia, PA: W.B. Saunders, 1979.

Yinger, J.M., Ikeda, K., Laycock, F., & Cutter, S.J. *Middle Start.* Cambridge, England: Cambridge University Press, 1977.

PART 5

Motor
Behavior

Part 5 contains a chapter on the emergence of research in the physical education discipline generally termed "motor learning" and another chapter on the current status of research in that field. Additionally, part 5 features a special chapter by Franklin M. Henry, a pioneer in the field. In his chapter, Dr. Henry describes the evolution of the memory drum theory of neuromotor reaction. This theory represents a cornerstone in motor learning research. Although it is particularly important for students to be familiar with the theory, perhaps even more important than the theory itself is the value of reading Dr. Henry's description of how the theory evolved.

Like the discipline of physical education itself, the subarea termed motor learning has other names, including motor control, motor integration, and motor behavior. Although these terms can have subtle differences in meaning, in general they all refer to the study of neural control of motor skills. These terms (learning, control, integration, behavior) describe functions determined primarily by the Central Nervous System (CNS). Use of these terms to describe motor function acknowledges the special role of CNS in controlling motor activities. In Chapter 14, Waneen Spirduso describes the emergence of research in this area. The roots of studies on how motor skills are learned, initiated, controlled, and modified lie in the disciplines of physiology, anatomy, psychology, and computer science. Therefore, it is not surprising that a number of terms are used to describe the motor learning field.

Also like the discipline of physical education, and other subareas within the discipline, research in motor learning carries a strong interdisciplinary component which has vastly enriched knowledge in the field of motor learning. As pointed out by Dr. Spirduso, development of the understanding of how motor tasks are controlled depended upon development of a basic understanding of brain and spinal cord function. Similarly, understanding how a computer functioned led to the development of hypotheses about how the brain operated. Contemporary study in motor learning frequently relies upon electrophysiological and computer technology. Therefore, even though a student or investigator may be primarily concerned with how motor tasks are performed, he or she is obligated to possess a solid grounding in the other previously mentioned disciplines. The interdisciplinary nature of motor learning requires that a serious student of motor learning read widely in journals of the various disciplines contributing to understanding in this subarea.

A comparison of Chapters 14 and 15 also reflects the interdisciplinary nature of contemporary research in motor learning. Chapter 14 is written from the perspective of a neurophysiologist and anatomist. This approach to understanding the control of motor activities involves the identification and categorization of the neural events which determine motor activities. It requires that hard data on neural events during activity be obtained. Chapter 15 (by Dr. Stelmach and his associates) is written from the perspective of a psychologist. This approach to understanding neural control of motor activities is perhaps more theoretical than that taken by a physiologist. The psychologist's approach relies upon the ability to observe motor behavior and to make inferences about the organization and control of neural mechanisms. The control systems analysis approach described in Chapter 15 is particularly useful in conceptualizing the operation of something as complex as the central nervous system. Much of the terminology used in Chapter 15 is also used in computer science, once again reflecting the inter- or multidisciplinary approach to contemporary studies in motor learning. The control systems approach to describing motor activity regulation not only provides a conceptual framework, but it also allows the formulation and testing of hypotheses. The testing of those hypotheses is then based not on invasive measurements, but on behavior or performance outputs. The combined efforts of anatomists, physiologists, psychologists, computer scientists, and control systems analysts have made significant recent progress in understanding neural control of motor behavior.

As suggested here, as well as in Chapters 14 and 15, Franklin Henry's contribution to the area of motor learning is probably more important than can be estimated from today's perspective. In Chapter 16, Henry provides an interesting description of his contribution to the memory drum theory of neuromotor reaction. He describes the events from the genesis of an idea, to the formulation of a working hypothesis, to actual experimentation, through data analysis, and to the point of confirmation of the hypothesis. As illustrated in Henry's narrative, considerable time may intervene between the first glow of an idea and the moment when the hypothesis bursts forth. Frequently, too, successful development and testing of a theory may depend upon the ability to state the theory in ways which can be tested experimentally.

Dr. Henry's description of the memory drum theory also includes bits of good advice for those who would be serious students, for example to review the literature thoroughly and rely only upon primary sources. Further, a scientist must be prepared to evaluate a theory in light of new evidence and to modify a theory if necessary.

The chapter contains a numerical example, with which Dr. Henry intends not only to illustrate a point, but also to challenge the interest of a more advanced student. For those students not yet sufficiently advanced to appreciate the numerical example, however, Henry has written the chapter so that the example need not be understood to appreciate the remainder of the chapter.

Some readers may enjoy a subtle repartee between Chapters 15 and 16. The memory drum theory was conceived when our knowledge of the working of the brain and spinal cord were not as advanced as today. It may be true that the memory drum theory is "simplistic" in view of other contemporary competing theories, but it is also true that some contemporaries are attempting to apply the memory drum theory to predict results in situations for which the theory was not intended. Several challenges to the memory drum theory have fallen very flat. Whether the theory is too specialized for broad application in describing motor performance is a question which can only be answered with time. Today, no other theory in motor learning is as well developed or has been as extensively tested. Adequacy of any theory or model is ultimately determined on the basis of how well it predicts. The future holds the answer of which motor control theory, specialized or complex, shall prove most effective.

The Emergence of Research in Motor Control and Learning

14 *W.W. Spirduso*

The recognition of motor control as a discrete and identifiable area of a discipline underpinning motor skill diagnosis, prescription and pedagogy has been a relatively recent spinoff from the emergence in the early 1960s of an academic discipline underpinning the physical education profession. At first blush, it seems strange that motor learning information, the subset content of motor control dealing with how humans improve control through practice and modulate control under fatigue conditions, should have been so long in finding its way into the research interest and pedagogy of those professing to teach others to move more efficiently. After all, what could be more intriguing than studying the "command center" of the enormously complex but tantalizingly challenging motor system of the human machine? Yet, although physical education as a profession was established in 1885, it was 1931 before any research questions were generated about motor learning, and not until the mid-forties before a significant number of studies appeared that could be recognized as falling within the current definitions of motor learning research.

What is Motor Learning Research?

Perhaps the slow development of motor control as a discipline occurred because an understanding of these constructs largely depended on an understanding of brain and spinal cord function, which in turn awaited the development of computor and electrophysiological technology. These technologies have only recently enabled psychologists and physiologists to ask questions that are highly interesting to the physical educator—how is purposive movement initiated, controlled, and modified? Consequently, some physical educators have recently joined the multidisciplinary search for comprehension of the human motor system. Within the profession in general, however, the body of knowledge relating to how humans control their movement is not defined by an invariant language system, subject to extensive research, or universally taught in programs for professional preparation. Academic courses relating to the topic may be found in university and college curricula under the various titles of Motor Behavior, Motor Control, Motor Performance, Motor Integration, and Motor Learning.

In 1978, when the *Research Quarterly* moved to a format which called for section editors, the problem was clearly apparent. Although it seemed clear there should have been two sections covering motor integration and learning—one section to review manuscripts pertaining to physiological motor systems as they relate to the control of movement, and another to pertain to the cognitive processes that describe and predict performance and the acquisition of skill—debate arose as to what each section should be labeled. Similarly, arguments about the "appropriate" descriptions of the interest areas have persisted for years among the members of the North American Society for Psychology of Sport and Physical Activity (NASPSPA), the society which attracts and nurtures the majority of serious researchers of motor behavior. Continually, terms like motor behavior, motor integration, motor performance, motor control, and motor learning are proposed as labels for the area focusing on research in human movement control. Most recently NASPSPA has adopted "Motor Learning and Control" as the title for this section.

Over the past several years, the terms motor control and motor learning have begun to appear more frequently, reflecting perhaps the gradual emergence—especially since 1970— of two basic strategies for understanding human movement. One of these strategies is investigating *motor learning,* in which the thrust is toward the conceptualization of cognitive processes underlying motor acts and performance associated with skill acquisition. Theories and techniques of psychology, bioengineering, linguistics, and cybernetics are used to explore the complexities of memory and learning as related to motor output. Although many research questions in the motor learning area deal directly with hypothesized basic mechanisms controlling performance, the majority of research is concerned with change in performance over trials, particularly with regard to interactions between human capacities and environmental demands. Research in the area leans heavily on an information processing model, and is conducted by professionals in all the disciplines mentioned previously as well as by physical educators. Because many of the research topics deal with the use of information that intervenes between the receipt of a stimulus and the emittance of a response in the decision-making process, the subjects of investigation in this area are largely human.

The other currently identifiable strategy is one in which techniques and theories of neurophysiology, neuropharmacology, neuropsychology, and behavioral biology are focused upon topics of reflex and voluntary mechanisms operative in human and animal movement. This area has increasingly been called *motor control*, and its research methodologies generally depend upon electrophysiological measurement of neuromuscular activity. A substantial proportion of researchers investigate human motor control mechanisms by electromyographic and electroencephalographic recording techniques. But an equally large number of researchers study questions requiring animal models, whose motor systems can be studied using the more invasive techniques of implanted electrodes, production of lesions, and drug application.

The motor learning and the motor control strategies supplement each other nicely; the motor learning findings suggest conceptual mechanisms of control, and the motor control findings identify neurophysiological phenomena as possible correlatives of the proposed mechanisms. Recently, the lines delineating the two strategies have become more and more ambiguous, with the information processing researcher proposing certain neurophysiological mechanisms for a specific model, and the neurophysiologist asking questions regarding "the control of goal-oriented behavior."

Research on motor control and motor learning has been conducted for many years by scientists in many disciplines. In the following sections the development of motor control and learning research is summarized, and the role that researchers in physical education have played in this development is discussed. Any classification scheme is arbitrary, but when motor control and learning research is viewed from the perspective of physical educators and their contributions, the research may be divided roughly into four periods: (a) early beginnings in psychology and physiology that preceded the contributions from physical educators' research (1890-1931), (b) the early period in which the primary focus was the descriptive study of motor learning (1931-1959), (c) the period in which motor control and learning were emerging as a distinct area and subset, respectively, of the discipline of physical education (1959-1970), and (d) the period in which physical education researchers joined scientists of other disciplines in the search for mechanisms (1970 to present).

Telegraph Keys and Reflexology: 1890-1931

As the primitive profession of physical education, interested largely in exercise as a preventive medicine, was beginning in the last decade of the 19th century, a few psychologists were curious about how men learn telegraphy. Acquisition curves of motor skill development were studied in men learning Morse Code on a telegraph key. These studies were largely exploratory and descriptive in nature, and the motivation was largely practical: "How can motor skill improvement be enhanced?" Thus, the primary targets of research tended to be topics such as the distribution of practice effects, reminiscence, and practice methodologies such as whole-part method. The classic volume recounting the work of this period was Woodworth's *Le Mouvement* (1903). Hollingsworth (1909) reported a series of studies in which he investigated the accuracy with which movements could be reproduced, as well as the nature of the errors committed. In effect, he was one of the earliest psychologists to ask questions about the motor control system. To answer his questions, he constructed the horizontal arm positioning instrument, known today as a kinesthesiometer and used widely in both behavioral and electrophysiological human and animal research. These studies represented a departure from the use of frequency responses or reaction latency responses as dependent variables in the study of human performance and learning. Another psychologist, Stetson, studied ballistic movement initiation in the 1920s (see Hartson [1932] for a review of analysis of skilled movements during this period). But these efforts failed to attract replication and interest in the motor control of movement reproduction and initiation, and for the most part, their work went unnoticed for many years.

Motor control mechanisms were of course being studied much earlier by physiologists. John Hughlings Jackson (1958) had long tried to convince his colleagues that the brain, rather than being solely a convolutional repository of "ideas," also contained a motor cortex which played a role in controlling movement. Studies of motor control at the turn of the century focused on attempts to label the motor and sensory areas of the cortex, and with the labeling came hypotheses regarding the nature of the brain's output. Whether various areas produced complex learned movements or components of movement was a topic of great interest. Meanwhile, from 1895 to 1935, Sherrington was formulating the components of sensorimotor integration at the spinal cord level. His conceptualization of spinal cord neural integration was, and is, fundamental in thinking regarding the basic components of motor system control. He coined the term "proprioception," which has been a topic of great interest to psychologists and physical educators interested in kinesthesis. In summary, during the period to 1931, research in motor learning was focused on the description of human and environmental factors influencing learning curves. Phenomena such as retention, massed or distributed practice, and reminiscence were described. Research in motor control, conducted by physiologists using primitive electrophysiological instrumentation on anesthetized animals, was used largely to describe crude cortical representation models of muscle function, spinal reflexes, and muscle receptor anatomy and function.

Describing, Measuring, and Applying: 1931-1959

During the 1930s, psychologists' experiments on motor learning topics increased in sophistication: a more theoretical orientation was accompanied by the introduction of new and more powerful statistical techniques for handling large masses of data. In the next decade, a substantial number of young experimental psychologists were prepared to investigate motor skills relevant to the war effort. Federal support for this research was impressive; grants were abundant and some laboratories were provided by the Department of Defense. In this time of high productivity, new conceptual strategies evolved for studying movement such as human engineering, ergonomics, and human performance theory. The period also was notable for the small cluster of English psychologists who were destined to have a profound and lasting impact on motor learning researchers from that time to the present. Barlett, Gibbs, Hicks, Poulton, Whiting, and Welford were giants in the area, formulating several now well-known models such as the psychological refractory period, Hicks-Hyman law, and anticipatory tracking. Topics like individual differences, knowledge of results, retention and attention (primarily vigilance) were investigated with prodigious energy during this period. Hull's theory (1943) of drive reduction presented a model which was easily tested by motor tasks, and in the fifties, a veritable flood of studies pertaining to the elucidation of factors operative in KR was unleashed: delay of KR, the KR interval, frequency of KR, and transformations of KR.

In the meantime, our understanding of the organization and function of the motor cortex was being advanced by physiologists. A "gunshot" wound methodology was used, exemplified by Teuber (1954), in which motor function was studied in individuals with brain injuries from the war. Motor function was linked to a specific area if motor dysfunction accompanied the damage. The sensorimotor humunculus was being carefully mapped by Woolsey. The energetically argued question of whether the motor cortex specified force of displacement was an example of the thrust toward establishing the functional relationships among the cortex, cerebellum, and spinal cord, particularly with regard to the control of voluntary movement. The parietal lobe of the cortex was suggested as an association area for learned movements. Alpha-gamma linkage, the forerunner of alpha-gamma coactivation, was proposed as a method by which the proprioceptive system is incorporated in voluntary control. Fledgling efforts at intracellular recording which began with Eccles' (1964) recording of single nerve cells provided information about excitation and inhibition of single motor neurons, their neuronal circuits, and basic spinal reflexive meahanisms. In the late forties and early fifties, concepts of spinal reflexive mechanisms were also applied to human work capacity by Hellebrandt (1951), who was active in conferences for physical educators, and who later suggested that motor learning accompanies strength development (1962).

While exciting progress was being made toward unraveling the mysteries of motor control and learning, to this point, physical educators had not seen their role as that of advancing knowledge about the topic. In the mid-1930s, a few physical educators became interested in studying motor learning and published reports of experiments in the American Association for Health, Physical Education, and Recreation's newly created *Research Quarterly*.

These experiments were largely addressing the pragmatic problems of teaching methodology of sports skills, measuring and comparing rhythm in discrete populations, and motor achievement in classes. As no studies of motor learning research were published in the first volume of *Research Quarterly,* the subject apparently did not captivate the interest of many of the physical educators at that time. The first study was one that could appropriately be classified as a descriptive study of motor control, and it was reported not by a physical educator but by W.R. Miles (1931a, 1931b) of the Stanford University's Psychology Laboratories. In the study, Miles investigated the individual and group reaction times in football charging. W.W. Tuttle, a physiologist at Iowa, was also prominent during the early 1930s, for he published several reaction-time studies in collaboration with physical educators, one of which dealt with the reation times of track runners of different distances (Westerlund & Tuttle, 1931). In fact, a large majority of the early *Research Quarterly* reports on the topic of motor control and learning were strongly influenced by scientists in other disciplines; for example, the experiments by K.J. McCristal (1933) and C.O. Jackson (1933) were conducted in the psychology laboratory of C.R. Griffith (1930). References used by physical educators were predominantly from psychology and physiology, and the studies were either exclusively descriptive in nature of applications of earlier psychological paradigms, such as the question of applying whole-part practice to sports skills.

Not surprisingly, the entire orientation of early *Research Quarterly* volumes was toward sports, dance, and health; the index titles in the early volumes included such items as "Basketball," "Football," "Aquatics," and "Rhythm." During this early period, the energies of several productive researchers who seemed to be at least indirectly interested in motor learning were committed to measuring a general level of student achievement in motor skills (1931) and motor capacity (1934). But from a more recent perspective, neither of these led to significant motor control and learning issues. However, Henry's (1960) model stressing the specificity of movement control may have been a reaction to the efforts of Brace and McCloy to develop a general motor quotient analogous to the then widely accepted intelligence quotient in psychology literature. With but a few notable exceptions, the majority of motor learning research from 1935 to 1959 was generally descriptive and pragmatic, dealing with the contribution of visual aids, manual guidance, and knowledge of mechanical principles underlying movement to the learning of sports skills. Theories of the transfer of training, whole-part learning, and a speed-accuracy trade off that were thoroughly explored by psychologists in the late 1920s and early 1930s were systematically reinvestigated within the context of teaching sports skills.

Two exceptions to the descriptive approach taken by physical education motor learning researchers up to 1959 were two studies which investigated motor control mechanisms. One was a study by Phillips (1941) in which kinesthesis and early learning were related to the acquisition of two perceptual motor skills, and the other was a study by Slater-Hammel (1941) in which neuromuscular mechanisms were proposed as the limiting factor for rate of leg movement in sprinting. Slater-Hammel, who conducted this study in the psychological laboratories at Oberlin College, was an early and influential figure in the field of motor learning. He introduced to the profession the experimental strategy of model testing in lieu of descriptive research in the area of motor control and learning.

Ushering in the "Discipline" with a "Memory Drum-Roll": 1959-1969

During the 1960s there was a decrease in motor control research on the part of psychologists, increased activity on the part of physical educators, and a slow growth of interest in the topic on the part of physiologists. Governmental support in the form of psychological research centers was drastically reduced, discouraging psychologists who required funding to conduct their work. Studies of motor learning continued to be published in psychology literature, but much less abundantly. Although there were a few attempts to formulate new theoretical approaches to the study of motor learning, these were only rudimentary; for the most part, research tended to elaborate in terms of further classifying such phenomena as knowledge of results, transfer of training, and retention. Cybernetics, although introduced in the late forties, was fully developed in the sixties by Wiener (1961), and had a strong influence on the later development of information processing theory.

With a quickening pace, neurophysiologists were generating questions about the nature of the commands given to the motor system in voluntary movement. They were broadening their scope by viewing neurophysiological constructs such as alpha-gamma coactivation, reciprocal innervation, and the size principle of motor unit recruitment as components of mechanisms by which voluntary motor commands could be integrated with spinal level control. From this perspective, higher brain centers were freed from many of the tedious details of precise spatial and temporal patterning, and the nature of voluntary commands controlling movement came to be of great interest. Evarts (1967) published and reported a series of fascinating studies in which questions were raised as to whether voluntary motor commands control specific muscles, reciprocal pairs of muscles, or the muscles with the responsibility for moving a joint. Studies of this nature represented only the beginning of a fruitful harvest of information made possible by the developing technology of electrode implantation in the brains of conscious, operationally conditioned primates. These techniques provided, for instance, the formulation of the alpha-gamma coactivation model, a model describing the exquisite integration of voluntary and servo mechanisms controlling goal-oriented movement. During this period, the increasing interest of many neurophysiologists in purposive movement and changes in the control of purposive movement with practice, was drawing them closer to questions similar to those traditionally asked by cognitive psychologists. For instance, the discovery of the readiness potential, present in electroencephalographic pattern analysis, was providing a neurophysiological correlate of the stimulus expectancy phenomenon, a factor which psychologists had previously proposed to facilitate response organization and execution (Kornhuber & Decker, 1973).

Interest in goal-oriented motor control led not only to speculation about the nature of the characteristics of the neural commands for execution, but also about the nature of the organization preceding the movement initiation. Notions about motor programs, which had previously been suggested by physiologists in generalized terms such as "motor plans," "motor images," "willful movement," "engrams," or "templates," now were seen by the multidisciplinary scholar in juxtaposition to the literature in which psychologists had made applications of computer analytic characteristics such as memory storage, retrieval, and executive programs with corresponding subroutines. It is not surprising, in retrospect, that someone familiar with both fields would perceive the utility of explaining motor programming and memory retrieval on the basis of a model derived from neurophysiological and psychological theory.

It was at this time that Franklin Henry published his now classic study on the memory drum theory to explain motor memory (1960). This represented the first time that a physical education researcher, rather than replicating experimental designs or describing behavior, refined and modified an existing model to account for behavioral differences specific to motor performance. It is difficult to ascertain from this relatively short perspective the full extent of the impact of Henry's work in the early sixties, but it can be conservatively said that it was profound. If it were necessary to identify a "father" of the study of motor skills control in physical education, Henry would have little competition for the honor. Attesting to its fruitfulness, a relatively large number of young researchers addressed their energies to testing Henry's memory drum model, a course of action that had serious consequences for the model, but had long lasting effects on the general strategy of motor learning research in physical education. As an educator, Henry equipped many researchers with careful laboratory techniques, modern statistical tools, and a theoretical strategy. He also developed a prototype motor learning laboratory and a graduate education protocol for preparing researchers. He articulated for physical educators the concept of the discipline of motor learning, and motivated many of them to develop the discipline by model testing. His students, in turn, had a substantial impact upon other researchers of the time.

Prior to Henry's influence, there were almost no motor learning laboratories in departments of physical education. Some might suggest that Coleman Griffith established the first laboratory in the gymnasium building at the University of Illinois as early as 1925 (Griffith, 1930). Developed as a cooperative and contributing enterprise with the athletic department, the Illinois laboratory was only in existence for seven years. Although several studies of reaction time were completed there, the majority of the experimental work was related to sports psychology. Perhaps because of its early and short existence, Griffith's laboratory seemed to have little impact upon the development of motor learning research and the establishment of motor learning laboratories.

In Kroll's (1971) comprehensive review of the development of research productivity and motor learning laboratories in the physical education profession, no laboratories titled "motor learning" or "motor control" were reported to be in existence during the period 1959-1964. His review of this subject included information from the American Academy of Physical Education's May 1965 study of laboratories in physical education. Therefore, as recently as 1965, the laboratories of F. Henry at Berkeley, A.T. Slater-Hammel at Indiana, W. Kroll at the University of Texas, and B. Cratty at UCLA were basically small rooms filled with home-made devices composed primarily of reaction timers, interval timers, and chronoscopes. Although they were primitive, these laboratories provided data that served to change the nature of physical education research in motor learning forever. Of course, the literature still contained descriptive investigations pertaining to distribution of practice, mental and physical practice, formal and informal learning, and the contribution of mechanical devices to learning. In a profession, there must always be those who struggle with the concerns of applying theoretical knowledge to professional problems. But the leading researchers in the field in the 1960s were a new breed, a group interested for the first time in the basic mechanisms of any type of motor control and learning, not just learning as it applied to sports skills or rhythm. Armed with the same basic knowledge relating to motor control that historically had been present in psychology and physiology, the serious doctoral students of motor control and learning were launched into the seventies where they would contribute substantially to the understanding of mechanisms underlying motor control and learning.

Peering Into the Black Box: 1970-

In the past decade, there has been a strong shift in motor learning research by both psychologists and physical educators from a product-performance orientation to a search for the processes underlying motor performance and learning. In other words, students of motor learning are trying to see into the black boxes (the boxes drawn in diagrammatic explanations of motor control) and speculate as to what mechanisms are operating. Rather than study the question "what does the motor response look like, under 'X' conditions or after 'Y' number of trials?", the research questions recently have been "how are the responses organized?", "how are they stored?", and "how are they retrieved?".

A signal paper that initiated substantial process-oriented research was that of Adams (1971) which described closed loop theory. In the ensuing years, there were more and more advocates of an information processing model as an efficient way to explain the control and learning of movement. Topics that have generated substantial interest are those of central-versus-peripheral control of movement, short-term motor memory, mechanisms of feed-forward, coding constructs, single channel theory, schema theory, and motor programming.

There is little question that the majority of physical education researchers concerned with mechanisms of control over the past 10 years have adopted the information processing strategy. This approach depends on four major assumptions: (a) a number of independent mental operations (processing stages) occur between a stimulus and a response, (b) each processing stage consumes a finite amount of time, (c) the stages only process available information, and (d) each stage makes transformed information available to the ensuing stage. Inasmuch as this approach focuses on mechanisms of behavior, it was not long before a growing number of investigators in physical education saw the value in also using neurological mechanisms to clarify the proposed mechanisms underlying behavior. Consequently, several investigators in the field have joined the very large number of neuroscientists investigating the motor system.

The seventies have seen neuroscientific information melded with behavioral observations and models in the attempt to understand motor control. Beginning in 1970, the Society for Neurosciences, with a membership of approximately 300 scientists from the disciplines of neurology, neuropharmacology, neurochemistry, neuroendocrinology, and physiological psychology, has grown to a membership of over 8,000. Interest in motor systems has greatly increased in these disciplines, so that conference proceedings reflect many programs related to brain control of motor output, electroencephalographic responses preceding movements, memory and learning, and brain plasticity.

With the advent of microelectrodes, sterotaxic devices, and implanted electrodes that allow electrophysiological recording in freely moving animals, central nervous system motor control is now being studied in conjunction with such constructs as intention, voluntary movement, expectancy, and error detection and correction. A substantial contribution by physical education researchers interested in motor control and learning is the use of some of these noninvasive techniques in the study of reflex phenomena, voluntary control, and use of perceptual information in human subjects. The integration of information theory, bioengineering, and neurophysiological recording exists now in all related disciplines, including physical education.

Several events in the recent past have strongly influenced and given a clear identity to the discipline of motor control and learning. The first of these was the publication of Cratty's *Movement Behavior and Motor Learning* (1964), one of the first books written by a physical educator in which information from several disciplines was synthesized and applied directly to understanding motor learning. This book was widely adopted as a textbook. Although a motor learning class was taught as early as 1962 by L. Locke and W. Anderson at Teachers College Columbia, no text written by a physical educator was available. Motor learning courses were almost nonexistent. The Cratty text was probably catalytic in generating graduate level motor learning courses at many universities. Another influential event was the establishment in 1966 of the North American Society for the Psychology of Sport and Physical Activity (NASPSPA). This learned society was appealing to both psychologists and physical educators whose research focus was in the area of motor behavior, and it was not long before the society sectioned into sport psychology, motor development, and motor control and learning.

The motor control and learning sections of the annual NASPSPA meetings provided a format for the presentation of papers, and the entire program encouraged intimate and lengthy discussions by persons separated by geography but not by interest and work techniques. Of greater importance, NASPSPA provided opportunities for interdisciplinary interaction. NASPSPA was and is a society organized to facilitate research on a specific topic rather than to facilitate interaction of members of a similar science of profession. Consequently, the business of understanding motor control and learning has always been a central issue in NASPSPA, and up to this point, the smallness of the society has enabled it to escape the energy consuming efforts of organizational management that have so handicapped many large associations. Most serious motor control and learning scholars in the physical education profession and many psychologists belong to NASPSPA and attend its annual conferences.

Another important influence on the area was the publication of the *Journal of Motor Behavior* in 1969. This journal has provided a vehicle for sharing research directly focused on motor control and learning, and includes papers that primarily reflect an information processing and bioengineering perspective. The journal also has accepted papers in which the control of movement has been addressed from a neurophysiological perspective.

Since 1970, interest in motor control and learning has dramatically increased. Two major scholarly periodicals of the physical education profession devoted a special issue to the topic of motor skill performance and learning (Locke, 1972). In January 1972, *Quest,* the scholarly publication of the National Association for Physical Education of College Women, in cooperation with the National College Physical Education Association for Men, published an issue focused on "Learning Models and the Acquisition of Motor Skills." This was followed nine months later by a special issue of the 1972 *Research Quarterly,* an important landmark because it introduced the writings of H.T.A. Whiting and A.T. Welford to the large number of physical educators subscribing to the journal. This issue also suggested implications of information processing models for physical education. The increased interest in motor control and learning research has enhanced expertise, produced sophistication of technique, and elevated productivity, as reflected by the excellent symposium on motor control and learning at the University of Wisconsin sponsored in 1977 by the Committee on Instructional Cooperation for the Big Ten Universities and the University of Wisconsin. Three books have been published since 1976 reflecting the new orientation of understanding the mechanisms of motor control and learning as prerequisite to the study of pedagogical problems related to acquiring motor skills (Martinuk, 1976; Stelmach, 1976, 1978).   Finally, the American College of Sports Medicine, long an association primarily concerned with the cardiovascular performance and intracellular metabolism and osteopathic respiratory, and skeletal muscular aspects associated with physical activity, has within the past few years shown an interest in central nervous system changes that may occur with training. Beginning in 1972, a small section of the program has consisted of papers relating to motor control. This association shows promise of making a strong contribution to the understanding of motor control in the future.

Much has happened in the last ten years to develop a discipline of control on the foundation established in the preceding seventy years, and physical educators have been making substantial contributions through publications and presentations. The topical study area of motor control and learning has existed since the turn of the century, but it has emerged within the perspective of the physical educator only within the past twenty years. As physical educators have become aware of the potential impact that understanding motor control and learning can have upon professional service, they have joined scientists from many disciplines in the common search for answers. Knowledgeable researchers in this area find it necessary to monitor the activities and publications of such associations as the Psychonomics Society, the American Psychological Association, the International Federation of Scientists, and the American Association for the Advancement of Science. Most serious scholars in the area attend and present papers in one or more of these associations in addition to those mentioned earlier.

The elucidation of the body of knowledge explaining motor control and learning is an important committment for the physical education profession to make. It seems intuitive that in order to change motor behavior, one must first understand it. The study of motor control and learning, growing healthily and already containing some powerful constructs, is a mandatory foundation for those who would teach motor skills, diagnose motor control problems, and prescribe learning or rehabilitative activities. The participation and contribution of physical educators in the development of this area is an exciting part of the process through which physical education is moving from an empirically to a theoretically based profession.

References

AAHPER. Special Issue: Skill learning and performance. *Research Quarterly,* 1972, **43**(3), 263-397.

Adams, J.A.   A closed-loop theory of motor learning. *Journal of Motor Behavior,* 1971, **3**, 111-149.

Brace, D.K.   The development of measures of pupil achievement in physical education. *Research Quarterly,* 1931, **2**, 14-31,

Cratty, B.J.   *Movement behavior and motor learning.* Philadelphia: Lea and Febiger, 1964.

Eccles, J.C. *The physiology of snapses.*   Heidelberg: Springer-Verlag, 1964.

Evarts, E.V.   Representation of movements and muscles by pyramidal tract neurons of the precentral motor cortex. In M.D. Yahr & D. Purpura, (Eds.), *Neurophysiological basis of normal and abnormal motor activities*, Hewlett, NY: Raven Press, 1967.

Griffith, C.R.   A laboratory for research in athletics.   *Research Quarterly,* 1930, **1**, 34-40.

Hartson, L.D.   Analysis of skilled movements. *Journal of Personality*, 1932, **11**, 28-43.

Hellebrandt, F.A., Houtz, S.J., & Eubank, R.N.   Influence of alternate and reciprocal exercise on work capacity. *Archives of Physical Medicine,* 1951, **32**, 766-776.

Hellebrandt, F.A. & Waterland, J.A.   Indirect learning—the influence of unimanual exercise on related muscle groups of the same and the opposite side. *American Journal of Physical Medicine,* 1962, **41**, 45-55.

Hollingsworth, H.L.   The inaccuracy of movement. *Archives of Psychology,* 1909, **2**, 1-87.

Henry, F.M. & Rogers, D.E. Increased response latency for complicated movements and a "memory drum" theory of neuromotor reaction. *Research Quarterly,* 1960, **31**, 448-458.

Hull, C.L. *Principles of behavior.* New York: Appleton-Century, 1943.

Jackson, C.O. Effect of fear on muscular coordination. *Research Quarterly,* 1933, **4**, 71-80.

Jackson, J.H. Observations on the localization of movements in the cerebral hemispheres, as revealed by cases of convulsion chorea, and "aphasia". In J. Taylor, G. Holmes, & F.M.R. Walshe (Eds.), *Selected writings of John Hughlings Jackson* (Vol. 1). New York: Basic Books, 1958.

Kornhuber, H.H. & Deeke, L. Event related slow potentials of the brain: Their relation to behavior. In C. McCallum & J.R. Knott (Eds.), *Electroencephalography and Clinical Neurophysiology* (Supp. 33), 1973.

Kroll, W.P. *Perspectives in physical education.* New York: Academic Press, 1971.

Locke, F. (Ed.). Learning Models and the acquisition of perceptual motor skills. *Quest,* 1972, **17**, 1-94.

Martinuk, R.G. *Information processing in motor skills.* New York: Holt, Rinehart, and Winston, 1976.

McCloy, C.H. Motor capacity and motor ability. *Research Quarterly,* 1934, **5**, 46-61.

McCristal, K.J. Experimental study of rhythm in gymnastic and tap dancing. *Research Quarterly,* 1933, **2**, 63-74.

Miles, W.R. Studies in physical exertion: II. Individual and group reaction time in football charging. *Research Quarterly,* 1931, **2**, 5-13. (a)

Miles, W.R. & Graves, B.C. Studies in physical exertion: III. Effect of signal variation on football charging. *Research Quarterly,* 1931, **2**, 14-31. (b)

Phillips, B.E. The relationship between certain phases of kinesthesis and performance, during the early stages of acquiring two perceptuo-motor skills. *Research Quarterly,* 1941, **12**, 571-586.

Slater-Hammel, A.T. Possible neuromuscular mechanism as limiting factor for rate of leg movement in sprinting. *Research Quarterly,* 1941, **12**, 745-756.

Stelmach, G.E. *Motor control: Issues and trends.* New York: Academic Press, 1976.

Stelmach, G.E. *Information processing in motor control and learning.* New York: Academic Press, 1978.

Teuber, H.L., & Mischkin, M. Judgment of visual and postural vertical after brain injury. *Journal of Psychology,* 1954, **38**, 161-175.

Westerlund, J.H. & Tuttle, W.W. Relationship between running events in track and reaction time. *Research Quarterly,* 1931, **2,** 95-100.

Wiener, N. *Cybernetics or control and communication in the animal and the machine* (2nd ed.), Cambridge. MA: The MIT Press, 1961.

Woodworth, R.S. *Le mouvement.* Paris: Doin, 1903.

Current and Prospective Issues in Motor Behavior

15 G.E. Stelmach, V.A. Diggles, L.D. Szendrovits, and B.G. Hughes

The psychological and physiological basis of motor action is perhaps the most dynamic and expanding area in the scientific core of physical education. One only has to look at the increasing number of researchers currently involved in the area or peruse any of the movement-oriented scientific journals to see the increased popularity. In recent years the motor behavior area has captured an inordinate amount of experimental and theoretical attention in the scientific community. There are several reasons for this new interest: First, there has been an increased realization that motor skills have a rich cognitive component intermediary to perception and action. Second, the motor behaviorists who have been traditionally linked only to psychology have developed, out of mutual necessity, a dialogue with the neuroscientists. Such multidisciplinary interchange has already begun to create new conceptual understandings and opportunities. Third, artificial intelligence has developed techniques enabling computers to exhibit aspects of intelligent behavior which has made insightful contributions to the comprehension of the nature of multipurpose control systems. Finally, motor skill research is no longer shackled by the requirement of practical applicability and has turned toward the processes underlying skilled behavior.

Along with the increasing popularity of motor skills research, there has been an accelerating trend away from research on skill acquisition and learning variables toward research on motor control processes. Because learning cannot be adequately characterized without an understanding of the structural and functional means of control, it appears that addressing processes rather than products is a more basic task for

The preparation of the present manuscript was supported in part by grants from the Research Committee of the Graduate School, University of Wisconsin-Madison, Project No. 190400, Biomedical Research Support Grants 144-G805 and 144-J432, and Air Force Grant AFOSR 78-3691 awarded to G.E. Stelmach.

research. Indeed, such a change is radical, especially since motor skill research was initially shaped by the attitude that learning is the primary aspect of skill which those in physical education should be concerned with. Previously, the conceptual structure for motor learning research was shaped by the overriding view that improvement in task performance (whether measured by speed, reduction of errors, or response consistency), was the sole criterion for successful learning. This approach produced voluminous amounts of empirical research that conveyed little knowledge regarding the acquisition and retention processes of motor skills.

If any worthy concept has emerged from motor behavior research over the years, it is the realization that the human as a behaving system is extremely complex. Yet the history of scientific inquiry has taught that the main path to generality and elegance is to search for measurable properties of behavior where the observable phenomena take on especially simple forms. After many years of attempts to simplify motor behavior through reductionistic paradigms, the emerging contemporary theme is that a complex system cannot be understood as a simple extrapolation from the properties of its elementary components, and that this form of scientific inquiry detracts from the integrity of the system being studied. When viewed mechanically, the human organism is a multisegmented, multilinked system whereby movement of one segment can influence the motion of an adjoining segment in a variety of ways. The plasticity, flexibility, and intricate organization of an acting human presents researchers with a many layered puzzle possessing an infinite number of pieces and combinations.

From the foregoing realizations, there is a trend emerging in motor behavior research which appears to be holistic and interdisciplinary in nature, and which considers the entire system in its attempts at understanding. There is a definite move toward more descriptive studies focusing on phenomena and away from "experiments on experiments." This expansive outlook indicates perhaps that motor behaviorists, who in the past pursued relatively parochial lines of research, have developed a common language with their colleagues in cognitive psychology, systems engineering, biomechanics, and the neurosciences. Of greatest import is the potential for a multidisciplinary approach which may lead us further than any other development toward solution of the puzzle.

If the area is to advance, it must be cognizant of the holistic and ecologically valid perspectives available. These perspectives are quite broad, and it is beyond the scope of this paper to cover all the possible applications to current issues. However, three issues are presented here which are central to progress in the motor behavior area. The remainder of the chapter is concerned with introducing the chosen topics, briefly explaining the present status of each, and speculating on their pertinence and potential for further investigation.

In the first section, control theory is introduced as a vehicle to enhance future conceptualization and experimentation. The viability of this perspective permits interdisciplinary interaction, providing a framework capable of encompassing the *entire* system and generating eloquent simulation techniques for testing and comparing theoretical models. However, because control theory provides only a conceptual referent for examining motor behavior, the second part of the chapter deals with the specification of action. As such, we speculate about the translation of higher level codes into the language of muscle dynamics, first in terms of action plan realization, and second at a less abstract level of discussion, with regard to the metrical and structural specifications between control levels. Last, automation is discussed in the light of the slow and difficult progress being made in the area. A number of contemporary ideas about automated skill are highlighted and future experimental possibilities, especially those using skilled actors in normal and/or natural situations, are offered.

Control Theory

Motor control has moved to the forefront of research interest in physical education. As a result, commonly used, although controversial models have become inadequate. Their insufficiency lies primarily in their simplistic portrayal of the human motor control system and the resulting limited investigation. The more common representation is that of a hierarchical, single-level control system; that is, movement resulting from the execution of motor commands issued from a single command generator. As seen in most information processing models (Massaro, 1975; Welford, 1968), conceptualizing the motor system in this way focused attention on events occurring prior to specification of the response. An example of this type of model was used in motor programs; Henry and Rogers (1960) employed such as information processing model to describe control of rapid movements. Keele (1968) subsequently popularized the same model. At that time, Keele defined a motor program as a centrally stored, prestructured set of motor commands specifying all parameters of the movement. He has since presented a more acceptable and less specific version in which the sequence of movements is represented in the motor program. However, the new version allows closed-loop adjustment when precision is required or corrections are necessary.

While the motor programming notion has produced much research for some time (Keele, 1977; Klapp & Irwin, 1976; Sternberg, Monsell, Knoll, & Wright, 1978), it has been a less than satisfying analogue for movement control. The complexity of the human motor control system far exceeds the explanatory capacity of this concept. The rigidity of motor programs cannot explain how muscles may vary their functional roles for the same joint or why the innervational states of an individual muscle and the movements it produces relate equivocally (Turvey, Shaw, & Mace, 1978). When one considers the possible degrees of freedom (Turvey, 1977) for humans involved in skilled movement, it is difficult to conceive of one structure (the executor) specifying the exact timing and combination of muscle contractions for all possible movements. Such a notion places considerable responsibility on the executor, prescribes total dependency of any lower portion of the system, and suggests a vulnerability to disturbances and malfunctioning not characteristic of the human performer.

Control Theory Perspectives

These paradoxical control problems unaddressed by single-level control models suggest a need to thoroughly reassess our traditional views of how the higher brain centers control coordinated movement. Researchers must adopt a conceptual framework that stresses the entire behaving system, unencumbered by methodologies and "hardware" considerations (Stelmach & Diggles, Note 1). The most useful framework for understanding the emerging theoretical positions is that of control theory, derived from systems analyses (Toates, 1975). Control theory can be viewed as a methodological or operational paradigm, focusing on the interactive behavior between or among the components of the physical system, whereas a system is defined as an interconnection of components forming a configuration to provide a desired response (Metz, 1974). Control theory is more than simply a methodology; it is an idealogy for studying "how things work," and by its nature, draws on many disciplines for application. A control theory perspective aids in conceptual thinking and provides a basis for constructive criticism and functional evaluations.

There are several facets of control theory which recommend it as a framework for understanding motor control in particular. As previously mentioned, an increased awareness of the complexity inherent in the control of action has served to demonstrate the inadequacy of many simple models in physical education literature. A control theory framework considers the entire system, attempting to represent complexity while at the same time refining it to a more digestible quality. Although it is an integral part of the engineering sciences, control theory is not bound to any one discipline; its utility is universal for identifiable physical systems. The common language provided by control theory promotes and facilitates interdisciplinary exchange and as well as an awareness that the principles educed are not dependent on the physical "hardware" of the system. Thus, it furnishes a superstructure for interpreting and comparing findings from multiple sources.

Classification of Systems

There are many diverse types of control systems, each with particular advantages and disadvantages in terms of the type of control they exert. Presented here are three characteristics for categorizing control models that go beyond simple open- and closed-loop notions. The first characteristic addresses the basic organization of the system and specifies the direction of control. This form of organization is hierarchical in that higher centers exert control directly or indirectly on lower structures or mechanisms. Because feedback is only meaningful relative to the desired outcome, it does not qualify as control in this sense; thus feedback loops can be included in a hierarchy without breaching the "top-down" flow of command.

The second categorical distinction is related to the number of levels of transformation which information must pass between the system reference signal and the achievement of the goal state. A transformation in this sense should be thought of as refinement, because of increasing specificity, and alteration, due to additional inputs at other levels. For simplicity's sake, the number of levels a system may possess has been dichotomized into single level and multilevel systems.

A third trait operationally distinguishes control processes into a meaningful dichotomy: lumped versus distributed control. This particular distinction focuses on control within a level of the system defined and the function of the structures at that level. A lumped model is defined where control processes or functions are homogeneous across structures at a single level. Examples of lumped systems can be found in most information processing models in which one structure is posited to operate on input at any given level. In a distributed control system, function at any one level is spread or distributed among a number of structures which may interact to achieve the desired output (Arbib, in press). Consequently, a distributed system does not require an executive command generator to initiate and control movement. An example of distributed control is found in industrial control systems, where a heirarchy of loosely coupled computers optimize production by sharing responsibilities to achieve overall plant goals. (Kahne, Lefkowitz, & Rose, 1979).

Each form of control possesses characteristics which are reflected in the theoretical models subsumed under it. As models are classified under a particular form of control, the advantages and disadvantages associated with that form may be anticipated in the model. Thus, one may evaluate the control capability of existing models based on their form of control. It should be noted that a taxonomy such as that layed out here is an arbitrary and operational convention to aid in theory comparisons and evaluation; thus, overlapping categorizations will occur because of the broad range of theories. For example, there are theories which address the entire behaving system and those which attempt to model some discrete aspect of the system; both can possess varying degrees of complexity and detail. Regardless of the scope of their intended description, models can be classified by their control characteristics. Thus, multilevel, lumped, or distributed control theories may encompass systems that vary widely in their control responsibilities: for example, the firing of a single neuron versus the regulation of a gross movement.

Examples of Systems

In opposition to the simplistic, single-level notions of movement control, the concept of functional groups of muscles, whether they are synergies (Bernstein, 1967), motor schemas (Arbib, in press), spinal automatism (Shik & Orlovsky, 1976) or generators (Smith, 1980), has been posited as intermediate levels of control describing the meaningful units by which the central nervous system specifies movement. Early on, Bernstein (1967) proposed these intermediate steps between the higher centers and individual muscle contractions. He suggested that movement may be specified in terms of muscle linkages; linkages being defined as a group of muscles that commonly work in synergy. This view, in one form or another, has been expressed by a number of people (Easton, 1972; Gelfand, Gurfinkel, Tsetlin, & Shik, 1971; Greene, 1972; Turvey, 1977). Easton (1972) more specifically suggested that a considerable amount of motor coordination was based on a repertoire of reflexes. Muscles engaged in associated movements could be functionally connected by combinations of reflexes or coordinative structures which could be activated by a single command of either central or peripheral origin. The notion of coordinative structures described by Easton refers to the pattern of connections between interneurons or motoneurons resembling those patterns elicited by reflexes (Easton, 1977). He arrived at this notion through observation of quadrupedal gaits, some athletic and art forms (Fukuda, 1961), and neurophysiological findings (Hellebrandt, Houtz, Partridge & Walter, 1956; Shik & Orlovsky, 1976).

Further support for these functional muscle combinations comes from the presence of interneuronal networks which may be activated to produce stereotypic movements and segmental reflexes. The autonomy connoted by this subsystem would be curbed slightly by the necessity of a smoothing or tuning function to choose and fit appropriate sets of muscles for achieving coordinated, volitional movement (Greene, 1972). Central systems, using the mechanisms proposed above, fall under the rubric of multilevel systems where transformations of the movement command intervene between intention and performance. The advantages of multiple levels of control over single level include (a) a reduction in the size and complexity of the command, and (b) the alleviation of the computational burden on the high level "executor" by delegating minor computation and processing to lower levels. However, these models are still simplistic in a control sense because they suggest that functioning is lumped within levels. The disadvantage of lumping control in this way is that plasticity and flexibility is lost if control is not interactive at a given level. Subsystems may not compensate for each other except through the next highest level of control. Lumped models of the central nervous system also require an executive controller or "command neuron" (Rosenbaum, 1977) to initiate commands, resulting in a rigid and vulnerable control system. In some cases, the lumped model may be a simplification of a more complex, distributed model, but the cost of simplicity is the elimination of plasticity and flexibility. One factor contributing to the use of lumped models is that the system's "hard wiring" is still poorly defined. When more is known about the interactions and interconnections of the central and peripheral nervous systems, lumped models will presumably become less common.

To circumvent the shortcomings of lumped behavioral models, it is necessary to postulate not only vertical interaction in the nervous system but horizontal interaction as well. In support of horizontal interaction, investigators have focused on the spinal cord as a complex mediator between supraspinal influences and muscle contraction (Berkinblit, Deliaginia, Feldman, Gelfand, & Orlovsky, 1978; Gurfinkel, Kots, Krinskiy, Paltsev, Feldman, & Tsetlin, 1971; Gurfinkel & Paltsev, 1965; Shik, Orlovsky, & Severin, 1966). For the most part, like Bernstein (1967), these investigators view muscle synergies as mechanisms for simplifying the control of movement by functioning as the external language of movement and the internal language of the nervous system. A number of investigators systematically examined the communication and interactions of subsystems involved in preparing a complex, kinematic chain like the body for movement (Belenkii, Gurfinkel, & Paltsev, 1967; Gurfinkel & Paltsev, 1965; Paltsev & Elner, 1967). For example, Gurfinkel and Paltsev (1965) demonstrated the presence of contralateral influences in the spinal cord; they observed that a knee jerk on one side altered the state of the segmentary structures of the opposite side by evoking both patterns of facilitation and inhibition depending on the time course of the task. Belenkii, Gurfinkel, and Paltsev (1967) also reported anticipatory activation of some muscles of the lower limbs and trunk involved in maintaining equilibrium. Recordings indicated that neural activity preceding movement was elicited not only from alpha motoneurons but also from the interneurons of the spinal segment. It appeared that supraspinal processes do not simply send direct movement commands, but that their basic role is the "appropriate rearrangement of the interaction organization of the individual subsystems at the spinal level" (Gelfand et al., 1971, p. 336). Thus, high-level processes prescribing the interactions of subsystems seem to implement feedforward and achieve tuning. It is the interactive and cooperative nature of these spinal processes that places them in the distributed category.

These findings suggest that movement is controlled by a multilevel, distributed system in which control is diffused across several structures interacting within and between levels to arrive at an output. In this context, a single "command neuron" or executor is not requisite; it may be replaced by the cooperative effort of a number of structures or collection of neurons. Thus cooperative computation, as Arbib (1975) terms it, is achieved through both vertical and horizontal interaction of neurons. This type of control offers an explanation of the adjustments seen in movement to compensate for variations in starting position, unexpected disturbances, and injury to a subsystem. In doing so, the system's reliability is greatly enhanced.

The advantages proffered by models of distributed control are convincing proponents of this concept. The flexibility and plasticity of such models closely resemble that of human performance and illustrate the adaptability of distributed control. However, there are disadvantages to the distributed control model which may detract from its usefulness, but increase its accuracy. When control is centralized through a high level controller with all available information, better performance results relative to specific situations and purposes. However, this achievement is at the cost of flexibility, reliability, and an extraordinary increase in responsibility of the single controller. When control is decentralized as in a multilevel, distributed model, greater flexibility is achieved through interacting systems, but there is also the potential for errors with each interaction, much like residual noise in the system. Although such noise would not be great enough to result in a system failure, it would increase the variability of the output. Noise-produced variability in this context could explain why humans never perform a task exactly the same way twice.

Perhaps the greatest disadvantage of the distributed control concept is the difficulty one encounters in trying to study it. The possible interactions and potential sources for input present the investigator with a Gordian knot, difficult to unravel and difficult to retie. The scarcity of research efforts directed at testing this model asserts the reluctance some researchers may feel in using such a model. However, control modeled as a multilevel, distributed system is worth the effort of examination. Phenomenologically, convincing parallels have already been identified between the human nervous system and this type of control, and future investigation should be aimed at empirical substantiation.

In the past, certain aspects of control theory have been applied to the study of motor behavior. Input-output relationships, block diagrams, and "black boxes" were commonly used conventions in systems modeling. This elementary application is in some ways responsible for the simplicity of earlier models. The true potential of a control theory perspective has not been realized due to this rather eclectic approach to its adaptation. If we are to progress toward more accurate representations, we must build models with the objective of simulating more closely the complexity of the system they are to represent. As stated previously, control theory has much to offer in the modeling of motor control systems, and as will be seen in subsequent sections, it offers a logical framework for consideration of specific control mechanisms.

Specification of Action

Unitization

Plans of Action. One of the most important issues to be addressed in motor control is the interface of abstract representations with movements in the construction of actions. This interface requires the translation of a higher level code to the language of muscle dynamics. The propagation of this control signal seems to be one of the most natural, albeit perhaps most elusive, objects for investigation because scientists are continuously seeking optimal and valid solutions for complex systems. Knowledge of the mechanisms used for the development and transformation of economical and expedient control signals would certainly increase our understanding of the motor system. In an effort to propose some questions which can stimulate and guide future research, transformation processes for a plan of action, tuning, and the language of muscle dynamics will be examined here.

Any theory of action must account for the obvious translation of intentions into purposeful movement. This is made possible, at least conceptually, through a plan of action. However, a study of action plans, per se, will not further the understanding of motor control, but a study of how the required process translates these abstract representations into action will invite a future direction for inquiry.

Psychologists have used a variety of explanations to describe plans of action in an attempt to explain purposeful interaction with the environment. Conventionally, they are described as general instructions prescribed for the regulation and integration of muscular coordination (Miller, Galanter, & Pribram, 1960; Norman, Note 2; Pew, 1974). Three attributes are characteristically ascribed to action plans. First, plans are derived from intention. Second, plans are general representations of action, and not detailed specifications. Third, they contain information concerning both the appropriate sequencing of movements and their temporal characteristics as they relate to the serial nature of the act. Unfortunately, these explanations have remained in a conceptual format and have not moved into an experimental setting, a necessary transition if we are to conceptually and behaviorally understand the course of action. Because this "translation" has not happened as yet, nor is it likely to happen in the near future due to the "slippery" nature of these constructs, it is proposed that a more fruitful approach would be to study the process by which these higher level control signals carry out their control functions.

Tuning. The development of action plans into a precise regulation of movements requires the translation of crude general commands to specific muscle activation. Assuming that a plan of action may be implemented through the process of tuning, two immediate questions must be answered. How is tuning effected, and where is it implemented? It has been proposed that tuning is accomplished through feedforward and feedback mechanisms, whereas the implementation seems to occur at an intermediate level of control, functional muscle groups (Arbib, in press).

It seems quite clear that a composition of coordinated movements is not controlled by commanding single muscle contractions. The advantage of this intermediate level of control, of course, lies in reducing the degrees of freedom of the system in its complex interaction with the environment, while simultaneously reducing the load on memory. Physiological evidence for the presence of functional muscle groups has come most notably from Russian research. Shik and Orlovsky (1976) found that the basic pattern of stepping could be generated by the spinal cord without input from the brain. This spinal automatism controls phases of activity of muscles in the stepping cycle, whereas the brain influences the overall level of muscle activity. The unmistakable presence of interlimb reflexes and the central coordination of limbs during locomotion indicated a higher level of automatism responsible for these events. Easton (1977) supplied a particularly appealing description of how such functional muscle groups could operate. According to Easton, movement commands activate reflex centers which, in turn, activate groups of motoneurons and/or interneurons. Once the pathways are facilitated, the central nervous system issues a general excitatory command to all motoneurons but triggers only the facilitated ones. The product of the reflex centers are fitted together and smoothed by a set of tuning transformations. Sources of input are accessible from direct cortical control of motoneurons, afferent feedback, and reflex recruitment.

From the neurosciences also emerged the realization that muscles engaged in associated movements, which may be functionally connected, could not be controlled simply by combining stereotypic actions. Although movement commands may activate functional muscle groups, coordinated volitional movement require a smoothing or tuning function to choose and fit appropriate sets of muscles (Easton, 1972). Greene (1972) specifically described tuning before movement as selecting an appropriate operating characteristic (feedforward). The highest control center selects an appropriate combination of movements appearing to provide the best fit for the desired outcome, while transformations at lower levels shape this combination into a more precise approximation through feedback. The parameters that appear to be controlled in the tuning process relate to selected functional muscle groups and their temporal characteristics.

Several ideas have been developed in an attempt to explain how plans of action are translated to coordinated movement, the most popular of which considers action plans to be implemented through a tuning process which in turn exerts its effects on functional muscle groups to orchestrate voluntary movement. Arbib (in press) suggested that coordinated control programs schedule and coordinate simultaneous action through the use of feedforward and feedback mechanisms so that successive actions are smoothly phased in order. This view posits feedforward as an agent for generating control signals to provide a functional relationship between desired output (e.g., muscle length) and necessary input (e.g., motoneuron firing). In this coactivated state, feedforward is continuously active to maintain the desired output, while feedback acts to refine this approximation. In discrete-activation feedforward, when feedforward and feedback are explicitly distinct, each activation of the feedforward signal brings the system into the right "ball park" so that feedback can operate effectively. Although these ideas are more characteristic of a complex behaving system, they are largely speculative and therefore warrant further scrutiny. For example, how can the system map one control signal to coordinate many signals; that is, how can we perform a single operation controlling independent components in a very detailed prescribed manner? At what levels of the nervous system are these transformations taking place? Future research will certainly revolve around these new issues and the related questions that they raise.

Parameterization of Action

The Language of a Control System. An additional contemporary issue is one which addresses control problems at closer proximity to the surface structures than to those commented on thus far. As a matter of necessity, control systems research should be combined with work aimed at defining the parameterization, or at least the degree of parameterization, of action. At least two reasons justify the necessity. First and foremost, a control system, in and of itself, cannot adequately describe action; it merely provides a framework or environment in which action, given suitable context, could occur. Clearly, a control system is unusable if its software is neither described nor appropriate, because it then has no *means* of control; it would be like a machine with no operating instructions. Furthermore, the greater the controlling influence assigned to lower centers, given their functional flexibility, the greater the need for specific understanding of parameters. One way to analogize parameterization is to consider a control system and the "language" with which it must produce, from a nonmotor plan of action, an overt motor act. The language can be considered the most mutually informative, concise, and immutable instruction relayed from one control level to any other. The language of one pair of control structures may be different from that of another pair, but over the entire system, structures which converse with each other do so in a common language.[1] For example, in an hypothetical control system, movement force is specified by an executive structure A. Structure B, in response, integrates the quantity and obtains a velocity specification which it might relay in turn to structure C. Through further quantity integration, C is therefore capable of obtaining a displacement value from A's original force specification by dealing only with B in their common language.

The second reason for improving the understanding of this language is the result of traditional motor behavior theories' inherent inability to represent known functional characteristics of the nervous system. Motor programs (and open-loop systems of similar ilk) additionally are rigid and energy-expensive even as theoretical models because of their single level, lumped control characteristics. Mounting physiological and behavioral data (see Stelmach & Requin, 1980, for a contemporary anthology) is suggestive of a multilevel control system with distributed and perhaps free-dominance characteristics (Turvey et al., 1978). Being address-specific, motor programs are cumbersome and top-heavy to the extent that even the simplest acts would overload the executive's storage and specification capability. In terms of the language analogy, rather than determining which part of the "vocabulary" would permit initiation and partial completion of any act, a motor program seems to need to determine and correctly order a huge number of different "letters," a situation uncharacteristic of an efficient and effective control system (and one also failing to resolve the degrees-of-freedom problem mentioned in the preceding section). In addition, both open- and closed-loop theories place imbalanced priority on efference (open-loop) and afference (closed-loop), when such a distinction is becoming increasingly redundant (see Evarts, 1971; Kelso, Holt, Kugler, & Turvey, 1980; Kelso & Stelmach, 1976 for further discussion).

Motor Programs. Recently, and in the light of more convincing evidence, the concept of motor programs has been revised. Schmidt, Zelaznik, Hawkins, Frank, and Quinn (1979), for example, have promoted the idea of a motor program as an abstract memory structure containing certain generalized and invariant properties, but which at some stage of

---

[1]The nature of the system's 'language' can be included in a broader analogy: basic subsystem control levels and simple neurophysiological mechanisms may be regarded as a 'vocabulary' of actions from which are developed more specific and unique movements. This 'vocabulary' represents a practical working repertoire of acts (and not the total 'dictionary' of possible variations in muscle dynamics or innervation) which may be grouped into 'words' whose number is smaller than the possible combinations of 'letters' (Gelfand et al., 1971).

action realization, requires the specification of other parameters in order to allow the act's unique characteristics to evolve (shades of vocabularies).

One obvious need in research is to determine whether every metrical and structural prescription is context-specific and dependent upon the muscle involvement or movement characteristics. In addition to pursuing this problem, other directions of research need to be examined; namely, the appealing arguments and models which have been proposed with regard to the physical and dynamic properties of muscle. Suffice to note here that at least one reason for their appeal is that muscle is the final component or filter through which all motor output must pass (Cooke, 1980; Turvey, 1977). The research on innate activities like gait reveal that there may indeed be centrally programmed parameters which are invariant over changes in the movement pattern. Shik and Orlovsky (1976) have noted that increases in locomotion speed are only the result of changes in force application during the stance phase and not in the phasing (relative timing) of the limbs. Grillner (1975) has provided a model which considers sequencing and relative timing to be invariants in the production of action, and Schmidt et al. (1979) have suggested that relative force within a sequence might also be specified in an act's abstract representation. There is not a great deal of research explicitly addressing this problem. One interpretation, derived from handwriting experimentation (e.g., Merton, 1972; Wing, 1978), has been suggestive of movement duration and spatial relationships being context-consistent, whereas overall force specifications are free to vary. This view has been supported by recent two-handed task data (Kelso, Southard, & Goodman, 1979), and Klapp (1977) has shown that muscle selection is parameterized at a relatively late stage in the specification process.

Mass Springs. A more accurate and attractive approach to control would be to develop a model based on the consistent finding that there is specification of final position. Supportive data has come from both behavioral research (e.g., Kelso, 1977; MacNeilage, 1970; Marteniuk & Roy, 1979) and from physiology. Feldman's work (Asatryan & Feldman, 1965; Feldman, 1966a, 1966b) in particular, is now being reinforced by a series of other research focusing on the dynamic characteristics of muscle. The original studies examined arm movements in response to sudden unresisted loadings or unloadings of external torques, and concluded that the arm acted like an elastic system whose mechanical properties were not influenced by the external force changes. The model suggests that the nervous system preselects equilibrium points by choosing the parameter of zero or resting length of a muscle, with movement occurring if actual length does not equal this value. Although more complex than a simple spring, the basic argument is that the muscles act upon a joint by virtue of their inherent nonlinear vibratory or oscillatory characteristics, so that regardless of initial location or external perturbations, the joint is capable of achieving the desired equilibrium point. Recent evidence strengthens this model. Bizzi's work (summarized in Bizzi, 1980) has revealed the primacy of an equilibrium point (between agonist and antagonist length-tension) specification. Bizzi and his associates found that learned arm and head target positions could be reproduced by normal and rhizotomized monkeys despite constant and acute load perturbations. Kelso (1977) found similar results in functionally deafferented human subjects.

This data, in addition to supporting an equilibrium hypothesis (Bizzi, 1980), effectively lays to rest some basic arguments by open- and closed-loop adherents and reveals some parameters and structures that cannot be involved in action specification. For example, details of the replication of target positions under deafferented conditions have long been a problem to closed-loop arguments, and open-loop theorists may have difficulty interpreting the achievement of final position under perturbed movement conditions. This finding is also contradictory (at least for unidirectional movements) to Schmidt et al's. (1979) remodeling of motor programs by the impulse-timing hypothesis. According to this hypothesis, and using the Bizzi paradigm, the perturbation of the moving arm would result in a shortened movement distance, since the force and duration specifications would have been met. Only if the precise length-tension ratio for agonist and antagonist muscles were made could a location be attained despite external torque application.

An important problem arising from the Bizzi (1980) hypothesis is that the system would require an immense storage capacity and computational capability for one specific equilibrium point to be specified for one movement: from all the possible length-tension curves for the agonist and for the antagonist, one value, at the intersection point of these curves, needs to be specified. Accepting that the muscle does act like a nonlinear spring, the problem of control of the spring is pivotal. Sakitt (Note 3) has suggested that an equivalent electrical means of overcoming this storage-computation overload would be a battery across a rheostat. The specification of the rheostat pointer would determine alpha motoneuron innervation (final position), and the battery would determine total innervation (overall muscle tension). Therefore, Sakitt suggested that after determining joint angle on the rheostat equivalent, any innervation will cause movement to the correct location. Does such an electrical circuit have a neural equivalent? Or is some other mechanism involved in this supplementary and necessary parameterization?

Houk's (1979) work is relevant to these problems. He suggested that descending motor commands act to shift the threshold length of the motor servo (a negative feedback system involving stretch and unloading reflexes), and that they could act to modify muscle stiffness (the ratio of force change to length change), rather than to regulate just muscle length or provide load compensation. Therefore, in response to the mechanical parameterization question (i.e., whether it is of length, force, or some derivative thereof), Houk suggests that none of these is specified individually "since a controlled change in threshold length acts to shift the entire relationship between length and force" (p. 112) which is then regulated by proprioceptive feedback. One might consider that the regulation of stiffness is not unlike regulating a rheostat pointer; the specification of resting length, by length-tension curves for example, is preset with other modifications (rate, acceleration and phasing) being made by altering stiffness and damping properties (Kelso et al., 1980). Such a system is advantageous in the contemporary body-environment perspective of action (e.g., Bernstein, 1967; Turvey, 1977) since it provides a springlike interface between the actor and the environment (Houk, 1979).

One pivotal direction that motor behaviorists appear to be taking is the depiction of movement control in terms of muscle dynamics and the coordination of groupings of muscles as single functional units. Recently gathered data, such as those of Bizzi, Cooke, Kelso et al., and Schmidt (all in Stelmach & Requin, 1980), when taken with those of Feldman (1966a, 1966b) reflect the convergence of conceptual, theoretical, and empirically based positions. A complete understanding of the positions must be a future goal. Presently, there are a number of aspects which remain problematic. The data mentioned above, although supporting contemporary theories of action, do not provide lucid explanations about multidirectional movements either in terms of control mechanisms or in terms of parameter specification. (It should be noted, however, that alternatives to these hypotheses have yet to be consistently substantiated.)

Schmidt's (1980) suggestion that relative timing is a dominant aspect of action specification in reversed movements warrants expanded investigation and elaboration, and Houk's (1979) description of the exact nature of skeletomotor reflexes requires further examination as well. Whether the parametrization of multilimbed movements is similar to that for single limbs is unclear (compare, for example, Kelso et al., 1979; Marteniuk & MacKenzie, 1980). The resolution of these questions is certainly a challenge for the 1980s.

Automation

Motor Skill Automation

As one progresses from an unskilled to a skilled state, dramatic changes occur in motor performance. It is widely believed that an unskilled performer must spend considerable time and effort to regulate the movements demanded by a particular task, a process requiring active and conscious participation. In contrast, conscious involvement is uncharacteristic of a skilled individual's performance.

Despite these known characteristics, our knowledge about how motor skills are automated is surprisingly scant and certainly incomplete. In many ways, psychologists know little more about the nature of automated motor skills than was known in the 19th century (Stelmach & Larish, 1980). There is really no clear empirical support for automation, yet such a capability seems to be necessary for an optimally designed motor control system. Perhaps this accounts for why so many researchers intuitively accept the idea or assumption that motor skill automation is possible. Past research, however, has assessed automation in a cursory way and has been confined to examining the motor act itself.

Over the years, it has been assumed that the way to understand attention is by documenting the limitations of processing capacity. Consequently, numerous attempts have been made to define factors involved in limiting, controlling, and directing attention (Kahneman, 1973; Keele, 1972; Moray, 1967; Norman, 1968). On the basis of this rationale, two distinct views on attention allocation have developed: one relating to capacity and the other to structure. A major problem plaguing the attention area is the inability of the capacity models (Kahneman, 1973; Norman & Bobrow, 1975) to provide a quantitative framework wherein the upper bounds of capacity can be determined. If a movement's attentional demand varies according to the nature of each task to be performed, it is difficult to pinpoint the reasons for processing limitations when an explicit theoretical framework is nonexistent. Lacking a definable limit of attention, capacity models are at best global, fostering predictions too imprecise to allow for a fair and adequate test. In contrast, structural models (Keele, 1972) have been subjected to rigorous tests because they are more concise, permitting clear-cut experiments to be designed for testing their validity. But capacity theorists contend that these tests include techniques insensitive to the small amounts of attention required by a process or that the difficulty of the tasks fails to exceed the limits of the capacity system. Circular arguments like these and the ability of each model to account for part or all of the other's research data are a major hindrance in revealing the nature and function of attention within the processing system.

However, the foregoing research and analysis still fail to provide definitive answers about the nature of automation. Important unsolved problems include the determination of the operational characteristics of this automatic state and the variables influencing the development of automation. Only after gaining an understanding of these problems can researchers begin to make substantive statements about the development and antecedent conditions of motor skill automation. The studies examining simultaneous motor performance were both equivocal and subject to numerous methodological criticisms (Bahrick, Noble, & Fitts, 1954; Brown, 1962; Vroon, 1973). Further, the reaction-time probe studies relate to automation only in the sense that they document which aspects of movement require attention (Ells, 1969; Posner & Keele, 1969; Salmoni, 1974).

Automatic Activation

In this section, a somewhat different perspective on motor skill automation is briefly presented, namely, the study of automatic sequences (for an expanded version, see Stelmach & Larish, 1980). In short, an automated sequence consists of memory associations which are activated in specific response configurations without active attention. Goal-directed movements are generally made in reference to some specific environmental context where the activating cue may be visual, auditory, or kinesthetic. As a result, repetitive association of a specific environmental cue with a specific motor act, or a finite number of responses, is quite common. In fact, what may explain automation is the development of an automatic sequence, such that the contextual situation automatically triggers the necessary action from the appropriate response class. Thus, a crucial aspect of automation involves the establishment of definite stimulus-response relationships with a specific context for action where the automatic processes activate the retrieval of overlearned associations from well-established memory structures. Therefore, researchers should no longer focus on just the motor act itself, but rather should emphasize the contiguity between context and action.

Associative and Automatic Learning

Recently, LaBerge (1975) and Shiffrin and Schneider (1977) developed models of perceptual and associative learning based on automatic activation. LaBerge viewed perceptual learning as a two-stage process: First, one learns to select among relevant and irrelevant stimulus features. Second, the relevant features are organized into higher order cognitive units. Initially, both stages are subservient to attention control for the identification and coding of unfamiliar stimuli or events. Each experience with the novel event increases the strength of this coding, such that less attention is required for perceptual organization. Finally, with repeated exposures, the necessity for attentional control to produce the codes is eliminated.

Schneider and Shiffrin (1977) and Shiffrin and Schneider (1977) extended LaBerge's ideas to include motor respones in automatic sequences. An automatic sequence consists of a systematic association of memory codes which have two properties: (a) the sequence of codes always becomes active in response to a particular input configuration, where the inputs may be externally or internally generated and include the general situational context, and (b) the sequence is activated automatically without needing active attention by the subject (Schneider & Shiffrin, 1977, p. 2). An example the authors give is that of a red traffic light initiating a braking response when someone is driving a car, yet a walking, halting, or traffic-scanning response when the same person is a pedestrian.

Perceptual learning, then, is analogous to the process of acquiring a new motor skill, where the learner must discriminate among relevant and irrelevant movements, and then organize the relevant movements into a patterned whole: the skill itself. As learning progresses, conscious selection and organization is eliminated, and the initially independent movements are performed as a smoothly sequenced action. Associative learning involves the temporal-spatial congruity between an environmental event and the optimal motor response schema (Schmidt, 1976). It must be reemphasized that there should be a mutual dependency between current context and action. It can be said that automatic sequences consist of over-learned spatial-temporal associations between a set of environmental conditions and a motor schema appropriate to the current situation. Norman (Note 2) seems correct in his statement:

Conscious awareness of schemas is not necessary for performance. The general idea is that well-learned plans need only be specified at the highest level. It is only with poorly learned acts or with novel rearrangements of well-learned components that conscious awareness of lower level components is required. When a plan is modified, however, there is a critical junction point at which the modification must occur, and if the required schema is not activated at that time, the regular, unmodified set will continue. (p. 24)

Examples of Automatic Sequences

The functional importance of automatic sequences can be illustrated by describing real-life behaviors that appear to be under automatic control and readers can gain insight into automatic sequencing by observing nonrandom errors in performance. It is apparent that motor slips most frequently occur when habituated or routine motor act must be altered in the absence of conscious processing.

A number of excellent examples of automatic sequencing can be identified in car-driving behaviors. While a general intent is usually to drive to a particular location, behaviors like unlocking the door, turning on the ignition, fastening the seat belt, releasing the parking brake, and shifting can be considered specific and routine elements in the driving scheme. For many, these actions are even completed in a pre-specified, unaltered sequence each time they get into the car. In fact, these behaviors are probably habituated to the point that attention need not be given to their actual performance. These actions are certainly simple enough, but what happens to them when one must drive an unfamiliar car? If the inside layout of the car is different, some very interesting, and sometimes dangerous, motor slips can occur.

The first example of a motor slip occurs when individuals switch from a car with the shifting lever on the floor above the drive shaft, to one in which the lever is situated on the steering column. In this instance, they often "automatically" reach down towards the floor, searching for the gear shift. Only after they cannot find it do they realize the lever is positioned in another location. A second example involves the placement of the parking brake. In some cars, the brake is off to the left below the steering wheel, and in others it is along side the driver's seat. Here again, when the car is unfamiliar, a common movement is to reach to the "normal" location of the parking brake only to find that it is not there.

Typewriting is the final example presented here. Anyone who has had to type with an unfamiliar typewriter having a different keyboard arrangement than their usual one can surely attest to these motor slips. That is, one continually reaches to the area habitually associated with one of the original keys. For skilled typists, the necessary adjustments between context and action are indeed difficult and tedious. To make an adjustment, typists must either slow their typing speed or stop completely to locate the new position of the key.

What these examples illustrate is that there appears to be a close association among the intent to act, the context for action, and the motor schema. The intention defines the context for action, which in turn activates the motor schema best suited for achieving this intent. However, variations in context require alterations of the habituated actions in the motor schema. Motor performance errors result if conscious processing is not allocated to this end. Therefore, these performance errors are not random occurrences.

In all the behaviors described, a conditioned response was triggered by the current context, but the necessary motor adjustments were not made because alterations in the context were not immediately realized. The automatic sequence is only incorrect relative to the changes in the environmental context. Hence, the normally associated actions were executed. The automatic responses were noticed only after attention and conscious processing were required for the situation.

Although the examples of automatic activation may be quite common and the arguments logical, researchers must go beyond mere intuition to develop an experimental framework in which questions about automation can be empirically assessed. The lack of a substantive knowledge base about automation and movement points out the difficulty in developing a suitable methodology. The study of automatic sequences, in conjunction with motor performance errors, has the potential to fill some of this void.

One characteristic of such a research endeavor is clear: automatic sequences must be examined in overlearned or highly practiced activities, a stipulation which poses a number of problems in an experimental setting. A possible solution is to use persons known to be highly skilled in tasks deemed suitable. Professional typists, concert pianists, and skilled athletes, for example, would make excellent choices. Almost any activity in which context and action are redundant should be potentially useful.

Providing suitable experimental tasks can be devised (see Stelmach & Larish, 1980), this approach should reveal important insights into the nature and structure of automated behaviors. Furthermore, we should be able to ascertain the operational characteristics of the automatic state, along with the critical variables for developing automatic sequences; thus, we should be able to better understand motor skill automation. This relationship between automation and automatic sequencing is both functionally and theoretically useful, and it provides an exciting prospect for future research. Although this empirical approach may not completely elucidate motor skill automation, it has the potential to advance the current state of the art.

Concluding Remarks

In this chapter, three topics possessing potential rewards for future investigations have been examined. However, if motor behaviorists are to take advantage of these directions and make headway in developing them, they must pay attention to the ramifications of studying a complex behaving system. To some extent, this concern is reflected in a current trend toward descriptive studies focusing on meaningful behavioral phenomena and using diverse dependent variables to capture some of the complexity that may escape the traditional measures of performance accuracy and response time. These additional variables provide information conducive to developing a conceptual framework stressing how a behaving system controls and regulates coordinated motor acts and encourages an holistic view of motor behavior. A multidisciplinary approach to research would go far in achieving this view and can be arrived at only through a functional understanding of key concepts from a number of disciplines studying the biological and behavioral determinants of movement. Behavioral models in the past have changed in accordance with developments in supporting disciplines, and motor control theorists should be prepared to take advantage of progress in each related discipline to advance their own.

Additionally, a system as complex as the human nervous system should be analyzed and conceptualized at different qualitative levels, a task accomplished only with a multidisciplinary approach. Marr and Poggio (1972) specified four important levels of understanding related to the object of scientific inquiry, equated here with the motor control system. At the first level, investigation centers around basic elements and components of the motor control system like neurons, muscle fibers, and motor units. The second level of inquiry concentrates on mechanisms, combinations, and composites of the basic components which act to perform specific functions, including sensory transducers, reflexes, synergies. At the third level, investigation focuses on the algorithm, describing the interaction and coordination of mechanisms. Sensorimotor integration, schema notions, cerebellar and cortical control of movement would all be representative of this level of inquiry. The remaining level is that of theory, that set of principles governing the interactions of a collection of algorithms. There are logical and causal relations among the four levels of description and each will have its place in the eventual understanding of motor behavior. However, individual disciplines often pursue research confined to one level with little consideration for the others. It should be be obvious that the information available at a particular level can support the findings of another while generating new directions for further research at either level. Appreciating the complexity of the motor control system as well as understanding it requires attention to these four levels and the relations between them.

It is clear that the emerging picture of what a motor behavior investigator needs to know and to pursue is a bit staggering. The evolution of the human organism has developed into a fantastically multilayered system which changes or is mediated in so many ways that it almost defies analysis. Unless diverse approaches encompassing a variety of concepts and methods are sought, our own insights will not go beyond some narrow province of the area. Research focused on the description and analysis of motor behavior requires increasingly specialized techniques often proceeding on a day-to-day basis with attention confined to the immediate demands of technical methodology and immediate theories. However, we need a broad, flexible, multidisciplinary framework which focuses on the conceptual understanding of motor behavior. Without it, there is a danger that the future will produce fragmented, isolated, and competitive subdisciplines where research ideas or situations become ends in themselves. If the future is to be bright, researchers must attempt to cumulate and synthesize research findings in a broad perspective that stresses the biological and psychological determinants of coordinated acts.

Reference Notes

1. Stelmach, G.E., & Diggles, V.A. *Control theories in motor control* (Tech. Rep. 2). University of Wisconsin, Motor Behavior Laboratory, 1980.
2. Norman, D.A. Slips of the mind and a theory of action. Unpublished manuscript, 1979.
3. Sakitt, B. A spring model and equivalent neural network for arm posture control. Unpublished manuscript, 1979.

References

Arbib, M.A. Artificial intelligence and brain theory: Unities and diversities. *Annals of Biomedical Engineering,* 1975, **3**, 238-274.

Arbib, M.A. Perceptual structures and distributed motor control. In V.B. Brooks (Ed.), *Handbook of physiology: Motor control* (Vol. 3). American Physiological Society, in press.

Asatryan, D.G., & Feldman, A.G. Functional tuning of the nervous system with control of movement or maintenance of a steady posture: I. Mechanographic analysis of the work on the joint on execution of a postural task. *Biophysics,* 1965, **10**, 925-935.

Bahrick, H.P., Noble, M., & Fitts, P.M. Extra-task performance as a measure of learning a primary task. *Journal of Experimental Psychology,*

1954, **58**, 298-302.

Belenkii, V. Ye., Gurfinkel, V.S., & Paltsev, Ye. I. Elements of control of voluntary movement. *Biophysics,* 1967, **12**, 154-161.

Berkinblit, M.B., Deliagina, T.G., Feldman, A.F., Gelfand, I.M., & Orlovsky, G.N. Generation of scratching: I. Activity of spinal interneurons during scratching. *Journal of Neurophysiology,* 1978, **41**, 1040-1056.

Bernstein, N. *The coordination and regulation of movement.* New York: Pergamon Press, 1967.

Bizzi, E. Central and peripheral mechanisms in motor control. In G.E. Stelmach & J. Requin (Eds.), *Tutorials in motor behavior.* Amsterdam: North-Holland, 1980.

Brown, I.D. Measuring the spare mental capacity of car drivers by a subsidiary auditory task. *Ergonomics,* 1962, **5**, 247-250.

Cooke, J.D. The organization of simple, skilled movements. In G.E. Stelmach & J. Requin (Eds.), *Tutorials in motor behavior.* Amsterdam: North-Holland, 1980.

Easton, T.A. On the normal use of reflexes. *American Scientist,* 1972, **60**, 591-599.

Easton, T.A. Coordinative structures—the basis for a motor program. In D.M. Landers & R.W. Christina (Eds.), *Psychology of motor behavior and sport.* Champaign, IL: Human Kinetics, 1977.

Ells, J.G. *Attentional requirements of movement control.* Unpublished doctoral dissertation, University of Oregon, 1969.

Evarts, E. Feedback and corollary discharge: A merging of the concepts. *Neurosciences Research Program Bulletin,* 1971, **9**, 86-112.

Feldman, A.G. Functional tuning of the nervous system with control of movement or maintenance of a steady posture: II. Controllable parameters of the muscles. *Biophysics,* 1966, **11**, 565-578. (a)

Feldman, A.G. Functional tuning of the nervous system with control of movement or maintenance of a steady posture: III. Mechanographic analysis of the execution by man of the simplest motor tasks. *Biophysics,* 1966, **11**, 766-775. (b)

Fukuda, T. Studies on human dynamic postures from the viewpoint of postural reflexes. *Acta Oto-Laryngologica* (Suppl. 161), 1961, 1-52.

Gelfand, I.M., Gurfinkel, V.S., Tsetlin, M.L., & Shik, M.L. Some problems in the analysis of movements. In I.M. Gelfand, V.S. Gurfinkel, S.V. Fomin, & M.L. Tsetlin (Eds.), *Models of the structural-functional organization of certain biological systems.* Cambridge, MA: MIT press, 1971.

Greene, P.H. Problems of organization of motor systems. In R. Rosen & F.M. Snell (Eds.), *Progress in theoretical biology* (Vol. 2). New York:

Academic Press, 1972.

Grillner, S. Locomotion in vertebrates: Central and reflex interaction. *Physiological Reviews,* 1975, **55**, 247-304.

Gurfinkel, V.S., Kots, Ya. M., Krinskiy, V.I., Paltsev, Ye. I., Feldman, A.G., Tsetlin, M.L., & Shik, M.L. Concerning tuning before movement. In I.M. Gelfand, V.S. Gurfinkel, S.V. Fomin, & M.L. Tsetlin, (Eds.), *Models of the structural-functional organization of certain biological systems.* Cambridge, MA: MIT Press, 1971.

Gurfinkel, V.S., & Paltsev, Ye. I. The effect of the state of the segmentary apparatus of the spinal cord on the realization of a simple motor reaction. *Biophysics,* 1965, **10**, 944-951.

Hellebrandt, F.A., Houtz, S.J., Partridge, M.J., & Walters, C.E. Tonic neck reflexes in exercises of stress in man. *American Journal of Physiology and Medicine,* 1956, **35**, 144-159.

Henry, F.M., & Rogers, D.E. Increased response latency for complicated movements and a "Memory Drum" theory of neuromotor reaction. *Research Quarterly,* 1960, **31**, 448-458.

Houk, J.C. Regulation of stiffness by skeletomotor reflexes, *Annual Review of Physiology,* 1979, **41**, 99-114.

Kahne, S., Lefkowitz, I., & Rose, C. Automatic control by distributed intelligence. *Scientific American,* 1979, **240**, 78-90.

Kahneman, D. *Attention and effort.* Englewood Cliffs, NJ: Prentice-Hall, 1973.

Keele, S.W. Movement control in skilled motor performance. *Psychological Bulletin,* 1968, **70**, 387-403.

Keele, S.W. Attention demands of memory retrieval. *Journal of Experimental Psychology,* 1972, **93**, 245-248.

Keele, S.W. Current status of the motor program concept. In D.M. Landers & R.W. Christina (Eds.), *Psychology of motor behavior and sport.* Champaign, IL: Human Kinetics, 1977.

Keele, S.W. Behavioral analysis of motor control. In V.B. Brooks (Ed.). *Handbook of physiology: Motor control* (Vol. 3). American Physiological Society, in press.

Kelso, J.A.S. Motor control mechanisms underlying human movement reproduction. *Journal of Experimental Psychology: Human Perception and Performance,* 1977, **3**, 529-543.

Kelso, J.A.S., Holt, K.G., Kugler, P.N. & Turvey, M.T. On the concept of coordinative structures as dissipative structures: II. Empirical lines of convergence. In G.E. Stelmach & J. Requin (Eds.), *Tutorials in motor behavior.* Amsterdam: North-Holland, 1980.

Kelso, J.A.S., Southard, D.L., & Goodman, D. On programming and coordinating two-handed movements. *Journal of Experimental Psychology: Human Perception and Performance,* 1979, **5**, 299-238.

Kelso, J.A.S., & Stelmach, G.E. Central and peripheral mechanisms in motor control. In G.E. Stelmach (Ed.), *Motor control: Issues and trends,* New York: Academic Press, 1976.

Klapp, S.T. Response programming as assessed by reaction time, does not establish the commands for particular muscles. *Journal of Motor Behavior,* 1977, **9**, 302-312.

Klapp, S., & Irwin, C.I. Relation between programming time and duration of the response being programmed. *Journal of Experimental Psychology,* 1976, **2**, 591-598.

LaBerge, D.H. Attention and automatic information processing. In P.M.A. Rabbit (Ed.), *Attention and performance V,* London: Academic Press, 1975.

MacNeilage, P.F. The motor control of serial ordering in speech. *Psychological Review,* 1970, **77**, 182-196.

Marr, D., & Poggio, T. From understanding computation to understanding neural circuitry. *Neurosciences Research Program Bulletin,* 1972, **15**, 470-488.

Marteniuk, R.G., & MacKenzie, C.L. A preliminary theory of two-hand co-ordinated control. In G.E. Stelmach & J. Requin (Eds.), *Tutorials in motor behavior.* Amsterdam: North-Holland, 1980.

Marteniuk, R.G., & Roy, E.A. The codability of kinesthetic location and distance information. *Acta Psychologica,* 1972, **36**, 471-479.

Massaro, D.W. *Experimental psychology and information processing.* Chicago: Rand McNally, 1975.

Merton, P.A. How we control the contraction of our muscles. *Scientific American,* 1972, **226**, 30-37.

Metz, D.L. The potential for systems theory application to studies of motor performance. *Human Factors,* 1974, **16**, 514-519.

Miller, G.A., Galanter, E., & Pribram, K.H. *Plans and the structure of behavior.* New York: Holt, 1960.

Moray, N. Where is capacity limited? A survey and a model. *Acta Psychologica,* 1967, **27**, 84-92.

Norman, D.A. Toward a theory of memory and attention. *Psychological Review,* 1968, **75**, 522-536.

Norman, D.A., & Bobrow, D. On data and resource limited processes. *Cognitive Psychology,* 1975, 7, 44-64.

Paltsev, Ye. I., & Elner, A.M. Preparatory and compensatory period during voluntary movement in patients with involvement of the brain of different localization. *Biophysics,* 1967, **12**, 161-168.

Pew, R.W. Levels of analysis in motor control. *Brain Research,* 1974, **71**, 393-400.

Posner, M.I., & Keele, S.W. Attention demands of movements. In *The proceedings of the 16th international conference of applied psychology* Amsterdam: Swets and Zeitlinger, 1969.

Rosenbaum, D. Selective adaptation of "command neurons" in the human motor system. *Neuropsychologia,* 1977, **15**, 81-91.

Salmoni, A.W. The attention demands of input monitoring. Unpublished doctoral dissertation, University of Michigan, 1974.

Schmidt, R.A. The schema as a solution to some persistent problems in motor learning theory. In G.E. Stelmach (Ed.), *Motor control: Issues and trends.* New York: Academic Press, 1976.

Schmidt, R.A. On the theoretical status of time in motor-program representations. In G.E. Stelmach & J. Requin (Eds.), *Tutorials in motor behavior.* Amsterdam: North-Holland, 1980.

Schmidt, R.A., Zelaznik, H.N., Hawkins, B., Frank, J.S., & Quinn, J.T. Motor-output variability: a theory for the accuracy of rapid motor acts. *Psychological Review,* 1979, **86**, 415-451.

Schneider, W., & Shiffrin, R.M. Controlled and automatic information processing: I. Detection, search, and attention, *Psychological Review,* 1977, **84**, 1-66.

Shiffrin, R.M., & Schneider, W. Controlled and automatic human information processing: II. Perceptual learning, automatic attending, and general theory. *Psychological Review,* 1977, **84**, 127-190.

Shik, M.L., & Orlovsky, G.N. Neurophysiology of locomotor automatism. *Physiological Reviews,* 1976, **56**, 465-501.

Shik, M.L., Orlovsky, G.N., & Severin, F.V. Organization of locomotor synergisms. *Biophysics,* 1966, **11**, 1011-1019.

Smith, J.L. Programming of stereotyped limb movements by spinal generators. In G.E. Stelmach & J. Requin (Eds.), *Tutorials in motor control.* Amsterdam: North-Holland, 1980.

Stelmach, G.E., & Larish, D.D. New perspective on motor skill automation. *Research Quarterly for Exercise and Sport,* 1980, **51**, 141-157.

Stelmach, G.E., & Requin, J. (Eds.), *Tutorials in motor behavior.* Amsterdam: North-Holland, 1980.

Sternberg, S., Monsell, S., Knoll, R.L., & Wright, C.E. The latency and duration of rapid movement sequences: Comparisons of speech and typewriting. In G.E. Stelmach (Ed.), *Information processing in motor control and learning.* New York: Academic Press, 1978.

Toates, F.M. *Control theory in biology and experimental psychology.* London: Hutchison, 1975.

Turvey, M.T. Preliminaries to a theory of action with reference to vision. In R. Shaw & J. Bransford (Eds.), *Perceiving, acting and knowing: Toward an ecological psychology.* Hillsdale, NJ: Erlbraum, 1977.

Turvey, M.T., Shaw, R.E., & Mace, W. Issues in the theory of action. In J. Requin (Ed.), *Attention and performance VII.* Hillsdale: NJ: Erlbaum, 1978.

Vroon, P.A. Tapping rate as a measure of expectancy in terms of response and attention limitations. *Journal of Experimental Psychology,* 1973, **101**, 183-185.

Welford, A.T. *Fundamentals of skill.* London: Methuen, 1968.

Wing, A.M. Response timing in handwriting. In G.E. Stelmach (Ed.), *Information processing in motor control and learning.* New York: Academic Press, 1978.

The Evolution of the Memory Drum Theory of Neuromotor Reaction

16 *F.M. Henry*

The Memory Drum Concept

It can readily be verified by one's own experience that a new and unlearned complicated motor act is carried out largely under conscious control, in an awkward step-by-step poorly coordinated fashion. When an act has become well-learned, it is executed skillfully with the details controlled nonconsciously; the movement "just does itself." Since the ability to perform the act skillfully is retained for a long time, it must be that some set of directions for its execution (i.e., a program) is stored in a motor memory. If the act is performed in response to a discrete signal to start, there is always a *latency period* of about 1½ or 2 10th-seconds before the movement begins; this is defined as the *reaction time* (RT) if (and only if) the response is made as quickly as possible (Woodworth, 1938).

According to the 1960 memory drum concept, certain major aspects of the neuromotor control system are analogous to the operations of an electronic computer. (In our present large computer, the rotating magnetic drum program storage of 1960 has been replaced by a multiple magnetic disc system of greater capacity, but the type of computer memory is of no consequence in the analogy). When it is needed, the stored motor program is accessed and read out to the neuromotor coordination centers (in computer terminology, to a *buffer* or temporary working memory). At these centers, circulating neural inputs are processed and integrated with and by appropriate subroutines (mostly innate) into the motor nerve outflow that implements the intended motor performance. This translation of the stored program into organized motor nerve commands to the muscles is called *programming.* In the case of a single discrete movement, programming is postulated to occur chiefly during the RT latency, although the outflow of course continues during the movement; it may be modified by afferent feedback if the movement requires a relatively long time. Consequently, a more complicated movement should be characterized by a longer latency period because the readout and programming process is also more complicated. Since RT could be measured accurately and the conditions of measurement could be controlled, experiments with RT offered a method to investigate the postulated programming as a function of the characteristics of the types of movements employed.

Emergence of a Tentative Theory

These ideas did not suddenly emerge full-fledged. I discovered early in the 1950s (Henry, 1952) that contrary to the common belief at that time, individual differences in reaction time (RT) and movement time (MT) for a standardized movement were uncorrelated. This result strongly suggested that the functioning of some sort of neural organizing mechanism (characteristic of the movement to be made) determined individual differences in RT, while the corresponding individual MT scores were determined by a different mechanism that might be called muscle effectiveness. Obviously the movement itself and the latency which preceded it were serial phases of a single continuous process. However, since there was no movement during latency, a different mechanism must have come into action during movement.

About this time I completed an experiment on kinesthetic perception that made me aware that extremely accurate movement control sometimes occurred at a level that was far below the stage of possible conscious awareness (Henry, 1953). I also engaged in intensive study of reaction time literature—one of the salutary results of this endeavor was that although the comprehensive volume on experimental psychology by Woodworth (1938) was useful, it was an inadequate substitute for examining the original research reports. For example, I found that the Telford (1931) data that he cited to show the influence of RT foreperiod variation were actually data on the psychological refractory period; the tabled intervals were not the equivalent of foreperiods. In addition, Woodworth's statement that a complex movement gives a relatively long RT was based on Freeman's 1907 observation that RT became longer when a geometric figure to-be-drawn was more complex (an increase which may have resulted from perceptual rather than movement complexity).

The lesson here is not that even a great scientist such as Woodworth cannot be trusted, but rather that one who is engaged in serious research simply *must* read the original reports; secondary sources are only useful aids. A second lesson is that doing so may pay unexpected dividends. For example, the Telford psychological refractory period discovery suggested to me that some sort of pre-response neural organizing was occurring during the RT period. This led me rather naturally to consideration of the motor control phenomena involved in transmitting information by the Morse code, a skill that I had acquired many years earlier. (In 1922, after months of practice, I passed the examination for the commercial radio operator's license, sending at 25 words/min and receiving at 20. Being relatively inexperienced, it was still necessary for me to send from previously typed copy, even at a relatively slow rate of 16 words/min; I also needed to hear the buzzing sound or tone that transmitted when the key was pressed). Each letter, made up of a unique combination of so-called dots and dashes, was mentally (and nonconsciously, considering the speed) translated into a distinctive and recognizable sound pattern; in sending, that pattern was nonconsciously translated into a unique pattern of motor action. It seemed obvious to me that for each letter there must be a stored and readily accessible sound-pattern memory trace, as well as a stored movement-pattern to control the corresponding unique motor action. This was getting close to the memory drum concept.

During the period 1952-58, experiments on the task-specificity of the transfer of motor learning were being performed by several of my graduate students; these were summarized in a brief report (Henry, 1958). If, during the learning of a motor skill task, there was interpolated practice on another motor skill task, that practice did not improve performance on the original task unless the interpolated task was almost *identical* with the original. While I was not yet ready to present the memory drum concept publicly, it seemed to me that these results suggested that there was, stored in the motor memory, a specific neural program for each task; this program would be changed and improved by practicing the original task, but it would otherwise be retained without alteration for a very long period of time. Experimental psychologists were already convinced of the long retention of motor skill; subsequent research has justified that belief. Long retention implies resistance to negative transfer from learning other skills during the retention period; such resistance would be a consequence of extreme task specificity of motor transfer effects.

If the stored motor program was extremely task specific, it seemed logical that *if* a considerable part of its processing into a neural outflow to motor nerves occurs during the latency period (i.e., during RT), some specific motor tasks should be characterized by different RTs. Use of the computer analogy to illustrate a preliminary model of a processing mechanism seemed a logical step at the time. The need for definitive (rather than suggestive) experimental evidence was clear.

Emergence of an Experimental Design

Prior to designing an experiment, however, it was necessary to place the concept into a reasonably explicit theoretical framework. Initially, it was stated as a "special" theory, applying to a certain class of movements and conditions, and certain types of movement variations. I reasoned that it could always be restated and explored in more general terms later if it should prove to be of value.

The first limitation was to large scale "gross" movements, since that was where my interest was centered, and "finger dexterity" types of movements might involve other factors. The second limitation was to discrete single movements, with time dimensions that would avoid the complications of "closed loop" feedback as well as conscious control of movement details while the motor act was in progress. The third limitation was that the movement was to be made in response to a definite stimulus signal; the response must be made as quickly as possible, as otherwise the stimulus-response interval would not constitute a genuine reaction time. The fourth limitation was that the movement be previously learned, so that the postulated motor program would have been developed and stored in the motor memory. Within these limitations, I could visualize the stored program being read out to the motor coordination centers and organized into motor nerve outflow during the RT period. More complicated programs would require the organizing of more information from memory storage and additional innate movement patterns, thus increasing the processing time during the RT period.

The most direct way to check the validity of the concept seemed to be to use simple versus complicated movements as the independent variable, and RT as the dependent variable. My early experiment (Henry, 1952), designed to determine RT-MT correlations in two independent samples of subjects tested by different experimenters using different movements and different amounts of practice, was definitely not suited to this purpose. The new experiments would need data under conditions of the finger-lift type (almost zero movement) that could be compared with well-established standard values (Woodworth, 1938), to insure that obtained results were not atypical, and to serve as a control or base value (designated A). Since the amount of added movement complexity needed to produce an observable effect was unknown, the largest amount that seemed practical (designated C) was employed, as well as an intermediate amount (designated B). At this pioneering stage of investigation, *com-*

plexity of movement had to be defined operationally. It was doubtful
if the mere change in length of a movement would influence the time
required for premovement processing (during RT); however, if muscular
guidance was required to hold the movement in the intended direction during the extended distance, an effect might be expected (Henry & Harrison,
1961). Similarly, a mere increase in guidance accuracy requirement would
probably not affect the processing time, since it would not require a more
complicated program or additional subroutines. However, the intertwined
requirement of directional guidance for an increased movement distance
could be thought of as involving additional muscles in the guidance, thus
increasing RT.

A larger effect would presumably occur if the movement was made
more complex by incorporating additional components, as compared with
the 1952 "ball snatch" used for Movement B. In preliminary experiments,
various combinations were tried; what eventually emerged was an added
ball target to be hit backhand and a button to be touched before striking down the ball of Movement B. This Movement C, made at maximum
speed, required nearly a half-second; Movement B required only a 10th-
second.

Movement C may be described as follows: The subject sits at a table,
with the right index finger resting on a sensitive reaction key. There are
two tennis balls, each hanging on a string which holds them 6 in. (15 cm)
above the table top. At the signal, the hand is moved diagonally upward
and to the right to backhand the first ball and continue diagonally downward and forward to slap a button target on the table top, and then move
diagonally upward and to the left to snatch the second ball before slow-
ing down. Each ball drops down when touched or snatched. The total
movement is continuous even though some direction changes are involved;
performance is at maximal speed throughout. For Movement B, the first
ball is removed; the movement is diagonally upward and forward 11 in.
(29 cm). For Movement A (the finger lift), both balls are removed. The
measurements of RT and MT are recorded automatically on 100th-second
electric timers.

Subjects were tested individually in rotating order A,B,C; A,B,C and
so on. Following 45 practice trials, there were 30 measurements (10 with
each movement for each subject). Since the apparatus was set up with
zero, one, or two balls in place before each trial, the subject always knew
in advance which of the three movements was to be made; this insured
that the time required for movement selection (which might involve a
conscious process) would not contaminate the RT. The automatic (nonconscious) retrieval, reading out, coordinating, and processing of the pro-

gram information stored in the motor memory was postulated to constitute part of the RT; this entire process would be triggered by the stimulus to respond. Since the stimulus was always the same (the sound of an
electric gong in this particular experiment) and the desired response movement was always and unequivocally known and selected in advance, the
measured RT was of the "simple" category.

Consideration was given to the possible use of the disjunctive or
"choice" RT method (Woodworth, 1938). The apparatus would have
incorporated three stimulus lights labeled A,B, and C, used in random
order. At each trial, the subject would have to identify which stimulus
had occurred, and then choose the movement appropriate to that stimulus. It was known that the requirement of stimulus identification increased RT and that the requirement of response choice also increased
RT (Woodworth, 1938). Moreover, movement selection time would
then necessarily be a part of the measured RT. Consequently, the
anticipated increase in RT from program processing would be mixed up
with the increases from these nonrelevant sources, so it would not be
possible to make a straightforward and meaningful interpretation of the
cause of an observed RT increase. These difficulties would be avoided
by using the simple RT method.

Factual Results Confirm the Theory

Using the experimental design and movements described above, I
tested 30 male university undergraduates, and then did a similar experiment with 30 women undergraduates. In both experiments, the RT for
A (the finger lift with minimal movement) was in excellent agreement
with the accepted value for an auditory stimulus (Woodworth, 1938).
The RT for Movement C was 2.3 standard scores longer than for A in
the men and 1.7 longer in the women. These are substantial increases.
While the increase was smaller for the less complex Movement B, it was
statistically significant at the .01 probability level, as was the increase
for C compared with B.

Before publishing these results, I had my assistant Don Rogers do the
experiment with 20 male subjects age 24, and similar sized samples of
12-year-old boys and 8-year-old boys. These three experiments were repeated on subsequent days. The results were substantially the same as
observed in the college students—mean RTs were significantly slower
for Movement B than for A, and significantly slower for C than for B.
It should be emphasized that all of the subjects in these experiments
were volunteers, who had been told how crucial it was to always start

the movement just as quickly as possible after the stimulus, and had frequently been exhorted to do so during the 45-trial training period. (RT data are meaningless unless every subject wants to do the experiment, and to do it as well as possible.)

A description of the memory drum theory and the detailed results from the experiments outlined above were published in 1960 (Henry & Rogers). Incidental to the investigation of another problem, a 1961 study (Henry & Harrison) reported RT data for an arm swing aimed at a target, and a later publication by one of my graduate students (Williams, 1971b) found the RT even longer for an extended arm swing—in both instances the RT for initiating the arm swing was considerably longer than the RT for a finger lift movement. These two experiments used a visual stimulus (in the previous experiments, the sound of a gong had been employed). Another Berkeley study (with which I was not involved) used movements similar to B and C described above, but employed a different experimental design (Norrie, 1967). The earlier results were confirmed—the simple RT was longer for the most complex movement, as predicted by the theory.

Another Line of Evidence:
The Psychological Refractory Period

The Telford (1931) discovery of the psychological refractory period (PRP) came to my attention about 1954; as stated earlier, this phenomena influenced my subsequent theorizing about the emerging memory drum concept. As pointed out by Harrison, this discovery seems to have been ignored until about 1948, when Vince (see Harrison, 1960) confirmed the existence of the PRP in a more extensive set of experiments. These investigators both used the *serial* RT method. In the Vince study, a long and continuous series of visual stimuli, occurring at randomly ordered intervals ranging from .05 to 1.6 sec, was presented to the subject; both the stimuli and the responses (small movements of a hand-held stylus) were recorded on a moving paper tape, so that the interstimulus intervals and the RT of the responses could be measured.

When the second of two serial stimuli occurred less than about .40 sec after the first, the RT for the second stimulus was longer than normal. For example, if the normal RT was .20 sec and the second stimulus occurred only .15 sec after the first, the RT for the second increased to .25 sec. This meant that there was a refractoriness of .05 sec that had to add on to the normal .20 sec RT for the second stimulus. It was also observed that when the two stimuli were separated by less than .40 or

.50 sec, the response to the second was sometimes omitted; this was another indicator of a refractory period. This discription is of course a much simplified version of the experiments and the results. The journal references to the work of the English investigators (Vince, Welford, and others) have been listed in the review by Harrison (1960); the reader is warned that the English authors employed the term *discrete* in a different sense than I have used it in the present article, where it indicates a movement made in response to an isolated stimulus (or, in the PRP situation, an intertwined pair of stimuli and responses) that constitutes a trial that is isolated from the next trial by 10 or 12 sec so as to avoid any interaction.

It seemed to me that the tentative memory drum concept would predict that if the movement is minimal, as for example a simple finger lift or key press, refractoriness to starting the programming process in response to a stimulus to start a second movement during the RT latency period of the first stimulus should be incomplete and relatively weak—the capacity of the processing mechanism would not be reached, and it should be possible to start the processing of the second response. On the other hand, if the first movement is complicated, there should be refractoriness to starting the processing of the second response, and its RT should also be longer.

The Refractoriness Experiments

While the serial RT method was appropriate to the interests of the English investigators, there were several reasons why it was not suited to the study of "programming." Consequently, I devised two experiments more pertinent to that purpose, and constructed the necessary apparatus. The first one required that the subject press a reaction key in response to the initial stimulus, and then slide the finger a few millimeters to the right or left in response to the second stimulus, depending on whether a stimulus light to the right or left of the key came on. The occurrence of right or left was in random order, as was the time interval between the first stimulus and the second. This interstimulus interval ranged from .05 to .60 sec, under the control of an electronic device; the RTs were measured by electric chronoscopes. One of the measures of refractoriness was the error rate, an error being defined as a failure to move in the correct direction in response to the second stimulus (this is quite different from the definition of an error in the English experiments). The other measure was of course the length of the second RT during the small interstimulus intervals. Since both of the movements were minimal, the purpose of this experiment was to establish a base against which to compare the results with complicated movements. One of my graduate students, John Harrison, performed the experiment and published the results (Harrison, 1960).

The second experiment, employing a relatively complicated movement, required a different apparatus configuration, but was the same in principle. The subject made a side-arm forward swing in the vertical plane, using the shoulder joint as a pivot with the stiffly extended arm starting from behind the body (with the hand on a reaction key) and ending in a forward and upward position after passing through the target (a pull-out string stretched between two uprights spaced 30 cm apart). The subject always made the arm swing at maximum speed in response to the first stimulus light; in about half of the instances (in a randomly determined order) the second stimulus light flashed on after a randomly determined interval of .10 to .35 sec after the first stimulus. The required response to the second stimulus was to immediately reverse the direction of the arm swing and slap the hand forcefully against the thigh. The instant of beginning reversal was of course deceleration of the forward movement; this was measured by an electric chronoscope controlled by a decelerometer held in the subject's hand.

In order to discourage any tendency to slow the first response in anticipation of the possible second stimulus, a mild electric shock was administered automatically if the first response was not started as quickly as the individual's average RT that had been established in a preliminary training series. Following the main experiment, there was a series of "normal" trials in which the subject knew there would be no reversal stimuli (these being the simple RTs for the arm swing movement), and also a series of simple finger lift or control RTs with which they could be compared. As in the first experiment, there were two measures of latency-period refractoriness, namely an error consisting of failure to initiate the movement reversal in response to the second stimulus, and a lengthening of the RT for the second stimulus when it occurred during the RT latency of the first stimulus. This study was published a year later (Henry & Harrison, 1961).

Inadequacy of the Apparatus. While the first arm swing experiment did establish *movement* refractoriness (since the individuals tested were unable to implement the reversal early enough to avoid hitting the target string), and did furnish some facts that tended to confirm the memory drum predictions, it was clear that a considerably longer movement was needed. Consequently, Williams (1971b) doubled the distance between the reaction key and the target and added a forward lunge to the arm swing, which increased the complexity of the total movement. This also made it possible to extend the length of the interstimulus intervals to cover the range .10 to .70 sec so that more extensive information was available on the error rates as well as on RTs for the second response.

Refractoriness Increased by Movement Complexity

The published reports of the three experiments outlined above were chiefly addressed to the refractoriness problem per se and the use of the second RT as a "probe"; in fact, the two that reversed the arm swing did not give the numerical values of RTs for the second stimulus. However, those values can be calculated from the first RT and the deceleration time (DT) for the shorter intervals where reversal starts before the hand passes the target. This restriction does not apply to a subsequent study where the reversal response was replaced by lifting the thumb from a microswitch held in the moving hand (Williams, 1973).

Thus we have available data from four studies done at the Berkeley Laboratory and using the same electronic control devices and the same apparatus except for the Harrison (1960) tests with the minimal finger movements. We will defer for the moment a discussion of the first arm swing experiment, since the movement was found to be too short for dependable results in the present frame of reference. In the two using the extended arm swing, the error rate at the .10 sec interstimulus interval using the thumb lift as the second response was 13.6% and the second RT was .54 sec; using the reversal response the corresponding values were 24.6% and .56 sec (Williams, 1971b, 1973). These are much larger than found for the simple finger movements, namely 1.2% and .30 sec (Harrison, 1960). A similar pattern was found at the .20 sec interstimulus interval; this effect of movement complexity on the error rate and RT was predicted by the memory drum theory.

While the results with the earlier and simpler arm swing (Henry & Harrison, 1961) were also of the predicted pattern, the values were somewhat atypical; the error rate was 42.2% and the RT calculated for the reversal stimulus was only .31 sec. Williams (1971a) repeated this experiment with similar results, although the error rate of 27% was lower. As noted above and explained in the Henry and Harrison (1961) article, the movement was not long enough to avoid a constraint on these measures. However, the "normal" RT for the arm swing movement itself was not subject to that constraint. I should mention that in going through my 1960-61 notes in order to find the finger lift control RT for these subjects (.171 sec), I discovered that the simple control value reported by Harrison (1960) on page 598 of his article was from the wrong data summary, namely the auditory RT of .158 sec for 24-year-old males (Henry & Rogers, 1960); he should have reported .171 sec.

It is interesting that the refractory period method, in the general configuration of the 1960 Harrison study and the arm swing experiments, is currently in use in investigations of movement programming (Glencross & Gould, 1979). The second stimulus is called a "probe"; there is a modern trend to use the term "movement planning" instead of "programming."

Delay in Perception of the Response

Experimental evidence that a skilled discrete movement is indeed performed under nonconscious control has been sparse. Because that postulate was an important aspect of the memory drum concept, Williams (1970) performed an experiment that addressed the problem. The original Henry and Harrison (1961) apparatus was used, with a further requirement: as soon as convenient after each reversal trial (4 or 5 sec) the subject reproduced the position reached by the arm and hand at the instant the second stimulus was perceived to have flashed on. A meter-stick placed alongside the movement made it possible for the experimeter to record the distance; this could later be converted into a time equivalent by using a velocity profile curve.

When the interstimulus interval was .10 sec, the average subject indicated that the hand had travelled to 83 cm (rather close to the target string) at the time the light flashed on; in fact the hand had not yet started to move at that instant, and the arm swing would not get into motion for another .10 sec. The conscious perception of that second stimulus occurred .27 sec *after the fact*—indeed, it coincided with the time of overt *response* to it (as revealed by calculations based on the DT and other data). Thus the preresponse processing of the reversal movement was done at a nonconscious level. It should be noted that the RT for the arm swing in this experiment (Williams, 1970) was appreciably faster than reported earlier by Henry and Harrison (1961), although the MTs and DTs were in close agreement; the same data were employed in a later article (Williams, 1971a) that reported the error rates, and included a detailed description of the apparatus. No data were obtained on the "normal" arm swing or the control or finger lift RT for these subjects.

The Williams article (1970) included a discussion of this result in relation to the views of other investigators who accepted the idea of perceptual delay as a factor that must be considered. He also reported highly reliable individual differences in arm swing RT and MT as well as DT (decelerometer time) and PD (perceptual delay). A substantial correlation between DT and PD was anticipated, but failed to materialize. Williams evidently felt the need to use a more extended movement, since the longer of the two interstimulus intervals (.20 sec) placed the second stimulus at the time of the first response and thus restricted meaningful interpretation to the .10 sec interval. The basic method is innovative and valid; with the extended movement it should produce data of additional value.

Independence of Reaction and Movement Times

Independence Explained and Confirmed

As mentioned at the beginning of this chapter, the discovery that the correlation between MT and the preceding latency or RT of the movement was approximately zero (Henry, 1952), even though strong and reliable individual differences were present in both variables, was one of the factors that led to the memory drum concept. Although it was stated that RT and MT were independent and uncorrelated, there was no intent to apply an esoteric mathematical definition to the word *independent* either then or later. The interpretation placed on the statistical results was that an individual characterized by a relatively fast and reproducible RT would be characterized by an associated MT that was also reproducible, but might be relatively fast or slow or anywhere between. Similarly a slow or medium reactor would be characterized by a consistent MT that might be fast or slow or anywhere between. It is easy to demonstrate the reality of this pattern with actual data if the number of individuals in the sample is sufficiently large. In the example which follows, 51 college women were given 50 trials, the measurements being simple RT and MT for a movement that was fairly long and complicated. I have used Trial 45 in order to avoid practice effect complications, the raw data being supplied by the original experimenter (Norrie, 1967). The explanation is unavoidably somewhat technical.

The mean scores for these data are 226 msec (SD = 37.9) for RT and 499 msec (SD = 88.2) for MT; the RT-MT correlation is .065; the reliability coefficients (r between Trials 44 and 45) are .662 for RT and .859 for MT. Using 100th-second units, the 10 subjects with fastest RT scores in Trial 45 have MTs ranging from 38 to 74 (SD = 9.9), the 10 with slowest RT scores have MTs ranging from 37 to 62 (SD = 7.5).

Table 1

RT and MT Scores (Hundredth Seconds) for the 10 Fastest and 10 Slowest Reactors in Trials 44 and 45

	Fastest						Slowest				
RT	MT	DIFF	RT	MT	DIFF	RT	MT	DIFF	RT	MT	DIFF
Trial 44			Trial 45			Trial 44			Trial 45		
17	45	28	15	42	27	22	49	27	25	49	24
15	45	30	16	46	30	25	46	21	25	46	21
18	47	29	17	49	32	24	44	20	25	43	18
19	45	26	17	41	24	29	38	9	26	37	11
20	39	19	18	42	24	25	60	35	26	62	36
18	75	57	19	74	55	22	52	30	27	51	24
20	50	30	19	49	30	27	39	12	28	37	9
17	40	23	19	38	19	30	53	23	32	51	19
18	45	27	20	42	22	33	44	11	33	45	12
19	54	35	20	55	35	28	59	31	35	56	21

The within-subject SDs are 2.2 and 1.5. In the total distribution of MTs, the fastest is associated with a medium RT, the next two with slow RT and the next two with fast RT; the slowest MT is associated with a medium RT, the second with a fast RT and the fourth slowest with a slow RT. This unordered RT-MT relationship is of course in agreement with the interpretation in the previous paragraph. It is not unique to these particular data. The scores from another sample of 51 subjects tested with a simpler movement exhibits this same pattern. If the reliability coefficients had been approximately zero the unordered pattern might have been present, although individual scores in RT and MT would no longer have characterized individual persons but would have varied randomly from trial to trial. However, the concern here is not with that circumstance, but rather with the high reliability (i.e., strong individual differences) situation.

In consequence of that situation, individuals who are fast in both RT and MT or fast in one and slow in the other or exhibit some intermediate pattern tend to maintain their individual pattern in a subsequent test, as shown in the data of Table 1. One may use the difference (MT - RT) as a crude index of individual pattern; the correlation between the individual indices in Trials 44 and 45 is $r = .96$ in the fast reaction group and

.91 in the slow group. Thus RT and MT characteristics of individuals are indeed independent when the correlation between them approximates zero, in the sense that each person has an *individual* characteristic relation between RT and MT that may be of any of the possible patterns as illustrated above.

Assuming that it is firmly established that the basic RT-MT correlation is low (approximating zero) and that there are reliable individual differences in both RT and MT, it becomes necessary to search out (or at least propose) the cause of this absence of correlation. Using a somewhat broader definition of the memory drum concept (to cover the disjunctive RT situation where both the movement and program selection processes are included in the latency), it was postulated (Henry, 1961) that ". . .response latency is determined by the nature and complexity of a stored neuromotor 'program' or motor memory that requires time to be selected and read out to the motor nerves. The speed of a movement is theoretically determined by a different factor, namely strength in action, which is controlled by the effectiveness of the program in causing the muscles to create or apply force to the limbs and cause the movement" (p. 353). This statement is overly brief and can be misinterpreted; it must be considered in the light of the original discussion of the memory drum concept (Henry & Rogers, 1960). In particular, time to be "read out" was intended to include "programming" (i.e., the processing of the stored motor program and subroutines, up to the stage of the motor nerve outflow that results in the first evidence of response movement). Indeed, in the present context (simple RT with prestimulus selection) the latency times (RTs) of individuals were postulated to reflect the processing time which is occupied by neural activity prior to muscle contraction; this time increased when the to-be-made movement was more complex. Since the limb movement was made at maximum speed, the MT would reflect the efficiency of the coordinated neural outflow in producing the effective force exerted against the mass of the limb by the muscles, and might involve such variables as their physiological capability to rapidly exert force, which could differ among individuals. Anatomical differences might also be involved. Thus while the muscle contraction is a response to the neural outflow, the mechanism of limb movement per se is obviously not the same as the mechanism of the neural activity of premovement "programming." This offers an explanation for low or zero correlation between RT and MT. Insofar as I am aware, no other explanation has been proposed.

Consistent with this explanation, Clarke and Henry (1961) found improved strength and speed of a standardized arm movement that was not practiced in a general strength development course; there was no change at all in the RT for the movement. A control group exhibited a nonsignificant loss in arm speed and no appreciable change in RT.

There remained the question of whether the evidence was adequate to establish that the basic RT-MT correlation was very low, approximating zero. Following the original study (Henry, 1952), Pierson (1958) reported correlations ranging from .27 to .86 in small samples of $N = 20$, differing in age. There was an immediate flurry of activity, culminating in the presentation of extensive data exhibiting near-zero correlations and reviewing several 1960 and 1961 studies by others, all reporting near-zero correlations using substantial sample sizes (Henry, 1961). That article included explanations and examples of how higher correlations would occur if the samples of subjects were heterogeneous as to age or sex, or if various special conditions were present. There was general agreement as to near-zero correlations in homogeneous samples of substantial size ($N = 50$ or more), although there were some instances of statistically significant RT-MT correlations, both positive and negative. The reliability coefficients (usually based on 10-trial mean scores) were .90 or higher.

Factor Analysis Confirms Independence

A subsequent study (Henry, Lotter & Smith, 1962) utilized different subjects, apparatus and limb movements. (This is the same as the reference no. 5 stated as "in press" with a tentative title in the Henry and Harrison 1961 article.) Two sets of RT-MT data ($N = 80$ with six limb movements and $N = 70$ with four limb movements) were subjected to factor analyses; they agreed in demonstrating that latency and movement speed were separate and uncorrelated factors. Before discussing this finding in more detail, it seems necessary to explain that a complete factor analysis yields evaluations of the item specificity component of individual differences. This requires the availability of the reliability coefficient for each item (i.e., for each of the movements) for each variable (RT and MT). Since the observed coefficient (unsquared) is theoretically the squared correlation between true scores and the observed scores that consists of individual differences; the remaining portion of the total variance of the scores is usually called error variance, since it is commonly assumed to consist of random variability that does not characterize individual persons. It may also be called the unreliability variance.

The individual difference variance is in turn fractionated into propor-

tions assigned to each of the factors extracted in the analysis, each proportion being the squared factor loading of an item in a factor. Thus the
sum of the squared factor loadings for an item (usually designated h^2)
is the portion of the individual differences that is "explained" by the
factors; the remaining proportion (usually designated b^2) is called the
item specificity; algebraically, $h^2 + b^2 = r_{ii}$ for each item, where r_{ii} is the
observed reliability coefficient of that item. In the present instance, two
factors emerged, namely A (latency) and B (speed of movement); we will
designate the factor loadings as r_a and r_b and the unreliability as e,
so we may write the proportions of total variance of an item
as $r_a^2 + r_b^2 + b^2 = r_{ii}$ and $e^2 + r_{ii} = 1$. As a concrete example, consider
the data of Table 3 in the reference cited above (Henry et al.,1962)
where Item 1 is RT for an arm movement; the values for r_a^2 and r_b^2 are
are .570 and .001, b_2 is .340, r_{ii} is .911, and e^2 is .089. Item 5 is MT
for that same movement; the values are .005 and .372 for the squared
factor loadings, the item specificity b^2 is .579, r_{ii} is .974 and e^2 is .026.

Although the discussion in that study did not consider the implications for the memory drum concept, that is our present concern. Thus
our immediate interest is in the tabled item specificity values. In the
first experiment ($N = 80$), they are .340, .239, .180 and .247 for the
RT items of the four discrete limb movements compared with .597,
.637, .575 and .473 for the MT items of these same movements. In the
second experiment ($N = 70$) the subjects and limb movements were different; the values for the RT items are .145, .211, .363, and .260 compared with the MT item values of .702, .550, .614, and .672. Clearly,
item specificity is relatively low for RT and moderately high for MT—in
fact, in seven of the eight instances the MT specificity is greater than the
corresponding factor loading variance, whereas RT specificity is only about
about half as large as the factor loadings in all instances and exhibits no
systematic relationship with the item-by-item pattern of MT specificity.
These findings support the idea that different mechanisms determine
individual differences in RT and MT scores. (Item specificity had been
ignored in other movement studies).

Without question, there are strong individual differences in RT latency
in these data—in fact, from 91 to 97% of the total score variance in the
several items is individual differences variance. Of course we do not know
what proportion can be assigned to preresponse "programming"; one
could argue that the programming time portion of the latency for a specific movement is constant for all individuals and thus does not contribute
to individual differences in RT. This would strengthen the case for the

postulation of different mechanisms in programming time as compared with MT (which exhibits strong and unequivocal individual differences), and would not invalidate the bases of the memory drum concept. But it seems more plausible to believe that there are individual differences in programming time for a specified movement; this would account for the considerable variation in the item specificity portion of individual difference which ranges from .145 to .363. (Remember that the within-subject variability e^2 is not involved, since it is a different component of the total variance.) This particular interpretation must be viewed as suggestive rather than conclusive since both arm and leg movements were used and there was no systematic variation in movement complexity. What is needed is a factor analysis using a single limb, with gross movements comparable to the Henry and Rogers (1960) types A, B, C and an extended C, and an adequate sample size. Or perhaps someone can devise a more effective way to determine if, and to what extent, there are reliable individual differences in the net programming time portion of RT latency. The problem is not crucial, but it *is* challenging.

Experimental Results at Other Laboratories

Up to this point, this chapter has been limited to the evolution of the memory drum theory and various lines of supporting evidence at the Berkeley Laboratory. Some 12 years after the published description of the theory in 1960, investigators at other laboratories began studies of the influence of RT latency of varying various specific aspects of a discrete movement. In a recent article (1978) Beth Kerr has listed and referenced the published reports of these studies through 1976, indicating which ones did or did not find that movement variation affected RT. She concluded that RT must be considered to be sensitive to differences in movement parameters, although clear-cut patterns have remained elusive.

The reason for this elusiveness may be that some of the investigators have not been aware that the theory predicted no effect if the movement itself remained unaltered (and thus did not require a noticeably more complicated or complex program). Thus a simple increase in extent (i.e., distance) or exerted force or the duration of the exerted force should not appreciably increase the simple RT; the reported results agree with this prediction. In contrast, when additional elements of complexity are incorporated in a movement, the required programming is more complex and the RT should increase; those studies that varied this parameter substantially in large movements did report the increase.

It is doubtful if variations such as altering target size (other factors remaining constant) should influence programming complexity very much; this matter was discussed earlier.

Quantification of the Independent Variable

Although some investigators are striving to define the movement variables according to external characteristics such as extent, directional constraint, resistance, duration and the like, it is not very likely that these are literally or independently involved in the programming process. It may well be more productive to respect operational definitions of the movement variables until more is known about the movement alterations that do and do not change RTs, and most importantly, about how much alteration is required for how much effect.

The outcome of the refractoriness experiments suggests there may be a "threshold" phenomenon—considerable alteration in small and relatively simple movements may involve differences in programming that can be accomodated within a minimal length RT. In other words, RT should not be thought of as a simple measure of programming; rather, certain types and aspects of that process are probably time-dependent to the extent of altering RT and others are not. While it may be useful and important to identify those that do and do not alter RT, it should be emphasized again, and strongly, that absence of RT effects does not constitute evidence that the memory drum concept is invalid. However, there *are* variations in movement complexity that *do* have well-established influences on latency. Consequently the RT observations offer a method that gives considerable insight into the programming process, even though simple quantitative measurement of external movement variables does not yield a satisfactory scale for the independent variable.

Current Status of the Memory Drum Theory

Terminology

In this chapter, the terminology has been consistent with that used in the 1960 article. For example, "to program" has meant *to store* in the motor memory (by practicing the skill) a memory trace that can be repeatedly accessed for processing into the neural outflow that executes the motor act; "programming" has meant *the processing* or translation of the stored information into that neural outflow to the muscles. The reader who is interested enough to pursue the subsequent published reports by other investigators should be warned that those terms (and others) have not uncommonly been used under definitions that differed from the 1960 usage; new terms replace the old (e.g., "planning" for "programming"). That could confuse the unwary.

I have used the word "theory" in the sense defined in my dictionary: "1: A plan or scheme subsisting in the mind, but based on principles varifiable by experiment"—under the assumption that replicated observation of an outcome predicted by the theory constitutes verification. In recent years, it has become fashionable to use the word *model*, sometimes as equivalent to the word theory and sometimes with a somewhat different connotation. Scientists have faith that a body of confirmed theories leads to an understanding of the laws of nature.

Theories Mutate. A careful study of the history of science will show that theories are not static; to the contrary, they undergo evolution. Sometimes this is in the direction of greater breadth and explanatory power; sometimes it involves weeding out of imperfections. In other instances, a theory may have to be discarded, but it will have served as a stimulus to the development of a more adequate replacement. If these evolutionary changes did not occur, it seems obvious that there could be no progress in scientific understanding.

Criticisms

There have, of course, been published criticisms of the 1960 experiments and the interpretation of the results; this is a normal and important part of the scientific process. A serious question was raised in 1974 and reiterated three years later (Klapp, 1977); it was echoed in some other recent publications. Since I was able to answer the criticisms by calling on previously published data and terminology that had not been taken into consideration, I wrote a formal "Reply" (Henry, 1980). The outcome of this exchange (Klapp, 1980) seems to be that the use of the *simple* RT method is legitimate within the domain of the 1960 theory (discrete gross limb movements), whereas the *choice* RT method seems appropriate for investigations of programming in the case of small scale movements and the motor aspects of vocalizing (Klapp, 1977). In the latter case, the 1960 theory (a "special theory") was deemed inadequate, and appropriate improvements were made. However, use of the choice RT in that area of study has also been criticized and simple RT favored (Sternberg, Monsell, Knoll, & Wright, 1978), so that issue, in my opinion is still not resolved. It should be mentioned that the RTs of the refractoriness experiments discussed earlier do not fall clearly into *either* the simple or choice RT categories.

Further Evolution of the 1960 Theory

Even if it should still be useful within its original domain, modification is needed to reflect subsequent advancement in knowledge. It seems likely that the motor skill program is stored in coded form, perhaps as a *schema* (Schmidt, 1976) or somewhat generalized (rather than detailed) neural plan for the movement. The question of whether this concept is compatible with the high task specificity of motor skill transfer needs to be considered, however.

Klapp (1977) recently presented an improved version of the theory, supported by experimental results in a variety of situations involving the articulation of words, and in small movements; Sternberg et al. (1978), have presented a refined and elaborated new version of the theory, supported by experimental evidence from the production of spoken words and the typing of words. Thus the scope of the original and rather specialized theory has been extended materially, including application to rapid movement sequences.

I must confess that I was surprised to learn that the original concept, and the use of RT latency to investigate it, had been profitable in these areas that are so different from those that I had contemplated. Nevertheless, it seems likely that the theory is destined to lose its identity eventually, since there are other aspects of movement control that are not incorporated within it.

Other theoretical approaches to the issue of programmed motor control of discrete movements have appeared during the past 20 years; with the advancement of neurophysiological knowledge concerning movement, much more comprehensive theoretical structures are emerging. The 1976 volume titled *Motor Control: Issues and Trends* (Stelmach, 1976) contains articles by 11 active investigators; while it offers an excellent view of current activity, much has happened in the ensuing 4 years. Indeed, another such volume appeared 2 years later (Stelmach, 1978).

References

Clarke, D.H. & Henry, F.M., Neuromotor specificity and increased speed from strength development. *Research Quarterly*, 1961, **32**, 315-325.

Glencross, D.J. Response complexity and the latency of different movement patterns. *Journal of Motor Behavior*, 1973, **5**, 95-104.

Glencross, D.J. & Gould, J.H. The planning of precision movements. *Journal of Motor Behavior*, 1979, **11**, 1-9.

Harrison, J.S. Psychological refractoriness and the latency time of two consecutive motor responses. *Research Quarterly,* 1960, **31**, 590-600.

Henry, F.M. Independence of reaction and movement times and equivalence of sensory motivators of faster response. *Research Quarterly,* 1952, **23**, 43-53.

Henry, F.M. Dynamic kinesthetic perception and adjustment. *Research Quarterly,* 1953, **24**, 176-187.

Henry, F.M. Specificity vs. generality in learning motor skills. *Proceedings of the National College Physical Education Association,* 1958, **61**, 126-128.

Henry, F.M. Stimulus complexity, movement complexity, age and sex in relation to reaction latency and speed in limb movements. *Research Quarterly,* 1961, **32**, 353-366.

Henry, F.M. Use of simple reaction time in motor programming studies: A reply to Klapp, Wyatt and Lingo. *Journal of Motor Behavior,* 1980, **12**, 163-168.

Henry, F.M. & Harrison, J.S. Refractoriness of a fast movement. *Perceptual and Motor Skills,* 1961, **13**, 351-354.

Henry, F.M., & Rogers, D.E. Increased response latency for complicated movements and a "memory drum" theory of neuromotor reaction. *Research Quarterly,* 1960, **31**, 448-458.

Henry, F.M., Lotter, W.S., & Smith, L.E. Factorial structure of individual differences in limb speed, reaction, and strength. *Research Quarterly,* 1962, **33**, 70-84.

Kerr, B. Task factors that influence selection and preparation for voluntary movements. In G.E. Stelmach (Ed.), *Information processing in motor control and learning.* New York: Academic Press, 1978.

Klapp, S.T. Reaction time analysis of programmed control. In R.S. Hutton (Ed.), *Exercise and sports sciences reviews* (Vol. 5). Santa Barbara, CA: Journal Publishing Affiliates, 1977.

Klapp, S.T. The memory drum theory after twenty years: Comments on Henry's note. *Journal of Motor Behavior,* 1980, **12**, 169-171.

Norrie, M.L. Practice effects on reaction latency for simple and complex movements. *Research Quarterly,* 1967, **38**, 79-85.

Pierson, W.R., & Montoye, H.J. Movement time, reaction time and age. *Journal of Gerontology,* 1958, **13**, 418-421.

Schmidt, R.A. The schema as a solution to some persistent problems in motor learning theory. In G.E. Stelmach (Ed.), *Motor control: issues and trends.* New York: Academic Press, 1976.

Stelmach, G.E. (Ed.). *Motor control: issues and trends.* New York: Academic Press, 1976.

Stelmach, G.E. (Ed.). *Information processing in motor control and learning.* New York: Academic Press, 1978.

Sternberg, S., Monsell, S., Knoll, R.L., & Wright, C.E. The latency and duration of rapid movement sequences: comparisons of speech and typewriting. In G.E. Stelmach, (Ed.), *Information processing in motor control and learning.* New York: Academic Press, 1978.

Telford, C.W. The refractory phase of voluntary and associative responses. *Journal of Experimental Psychology,* 1931, **14,** 1-36.

Williams, L.R.T. Perceived occurrence of the second of two closely spaced stimuli in a long movement. *Journal of Motor Behavior,* 1970, **2,** 175-181.

Williams, L.R.T. Refractoriness of a long movement. *Research Quarterly,* 1971, **42,** 212-219. (a)

Williams, L.R.T. Refractoriness of an extended movement to directional change. *Journal of Motor Behavior,* 1971, **3,** 289-300. (b)

Williams, L.R.T. Psychological refractoriness of two serial motor responses. *Research Quarterly,* 1973, **44,** 24-33.

Williams, L.R.T. & Sullivan, S.J. Effects of movement speed on the refractoriness of an extended movement to reversal. *Journal of Human Movement Studies,* 1978, **4,** 70-84.

Woodworth, R.S. *Experimental psychology.* New York: Holt, 1938.

PART 6

Sport Psychology and Sociology

Of the several subdisciplines of physical education reviewed in this volume, sport psychology and sociology have had the greatest difficulty establishing themselves as legitimate fields worthy of serious study. It was not that coaches, athletes, or physical educators thought that psychology or sociology of sport were unimportant, but that these fields were at the time too complex for systematic study. Although these fields are complex, the scientific method has been successfully adapted to the study of complex individual and group behavior within a physical activity context. As shown in the next 3 chapters, modest gains have been made in both subdisciplines. Consequently, sport psychology and sociology have become important subdisciplines within physical education in the last 15 years.

Today, most physical education departments offer course work in both sport psychology and sociology at the undergraduate and graduate levels, and many have specialized master's and doctoral programs. As interest in the study of these subdisciplines grew, national and international scholarly societies formed and flourished. For example, the North American Society for the Psychology of Sport and Physical Activity has grown from 11 original members in 1967 to 450 members in 1980. In sport sociology, the North American Society for Sociology of Sport was formed in 1980 and now has approximately 110 members. Scholarly journals and at least a half-dozen texts in each field now exist.

As these fields have developed, scholars from the parent disciplines of psychology and sociology have come to recognize the value of studying behavior in sport and the role of sport in American life. Consequently, the scholarly pursuits of sport psychologists and sociologists are not only gaining acceptance by academicians within the parent disciplines, but in some cases, these academicians are collaborating with sport psychologists and sociologists in the study of sport.

Sport psychology has two broad areas of concern: (a) how participation in sport or physical activity influences the individual, and (b) how the individual's personality and other individual attributes combine with situational factors to influence participation in sports. Thus, sport psychologists are interested primarily in the behavior of individuals as they function within sport, but they also rub shoulders with sport sociologists when studying small groups in sport. Unlike sport psychologists, however, sport sociologists are interested primarily in the team or group as a whole rather than the individual members of the team. But the sport sociologist's interest is not just limited to small groups; it also includes larger organizations and institutions, as well as the intriguing question about what role sport plays in our society.

Part 6, then, opens with a chapter by Dean Ryan, a pioneer in contemporary sport psychology research, who presents a succinct account of the historical development of the sport psychology field. He discusses the more prominent lines of research in the recent past and identifies the field's major contributions. Finally, Dr. Ryan exposes some of the myths of sport psychology.

Diane Gill, in Chapter 18, presents an overview of many current areas of sport psychology research. She concisely discusses the research on personality; motivation; social influence processes such as social facilitation, limitation, and social reinforcement; group dynamics including team cohesiveness and leadership; and such applied topics as women, children, and elite athletes' participation in sport. The careful reader will find many ideas for future study in this chapter.

In Chapter 19, Susan Greendorfer presents a comprehensive discussion of both the emergence and future prospects of sport sociology. Although sport sociology can trace its origin back as early as the 1920s, the actual emergence of the field as an active subdiscipline occurred in the mid-1960s. This was a time when America's value structure and its social and political systems, including sport, were being questioned as never before. Thus, although the history of the field is short, Dr. Greendorfer helps the reader gain a perspective on the emergence of this field and its recent struggles from infancy to childhood. Her chapter is incisive and critical, but also includes constructive evaluation of sport sociology research, revealing both its discoveries and shortcomings.

Chapter 19 on sociology of sport completes the tour of the major subdisciplines comprising the academic discipline known as physical education. The subdisciplines included in this volume are those which have already made substantive contributions to the discipline's body of knowledge. They run the gamut of specialized fields—from the hard to the soft, from the old and established to the new and emerging. Yet other fields of interest, such as the political science, economics, anthropology, and management of sport, are embryos that may emerge as future subdisciplines.

Thus, as you finish reading Part 6, it is hoped you will have acquired an appreciation for the history and breadth of the discipline you shall now begin to study in-depth. On this point, it is fitting to close with some wisdom from G. Lawrence Rarick (1967).

> If, in fact, we are serious in our belief that there is an identifiable body of knowledge which belongs to what we call physical education, we need to begin at once to build the general framework for structuring this body of knowledge. With this accomplished, we can perhaps more clearly pinpoint the future direction of our research and other scholarly efforts. (p. 52)

Reference

Rarick, G.L. The domain of physical education as a discipline. *Quest,* 1967, **9**, 49-52.

The Emergence of Psychological Research as Related to Performance in Physical Activity

17 *E.D. Ryan*

When we speak of the emergence of psychology in the field of physical education we are faced with somewhat of a paradox. In a sense there have already been *two* emergences. The first was at the turn of the century, the second was after World War II. The earliest studies in social psychology, published in 1897, dealt with the influence of competition on bicycle performance (Triplett, 1897); the first laboratory, established in 1925 and devoted to the study of sport and physical education in the United States, focused primarily on psychology of sport (Griffith, 1930). In spite of these early beginnings, however, there was little follow-up, and attempts to study psychology of sport and physical activity were infrequent. But because of its presumed psychological benefits, the lack of research did not stop early educators from advocating sport and physical activity.

In 1895, Rev. William Augustus Stearn, the President of Amherst College said, "If a moderate amount of physical exercise could be secured to every student daily, I have a deep conviction. . .that not only would lives and health be preserved, but animation and cheerfulness, and a higher order of efficient study and intellectual life would be secured" (Leonard & Afflect, 1947, p. 275). Amos Alonzo Stagg in 1911 stated, ". . . the work of the gymnasium and the athletic field ranks as the greatest moral force in the university. Certain it is that the department of physical training has done more to preserve sane morals among college students than any others influence" (Stagg, 1911, p. 184). G. Stanley Hall said, "Physical education is for the sake of mental and moral culture and not an end in itself. It is to make the intellect, feelings, and will more vigorous, sane supple and resourceful" (Hall, 1908, pp. 1015-1016). More recently, C.H. McCloy wrote,

> He [the student] is encouraged to participate in physical activity in such a way as gradually to develop self-confidence, self-reliance, and better morals. He is trained to be cool-headed and to control his temper, to

cooperate with his fellow students and to be loyal to his team and his school; to be magnanimous, to respect the rules, to play fairly, to be thorough and dependable—to be in other words, a good sportsman. (Mc-Cloy, 1941, p. 5)

Earliest Studies

One of the earliest psychological studies reported in physical education literature was by Arthur McDonald, a criminologist who studied baseball because he considered it one of the greatest existing moral tonics for boys and young men. He felt it directed the surplus physical energy of young men into the right channel, which otherwise might be employed in ways detrimental to moral and physical life. While McDonald made no attempt to test the assumption concerning the value of sport, his observation on the psychological aspects of the sport are interesting. Among the topics discussed were "power of the mind in baseball," "confidence," and "mental influence." McDonald said, "There are three general mental states in which a player may be; over confident, lack of confidence or nervousness." "Nervousness is the worst condition of all, for even the best player when in such a state may play the worst" (MacDonald, 1914, p. 222). While the article has a number of interesting and pertinent psychological observations similar to those made by coaches today, the only actual data were anthropological in nature.

An even earlier psychological study of football by Professor G.T.W. Patrick appeared in the *American Journal of Psychology* in 1903. The paper was theoretical in nature and attempted to explain the motives which draw throngs of people to witness football games.

> We understand fairly well the impulses which determine a man to work for bread or steal it, to scramble for money, fortune, social position, the favor of women; but what is the motive which prompts the English workman to spend fifty-five minutes of his precious noon recess in watching a local football game, and devoting five minutes to his dinner? Or why does the busy professional man, leaving his office, journey a hundred miles to see an intercollegiate match lasting an hour and a half? (Patrick, 1903, p. 105)

He discussed the theories of play current at the time and found them wanting. He concluded by saying,

> . . . it should be observed that the psychology of football and similar sports does not teach that in those games there is a return to savagery. There is a momentary return in the form of sport to the serious manners of former days in order that in the serious affairs of today, these manners may be more completely left behind. The intense passion for such games is in itself an indication that they answer to some present need. This need we

have already indicated in the psychology of work and play. In those countries where serious life is taken most seriously, as among the Anglo-Saxon nations, there is exhibited greater occasional abandonment to those sports which afford the greatest relief from mental tention.   (p. 117)

Perhaps the first direct experimental attack on the question of the value of sport and physical activity was made by R.A. Cummins (1914).

Much discussion has been published in recent years as to the probable value of athletics for college students, especially certain forms of exercise as that of football and basketball. In this connection it occurred to the writer that by singling out certain physical and mental traits it would thus be possible to reduce the problem to a measurable basis. Accordingly, the physical trait of motor reaction and the psychological traits of attention and suggestibility were selected as those which might reasonably be expected to show change through basketball practice when persistently followed up for a season?   (p. 356)

First Emergence

Probably the first psychologist to devote his full attention to the problems of physical education and athletics was Coleman Giffith of the University of Illinois. A course entitled "Psychology and Athletics" was first taught at Illinois in 1923. The new course sought to make a serious psychological analysis of all phases of athletic competition, to review the literature already available which bore upon such problems as skill, learning habits, attention, vision, emotion, and reaction time, and to gain, whenever possible, such new knowledge as time and facilities warranted. This led to the first text on the subject, *Psychology of Coaching* (Griffith, 1926). According to Griffith the text was ". . .really a series of observations on the way in which Illinois coaches went about it to produce their teams" (p. 36). A second book, *Psychology and Athletics,* was published soon after (Griffith, 1928).

The first laboratory for research in physical education and athletics in the U.S. was also established at the University of Illinois by Coleman Griffith in 1925 (Griffith, 1930). According to Griffith, George Huff, Director of Physical Welfare for Men at Illinois, advanced the idea to develop a laboratory which would devote itself to problems in the psychology and physiology of athletic activity quite independently of any attempt to create bigger and better athletic teams. Griffith noted that Huff appeared to be interested in the contribution such research might make to pure science rather than to building better teams. Griffith also reported that to the best of his knowledge, the Illinois laboratory was the second psychological laboratory to be devoted wholly to problems in athletics. At the time Griffith wrote, there was also a psychological laboratory in Berlin, Germany, in connection with a coaching school.

A quote by Griffith in 1925 sounds as fresh and topical as if it had been written today.

> A great many people have the idea that the psychologist is a sort of magician who is ready, for a price, to sell his services to one individual or to one group of men. Nothing could be further from the truth. Psychological facts are universal facts. They belong to whoever will read them. There is another strange opinion about the psychologist. It is supposed that he is merely waiting until he can jump onto the athletic field, tell the old time successful coach that he is all wrong and begin, then, to expound his own magical and fanciful theories as to proper methods of coaching, the way to conquer overconfidence, the best forms of strategy, and so on. This, of course, is far from the truth, although certain things have appeared in the applications of psychology to business and industry to lead to such an opinion. During the last few years and at the present time, there have been and are many men, short in psychology and training and long in the use of the English language, who are doing psychological damage by advertising that they are ready to answer any and every question that comes up in any and every field. No sane psychologist is deceived by these self-styled apostles of a new day. Coaches and athletes have a right to be weary of such stuff. (Griffith, 1925, p. 194)

In spite of Griffith's work, however, and the few studies alluded to here, there was little follow-up.

Psychology was in the midst of a movement for mental assessment so it isn't surprising that much of the early work in physical education centered around the relationship between physical and mental abilities. In an extensive review of 34 articles prior to 1927 which examined the question, Cozens concluded there was little or no relationship between mental and physical performance (Cozens, 1927). Closely related to this research were studies comparing athletes and nonathletes. A study by Ruble compared athletes and nonathletes at one university and concluded, "There is a very close relationship between intelligence and success in athletics" (Ruble, 1928), while a study by Hall appearing in the same volume concluded that, "Athletics slightly decrease the scholastic efficiency of students" (Hall, 1928). This line of research was to continue well into the 60s. McCloy, an early advocate of physical activity as a means of developing personality and self-confidence, and several of his students did a number of studies in an early attempt to measure character and personality (Blanchard, 1936; McCloy, 1930; O'Neal, 1936). However, he acknowledged "It [the series of studies] has suggested more problems than it has solved. There is apparently a need for further research in the field of character and personality studies" (Blanchard, 1936,

p. 66). But programs of research in the psychological area that involved several different studies by a single author, or studies that built on each other were infrequent. Most of the research that appeared prior to WW II was limited to a single study on a specific topic. This trend is just now beginning to change. Kroll noted that "Fewer than a dozen published articles could gain entrance into the top ten list for all time contributions" (Kroll, 1971, p. 153).

In spite of the fact that research programs by physical educators were infrequent, most texts in physical education had chapters or sections on the psychological aspects of physical education, and as pointed out earlier, many of the objectives in physical education were psychological in nature, (i.e., to build character, honesty, etc.). Lacking research in physical education, leaders made sincere efforts to use research findings from psychology for their own areas of interest. A significant statement indicating both the desire of physical educators to use information of a psychological nature and the frustration caused by the imprecise nature of psychology as an applied field, appeared in a 1934 introductory text in physical education.

> In the field of psychology as applied to teaching and learning the present century has seen startling changes of a radical character. These changes have tended to confuse the student of education who is not primarily a psychologist, because he has no sooner established a set of psychologic principles to guide him in his teaching methods when he is asked to modify these methods to make them consistent with some new advances in psychology. Just as we have adopted our methods, almost perfectly, we feel, to this 'bond psychology,' the Gestalt psychology appears with radically different theories about human learning, backed by experiments of such significance that the educator who is willing to learn must at least give these new theories thoughtful consideration with the idea of utilizing in his work any new ideas which give promise of greater success in teaching technique.
>
> This state of continuous change in this field of psychology has caused a number of practical-minded people to discard the whole subject in disgust. (Nixon & Cozens, 1934, pp. 55-56)

Later the authors say, ". . .it is a pleasure to point out that on many important points all rational schools of psychology are in substantial agreement" (p. 56).

In 1943, Davis and Lawther published a text, *Successful Teaching in Physical Education,* that had five chapters dealing with psychology, including an excellent chapter on motor learning (Davis & Lawther, 1941). It might be pointed out, however, that none of the references quoted in the psychological sections were from research published in physical education literature. The situation was basically unchanged nine years later when Esslinger wrote,

There have been very few investigations to determine the better methods of teaching physical education activities, and the value of some of those reported is nullified by errors in experimental procedures or by the small number of cases involved. The investigations made thus far have been chiefly concerned with the relative merits of the whole *versus* the part method of learning. (Esslinger, 1952, p. 821)

Second Emergence

The second emergence of psychology in the field of physical education occurred at the end of WW II. For the first time, courses in motor learning and motor performance began to be taught. Most prominent were classes at the University of California, Berkeley, under Franklin Henry; the University of Indiana under Arthur Slater-Hammel, and at Penn State under John Lawther. The early courses dealt almost exclusively with motor learning, but motivational factors and material related to sport psychology were occasionally included.

Research on better methods of teaching physical education continued, but for the first time a few individuals were beginning to make consistent contributions and a series of systematic studies began to appear (Knapp & Dixon, 1950, 1952; Knapp, Dixon, & Lazier, 1958). A series of studies by Franklin Henry (Henry, 1951, 1952), Arthur Slater-Hammel (Slater-Hammel & Andres, 1952; Slater-Hammel & Stumpner, 1950), and "Fritz" Hubbard (Hubbard & Seng, 1954) on reaction time in sport was probably the precursor to what is now referred to as "motor learning" or "motor control." In spite of the fact that most of the work by these three men were in areas not directly related to the topic of this paper, their contribution must not be overlooked. It was during the period between 1949 and 1965 when students of these three professors were contributing heavily to research in the psychological area.

Warren Johnson (1949) published a study on "emotion" and athletics. As early as 1933, C.O. Jackson had explored "The effect of fear on muscular contraction" (Jackson, 1933), but Johnson's study was the first since that time. Subsequently, Johnson and his colleagues published a series of five or six articles extending the initial finding (Harmon & Johnson, 1952; Husmann, 1955; Johnson, Hutton, & Johnson, 1954; Johnson & Hutton, 1955). Students of F.M. Henry working from a slightly different perspective, began to investigate similar problems. Howell (1953), Ryan (1961, 1962a, 1962b) and Carron (1968) examined motor performance under stress, but related the research to Hullian Drive theory. The Carron study used both situational stress and personality measures of anxiety at approximately the same time Ulrich was making still another approch to the influence of stress on performance (Hennis & Ulrich, 1958; Ulrich, 1957; Ulrich & Burke, 1957).

Textbook material specifically designed for physical education began to appear, greatly facilitating the expansion of courses in this area. John Lawther published *The Psychology of Coaching,* (1951) and the very influential *Science and Medicine in Sport* was published in 1960 (Johnson, 1960). The four chapters devoted to psychology in this volume effectively integrated most of the available psychological research in the area—a "landmark" in the emergence of psychological research in physical education. Perhaps the most notable text on the subject has been B.J. Cratty's text, *Motor Behavior and Motor Learning* (1964). For the first time, the research literature relating psychology to motor learning and performance was available in a single volume. It was no longer necessary for teachers or professors to be an expert in all areas. The text was more than a collection of research findings, however. As E.A. Fleshman stated in the forward, "Cratty shows how these studies bear on problems of concern to physical educators. His real contribution is in pulling the studies together, interpreting them, and synthesizing them in meaningful ways" (p. 6).

At approximately the same time, another event occurred which had an important effect on the emergence of the field. In 1965, just prior to the First International Congress of Psychology of Sport held in Rome, Warren Johnson suggested the possible formation of a society for sport psychology in the US. The first meeting of the North American Society for the Psychology of Sport and Physical Activity (NASPSPA) was held just prior to the AAHPER Convention in Chicago in 1966, and Arthur Slater-Hammel was elected president. The organization continued to meet for one or two day sessions just prior to the AAHPER Convention until 1973, when the members, making a very important decision, voted to hold their meeting independently of the AAHPER. The first such meeting was at Allerton Park, Illinois in 1973. To paraphrase a statement made at that time by the president of the organization, the change made the NASPSPA meeting the primary meeting for presentations of research and ideas in the area of psychology as it related to sport and physical activity. This organization encourages and permits intimate and intense academic interchange by the participants as well as extensive discussion of theoretical issues, and it also encourages coordination of research efforts by members (Loy, 1974).

Sustained Contributions

Earlier in the paper it was noted that very few programs of sustained research on a single topic had been developed. Most researchers who made more than a single contribution had skipped from one area of interest to another without completely answering the question raised by the initial study. Many, if not most, of the studies published in the *Research Quarterly* through the 1960s concluded with a statement that "more research needs to be done on this topic," but the "more research" was typically left to someone else. The result was that, more often than not, the research was never done.

There have been notable exceptions to this situation. Two of the more productive workers in the field during the past 10 years have been Rainer Martens and Daniel Landers. In 1969, they started a series of studies on "Social Facilitation" that continued for 10 years (Landers & McCullagh, 1976). A very recent series of studies that should have an impact on the profession, and is notable for its unique approach, has been undertaken by Ron Smith and Frank Smoll of the University of Washington. Working with Little League baseballers, they have developed a behavioral assessment system used to categorize the behaviors of Little League coaches devised a series of behavioral guidelines based on these observations, and then instituted a program to train the coaches to use the behaviors (Smith Smoll, & Carter, 1979; Smoll, Smith, Curtis, & Hunt, 1978).

Undoubtedly, the influence of personality was the area of research that had the longest history and generated more studies than any other. There were at least two reasons for the *quantity* of research in this area. First, virtually everyone believed there were individual differences in personality distinguishing between good performers and poor performers, between athletes and nonathletes, between persons of high-motor ability and low-motor ability, and perhaps between persons who participate in one sport rather than another. Also, it was considered that simply participating in athletics made for more wholesome personalities (each of these has been investigated *no less than* once). The second reason for the large number of studies was that it was very simple to take a well-established objective test, administer it to at least two groups presumed to differ on at least one dimension, then see if and how the groups actually differed. During the 50s and 60s, studies of this type were common (Cooper, 1969; Husmann, 1969), and the results quite contradictory (Ryan, 1969). Franklin Henry, in a statement during a conference, said, "I wonder why psychology in this area as well as others has gained so little in such a long time" (Henry, 1970, p. 373).

During the mid-60s Bruce Ogilvie and Tom Tutko, with the help of others, developed a personality scale—Athletic Motivation Inventory (AMI)—specifically designed to assess behaviors and attitudes pertinent to athletic participation (Tutko, Lyon, & Ogilvie, 1975). Because the scale was the first personality measure designed specifically for athletes it generated a great deal of interest, and with it, more than a little controversy. In the long run, the AMI was good for the area of sport psychology because it forcefully brought before the researchers in the area questions that had to be faced. An apparent dichotomy developed in the field; one group suggested that trait psychology as it relates to sports should be abandoned, while another group seemed to accept trait psychology completely and unquestioningly. It was not unusual at research meetings to have half of the papers based on the trait approach, and the other half trying to show why the approach was inappropriate. Two persons with extensive research in personality, who seemed at first glance to represent the extremes of the dichotomy, were Walter Kroll (1970) and William Morgan (1978). Reading their more recent papers indicates the field has made great progress since the mid-60s and is asking much better and more sophisticated questions—the dichotomy is not as apparent as it once seemed. The importance of "states" as well as "traits" has been emphasized, and the interaction of both of these, with environmental or situational factors, has been recognized and acknowledged. I took a somewhat different approach to personality as it relates to physical activity (Ryan, 1966, 1969; Ryan & Foster, 1967). The basic premise was that there seems to be certain consistent perceptual characteristics that distinguish athletes from nonathletes. Athletes tend to tolerate more pain, perceive time as passing more quickly, and show more reduction in kinesthetic-figural-after-effects than their nonathletic counterparts.

One of the better research programs to date in the area of physical activity psychology is the work of Rainer Martens and his colleagues at the University of Illinois on competitive anxiety. In a sense their work has focused on some of the same questions asked earlier (Carron, 1968; Harmon & Johnson, 1952; Howell, 1953; Ryan, 1961), but from a new perspective. It also addresses many of the questions raised by the personologists. In brief, this research has looked at a specific personality trait-anxiety in competitive situations. The research first developed the "Sport Competitive Anxiety Test" (SCAT) to measure the trait of competitive anxiety, then proceeded to test the interactions of this trait with anxiety "states" brought about under specific conditions in the competitive situation (Martens, 1977). The research program has been important for several reasons. First, it is theoretically based. Second, the SCAT scale was developed specifically for athletic situations and the theory under investigation. Third, it met the criticism and suggestions of both Morgan and Kroll in the integration of "situation-specific trait" and "states brought about by the situation," then investigated how both interacted with various environmental factors. Fourth, unlike most of the work in the area, the research of Martens and his colleagues had a logical beginning based on theory and progressed methodically and logically through a series of studies designed to contribute specific details to a more complete understanding of the theoretical model. Finally, while the program is theoretical in orientation, it has practical implications for the practitioner.

The continued work of William Morgan should also be noted. Morgan's work differs from most of the researchers in the field because he has been less interested in sport and athletics per se, and more involved with the psychological correlates of physical activity for all. In a sense, Morgan is attempting to test in a definitive way the speculations and assumptions which the pioneers in the field alluded to earlier (Morgan, 1969, 1976, 1979).

One thing that has limited research in this area has been the lack of publication outlets. The vast majority of the work has been published in *Research Quarterly.* A few articles have appeared in *Perceptual and Motor Skills, Medicine and Science in Sports,* and *Journal of Motor Behavior.* A handful of researchers have published occasionally in the *Journal of Personality and Social Psychology.* Outside of *Research Quarterly,* however, none of these are appropriate for many of the topics that should be investigated. Recently, a new publication, *Journal of Sports Psychology* published by Human Kinetics Publishers and edited by Daniel Landers, has emerged and seems to fill the need for a publication outlet for this area. Hopefully, this new outlet will encourage even more quality research in the area of psychology of sport and physical activity.

Conclusion

Probably the most important factor in changing the field and ensuring its continued growth and maturity has been the quality of young people coming into the area. Initially, most of the research was done by persons with few, if any, courses in psychology. Only a handful of researchers in physical education had adequate backgrounds in psychology. Recently, several universities have started to offer PhD programs with a specialty in psychology of physical activity, and students are graduating as competent research psychologists. It isn't uncommon today for graduate students to have a far better background in psychology than the leaders in the field had just a few years ago. In addition, persons in departments of psychology are beginning to be interested in the same questions that only the coach or physical educator were asking a few years ago. In the very near future, the major emphasis or focus of research in psychology of physical education may well become more pragmatic and applied. Combined with the increased competence of the young researchers in the field, we are ready for our "third emergence."

References

Blanchard, E.B. A behavior frequency rating scale for measurement of character and personality in physical education. *Research Quarterly,* 1936, **7**, 57-66.

Carron, A.V. Motor performance under stress. *Research Quarterly,* 1968, **39**, 463-469.

Cooper, L. Athletics, achievement, and personality: A review of the literature. *Research Quarterly,* 1969, **40**, 17-22.

Cozens, F.W. Status of the problem of the relation of physical and mental ability. *American Physical Education Review,* 1927, **32**, 127-155.

Cratty, B.J. *Movement behavior and motor learning.* Philadelphia: Lea and Febiger, 1964.

Cummins, R.T. A study of the effect of basketball practice on motor reaction and suggestibility. *Psychology Reviews,* 1914, **21**, 356-369.

Davis, E.C., & Lawther, J.D. *Successful Teaching in Physical Education.* New York: Prentice-Hall, 1941.

Esslinger, A.A. Methods of teaching. In W.S. Monroe (Ed.), *Encyclopedia of educational research.* New York: MacMillan 1952.

Fairclaugh, R.H. Transfer of motivation: Improvement in speed of reaction and movement. *Research Quarterly,* 1952, **23**, 20-27.

Griffith, C.R. Psychology and its relation to athletic competition. *American Physical Education Review,* 1925, **30**, 193-198.

Griffith, C.R. *Psychology of coaching.* New York: Scribners, 1926.

Griffith, C.R. *Psychology of athletics.* New York: Scribners, 1928.

Griffith, C.R. A laboratory for research in athletics. *Research Quarterly,* 1930, **1**.

Hackensmith, C.W. *History of physical education.* New York: Harper and Row, 1966.

Hall, G.S. Physical education in colleges. *Report of the National Education Association.* Chicago: University of Chicago Press, 1908.

Hall, R.T. How athletes and non-athletes compare in mental ability and educational achievement. *American Physical Education Review,* 1928, **33**, 388-389.

Harmon, J.M., & Johnson, W.R. The emotional reactions of college athletes. *Research Quarterly*, 1952, **23**, 391-397.

Hennis, G.M., & Ulrich, C. Study of psychic stress in freshman college women. *Research Quarterly*, 1958, **29**, 172-179.

Henry, F.M. Increase in speed of movement by motivation and transfer of motivational improvement. *Research Quarterly*, 1951, **22**, 219-228.

Henry, F.M. Independence of reaction and movement times and equivalence of sensory motivators of faster response. *Research Quarterly*, 1952, **23**, 43-53.

Henry, F.M. Discussion of current strategies and problems in personality assessment of athletics. In L.E. Smith (Ed.), *Psychology of Motor Learning*. Chicago: Athletics Institute, 1970.

Hetherington, C.W. The objectives of physical education. *American Physical Education Review*, 1922, **27**, 405-414.

Howell, M.L. Influence of emotional tension on speed of reaction and movement. *Research Quarterly*, 1953, **24**, 22-32.

Hubbard, A.W., & Seng, C.N. Visual movements of batters. *Research Quarterly*, 1954, **25**, 42-57.

Husmann, B.F. Aggression in boxers and wrestlers as measured by projective techniques. *Research Quarterly*, 1955, **26**, 421-425.

Husmann, B.F. Sport and personality dynamics. *NCPEAM Proceedings*. 1969, **72**, 56-70.

Jackson, C.O. An experimental study of the effect of fear on muscular contractions. *Research Quarterly*, 1933, **4**, 71-79.

Johnson, W.R. A study of emotion revealed in two types of athletic sport contests. *Research Quarterly*, 1949, **20**, 72-79.

Johnson, W.R. (Ed.). *Science and medicine of exercise and sports*. New York: Harper and Row, 1960.

Johnson, W.R., & Hutton, D.C. Effect of a competitive sport upon personality dynamics as measured by a projective test. *Research Quarterly*, 1955, **26**, 491-531.

Johnson, W.R., Hutton, D.C., & Johnson, G.B. Personality traits of some champion athletes as measured by two projective tests: The Rorschach and H.T.P. *Research Quarterly*, 1954, **25**, 484-485.

Knapp, C.G., & Dixon, W.R. Learning to juggle: I. A study to determine the effect of two different distributions of practice on learning efficiency. *Research Quarterly*, 1950, **21**, 331-336.

Knapp, C.G., & Dixon, W.R. Learning to juggle: II. A study of whole and part methods. *Research Quarterly*, 1952, **23**, 393-401.

Knapp, C.G., Dixon, W.R., & Lazier, M. Learning to juggle: III. A study of performance of two different age groups *Research Quarterly,* 1958, **29,** 32-36.

Kroll, W. Current strategies and problems in personality assessment of athletics. In L.E. Smith (Ed.), *Psychology of motor learning.* Chicago: Athletic Institute, 1970.

Kroll, W. *Perspectives in physical education.* New York: Academic Press, 1971.

Landers, D.M., & McCullagh, P.D. Social facilitation and motor performance. In J.R. Keogh (Ed.) *Exercise and sport science reviews* (Vol. 4). Santa Barbara, CA: Journal Publishing Affiliates, 1976.

Lawther, J.D. *The psychology of coaching.* Englewood Cliffs, NJ: Prentice-Hall, 1951.

Leonard, F.E., & Afflect, G.B. *A guide to the history of physical education.* Philadelphia: Lea and Febiger, 1947.

Loy, J.W. A brief history of the North American Society for the Psychology of Sport and Physical Activities. In M.G. Wade & R. Martens (Eds.), *Psychology of motor behavior and sport* (Vol. 1). Champaign, IL: Human Kinetics, 1974.

MacDonald, A. Scientific study of baseball. *American Physical Education Review,* 1914, **19,** 220-241.

Martens, R. Effect on performance of learning a complex motor task in the presence of spectators. *Research Quarterly,* 1969, **40,** 317-323.

Martens, R. *Sport Competition Anxiety Test.* Champaign, IL: Human Kinetics, 1977.

McCloy, C.H. Character building through physical education *Research Quarterly,* 1930, **1,** 41-61.

McCloy, C.H. What is modern physical education? *University of Iowa Extension Bulletin* (No. 505), State University of Iowa. Iowa City, IA: 1941.

Morgan, W.P. Physical fitness and emotional health: A review. *American Correctional Theraphy Journal,* 1969, **23,** 124.

Morgan, W.P. Psychological consequences of vigorous physical activity and sport. In M.G. Scott (Ed.), *The Academy Papers.* Iowa City, IA: American Academy of Physical Education, 1976.

Morgan, W.P. Sport personology: The credulous-skeptical argument in perspective. In A.A. Ismail (Ed.), *Psycho-social behavior of sport and play: Proceedings of 3rd symposium on intellectual development.* Indiana State Board of Health, 1978.

Morgan, W.P. Anxiety reduction following acute physical activity. *Psychiatric Annals,* 1979, **9,** 34-40.

Nixon, E.W., & Cozens, F.W. *An introduction to physical education.* Philadelphia: W.B. Saunders, 1934.

O'Neal, F.W. A behavior frequency rating scale for the measurement of character and personality in high school physical education classes for boys. *Research Quarterly,* 1936, **7**, 67-76.

Patrick, G.T.W. The psychology of football. *American Journal of Psychology,* 1903, **14**, 104-117.

Ruble, V.W. A psychological study of athletes. *American Physical Education Review,* 1928, **33**, 219-234.

Ryan, E.D. Motor performance under stress as a function of the amount of practice. *Perceptual Motor Skills,* 1961, **13**, 103-106.

Ryan, E.D. Relationship between motor performance and arousal. *Research Quarterly,* 1962, **33**, 279-287. (a)

Ryan, E.D. Effect of stress on motor performance and learning. *Research Quarterly,* 1962, **33**, 111-119. (b)

Ryan, E.D. Perceptual characteristics of vigorous people. In R.C. Brown & B.J. Cratty, (Eds.), *New prospectives of man in action.* Englewood Cliffs, NJ: Prentice-Hall, 1969.

Ryan, E.D. Reaction to sport and personality dynamics. *NCPEAM Proceedings,* 1969, **72**, 70-75.

Ryan, E.D., & Foster, R.L. Athletic participation and perceptual augmentation and reduction. *Journal of Personality and Social Psychology,* 1967, **2**, 272-276.

Ryan, E.D., & Kovacic, C.R. Pain tolerance and athletic participation. *Perceptual Motor Skills,* 1966, **22**, 383-390.

Singer, R.N. Effect of spectators on athletes and non-athletes performing a gross motor task. *Research Quarterly,* 1965, **36**, 473-482.

Slater-Hammel, A.T., & Stumpner, R.L. Batters reaction times. *Research Quarterly,* 1950, **21**, 353-356.

Slater-Hammel, A.T., & Andres, E.H. Velocity measurement of fastballs and curveballs. *Research Quarterly,* 1952, **23**, 95-97.

Smith, R.E., Smoll, F.L., & Carter, B. Coach effectiveness training: A cognitive-behavioral approach to enhancing relationship skills in youth sport coaches. *Journal of Sport Psychology,* 1979, **1**, 59-75.

Smoll, F.L., Smith, R.E., Curtis, B., & Hunt, E. Toward a mediational model of coach-player relationship. *Research Quarterly,* 1978, **49**, 528-541.

Sperling, A.P. The relationship between personality adjustment and achievement in physical activity. *Research Quarterly,* 1952, **13**, 351-363.

Stagg, A.A.   Some comments on physical education. *American Physical Education Review,* March 1911, p. 184.

Triplett, N. The dynamogenic factors in pacemaking and competition. *American Journal of Psychology,* 1897, **9,** 507-553.

Tutko, T.A., Lyon, L.P., & Ogilvie, B.C. *Athletic Motivation Inventory Manual.* San Jose, CA: Institute of Athletic Motivation, 1975.

Ulrich, C. Measurement of stress evidenced by college women in situations involving competition. *Research Quarterly,* 1957, **28,** 160-172.

Ulrich, C., & Burke, R.K. Effect of motivational stress upon physical performance. *Research Quarterly,* 1957, **28,** 403-412.

Current Research and Future Prospects in Sport Psychology

18

D.L. Gill

Sport psychology emerged as a recognizable subdiscipline within physical education in the late 1960s and early 1970s, and therefore, nearly all of the research in sport psychology is current. Even in the relatively short time of 15 years, however, research emphases in the field have changed dramatically. Early sport psychology research consisted of a few isolated, largely atheoretical studies; often these were graduate theses involving personality measures. Social psychological concepts and experimental paradigms dominated sport psychology through the 1970s, with the influence of social factors on motor performance being especially popular. Recently, sport psychologists have moved to more field research and an emphasis on applied issues. In the sections to follow, I have reviewed the major issues and findings in the major research areas of sport psychology, including personality, motivation, social influence processes, group dynamics, and applied sport psychology.

Personality

Individual differences in psychological characteristics, especially the common personality traits, have been part of sport psychology from the beginning of the field or the "first emergence" described by Ryan (chap. 17). Much of the early research consisted of administering standard personality inventories to samples of athletes. That largely atheoretical research, which is criticized elsewhere (Kroll, 1970; Martens, 1975a; Rushall, 1970), has subsided in recent years and much of the current writing on sport personality consists of reviews and position papers.

One popular conceptual debate is the trait-situation-interaction controversy, which is concerned with whether individual differences or environmental factors are the more important determinants of behavior.

Reviewers typically present these approaches as though researchers actually held extreme trait or situation views. In fact, virtually all active sport psychologists adopt an interaction approach, acknowledging the joint contributions of person factors (traits or dispositions) and situational factors as determinants of sport behavior, and recognize that all personality characteristics are not equally relevant to sport. Morgan (1978b, 1980) and Kane (1978) emphasize personality factors more than other sport psychologists, but neither is an extreme trait theorist. Likewise, most sport psychologists who have criticized sport personality research (e.g., Kroll, 1970; Martens, 1975a) recognize the importance of at least some individual differences and personality dispositions.

Morgan (1979, 1980) suggests that a personality pattern termed the "iceberg" profile characterizes highly successful athletes and cites evidence showing that elite athletes exhibit low levels of tension, depression, fatigue, and confusion and high levels of vigor. Alderman (1978) describes seven basic incentive systems in sport as affiliation, success, excellence, aggression, stress, independence, and power and suggests that individuals differ in those basic incentive systems. Most recent sport personality research, however, focuses on selected individual characteristics deemed relevant to sport behavior. Recently, Dishman, Ickes, and Morgan (1980) developed a measure of self-motivation with demonstrated reliability and validity that discriminates between dropouts and those who adhere to exercise programs.

Competitive Anxiety

Investigations of sport-specific individual differences, such as the competitive anxiety work of Martens (1977), appear especially promising. Martens's competitive anxiety work is a theory-based, systematic line of research that focuses on specific behaviors related to anxiety which are common in sport. Martens used the available theory and empirical base in psychology and also incorporated sport-specific constructs. Martens's major contribution is the development of the Sport Competition Anxiety Test (SCAT), which measures competitive trait anxiety, the predisposition to exhibit high levels of state anxiety in competitive situations, and the empirical demonstration of SCAT's validity. Martens's systematic series of laboratory and field investigations did much to further our understanding of competitive anxiety, but many questions remain unanswered. Although Martens focused on competitive trait anxiety (a person factor), subsequent studies have attempted to further delineate competitive state anxiety (Gruber &

Beauchamp, 1979; Martens, Burton, Rivkin, & Simon, 1980) and to identify situational factors that influence competitive anxiety, particularly win/loss or success/failure which has a dramatic effect on state anxiety. This research has found that state anxiety is substantially greater after losing than it is after winning (Martens & Gill, 1976; Scanlan & Passer, 1978a, 1979). The research has also shown that state anxiety increases significantly as the time to compete nears, especially so for high competitive trait anxious persons. Competitive anxiety is currently an active sport psychology research area and conferences and publications often include several papers, typically following an interaction approach that combines person factors (often SCAT) with varying situational factors.

Achievement Motivation

Achievement motivation and achievement behavior in sport, which has much in common with competitive anxiety, is a likely candidate for systematic research following an interaction approach. Indeed, the achievement motivation constructs and predictions of Atkinson's classic model have been applied to sport and motor behavior. Atkinson's approach is an interaction approach, although a limited one, which predicts that high and low achievement-oriented persons differ in behavior in achievement situations. In brief, the theory predicts that high achievers approach, perform well, and persist in achievement situations, especially the most challenging situations, whereas low achievers avoid challenging situations and suffer performance decrements when forced into them. In motor performance research, several investigators (Ostrow, 1976; Roberts, 1974; Scanlan & Ragan, 1978) report that high achievers do indeed prefer challenging situations more than low achievers, but the predicted difference between high and low achievers in actual performance is less consistently supported. Ryan and Lakie (1965) reported that high achievers improved performance from noncompetitive to competitive situations more than low achievers, but others (Healey & Landers, 1973; Ostrow, 1976; Roberts, 1972) report weak or no performance differences.

Although Atkinson's model encouraged research, especially in relation to choice of achievement situation, the model provides little insight into sport and motor performance achievement. Social psychologists have recognized the limits of Atkinson's original model and turned to more cognitive approaches, particularly attributional explanations of individual differences in achievement behavior, and sport psychologists are following suit. Development of sport-specific achievement constructs analagous to competitive trait anxiety is another logical approach. Coaches and athletes often refer to individual differences in competitiveness, and competitiveness seems to imply achievement motivation specific to sport competition. To date, however, sport psychology work on competitiveness is quite limited. An important beginning was made by Scanlan (1978), who incorporated Veroff's (1969) model of the development of achievement motivation, Martens's (1975b) model of the competition process, and research on the development of achievement motivation in her discussion of the antecedents of competitiveness. Cross-cultural research by Nelson and Kagan (1972) suggests that child-rearing practices in our culture (particularly contingent reinforcement systems) tend to make American children more competitive than children of other cultures. Orlick, McNally, and O'Hara (1978), working with native children of the northern Canadian territories and southern Canadian children, report that northern children were much more accepting of cooperative game structures than children in southern Ontario who preferred competitive structures.

Other Personality Dispositions

The interaction approach has been applied to a limited number of personality characteristics in addition to achievement motivation and competitive anxiety. Tu and Rothstein (1979) reported that dependency motive-oriented individuals did better in a jogging program with teacher-imposed goals, whereas independency motive-oriented persons did better with self-imposed goals. Loy and Donnelly (Donnelly, 1975; Loy & Donnelly, 1976) advocate an interaction model to look at the relationship of need for stimulation or stimulus seeking to sport participation.

Need for stimulation is primarily a perceptual characteristic, and recent work suggests that individual differences in cognitive and perceptual styles and strategies may be a more promising line of research for sport psychology than the typical social/personality characteristics studied in the past. Mischel (1968, 1973), one of the most cited critics of trait approaches in personality psychology, suggests that cognitive strategies are more consistent individual differences than social/personality characteristics, and Morgan (1980) suggests that the study of cognitive/perceptual styles holds promise for sport psychology. Ryan (Ryan, 1969; Ryan & Foster, 1967; Ryan & Kovacic, 1966) reported relationships between perceptual style, pain tolerance, and participation in contact sports, and Morgan (Morgan, 1978a; Morgan & Pollock, 1977) identified differences in the cognitive strategies of elite and average marathon runners. Average runners typically use a dissociative strategy, focusing on external cues or distracting ideas, whereas elite runners use an associative strategy, focusing on and monitoring body sensations. Nideffer has developed a measure of individual differences in attention styles (1976a) and discussed the relationship of varying attention styles to sport performance (1976b). The work of Ryan, Morgan, and Nideffer suggests that cognitive/perceptual characteristics play a role in sport and motor behavior, but considerable empirical work is needed to clarify that role.

Attitudes

Sport psychology research on attitudes closely parallels the personality research with attitudes toward physical activity as the primary focus. Early research on attitudes, like the research on personality, was atheoretical, plagued by methodological problems, and lacked the standard measures available for personality studies. The limited findings of sport attitude research, reviewed elsewhere (Martens, 1975b), indicate that persons generally hold positive attitudes toward sport, physical activity, and physical education, but those attitudes do not relate well to specific behaviors. Kenyon's (1968a, 1968b) conceptual dimensions of physical activity and empirically developed measure of attitudes toward physical activity was a major advance in sport attitude research, but subsequent studies have advanced little beyond the descriptive level. A recent longitudinal study by Smoll and Schutz (1980) indicates that attitudes measured by Kenyon's scale are *not* stable individual characteristics and thus sport psychologists could not logically expect consistent relationships between attitudes and sport behavior.

The Future of Personality Research

In light of the problems with previous attitude and personality studies, future research on individual differences will likely focus on sport-specific personality factors, such as competitive trait anxiety, or specific characteristics that are logically related to sport behavior. Perceptual and cognitive styles may well exert a consistent influence on some sport behaviors. In any event, future sport psychology research should follow models that consider the interactive influence of selected person variables and situational factors on psychological states and behaviors in sport and physical activity settings.

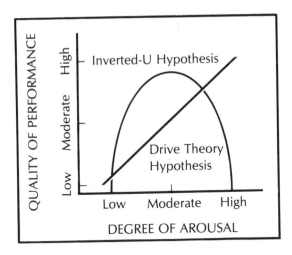

Figure 1.   The drive theory and inverted-U hypotheses.

Motivation

Motivation constructs overlap with personality as individual characteristics certainly exert a directive and energizing influence on behavior.
Motivation is, however, a more general term and this section focuses on
the intensity dimension of behavior, termed arousal. Within sport psychology, the relationship of arousal to motor performance is a popular
research and discussion topic. Much sport psychology work on arousal
stems from drive theory concepts of motivation, although other sport
psychologists follow more behavioristic approaches, and recently some
sport psychologists have incorporated more cognitive motivational constructs into their research.

Arousal and Motor Performance

The literature on arousal and motor performance, reviewed elsewhere
(Landers, 1980; Martens, 1974), generally is incorporated within two theories: drive theory and the inverted-U (see Figure 1). Drive theory, based on
the classic work of Hull and Spence, essentially predicts that increases
in drive or arousal increase the probability of the dominant response
being emitted. If the task is simple or well-learned, then the dominant
response will be the correct response and thus increased arousal should
improve performance; if the task is complex and not well-learned, how-

ever, the dominant response is likely to be an incorrect response and increased arousal impairs performance. The inverted-U model states that performance is best at a moderate, optimal level of arousal, and either increases or decreases in arousal from that optimal level decrease performance.

The inverted-U model can accommodate task differences by noting that different tasks have different optimal levels of arousal. Oxendine (1970), for example, suggested that complex skills involving fine movements and coordination (such as putting in golf) have low optimal arousal levels, whereas less complex endurance and strength tasks (such as weight lifting) have high optimal arousal levels. Although drive theory and the inverted-U models at first appear quite different, both suggest that the performance of simple or well-learned tasks is enhanced by higher arousal levels and the performance of novel, complex skills is impaired by high arousal levels. A laboratory experiment with three levels of stress (Martens & Landers, 1970), Lowe's (1973) investigation of stress and Little League batting, and a recent study by Weinberg and Ragan (1978) support the inverted-U model for motor performance, and Martens (1974) concluded his review of the arousal-motor performance literature by suggesting that the inverted-U had more support than drive theory. Carron (1980) and Landers (1980), however, suggest that drive theory may indeed be useful, and considerable social facilitation research provides empirical support for drive concepts.

As well as examining drive and inverted-U theories, some researchers have incorporated other constructs. Landers (1980) discussed Easterbrook's (1959) cue utilization theory and suggested the narrowing of attentional focus as a possible mediator between arousal and performance. Weinberg (Weinberg, 1978; Weinberg & Hunt, 1976), using EMG patterns to delve into the anxiety-performance relationship, noted that high anxious persons and persons in arousal-provoking situations used more muscular energy and exhibited less efficient movement patterns than low anxious persons. In a series of innovative studies involving the continuous monitoring of arousal with parachute jumpers, Fenz (1975) observed that novice parachutists increased in arousal from the night before the jump up to the time of the jump and were at their highest arousal level when performing. Experienced jumpers, on the other hand, reached their highest arousal levels early in the jump sequence and decreased or controlled arousal immediately before the jump (see Figure 2). This suggests that absolute levels of arousal are not necessarily related to performance. Instead, arousal patterns and the ability to control arousal seem to differentiate successful and less successful performers. Fenz's

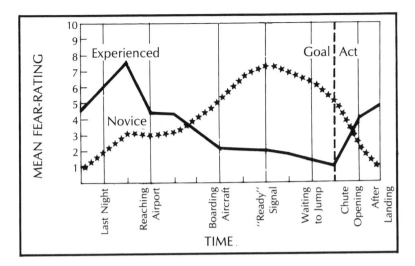

Figure 2. Arousal levels of experienced and novice parachutists prior to, during, and after a jump.

work and similar findings with Olympic gymnasts (Mahoney & Avener, 1977) imply that better performers are more task-oriented and able to control arousal, whereas poorer performers tend to think about their fears. These apparent cognitive differences may provide guidance for future arousal-performance research and for intervention strategies in applied sport psychology.

Behavior Modification

Behavioral approaches to motivation in sport, well represented by the work of Rushall and Siedentop (1972), emphasize the application of reinforcement principles and ignore drive, personality, and cognitive constructs. Siedentop (1978) cites a number of cases in which contingency management principles have been applied to improve performance or alter nonperformance behaviors in sport, and also presents guidelines for the effective use of contingency management.

Cognitive Approaches

In 1975, Wankel advocated the application of cognitive approaches to a number of sport psychology issues, and indeed, many sport psychologists have incorporated cognitive constructs, particularly causal attribu-

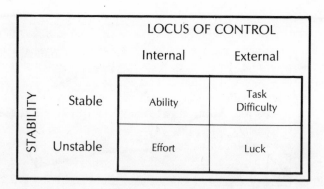

Figure 3. The two-dimensional classification system of causal attributions based on the model of Weiner et al. (1971).

tions, into their research. Much of the sport attribution research emanates from the model of Weiner, Frieze, Kukla, Reed, Rest, and Rosenbaum (1971), who identified four standard causal attributions—ability, effort, luck, and task difficulty—and proposed the two-dimensional classification system shown in Figure 3. Attributions are classified as internal (ability and effort) or external (luck and task difficulty) and stable (ability and task difficulty) or unstable (effort and luck). Researchers consistently observe that individuals tend to make internal attributions for success but attribute failure to external factors. This tendency to take personal credit for success and shift blame for failure to external factors, generally interpreted as an egocentric bias, has also been observed in sport settings, including Little League baseball (Iso-Ahola, 1975, 1977; Roberts, 1975, 1978), tennis (Forsyth & Schlenker, 1977), intercollegiate basketball (Bird & Brame, 1978), and game write-ups in newspapers (Lau & Russell, 1980).

Thus far, most sport attribution research has been at the descriptive level and simply replicated the egocentric tendency in success/failure attributions. Attribution theorists within social psychology have gone beyond the descriptive level, however, to investigate affective and behavioral implications of varying attributions. Sport psychologists need to do the same.

Mounting evidence suggests that the four basic attributions, typically accepted without question, are not the most appropriate attributions for sport. Roberts and Pascuzzi (1979), using open-ended win/loss attributions, reported that only 40% could be classified into the four basic attributions. Bukowski and Moore (1980) similarly stress the need to consider attributions other than the traditional four in sport situations. In his more recent work, Weiner himself (Weiner, 1979; Weiner, Russell, & Lerman, 1978) points out that the four traditional attributions were never intended to be the only attributions and the specific situation must be considered to determine appropriate attributions.

Recent evidence indicates that egocentric attributions in sport are not as prevalent as previously believed. Bukowski and Moore (1980) observed that winners did not take any more credit for success than losers gave them and found no evidence for an egocentric bias. Scanlan (1977) observed that competitors on a maze task attributed failure to the self more than success and interpreted such attributions as examples of "good winner" and "good loser" norms (Scanlan, 1977; Scanlan & Passer, 1978a). Scanlan and Passer (1980) also reported that losers in youth soccer were not more external in their attributions than winners, and Duquin (1978b) found both success and failure in elementary physical education to be attributed internally. Gill (1980) reported within-team attributions in team competition that exhibited a reverse-egocentric pattern, with members of winning teams assigning primary responsibility to their teammates and losing team members accepting primary responsibility for the loss themselves. Such findings suggest that attributions in sport are not necessarily subject to the same rules as attributions in social psychology laboratory and classroom studies. All this suggests that adopting the four traditional attributions and measures from social psychology and assuming an egocentric bias is not adequate for understanding the role of causal attributions in sport. Some innovative approaches for investigating attributions in sport will need to be developed by sport psychologists if this area is to prove helpful.

Although sport psychology research on cognitive factors is focused on success/failure attributions, a number of related areas also show considerable promise. The relationship of extrinsic rewards, such as trophies or scholarships, to intrinsic motivation is typically discussed in cognitive terms. Research by Lepper, Greene, and Nisbett (1973) and Deci (1975) dramatically demonstrated that extrinsic rewards can undermine intrinsic motivation. The reduction of intrinsic motivation following extrinsic rewards is generally interpreted in cognitive terms in that persons presumably interpret the rewards as controlling their behavior, and thus, when rewards are withdrawn, they no longer have a reason for doing the activity. This undermining of intrinsic motivation has obvious implications for sport, and sport psychologists have begun to investigate intrinsic motivation. Weinberg and Jackson (1979) and Weinberg and Ragan (1979) report that success in competition enhances while failure detracts from intrinsic motivation. Of particular significance is the research by Ryan who recently began to investigate the relationship of athletic scholarships to intrinsic motivation in intercollegiate athletics. His initial findings (Ryan, 1977, 1980) suggest that scholarship athletes do indeed display less intrinsic motivation to play than nonscholarship athletes, but also suggest some sex and sport differences that call for further study.

Cognitive concepts of perceived control and self-efficacy, concepts closely related to self-confidence, may well prove to be key factors in sport. Weinberg, Gould, and Jackson (1979) demonstrated that the manipulation of self-efficacy can affect motor performance, but to date, neither perceived control nor self-efficacy has received much attention from sport psychologists. Dweck (1980) recently discussed her extensive research on cognitive characteristics of mastery-oriented children (those who seek out and perform well in challenging achievement situations) and helpless-oriented children (those who feel they have no control and feel helpless in achievement situations) and suggested applications to sport. Further investigation of these suggestions within sport offers a promising direction for future research.

Social Influences on Motor Performance

The influence of social factors, particularly the presence of others, on motor performance was at the center of sport psychology research in the late 1960s and early 1970s. Although other issues have become dominant research themes, social influence processes remain a key aspect of sport psychology.

Social Facilitation

Martens (1969) initiated a series of laboratory studies on social facilitation concerned with the influence of the presence of others as a passive audience or coactors. Using a motor skill task, Martens supported Zajonc's (1965) theory which states that the presence of an audience creates arousal and thus impairs initial learning of a complex task but facilitates later performance on the same task. Later, a number of investigators varied the task, audience, and subject characteristics within the basic social facilitation paradigm, with the findings varying depending on the specific variables studied. Landers and McCullagh (1976) present a comprehensive review of those findings.

The controlled laboratory experiment approach that characterized sport psychology research in the 1970s did much to further the field, but it also led to a rather restricted approach to some issues, social facilitation being a prime example. Many of the research variations were trivial and the value of even Martens's clear findings may be questioned. A recent replication and critical analysis of Martens's (1969) audience study by Landers, Bauer, and Feltz (1978), along with the reply (Martens, 1979) and rejoinder (Landers, Bauer, & Feltz, 1979), provides a fine example of coherent critical exchange in sport psychology and sheds light on several theoretical and methodological issues in social facilitation research. One point upon which Landers et al. and Martens agree is that even with Martens's highly statistically significant effects, the practical significance of the audience effect is much more limited and accounts for only a small proportion of performance variance. Furthermore, the audience effect that seemed so clear in the controlled laboratory situation has not been replicated in the field; the few studies that have attempted to look at spectator or crowd effects at sports events have generally failed to find significant performance effects (Paulus & Cornelius, 1974; Paulus, Judd, & Bernstein, 1977).

The failure to advance substantially beyond the initial findings of Martens is probably one reason for the decline in popularity of social facilitation research, and undoubtedly, many believe the decline is long overdue. On the other hand, perhaps sport psychologists could glean findings of theoretical and practical value by adopting different approaches to investigations of the influence of the presence of others on motor performance and behavior in sport settings. Wankel (1980) advocates a more cognitive approach rather than reliance on the drive approach of Zajonc. On a more applied line, limited empirical work suggests that the home/away effect that many intuitively accept does have support. Schwartz and Barsky (1977) observed an advantage for home teams and reported that the advantage is greater for the offense than the defense and greater for indoor sports where the fans are close (e.g., ice hockey, basketball) than for outdoor sports (e.g., football, baseball). Varca (1980) suggested that the home advantage is due to more "aggressive" play by the home team and cited evidence from high school basketball teams indicating that the home team has an advantage in "aggressive" statistics (e.g., rebounds, steals) but not in shooting percentages.

Of course, home/away effects are not simply due to the presence of others, but probably involve social support and criticism. In experimental work the influence of praise and criticism or social reinforcement on motor performance has been examined separately from social facilitation effects.

Social Reinforcement

About the same time social facilitation research was getting underway, a series of laboratory experiments looking at the influence of social reinforcement in the form of positive and negative comments on motor performance was conducted (Martens, 1970, 1971, 1972; Roberts & Martens, 1970). Unlike social facilitation studies, that series did not yield statistically significant findings, although later studies did show some weak social reinforcement effects. Martens, Burwitz, and Newell (1972) reported limited motivational effects of social reinforcement in later performance stages; Gill and Martens (1975) found that social reinforcement improved performance when other information was not available; and Harvey and Parker (1972) reported motivational effects for frequent, intense social reinforcement. In general, though, laboratory studies yielded weak effects at best and few findings of practical significance.

Other lines of research related to social reinforcement show more promise. The contingency management approach advocated by Rushall and Siedentop appears effective with at least some specific sport behaviors. One of the most promising research programs is the work of Ron Smith and Frank Smoll with youth sport coaches. Rather than focusing on isolated praise and reproof comments, Smoll and Smith have taken a broader look at communication styles of coaches. An initial phase of their work involved observing and classifying coaching behaviors and the development of a standard system for assessing those behaviors (Smith, Smoll, & Hunt, 1977). Subsequent studies within their systematic line of research indicated that coaching behaviors did not affect win/loss records, but coaches who used more supportive comments and instruction and less punitive communication were rated more positively by players. More important, they also demonstrated that a training program for coaches was effective in that trained coaches used the positive approach more than a control group of coaches, and consequently, had players who not only rated the coaches positively, but also rated their teammates more positively and generally had a more positive outlook on the sport program (Smith, Smoll, & Curtis, 1979; Smoll & Smith, 1980). The training program had no effect on win/loss records, suggesting that sport psychologists interested in social reinforcement or general coaching styles should consider nonperformance variables to understand the role of such factors in sport.

Competition

Although competition has received less research attention than social facilitation, findings suggest similar effects on performance. That is, like social facilitation, competition is a social evaluation situation that creates arousal which facilitates performance on simple or well-learned tasks and impairs performance of complex skills that are not well learned. Competition especially seems to facilitate performance on speed and endurance tasks. Experimental findings indicate that competition improves performance over noncompetition on a dynamometer task (Berridge, 1935), reaction time tasks (Church, 1962; Gaebelein & Taylor, 1971). and a bicycle ergometer task (Wilmore, 1968).

As is true for social facilitation research, competition research has not yielded consistent findings for more complex sport and motor skills. Gill (1978b) observed that both individuals and two-person groups performed a well-learned complex maze task better in competition than noncompetition, but few sport psychologists have looked at the influence of competition on complex skills. A number of early studies suggested that speed is facilitated and accuracy impaired under competition (Church, 1968; Dashiell, 1930; Whittemore, 1924). A recent study (Gross & Gill, in press) of competition effects on the speed/accuracy components of dart-throwing performance, however, suggests that the influence of competition is not a simple facilitation of speed and impairment of accuracy. Using a range of instructions, Gross and Gill found that competition facilitated speed when task instructions emphasized speed, but competition had no apparent effect on accuracy, even when subjects slowed down under task instructions that emphasized accuracy. Earlier work (Church, 1968) also suggested that competition effects on speed are more reliable and consistent than competition effects on accuracy. More investigations looking into specific components of complex motor performance, such as speed and accuracy or EMG patterns as in Weinberg's (1978) anxiety work, may provide more insight into the specific effects of competition on motor performance.

Although competition effects on performance may be considered an extension of social facilitation, Martens (1975b) has pointed out that competition is really a complex social evaluation process involving much more than effects on performance. Competition is a key situation for sport psychology, and individual differences that influence and are influenced by the competition process, behavior within the competitive situation, and nonperformance outcomes of the competition process all need to be investigated.

Many of the issues discussed in the other sections (e.g., aggression, competitive anxiety) could be discussed within the framework of the competition process. Competition typically results in winning and losing or success and failure and the powerful effects of success/failure set competition apart from other social influence processes. As noted previously, laboratory and field studies indicate that winning decreases and losing increases state anxiety, and research also indicates that winners report greater satisfaction and perceived ability than losers (Gill, 1977). Martens and White (1975) systematically varied the win/loss ratio with a maze task and reported performance best when the win/loss ratio was 50%, and task satisfaction was higher when individuals won 50% or more of the time. More investigations of cognitive outcomes, as well as behavioral and affective consequences of competition may provide insight into both short-and long-term influences of competition on participants.

Modeling

Modeling refers to any increased behavior similarity between the model and the observer. It is a key social influence process for teachers and coaches who typically use demonstration as a primary instructional technique. Surprisingly, sport psychologists and motor learning researchers have seldom investigated the influence of models on sport-related or motor behavior. A few studies do indicate that observing a model can provide information to facilitate motor performance (Feltz & Landers, 1977; Gould, 1978; Martens, Burwitz, & Zuckerman, l976). Gould (1978) has suggested that the informational value of modeling varies with the task; tasks with a high information load (involving several possible strategies and procedural steps that must be executed correctly) are especially susceptible to modeling influences. Thomas, Pierce, and Ridsdale (1977) have reported age differences in modeling effects, suggesting that processing capacity mediates modeling effects. As well as serving as a source of information, models may also play a motivational role. Landers and Landers (1973), in their study of skilled and unskilled teacher and peer models, observed that subjects were more likely to imitate a teacher model regardless of the model's skill level, and Gould (1978) reported that model sex influenced the modeling process, both suggesting motivational effects.

Conclusion

Social influence and motor performance was probably the most productive line of research in sport psychology through the 1970s as many studies examined the influence of social factors (audience presence, praise, and reproof comments, etc.) on motor tasks in laboratory settings. That line of research contributed to our understanding of social phenomena in sport and physical activity, and the emphasis on theory-based, controlled laboratory experimentation was an important advance for sport psychology, but the practical value of much of this research is limited. Many of the issues and questions raised about social influence processes in sport and motor performance are still important, and new lines of research, including field as well as laboratory settings and alternative approaches that incorporate cognitive constructs, may add greatly to sport psychology.

Social Interaction

Although much sport psychology research focuses on the influence of others on individual motor performance, social interaction within sport and physical activity settings is also a concern of sport psychologists. Aggression or violence in sport is a prevalent social behavior of concern to the general sport public.

Aggression and Altruism

A number of position papers and reviews exist, but empirical studies of aggression in sport are rare. Most sport psychologists who investigate or discuss aggression adopt some form of the social learning approach, following the theoretical work of Bandura (1973) or Berkowitz (1962, 1972). Both Bandura and Berkowitz stress the role of social learning and situational cues in determining aggressive behavior, although Berkowitz also emphasizes the role of arousal as a precipitating factor.

Earlier literature often stressed the role of competitive athletics as a catharsis that allowed participants to release their aggressive energies. Research on the catharsis notion, however, indicates that participation in strenuous activity does not reduce and may increase subsequent aggression (Ryan, 1970; Zillman, Katcher, & Milavsky, 1972).

Michael Smith (1978, 1979) has written extensively on aggression and violence in hockey and his work is probably the most concerted effort to investigate aggressive behavior in sport. Smith follows a social learning approach, proposing that aggressive behavior is learned in youth hockey. He specifically cites the emphasis on aggression as a means to advance in the hockey system, media reinforcement of aggresive behavior, and the influence of significant others (parents, coaches, teammates) as factors that encourage aggression in youth hockey. Silva (1978, 1980), a sport psychologist who has recently investigated aggression in sport, stresses the need to precisely define aggression and to differentiate aggression from assertive behavior. Silva also notes that aggression, like arousal and stress, may be distracting and thus affect performance.

Although many sport psychologists have discussed aggression at length, few have given attention to the opposite behavior in sport, namely altruism, more popularly referred to as sportsmanship. Kroll (Note 1) reviewed the rather fragmented work on sportsmanship and concluded that such moral behavior in sport is not developed by avoiding competition or emphasis on win/loss outcomes. Instead, sportsmanship is developed precisely in those situations in which moral behavior conflicts with behaviors directed toward important and valued outcomes. Martens (1978b) incorporated Kroll's concepts along with developmental psychology work on moral development to suggest that development of sportsmanship in youth sports does not demand elimination of competition, but a competitive environment that emphasizes moral behaviors.

Clearly, a number of issues related to aggression and sportsmanship could be investigated, including the immediate situational factors and individual differences that influence aggressive and altruistic behavior in sport, the affective, cognitive and behavioral consequences of such behaviors, and the development of aggressive or moral behavior through sports. Aggression and sportsmanship, however, are not as easily defined and measured as performance outcomes. Methodological problems have undoubtedly hindered sport psychology research on those topics in the past and present a challenge for future investigators.

Group Performance

Most existing sport psychology research involves individuals, but group dynamics concepts are certainly a component of sport psychology because many sport activities, from recreational youth sports to highly competitive professional athletics, occur in groups. The relationship of individual performance to group performance is a practical concern when a coach selects individuals for a team as well as a research issue that has received some attention.

Steiner's (1972) model of group process and productivity provides a theoretical background for research on group performance, and Landers (1974) has applied Steiner's model to motor performance tasks. Steiner's basic proposition is that a group's actual performance is a function of the group's potential performance (when available resources and abilities are optimally used to meet task demands) minus motivation and group coordination process losses. Gill (1979), incorporating Steiner's concepts, examined individual and group performance on a maze task requiring either maximum cooperation and interaction between partners or no cooperation. Results indicated a moderate, positive prediction from individual performance to group performance, and further suggested that a wide range of individual abilities within a group could have detrimental effects because group performance on the cooperative or interactive task was dominated by the lower ability partner. Although the reported positive relationship supports earlier findings (Comrey, 1953; Wiest, Porter, & Ghiselli, 1961), research has shown that the relationship is highly dependent on the reliability of both individual and group performance, and in actual sport situations a number of factors influence group performance variability limiting the predictive power of the individual-group performance relationship.

Steiner's model also provided the conceptual basis for work on group size and group performance. The most important finding in this area is known as the Ringlemann effect, which is a progressive decline in average individual performance as group size increases. Ingham, Levinger, Graves, and Peckham (1974) using a rope-pulling task demonstrated that performance decrements were a result of losses in motivation among individuals and not due to coordination problems among the group members. More recently, Latané, Williams, and Harkins (1979a, 1979b) investigated the same phenomenon, which they term "social loafing," with clapping and shouting tasks. Latané et al., replicated the effect, but unlike Ingham et al., reported evidence for both coordination and motivation losses in group performance, suggesting the causes for the Ringlemann effect are task specific.

Group Cohesion

Sport psychology research also includes several nonperformance group dynamics variables, with cohesiveness perhaps being the most extensively researched construct. (For a more extensive review of the literature and research on cohesiveness see Gill, 1978a). A number of studies have examined the relationship of cohesiveness, generally measured with a questionnaire, to group performance, generally defined by a season win/loss record, but findings are equivocal. Several studies report positive cohesiveness-performance relationships (e.g., Ball & Carron, 1976; Bird, 1977; Landers & Crum, 1971; Martens & Peterson, 1971; Peterson & Martens, 1972; Widmeyer & Martens, 1978), but several studies report negative or no relationships (e.g., Landers & Luschen, 1974; Lenk, 1969; Melnick

& Chemers, 1974).

Some sense can be made of the equivocal findings by close examination of the cohesiveness literature. Generally, positive cohesiveness-performance relationships are observed when cohesiveness is defined and measured as attraction to the group as a whole rather than attraction to individuals within the group, and when the group activities require interaction among team members (e.g., basketball as compared to rowing). In terms of the causal direction of the cohesiveness-performance relationship, current evidence, especially studies explicitly designed to look at causality (Bakeman & Helmreich, 1975; Carron & Ball, 1978), indicates that performance success is more likely to lead to cohesiveness than vice versa. Future research, using definitions and measures that reflect cohesiveness as a group construct relevant to sport, may further clarify the cohesiveness-performance relationship and the factors that mediate that relationship in sport and physical activity settings.

Leadership

Like cohesiveness, leadership is a common discussion topic in sport psychology, but much of the actual research on leadership in sport focuses on a single issue—Grusky's (1963) proposal that leadership in sport organizations is related to formal task structure. Specifically, Grusky cited data demonstrating that baseball managers are more likely to come from the centrally located, high interaction positions (infielders and catchers) than from the low interaction positions (pitchers and outfielders). Several subsequent studies (e.g., Loy & Sage, 1970) confirmed Grusky's original findings, although some investigators (Chelladurai & Carron, 1977) suggest modification of Grusky's concepts. Tropp and Landers (1979) applied Grusky's model to field hockey and observed that interaction patterns did *not* parallel centrality of position as Grusky proposed. Their observation that goalies were especially high on leadership led to the further suggestion that the performance of independent tasks and functional centrality are more important determinants of leadership than spatial location of playing positions.

Investigations of leadership in sport other than tests of Grusky's model are rare. Chelladurai and Saleh (1980) developed a leadership scale and attempted to identify dimensions of leader behavior in sport. Chelladurai and Saleh related their work to coaching behavior, and their dimensions are similar to the dimensions of coaching behavior identified by Danielson, Zelhart, and Drake (1975). Nevertheless, coaching behavior and leadership are not identical; coaching involves many roles and relationships in addition to the leadership role, and many forms of leadership other than coaching occur within sport. Future investigations of coaching roles and behaviors should keep in mind the uniqueness of the coach ing role and not simply equate coaching with leadership.

Conclusion

Similar cautions could be stated about most issues in group dynamics; sport teams are prominent and unique groups, and many findings from research with discussion groups, problem-solving groups, or other social psychology research groups are not necessarily applicable to sport groups. The investigation of group dynamics in sport presents a number of obstacles; studies must involve large numbers, extraneous variables are difficult to control, and neither conceptual models nor standard measures and procedures exist in sport psychology or social psychology. Some sport psychologists will perhaps persist in spite of the obstacles and advance our understanding of the dynamics of sport groups, an area long slighted.

Applied Sport Psychology

Most of the sport psychology research discussed to this point involves basic sport psychology and social psychology constructs. Some investigators have followed a more applied approach, drawing upon several of the subareas within sport psychology to study particular populations or issues. Within the last 5 years, a number of sport psychologists have studied two groups, women and children. Even more recently some sport psychologists have initiated applied work with elite athletes.

Women in Sport

Investigations of the psychological aspects of women in sport generally follow social psychology work on sex differences in personality and achievement behavior. Bem's (1978) and Spence and Helmreich's (Helmreich & Spence, 1977; Spence & Helmreich, 1978) work on the personality constructs of masculinity, femininity, and androgyny gained a popular following and spurred considerable research, particularly by persons interested in the psychology of women and, to a limited extent, psychology of women in sport.

Both Bem, and Spence and Helmreich treat masculinity and femininity as separate, independent personality dimensions comprised of positively valued traits. Possession of masculine characteristics (primarily instrumental characteristics such as active, competitive) purportedly relates to the performance of masculine or instrumental behaviors, whereas possession of feminine characteristics (generally expressive or nurturant characteristics such as warm, supportive) relates to the performance of feminine or nurturant behaviors, and possession of both characteristics (androgyny) is especially desirable as the androgynous person performs well both masculine and feminine behaviors. Sport is typically an instrumental activity that requires behaviors associated with the masculine personality orientation, and therefore, persons (either male or female) with masculine or angrogynous personality types should dominate in sport. Indeed, Helmreich and Spence (1977) report that female athletes tended to fall into masculine and androgynous categories more than a control sample of university females. A number of sport psychologists have used either the Bem Sex Role Inventory (BSRI) (Bem, 1974) or the Personality Attributes Questionnaire (PAQ) (Spence & Helmreich, 1978) with athlete samples and results generally concur with Helmreich and Spence. (Readers are referred to Birrell [1978] or Duquin [1978a] for more extensive discussions of androgyny and sport participation.)

Students interested in angrogyny research should note that despite the popularity of the work, both the concepts and measures are controversial and have been justifiably criticized (Locksley & Colten, 1979; Pedhazur & Tetenbaum, 1979). Recent work also suggests that the relationship of androgyny, as measured on the BSRI or PAQ, to sex role behaviors and flexibility is weak, and interaction approaches considering situational cues are desirable (Helmreich, Spence, & Holohan, 1979).

Other investigators have examined sex differences in achievement behavior from a variety of perspectives. The most promising work involves cognitive constructs, including achievement attributions and the evaluation of men's and women's achievements by others. As an excellent review by McHugh, Frieze, and Duquin (1978) notes, the literature is rather fragmented and inconclusive, but some evidence does suggest that females are less likely to take personal credit for success than males (Deaux, 1976; Deaux & Farris, 1977); females are more likely than males to exhibit helplessness characteristics (Dweck, Davidson, Nelson, & Enna, 1978); and both women and men evaluators tend to give more personal credit for success to males than females (Brawley, Landers, Miller, & Kearns, 1979; Deaux, 1976).

Children in Sport

Children in sport emerged as a popular topic for sport psychology in 1978 with the publication of several books specifically devoted to youth sports (Magill, Ash, & Smoll, 1978; Martens, 1978a; Smoll & Smith, 1978). Recent sport psychology conferences also include a number of papers on youth sports, but to date the work largely consists of position papers and descriptive studies. Orlick has commented at length about the problems of youth sports, particularly dropouts and the overemphasis on competition at the expense of cooperative skills (Orlick & Botterill, 1975). Recent examples of youth sport research include an assessment of physical and psychological characteristics that indicated no differences between youth sports participants and nonparticipants (Magill & Ash, 1979) and Gould and Martens's (1979) descriptive data on youth sport coaches indicating that the coaches are quite task-oriented and positive toward their programs. It should also be noted that some of the research in other sport psychology areas (e.g., attributions, competitive anxiety) involves samples of children.

Elite Athletes

Although youth sports seemed the "hot" topic at sport psychology conferences a few years ago, applied sport psychology with elite athletes seems to have taken its place in the last 2 years. In an article appropriately titled "About Smocks and Jocks," Martens (1979a) advocated a shift from the sport psychology laboratory research of the past to field research on more applied techniques with athletes. A number of sport psychologists have made that shift, not only in research, but also as sport psychology consultants with athletic teams or organizations. Such work, however, raises a number of ethical issues regarding qualifications of sport psychologists to do such consulting as well as the techniques they use. The North American Society for the Psychology of Sport and Physical Activity (NASPSPA), the primary sport psychology organization, is currently delving into those issues, and recent articles present some of the arguments (Harrison & Feltz, 1979; Nideffer, DuFresne, Nesvig, & Selder, 1980).

The move to apply psychology with elite athletes has proceeded much faster than the empirical research on such applied techniques. Generally, the techniques involve cognitive-behavioral principles rather than psychodynamic techniques. Mahoney (1979) specifically advocated the application of cognitive skills to athletics, and Suinn (1976, 1980) has written extensively on his work with athletes using visuo-motor behavior rehearsal (VMBR) and anxiety management training. Both Mahoney and Suinn are clinical psychologists, but nonclinical sport psychologists have begun to explore their suggestions.

For example, Epstein (1980) investigated imagery and mental rehearsal and Noel (1980) studied the VMBR technique with tennis players, but neither reported significant findings. Meyers and Schleser (1980) reported that a cognitive-behavioral intervention effectively improved basketball performance, although their study consisted of a case report of one athlete. Smith (1980), a clinical psychologist who has also done considerable sport psychology work, has developed a cognitive-affective stress management program and cited support for the effectiveness of the program in sport.

The shift to applied sport psychology issues will probably continue in the immediate future, a trend which offers both promise and danger. One of the most promising aspects of recent sport psychology research is the shifting of attention to sport-specific issues. Too much of the past sport psychology research simply adopted the most current social psychology concepts and methods with little concern for the uniqueness of sport and physical activity settings. Sport psychologists need to look to sport to find the issues and questions specific to the field of sport.

Unfortunately, the current move to applied sport psychology is restricted to a few psychological techniques and to elite athletes. The focus on elite athletes may be due to several factors, including the expressed interest of some Olympic and professional sport organizations in psychology, the availability of limited funds earmarked for immediate application with top competitors, and perhaps the public attention and prestige associated with top-level athletics. Nevertheless, sport psychology should not restrict itself to an elite segment of the population. The principles that apply to the Olympic runner do not necessarily apply to the 10-year-old soccer player. Sport psychologists should keep in mind that work with elite athletes is only one application of the discipline of sport psychology. For example, the percentage of older Americans in the population is increasing and research on the needs and wishes of this segment of the population could prove timely.

Another positive aspect of the current applied sport psychology trend is the shift to more field research and studies with sport participants. Previous sport psychology research was dominated by lab experiments and even by specific prototypes within experimental lab research. A better balance between field and laboratory research was needed, and current research reflects a balance. The danger, of course, is going to the other extreme and failing to recognize the contribution of controlled laboratory experimentation. Without a basic discipline or body of knowledge, applied sport psychology has little value.

Finally, just as some social psychological experimental findings have limited applicability in sport, some clinical techniques useful in clinical practice undoubtedly have little value in sport. Right now the most pressing need in sport psychology is for research on applied techniques, not for people to apply untested techniques to athlete samples. Sound research conducted within a theoretical framework, and incorporating both laboratory and field investigations, is the answer.

Conclusions

Personality, motivation, social influences on motor performance, social interaction processes, and the application of sport psychology to particular samples and activities have been active research areas as long as sport psychology has been an identifiable subdiscipline. Research continues in all of these areas, although emphases have shifted over the last 15 years. Many of the changes parallel social psychology, including a trend to more cognitive approaches and increased emphasis on field research, but sport psychologists increasingly have become more concerned with the uniqueness of the sport situation.

Personality and motivation constructs have been investigated from the beginning of sport psychology; personality research continues today, but current sport psychologists typically forsake general personality inventories for sport-specific personality and motivation constructs and adopt interaction models incorporating both individual differences and situational variables. Social influences on motor performance, which formed the core of sport psychology in the late 1960s and 1970s, brought increased emphasis on theoretical constructs and controlled laboratory experimentation to the discipline. That research continues, but dissatisfaction with the restricted laboratory paradigms and findings of limited practical significance led sport psychologists to consider alternative approaches and other research areas. Social interaction processes, including interpersonal relations and group dynamics, have always been recognized as components of sport psychology, but that research has never developed within a systematic line, probably because of methodological obstacles and the lack of theoretical and empirical models.

Currently, sport psychologists are increasingly turning to applied sport psychology, particularly the application of cognitive-behavioral techniques with athletes. That trend has brought several positive changes to the field, including greater emphasis on sport-relevant issues and questions, more field research with sport participants, and consideration of clinical psychology theories and findings. I share Ryan's (Chapter 17) conclusion that the major focus of resarch in this field may become more pragmatic and applied, with the admonition that the efforts of sport psychologists in the "third emergence" are not confined to application but are directed toward developing the theoretical and empirical base of sport psychology.

Reference Note

1. Kroll, W. *Psychology of sportsmanship.* Paper presented at the Sport Psychology meeting, National Association for Sport and Physical Education (NASPE), American Association for Health, Physical Education and Recreation, Atlantic City, NJ, March 1975.

References

Alderman, R.B. Strategies for motivating young athletes. In W.F. Straub (Ed.), *Sport psychology: An analysis of athlete behavior.* Ithaca, NY: Mouvement Publications, 1978.

Bakeman, R., & Helmreich, R. Cohesiveness and performance: Covariation and causality in an underseas environment. *Journal of Experimental Social Psychology,* 1975, **11**, 478-489.

Ball, J.R., & Carron, A.V. The influence of team cohesion and participation motivation upon performance success in intercollegiate ice hockey. *Canadian Journal of Applied Sport Sciences,* 1976, **1**, 271-275.

Bandura, A. *Aggression: A social learning analysis.* Englewood Cliffs, NJ: Prentice-Hall, 1973.

Bem, S.L. The measurement of psychological androgyny. *Journal of Consulting and Clinical Psychology,* 1974, **42**, 155-162.

Bem, S.L. Beyond androgyny: Some presumptuous prescriptions for a liberated sexual identity. In J. Sherman & F. Denmark (Eds.), *Psychology of Women: Future directions for research.* New York: Psychological Dimensions, 1978.

Berkowitz, L. *Aggression: A social-psychological analysis.* New York: McGraw-Hill, 1962.

Berkowitz, L. Sports competition and aggression. In I.D. Williams & L.M. Wankel (Eds.), *Proceedings of the fourth Canadian symposium on psycho-motor learning and sport psychology.* Ottawa: Department of National Health and Welfare, 1972.

Berridge, H.L. An experiment in the psychology of competition. *Research Quarterly,* 1935, 37-42.

Bird, A.M. Development of a model for predicting team performance. *Research Quarterly,* 1977, **48**, 24-32.

Bird, A.M., & Brame, J.M. Self versus team attributions: A test of the "I'm OK, but the team's so-so" phenomenon. *Research Quarterly,*

1978, **49**, 260-268.

Birrell, S. Achievement related motives and the woman athlete. In C.A. Oglesby (Ed.), *Women and sport: From myth to reality.* Philadelphia: Lea & Febiger, 1978.

Brawley, L.R., Landers, D.M., Miller, L., & Kearns, K.F. Sex bias in ·evaluating motor performance. *Journal of Sport Psychology,* 1979, **1**, 15-24.

Bukowski, W.M., Jr., & Moore, D. Winners' and losers' attributions for success and failure. *Journal of Sport Psychology,* 1980, **2**, 195-210.

Carron, A.V. *Social psychology of sport.* Ithaca, NY: Mouvement Publications, 1980.

Carron, A.V., & Ball, J.R. Cause-effect characteristics of cohesiveness and participation motivation in intercollegiate hockey. *International Review of Sport Sociology,* 1977, **12**, 49-60.

Chelladurai, P., & Carron, A.V. A reanalysis of formal structure in sport. *Canadian Journal of Applied Sport Sciences,* 1977, **2**, 9-14.

Chelladurai, P., & Saleh, S.D. Dimensions of leader behavior in sports: Development of a leadership scale. *Journal of Sport Psychology,* 1980, **2**, 34-45.

Church, R.M. The effects of competition on reaction time and palmar skin conductance. *Journal of Abnormal and Social Psychology,* 1962, **65**, 32-40.

Church, R.M. Applications of behavior theory to social psychology: Imitation and competition. In E.C. Simmel, R.A. Hoppe, & G.A. Milton (Eds.), *Social facilitation and imitative behavior.* Boston: Allyn & Bacon, 1968.

Comrey, A.L. Group performance in a manual dexterity task. *Journal of Applied Psychology,* 1953, **37**, 201-210.

Danielson, R.R., Zelhart, P.F., & Drake, C.J. Multidimensional scaling and factor analysis of coaching behavior as perceived by high school hockey players. *Research Quarterly,* 1975, **46**, 323-334.

Dashiell, J.F. An experimental analysis of some group effects. *Journal of Abnormal and Social Psychology,* 1930, **25**, 190-199.

Deaux, K. *The behavior of women and men.* Monterey, CA: Brooks/Cole, 1976.

Deaux, K., & Farris, E. Attributing causes for one's own performance: The effects of sex, norms, and outcome. *Journal of Research in Personality,* 1977, **11**, 59-72.

Deci, E.L. *Intrinsic motivation.* New York: Plenum Press, 1975.

Dishman, R.K., Ickes, W., & Morgan, W.P. Self-motivation and adherence to habitual physical activity. *Journal of Applied Social Psychology,*

1980, **10**, 115-132.

Donnelly, P. Need for stimulation: Some possible antecedents of individual differences and its relation to sport involvement. In C. Bard, M. Fleury, & J. Salmela (Eds.), *Mouvement: Actes du 7e symposium Canadien en apprentissage psycho-moteur et psychologie du sport.* Québec: Association des professionnels de l' activité physique du Québec, 1975.

Duquin, M.E. The androgynous advantage. In C.A. Oglesby (Ed.), *Women and sport: From myth to reality.* Philadelphia: Lea & Febiger, 1978. (a)

Duquin, M.E. Attributions made by children in coed sport settings. In D.M. Landers & R.W. Christina (Eds.), *Psychology of motor behavior and sport—1977.* Champaign, IL: Human Kinetics, 1978. (b)

Dweck, C.S. Learned helplessness in sport: In C.M. Nadeau, W.R. Halliwell, K.M. Newell, & G.C. Roberts (Eds.), *Psychology of motor behavior and sport—1979.* Champaign, IL: Human Kinetics, 1980.

Dweck, C.S., Davidson, W., Nelson, S., & Enna, B. Sex differences in learned helplessness: II. The contingencies of evaluative feedback in the classroom and III. An experimental analysis. *Developmental Psychology,* 1978, **14**, 268-276.

Easterbrook, J.A. The effect of emotion on cue utilization and the organization of behavior. *Psychological Review,* 1979, **66**, 183-201.

Epstein, M.L. The relationship of mental imagery and mental rehearsal to performance of a motor task. *Journal of Sport Psychology,* 1980, **2**, 211-220.

Feltz, D.L., & Landers, D.M. Informational-motivational components of a model's demonstration. *Research Quarterly,* 1977, **48**, 525-533.

Feltz, D.L., Landers, D.M., & Raeder, U. Enhancing self-efficacy in high-avoidance motor tasks: A comparison of modeling techniques. *Journal of Sport Psychology,* 1979, **1**, 112-122.

Fenz, W. Coping mechanisms and performance under stress. In D.M. Landers (Ed.), *Psychology of sport and motor behavior II.* University Park, PA: Pennsylvania State University, 1975.

Forsyth, D.R., & Schlenker, B.R. Attributional egocentrism following performance of a competitive task. *The Journal of Social Psychology,* 1977, **102**, 215-222.

Gaebelein, J., & Taylor, S. The effects of competition and attack on physical aggression. *Psychonomic Science,* 1971, **24**, 65-67.

Gill, D.L. Influence of group success-failure and relative ability on intrapersonal variables. *Research Quarterly,* 1977, **48**, 685-694.

Gill, D.L. Cohesiveness and performance in sport groups. In R.S. Hutton (Ed.), *Exercise and sport sciences reviews* (Vol. 5). Santa Barbara, CA: Journal Publishing Affiliates, 1978. (a)

Gill, D.L. The influence of competition on individual and group motor performance. *Journal of Human Movement Studies,* 1978, **4**, 36-43. (b)

Gill, D.L. The prediction of group motor performance from individual member abilities. *Journal of Motor Behavior,* 1979, **11**, 113-122.

Gill, D.L. Success-failure attributions in competitive groups: An exception to egocentrism. *Journal of Sport Psychology,* 1980, **2**, 106-114.

Gill, D.L., & Martens, R. The informational and motivational influence of social reinforcement on motor performance. *Journal of Motor Behavior,* 1975, **7**, 171-182.

Gould, D.R. *The influence of motor task types on model effectiveness.* Unpublished doctoral dissertation, University of Illinois at Urbana-Champaign, 1978.

Gould, D., & Martens, R. Attitudes of volunteer coaches toward significant youth sport issues. *Research Quarterly,* 1979, **50**, 369-380.

Gross, J.B., & Gill, D.L. Competition and instructional set effects on the speed and accuracy of a throwing task. *Research Quarterly for Exercise and Sport,* in press.

Gruber, J.J., & Beauchamp, D. Relevancy of the Competitive State Anxiety Inventory in a sport environment. *Research Quarterly,* 1979, **50**, 207-214.

Grusky, O. The effects of formal structure on managerial recruitment: A study of baseball organization. *Sociometry,* 1963, **26**, 345-353.

Harney, D.M., & Parker, R. Effects of social reinforcement, subject sex, and experimenter sex on children's motor performance. *Research Quarterly,* 1972, **43**, 187-196.

Harrison, R.O., & Feltz, D.L. The professionalization of sport psychology: Legal considerations. *Journal of Sport Psychology,* 1979, **1**,182-190.

Healey, R.R., & Landers, D.M. Effect of need achievement and task difficulty on competitive and noncompetitive motor performance. *Journal of Motor Behavior,* 1973, **5**, 121-128.

Helmreich, R., & Spence, J.T., Sex roles and achievement. In R.W. Christina & D.M. Landers (Eds.), *Psychology of motor behavior and sport—1976.* (Vol. 2). Champaign, IL: Human Kinetics, 1977.

Helmreich, R.L., Spence, J.T., & Holohan, D.K. Psychological andrognyny and sex role flexibility: A test of two hypotheses. *Journal of Personality and Social Psychology,* 1979, **37**, 1631-1644.

Ingham, A.G., Levinger, G., Graves, J., & Peckham, V. The Ringlemann effect: Studies of group size and group performance. *Journal of Ex-*

perimental Social Psychology, 1974, **10**, 371-384.

Iso-Ahola, S. A test of the attribution theory of success and failure with Little League baseball players. In C. Bard, M. Fleury, & J. Salmela (Eds.), *Mouvement: Actes du 7e symposium en apprentissage psycho-moteur et psychologie du sport.* Québec: Association des profession-nels de l'activité physique du Québec, 1975.

Iso-Ahola, S. Effects of team outcome on children's self-perception: Little League baseball. *Scandinavian Journal of Psychology,* 1977, **18**, 38-42.

Kane, J.E. Personality research: The current controversy and implica-tions for sports studies. In W.F. Straub (Ed.), *Sport psychology: An analysis of athlete behavior.* Ithaca, NY: Mouvement Publications, 1978.

Kenyon, G.S. A conceptual model for characterizing physical activity. *Research Quarterly,* 1968, **39**, 96-105. (a)

Kenyon, G.S. Six scales for assessing attitudes toward physical activity. *Research Quarterly,* 1968, **39**, 366-574. (b)

Kroll, W. Current strategies and problems in personality assessment of athletes. In L.E. Smith (Ed.), *Psychology of motor learning.* Chicago: Athletic Institute, 1970.

Landers, D.M. Taxonomic considerations in measuring group performance and the analysis of selected group motor performance tasks. In M.G. Wade & R. Martens (Eds.), *Psychology of motor behavior and sport.* Urbana, IL: Human Kinetics, 1974.

Landers, D.M. The arousal-performance relationship revisited. *Research Quarterly for Exercise and Sport,* 1980, **51**, 77-90.

Landers, D.M., Bauer, R.S., & Feltz, D.L. Social facilitation during the initial stage of motor learning: A re-examination of Martens' audience study. *Journal of Motor Behavior,* 1978, **10**, 325-337.

Landers, D.M., Bauer, R.S., & Feltz, D.L. The significance of "signifi-cant" results: A reply to Martens. *Journal of Motor Behavior,* 1979, **11**, 229-231.

Landers, D.M., & Crum, T.F. The effect of team success and formal structure on interpersonal relations and cohesiveness of baseball teams. *International Journal of Sport Psychology,* 1971, **2**, 88-96.

Landers, D.M., & Landers, D.M. Teacher versus peer models: Effects of model's presence and performance level on motor behavior. *Journal of Motor Behavior,* 1973, **5**, 129-139.

Landers, D.M., & Luschen, G. Team performance outcome and cohesive-ness of competitive co-acting groups. *International Review of Sport Sociology,* 1974, **2**, 57-69.

Landers, D.M., & McCullaugh, P.D. Social facilitation of motor performance. In J. Keogh & R.S. Hutton (Eds.), *Exercise and sport sciences
reviews* (Vol. 4). Santa Barbara, CA: Journal Publishing Affiliates,
1976.

Latané, B.,Williams, K., & Harkins, S. Many hands make light the work:
The causes and consequences of social loafing. *Journal of Personality
and Social Psychology,* 1979, **37**, 822-832. (a)

Latané, B., Williams, K., & Harkins, S. Social loafing. *Psychology Today,*
October 1979, pp. 104-110. (b)

Lau, R.R., & Russell, D. Attributions in the sports pages. *Journal of
Personality and Social Psychology,* 1980, **39**, 29-38.

Lenk, H. Top performance despite internal conflict. In J.W. Loy & G.S.
Kenyon (Eds.), *Sport, culture and society.* New York: Macmillan, 1969.

Lepper, M.R., Greene, D., & Nisbett, R.E. Undermining children's intrinsic interest with extrinsic reward: A test of the "overjustification"
hypothesis. *Journal of Personality and Social Psychology,* 1973, **28**,
129-137.

Locksley, A., & Colten, M.E. Psychological androgyny: A case of mistaken
identity? *Journal of Personality and Social Psychology,* 1979, **37**,
1017-1031.

Lowe, R. *Stress, arousal, and task performance of Little League baseball players.* Unpublished doctoral dissertation. University of Illinois
at Urbana-Champaign, 1973.

Loy, J.W., & Donnelly, P. Need for stimulation as a factor in sport involvement. In T. Craig (Ed.), *The humanistic and mental health aspects of sports, exercise, and recreation.* Chicago: American Medical
Association, 1976.

Loy, J.W. Jr., & Sage, J.W. The effects of formal structure on organiza-
tional leadership: An investigation of interscholastic baseball teams.
In G. Kenyon (Ed.), *Contemporary psychology of Sport.* Chicago:
Athletic Institute, 1970.

Magill, R.A., & Ash, M.J. Academic, psycho-social, and motor characteristics of participants and nonparticipants in children's sport. *Research
Quarterly,* 1979, **50**, 230-240.

Magill, R.A., Ash, M.J., & Smoll, F.L. (Eds.). *Children in sport: A contemporary anthology.* Champaign, IL: Human Kinetics, 1978.

Mahoney, M.J. Cognitive skills and athletic performance. In P.C.
Kendall & S. D. Hollon (Eds.), *Cognitive-behavioral interventions:
Theory, research and procedures.* New York: Academic Press, 1979.

Mahoney, M.J., & Avener, M. Psychology of the elite athlete: An
exploratory study. *Cognitive Therapy and Research,* 1977, **1**,

135-141.

Martens, R. Effects of an audience on learning and performance of a complex motor skill. *Journal of Personality and Social Psychology*, 1969, **12**, 252-260.

Martens, R. Social reinforcement effects on preschool children's motor performance. *Perceptual and Motor Skills*, 1970, **31**, 787-792.

Martens, R. Internal-external control and social reinforcement effects on motor performance. *Research Quarterly*, 1971, **42**, 107-113.

Martens, R. Social reinforcement effects on motor performance as a function of socio-economic status. *Perceptual and Motor Skills*, 1972, **35**, 215-218.

Martens, R. Arousal and motor performance. In J. Wilmore (Ed.) *Exercise and sport sciences reviews* (Vol. 2). New York: Academic Press, 1974.

Martens, R. The paradigmatic crisis in American sport personology. *Sportwissenschaft*, 1975, **5**, 9-24. (a)

Martens, R. *Social psychology and physical activity*. New York: Harper & Row, 1975. (b)

Martens, R. *Sport competition anxiety test*. Champaign, IL: Human Kinetics, 1977.

Martens, R. *Joy and sadness in children's sports*. Champaign, IL: Human Kinetics, 1978. (a)

Martens, R. Kid sports: A den of iniquity or land of promise. In R.A. Magill, M.J. Ash,& F.L. Smoll (Eds.), *Children in sport: A contemporary anthology*. Champaign, IL: Human Kinetics, 1978. (b)

Martens, R. About smocks and jocks. *Journal of Sport Psychology*, 1979, **1**, 94-98. (a)

Martens, R. The significance of nonsignificant findings: A reply to Landers, Bauer, and Feltz. *Journal of Motor Behavior*, 1979, **11**, 225-228. (b)

Martens, R., Burton, D., Rivkin, F., & Simon, J. Reliability and validity of the Competitive State Anxiety Inventory (CSAI). In C. H. Nadeau, W.R. Halliwell, K.M. Newell, & G.C. Roberts (Eds.), *Psychology of motor behavior and sport - 1979*. Champaign, IL: Human Kinetics, 1980.

Martens, R., Burwitz, L., & Newell, K.M. Money and praise: Do they improve motor learning and performance? *Research Quarterly*, 1972, **43**, 429-442.

Martens, R., Burwitz, L., & Zuckerman, J. Modeling effects on motor performance. *Research Quarterly*, 1976, **47**, 277-291.

Martens, R., & Gill, D.L. State anxiety among successful and unsuccessful competitors who differ in competitive trait anxiety. *Research Quarterly,* 1976, **47**, 698-708.

Martens, R., & Landers, D.M. Motor performance under stress: A test of the inverted-U hypothesis. *Journal of Personality and Social Psychology,* 1970, **16**, 29-37.

Martens, R., & Peterson, J.A. Group cohesiveness as a determinant of success and member satisfaction in team performance. *International Review of Sport Sociology,* 1971, **6**, 49-61.

Martens, R., & White, V. Influence of win-loss ratio on performance, satisfaction and preference for opponents. *Journal of Experimental Social Psychology,* 1975, **11**, 343-362.

McHugh, M.C., Frieze, I.H.,& Duquin, M.E. Beliefs about success and failure: Attribution and the female athlete. In C.A. Oglesby (Ed.), *Women and sport: From myth to reality.* Philadelphia: Lea & Febiger, 1978.

Melnick, M.J., & Chemers, M.M. Effects of group social structure on the the success of basketball teams. *Research Quarterly,* 1974, **45**, 1-8.

Meyers, A.W., & Schleser, R. A cognitive behavioral intervention for improving basketball performance. *Journal of Sport Psychology,* 1980, **2**, 69-73.

Mischel, W. *Personality and assessment.* New York: Wiley, 1968.

Mischel, W. Toward a cognitive social learning reconceptualization of personality. *Psychological Review,* 1973, **80**, 252-283.

Morgan, W.P. Mind of the marathoner. *Psychology Today,* 1978, **11**, 38-49. (a)

Morgan, W.P. Sport personology: The credulous-skeptical argument in perspective. In W.F. Straub (Ed.), *Sport psychology: An analysis of athlete behavior.* Ithaca: Mouvement Publications, 1978. (b)

Morgan, W.P. Prediction of performance in athletics. In P. Klavora & J.V. Daniel (Eds.), *Coach, athlete, and the sport psychologist.* Champaign, IL: Human Kinetics, 1979.

Morgan, W.P. The trait psychology controversy. *Research Quarterly for Exercise and Sport,* 1980, **51**, 50-76.

Morgan, W.P., & Pollock, M.L. Psychologic characterization of the elite distance runner. *Annals of the New York Academy of Sciences,* 1977, **301**, 382-403.

Nelson, L.L., & Kagan, S. Competition: The star-spangled scramble. *Psychology Today,* September 1972, pp. 53-56; 90-91.

Nideffer, R.M. Test of attentional and interpersonal style. *Journal of Personality and Social Psychology,* 1976, **34**, 394-404. (a)

Nideffer, R.M. *The inner athlete.* New York: Thomas Y. Crowell, 1976. (b)

Nideffer, R.M., DuFresne, P., Nesvig, D., & Selder, D. The future of applied sport psychology. *Journal of Sport Psychology,* 1980, **2**, 170-174.

Noel, R.C. The effect of visuo-motor behavior rehearsal on tennis performance. *Journal of Sport Psychology,* 1980, **2**, 221-226.

Orlick, T.D., & Botterill, C. *Every kid can win.* Chicago: Nelson-Hall, 1975.

Orlick, T.D., McNally, T., & O'Hara, T. Cooperative games: Systematic analysis and cooperative impact. In F.L. Smoll & R.E. Smith (Eds.) *Psychological perspectives in youth sports.* Washington, DC: Hemisphere, 1978.

Ostrow, A.C. Goal-setting behavior and need achievement in relation to competitive motor activity. *Research Quarterly,* 1976, **47**, 174-183.

Oxendine, J.B. Emotional arousal and motor performance. *Quest,* 1970, **13**, 23-32.

Paulus, P.B., & Cornelius, W.L. An analysis of gymnastic performance under conditions of practice and spectator observation. *Research Quarterly,* 1974, **45**, 56-63.

Paulus, P.B., Judd, B.B., & Bernstein, I.H. Social facilitation and sports. In R.W. Christina & D.M. Landers (Eds.), *Psychology of motor behavior and sport - 1976* (Vol. 2). Champaign, IL: Human Kinetics, 1977.

Pedhzur, E.J., & Tetenbaum, T.J. BSRI: A theoretical and methodological critique. *Journal of Personality and Social Psychology,* 1979, **37**, 996-1016.

Peterson, J.A., & Martens, R. Success and residential affiliation as determinants of team cohesiveness. *Research Quarterly,* 1972, **43**, 62-76.

Roberts, G.C. Effect of achievement motivation and social environment on performance of a motor task. *Journal of Motor Behavior,* 1972, **4**, 37-46.

Roberts, G.C. Effect of achievement motivation and social environment on risk taking. *Research Quarterly,* 1974, **45**, 42-55.

Roberts, G.C. Win-loss causal attributions of Little League players. In C. Bard, M. Fleury, & J. Salmela (Eds.), *Mouvement: Actes du 7ᵉ symposium Canadien en apprentissage psycho-moteur et psycholo-*

gie du sport. Québec: Association des professionels de l'activité physique de Québec, 1975.

Roberts, G.C. Children's assignment of responsibility for winning and losing. In F.L. Smoll & R.E. Smith (Eds.), *Psychological perspectives in youth sports.* New York: Halsted Press, 1978.

Roberts, G.C., & Martens R. Social reinforcement and complex motor performance. *Research Quarterly,* 1970, **41**, 175-181.

Roberts, G.C., & Pascuzzi, D. Causal attributions in sport: Some theoretical implications. *Journal of Sport Psychology,* 1979, **1**, 203-211.

Rushall, B.S.. An evaluation of the relationship between personality and physical performance categories. In G.S. Kenyon (Ed.), *Contemporary psychology of sport.* Chicago: Athletic Institute, 1970.

Rushall, B.S., & Siedentop, D. *The development and control of behavior in sport and physical education.* Philadelphia: Lea & Febiger, 1972.

Ryan, E.D. Perceptual characteristics of vigorous people. In R.C. Brown Jr. & B.J. Cratty (Eds.), *New perspectives of man in action.* Englewood Cliffs, NJ: Prentice-Hall, 1969.

Ryan, E.D. The cathartic effect of vigorous motor activity on aggressive behavior. *Research Quarterly,* 1970, **41**, 542-551.

Ryan, E.D. Attribution, intrinsic motivation, and athletics. In L.I. Gedvilas & M.E. Kneer (Eds.), *Proceedings of the NCPAEM/NAPECW National Conference, 1977.* Chicago: Office of Publications Services, University of Illinois at Chicago Circle, 1977.

Ryan, E.D. Attribution, intrinsic motivation, and athletics: A replication and extension. In C.H. Nadeau, W.R. Halliwell, K.M. Newell, & G.C. Roberts (Eds.), *Psychology of motor behavior and sport - 1979.* Champaign, IL: Human Kinetics, 1980.

Ryan, E.D., & Foster, R. Athletic participation and perceptual augmentation and reduction. *Journal of Personality and Social Psychology,* 1967, **6**, 472-476.

Ryan, E.D., & Kovacic, C.R. Pain tolerance and athletic participation. *Perceptual and Motor Skills,* 1966, **22**, 383-390.

Ryan, E.D., & Lakie, W.L. Competitive and noncompetitive performance in relation to achievement motive and manifest anxiety. *Journal of Personality and Social Psychology,* 1965, **1**, 342-345.

Scanlan, T.K. The effect of success-failure on the perception of threat in a competitive situation. *Research Quarterly,* 1977, **48**, 144-153.

Scanlan, T.K. Antecedents of competitiveness. In R.A. Magill, M.J. Ash, & F.L. Smoll (Eds.), *Children in sport: A contemporary anthology.* Champaign, IL: Human Kinetics, 1978.

Scanlan, T.K., & Passer, M.W. Anxiety-inducing factors in competitive youth sports. In F.L. Smoll & R.E. Smith (Eds.), *Psychological perspectives in youth sports.* Washington, DC: Hemisphere, 1978. (a)

Scanlan, T.K., & Passer, M.W. Factors related to competitive stress among male youth sport participants. *Medicine and Science in Sports,* 1978, **10**, 103-108. (b)

Scanlan, T.K., & Passer, M.W. Sources of competitive stress in young female athletes. *Journal of Sport Psychology,* 1979, **1**, 151-159.

Scanlan, R.K., & Passer, M.W. Self-serving biases in the competitive sport setting: An attributional dilemma. *Journal of Sport Psychology,* 1980, **2**, 124-136.

Scanlan, T.K., & Ragan, J.T. Jr. Achievement motivation and competition: Perceptions and responses. *Medicine and Science in Sports,* 1978, **10**, 276-281.

Schwartz, B., & Barsky, S.F. The home advantage. *Social Forces,* 1977, **55**, 641-661.

Siedentop, D. The management of practice behavior. In W.F. Straub (Ed.), *Sport psychology: An analysis of athlete behavior.* Ithaca, NY: Mouvement Publications, 1978.

Silva, J.M. III. Understanding aggressive behavior and its effects upon athletic performance. In W.F. Straub (Ed.), *Sport psychology: An analysis of athlete behavior* (2nd ed.). Ithaca, NY: Mouvement Publications, 1978.

Silva, J.M. III. Assertive and aggressive behavior in sport: A definitional clarification. In C.H. Nadeau, W.R. Halliwell, K.M. Newell, & G.C. Roberts (Eds.), *Psychology of motor behavior and sport - 1979.* Champaign, IL: Human Kinetics, 1980.

Smith, M.D. Hockey violence: Interring some myths. In W.F. Straub (Ed.), *Sport psychology: An analysis of athlete behavior.* Ithaca, NY: Mouvement Publications, 1978.

Smith, M.D. Social determinants of violence in hockey: A review. *Canadian Journal of Applied Sport Sciences,* 1979, **4**, 76-82.

Smith, R.E. A cognitive-affective approach to stress management training for athletes. In C.H. Nadeau, W.R. Halliwell, K.M. Newell, & G.C. Roberts (Eds.), *Psychology of motor behavior and sport - 1979.* Champaign, IL: Human Kinetics, 1980.

Smith, R.E., Smoll, F.L., & Curtis, B. Coach effectiveness training: A cognitive-behavioral approach to enhancing relationships in youth sport coaches. *Journal of Sport Psychology,* 1979, **1**, 59-75.

Smith, R.E., Smoll, F.L., & Hunt, E. A system for the behavioral assessment of athletic coaches. *Research Quarterly*, 1977, **48**, 401-407.

Smoll, F.L., & Schutz, R.W. Children's attitudes toward physical activity: A longitudinal analysis. *Journal of Sport Psychology*, 1980, **2**, 137-147.

Smoll, F.L., & Smith, R.E. *Psychological perspectives in youth sports.* Washington, DC: Hemisphere, 1978.

Smoll, F.L., & Smith, R.E. Psychologically-oriented coach training programs: Design, implementation, and assessment. In C.H. Nadeau, W.R. Halliwell, K.M. Newell, & G.C. Roberts (Eds.), *Psychology of motor behavior and sport - 1979.* Champaign, IL: Human Kinetics, 1980.

Spence, J.T., & Helmrich, R.L. *Masculinity and femininity.* Austin, TX: University of Texas Press, 1978.

Steiner, I.D. *Group process and productivity.* New York: Academic Press, 1972.

Suinn, R.M. Body thinking: Psychology for Olympic champs. *Psychology Today*, July 1976, pp. 38-43.

Suinn, R.M. *Psychology in sports: Methods and applications.* Minneapolis, MN: Burgess, 1980.

Thomas, J.R., Pierce, C., & Ridsdale, S. Age differences in children's ability to model motor behavior. *Research Quarterly*, 1977, **48**, 592-597.

Tropp, L.J., & Landers, D.M. Team interaction and the emergence of leadership and interpersonal attraction in field hockey. *Journal of Sport Psychology*, 1979, **1**, 228-240.

Tu, J., & Rothstein, A.L. Improvement of jogging performance through application of personality specific motivational techniques. *Research Quarterly*, 1979, **50**, 97-103.

Varca, P.E. An analysis of home and away game performance of male college basketball teams. *Journal of Sport Psychology*, 1980, **2**, 245-257.

Veroff, J. Social comparison and the development of achievement motivation. In C.P. Smith (Ed.), *Achievement-related motives in children.* New York: Russell Sage Foundation, 1969.

Wankel, L.M. Social facilitation of motor performance: Perspective and prospective. In C.H. Nadeau, W.R. Halliwell, K.M. Newell, & G.C. Roberts (Eds.), *Psychology of motor behavior and sport - 1979.* Champaign, IL: Human Kinetics, 1980.

Weinberg, R.S. The effects of success and failure on the patterning of neuro-muscular energy. *Journal of Motor Behavior,* 1978, **10**, 53-61.

Weinberg, R., Gould, D., & Jackson, A. Expectations and performance: An empirical test of Bandura's self-efficacy theory. *Journal of Sport Psychology,* 1979, **1**, 320-331.

Weinberg, R.S., & Hunt, V.V. The interrelationships between anxiety, motor performance and electromyography. *Journal of Motor Behavior,* 1976, **8**, 219-224.

Weinberg, R.S., & Jackson, A. Competition and extrinsic rewards: Effects on intrinsic motivation and attribution. *Research Quarterly,* 1979, **50**, 494-502.

Weinberg, R.S., & Ragan, J. Motor performance under three levels of trait anxiety and stress. *Journal of Motor Behavior,* 1978, **10**, 169-176.

Weinberg, R.S., & Ragan, J. Effects of competition, success-failure, and sex on intrinsic motivation. *Research Quarterly,* 1979, **50**, 507-510.

Weiner, B. A theory of motivation for some classroom experiences. *Journal of Educational Psychology,* 1979, **71**, 3-25.

Weiner, B., Frieze, I.H., Kukla, A., Reed L., Rest, S., & Rosenbaum, R.M. *Perceiving the causes of success and failure.* Morristown, NJ: General Learning Press, 1971.

Weiner, B., Russell, D., & Lerman, D. Affective consequences of causal ascriptions. In J.H. Harvey, W.J. Ickes, & R.F. Kidd (Eds.), *New directions in attribution research* (Vol. 2). Hillsdale, NJ: Erlbaum, 1978.

Whittemore, J.C. Influence of competition on performance: An experimental study. *Journal of Abnormal and Social Psychology,* 1924, **19**, 236-253.

Widmeyer, W.N., & Martens, R. When cohesion predicts performance outcome in sport. *Research Quarterly,* 1978, **49**, 372-380.

Wiest, W.M., Porter, L.W., & Ghiselli, E.E. Relationships between individual proficiency and team performance and efficiency. *Journal of Applied Psychology,* 1961, **45**, 435-440.

Wilmore, J.H. Influence of motivation on physical work capacity and performance. *Journal of Applied Physiology,* 1968, **24**, 459-463.

Zajonc, R.B. Social facilitation. *Science,* 1965, **149**, 269-274.

Zillmann, D., Katcher, A.H., & Milavsky, B. Excitation transfer from physical exercise to subsequent aggressive behavior. *Journal of Experimental Social Psychology,* 1972, **8**, 247-259.

Emergence of and Future Prospects for Sociology of Sport

19

S. Greendorfer

The loose beginnings of sociology of sport can be linked to the scholarly works of mid-19th as well as 20th century anthropologists (Stewart Culin, E.B. Tylor), sociologists (Herbert Spencer, Thorstein Veblen, George Simmel, Max Weber, George Herbert Mead), philosophers (Friedrich Schiller, Karl Groos, Johan Huizinga), and psychologists (M. Triplett, G.T.W. Patrick, George Elliot Howard). On the one hand sociology of sport has as its roots extensive theoretical discussions based on general concepts; however, it also has empirical roots. Empiricism in the sociology of sport began with the experimental investigations of Triplett in 1898 on the influence of competition on bicycle performance and other motor tasks such as reel winding (Lueschen, 1980). Thus, sociology of sport is a product of the efforts of scholars in several social sciences, scholars who were concerned with the phenomena of either play, games, or sport.[1] Furthermore, it developed from two distinct orientations: theoretical and conceptual discussion, and empirical investigation. Despite the continued presence of theories of play, debates over the function of games, ethnographic descriptions of games in culture, and isolated empirical studies—all extending from the 1850s to the late 1950s—it was not until 1965 that sociology of sport became an identifiable subdiscipline of physical education in the United States.

In a landmark paper, Kenyon and Loy (1965) formally called for

---

[1]For a more detailed description of the historical development of scholarly works pertaining to play, games and sport, the reader is referred to the CAHPER Monograph by Loy, McPherson and Kenyon. However, for first-hand insight into the ideas or theories of these scholars, the reader is referred to the original sources (e.g., Karl Groos, *Play of Animals* and *Play of Man;* Thorstein Veblen, *The Theory of The Leisure Class;* Johan Huizinga, *Homo Ludens;* E.B. Tylor, On the game of patolli in ancient Mexico and its probable Asiatic origin, *Journal of the Anthropological Institute of Great Britain and Ireland,* 1878, **8.**

the study of physical activity as a sociological phenomenon and as a value-free science. In their paper they: (a) lodged a plea for the serious study of sport *sui generis*, because sport was a pervasive social phenomenon and had social significance; (b) described the nature of sport sociology as the study of the regularity and departures from it of human social behavior in a sports context; (c) identified the field as an empirical science, and as such they identified possibilities for future research; and (d) defined sociology of sport as a subdiscipline. Relative to the fourth point, in subsequent papers by Kenyon (1968, 1969) and Loy (Note 1), they both described sociology of sport as having a specific focus or knowledge base, a frame of reference, and a mode of inquiry. The specific focus was sport; the frame of reference was sociology (because concepts and social theory provided the framework); and the mode of inquiry was associated with sociological methods (e.g., survey—questionnaires and interviews; secondary data analysis—content analysis, examination of data already collected such as census data or material in guidebooks; and field studies) (Kenyon, 1969; Loy, Note 1; McPherson, 1975).

Although the original Kenyon and Loy article (1965) prompted a series of papers which further delineated the subdiscipline and introduced sociology of sport to graduate curricula in the United States, their article was not without a context. Interest in sport as a social phenomenon had been growing in Europe as well as in the United States, and isolated papers began to appear in print between 1950 and the late 1960s (e.g., Lueschen, 1966; Stone, 1955; Wohl, 1953). Furthermore, Charles Cowell's article in the May 1960 supplement to the *Research Quarterly* included sociological as well as psychological and historical concerns; Cowell's paper may have been a direct stimulus to the Kenyon and Loy statement.[2] Concurrently, at the international level, sociology of sport was institutionalized through the creation of an International Committee on Sport Sociology (ICSS) formed by members from two UNESCO-affiliated associations, the International Council of Sport and Physical Education (ICSPE) and the International Sociological Association (ISA). The ICSS, composed of both sociologists and physical educators, sponsored semi-

---

[2]This special edition commemorated the 75th anniversary of the American Association for Health, Physical Education, and Recreation. The intent of the reviews in this issue was to examine the validity of objectives endorsed by physical education and its allied fields. The publication reviewed research pertaining to physical activity and its effects on well being, with emphasis placed on the demonstrated values or contributions of physical activity.

nars and symposia, and in 1966 published the first issue of the *International Review of Sport Sociology*. Whereas the first publication of this annual journal was devoted to conceptualization of the subdiscipline, justification of its existence, presentation of concepts and methodologies, and description of the social organization of sport sociology in various countries (McPherson, 1975, p. 64), heightened interest in a variety of topics led to a proliferation of theoretical considerations and empirical investigations, such that this annual journal became a quarterly in 1973.

Whereas early position papers were concerned with the definition and description of the scope of sociology of sport, perhaps such concerns also shaped the nature of early investigations as well as the topics selected for research. For example, sociology of sport was concerned with the study of basic social units (individuals, groups, institutions, or societies), fundamental social processes (socialization, stratification, discrimination), and structural or organizational patterns of social behavior in sport situations (Kenyon, 1969; Kenyon & Loy, 1965; McPherson, 1975). Thus, early studies in sociology of sport could be classified according to these general themes. Studies pertaining to attitudes toward physical activity and personal attributes of athletes (e.g., personality traits) did represent one line of inquiry regardless of the fact that such research was more psychological in nature. After a period of time, however, these research concerns were discontinued by most core sociologists of sport. Nowadays, the appearance of such investigations seems to reflect the interest of isolated individuals who may not be classified as either sociologists or psychologists of sport.

More prominent examples of sport sociology research encompassed topics examining the relationship between sport and other social institutions, such as education, politics, economics, religion, and the mass media. Because sport had been defined as a social institution (Loy & Kenyon, 1969), patterns within sport could be compared with patterns found in other social institutions. This was typical of the early research concerned with the relationship between sport and politics as well as that dealing with sport and economics. Efforts related to politics were mainly descriptive in nature, and discussions focused on the relationship between political ideologies of specific nations and how sport served as a political tool for espousing such ideologies. Although early research on economics was also descriptive, it provided insight into the structure of professional sport and explained the complexities embedded in the definition of monopolistic practices, interstate commerce, and anti-trust legislation. Even though political or legislative implications were not fully developed in this research, such economic considerations served as a basis for current research which delves into the complexities of salary structure of athletes,

profits and losses of professional sport, and financial curiosities of intercollegiate sport.

By far, the topic receiving disproportional research attention was that
related to sport and education. Several investigations attempted to demonstrate the functional role of sport in the school. For example, in research which supported the notion that sport was consonant with the
goals of education, several studies found that high school athletes not
only earned higher grades than nonathletes, but they also had higher
educational aspirations than did their nonathletic counterparts. Moreover,
these early research efforts relating to sport and education are directly
responsible for current research interests concerning the social mobility, and
educational and occupational attainment of athletes. In contrast to this
popular topic, however, other areas have received minimal attention. Despite some interest in sport and politics, sport and religion, and sport
and the mass media, research efforts have been sadly lacking. More extensive theoretical and empirical research needs to be developed in each
of these areas.

Relative to investigations of sport and social processes, a substantial
number of studies examined how individuals are socialized into or through
sport, the relationship between social class background and sport participation (e.g., stratification), and racial segregation in sport. Whereas the
sport socialization research used theoretical bases for empirical investigation, very few studies in social stratification or racial segregation eman-
ated from a conceptual framework. Instead, stratification questions were
superficial; researchers were content to simply demonstrate that the lower
classes are poorly represented in sport and that participants in team and
combative sports come mainly from the lower social classes whereas those
in individual and dual sports are from the upper classes. Thus, the majority of these studies remained at the descriptive level; discovered relationships were not explained; and replication of these studies, although frequent, added little to the existing literature. Although the notion of
racial segregation in sport originally used a theoretical framework (Loy
& McElvogue, 1970) in its attempt to test Grusky's (1963) theory of
formal organizations, subsequent studies were mere replications. Results
were used to debate the issue relative to the existence of racial discrimination
in sport. This research was concerned with the playing positions occupied
by black athletes in professional baseball and football. The original investigation attempted to explain why few blacks became managers or coaches
by linking the centrality of playing position with leadership. Unfortunately, replication studies were preoccupied with the descriptive data, such as
how many blacks occupy central or peripheral positions. Although the re-

plications provided an excellent source of longitudinal data, very few attempts were made at explaining the presence or lack of social change. In fact, the patterns of proportional shifts in playing position were never closely examined.

The first symposium sponsored by the ICSS was devoted to "Small Group Research and the Group in Sport." The conference was held in 1966 in Cologne, West Germany. The topics considered at this conference were those which were popular and appeared in textbooks, and focus was on the structural and organizational patterns of teams. Several early studies investigated aspects of group structure and interaction processes within teams. One topic receiving considerable attention concerned the relationship between interpersonal relations of team members and team performance. Thus, a popular research question related to this topic asked if members of winning teams liked each other, or if they had to get along for the team to be successful. Another popular topic was whether or not cohesiveness was necessary for team success. Although some useful concepts emerged from this research, such as the distinction between task and affect structure, results from the cohesion research were often ambiguous and inconclusive. Perhaps this confusion was due to inconsistent definitions and operationalization of the concept of cohesiveness, which seemed to differ from one investigation to the next.

Despite the usefulness of several small group concepts, sociologists of sport have practically abandoned research from a small group perspective. Reasons for this decline in interest were probably due to the failure to organize research findings into a meaningful theoretical structure and because of the "shotgun" nature of empirical investigations. Interest has not been totally lost, however, because current research questions focus on whether cohesiveness leads to success or whether success leads to cohesiveness. In addition, other aspects of group structure have received attention. For instance, research examining the relationship between centrality and leadership has demonstrated that captains, managers, and coaches come from central rather than peripheral positions in basketball, football, and ice hockey as well as baseball. More recently, focus has shifted to a formal organization and systems approach to the analysis of sport teams, and research questions have been devoted to the rate of managerial replacement and how team success relates to hiring and firing of coaches/managers. Other research concerns have concentrated on team or organizational effectiveness and the factors contributing to such effectiveness, such as player turnover and performance levels of teams.

Issues Related to the
Development of Sociology of Sport

Although the first few years of the subdiscipline demonstrated a growth in interest and a proliferation of research endeavors, some of the early work has been severely criticized (Gruneau, 1978; Loy, 1980; Lueschen, 1980; McPherson, 1975, 1978). As previously mentioned, several studies were descriptive and atheoretical because they did not emanate from a conceptual framework. As such, results were not integrated into a theoretical structure, and the "body of knowledge" consisted of unrelated facts. Quite often individuals selected certain sociological variables (e.g., sex, race, social class) on which to compare subsamples; yet the rationale for undertaking the study was not clear. Further, there was little attempt at explanation, and results could not be generalized (McPherson, 1975). In addition, many statements relating to social problems and social issues began to appear in the literature, and quite frequently, they were classified as sociology of sport. These statements, however, were more a reflection of social philosophy than of scientific inquiry. As such, the shotgun studies as well as philosophical statements could not appropriately be labeled as sociology of sport because they did not apply sociological theory or concepts to empirical investigations.

Thus, the early history of sociology of sport was checkered with serious research endeavors using a systematic approach and a conceptual framework mixed with atheoretical studies having no apparent context, or mixed with rhetorical statements espousing the values (good or bad) of sport. Nevertheless, a consistency in approach by core sociologists of sport existed; objectives, definitions, and purposes were clearly delineated, and these individuals were not bashful in their declarations as to what was sociology of sport and what was not.

Particularly noteworthy are the recent "state of the field" papers appearing in the literature (Loy, 1980; Loy, McPherson, & Kenyon, 1978b; Sage, 1979; Snyder & Spreitzer, 1979). Although reasons for this recent appraisal are not clear, it is interesting that some 15 years after its inception, the subdiscipline has again been inundated with position papers. Again, the consistency of topics and concerns in these statements is noticeable and worthy of mention: development of the subdiscipline, analysis of critical issues, and prognosis relative to future prospects. Considerable agreement exists among these papers about the emergence of the the subdiscipline, and a brief outline of their content is included in this chapter.

Although there are various interpretations as to the historical events which may have led to the present status of sociology of sport, the approach by Loy and his colleagues (Loy, McPherson, & Kenyon, 1978b; Loy, 1980) has been the one most frequently quoted. Using Mullins's (1972) description of developmental stages for scientific specialties, the authors traced the development of sociology of sport over the last two decades and outlined the transitions in four stages: (a) The Normal Stage (1951-1964), (b) The Network Stage (1965-1972), (c) The Cluster Stage (1973-1978), and (d) The Specialty Stage (19??).

The first stage, characterized by a low degree of organization among scholars and within the literature, ends with the establishment of the International Committee on Sport Sociology (Loy, 1980). The major outlet or journal for research was the *International Review of Sport Sociology,* and the scholars represent the *first generation* of sport sociologists. Most were trained in physical education and sport and had a strong interest in social phenomena, or they received formal training in sociology and had a strong interest in sport (McPherson, 1975).

The second stage of development is characterized by more frequent communication among sport sociologists, increased rates of publication, and more conferences. During this period several books were published, such as *Sport, Culture and Society* (Loy & Kenyon, 1969), *Sport and American Society* (Sage, 1970), *Cross Cultural Analysis of Sport and Games* (Lueschen, 1970), and *Sport in the Socio-Cultural Process* (Hart, 1972). These texts were collections of readings pertaining to a variety of topics; most paralleled the early research thrusts (e.g., definitions, sport and education, sport and culture, sport and social class, race and sport, etc.). Increased interest in sociology of sport during this stage led to the development of the first newsletter in North America, the *Sport Sociology Bulletin,* which contained short items on activities and meetings and also included brief commentaries. The proliferation of research, however, created undue pressures on this newsletter, and soon it was publishing empirical studies as well as theoretical discussions. These increased publication demands led to a new journal, *The Review of Sport and Leisure,* which replaced the *Bulletin* in 1976. Although increased scholarly interest was reflected by the growing cadre of graduate students in the subdiscipline during this period, those who earned a doctorate in the early 1970s are still considered members of the first generation (Loy, McPherson, & Kenyon, 1978b), despite the fact that they received training in departments of sociology as well as in physical education.

The third state (Cluster) represents an extension and growth in practically all domains: accelerated research efforts, increased number of scholars, more conferences, a growing number of journals, and authored textbooks. During this period the *International Review of Sport Sociology* became a quarterly, *The Review of Sport and Leisure, Journal of Sport and Social Issues,* and *Arena Review* were established. Also during this time period journals in related areas were established (e.g., *Leisure Sciences, Journal of Popular Culture, Journal of Leisure Research, Sportswissenschaft,* to mention a few). Although the *Research Quarterly* as well as journals in sociology (e.g., *Pacific Sociological Review, Social Science Quarterly, Sociological Quarterly*) occasionally published manuscripts related to the sociological nature of sport, prior to this period appearance of sport articles was not frequent. Thus, the presence of a section editor in sport sociology or specialists reviewing manuscripts related to the sub-discipline represents progress. Equally worthy of notice is the proliferation of textbooks, monographs, and conference proceedings during this stage. In 1978 alone, four co-authored or authored texts were published (e.g., *Sport and Social Systems* by Loy, McPherson & Kenyon; *Social Aspects of Sport* by Snyder & Spreitzer; *Sociology of American Sport* by Eitzen & Sage; and *Sport in Society* by Coakley). In contrast to earlier anthologies, these texts did not approach the subject matter from a purely topical perspective. Rather, they were more theory based and integrated theoretical perspectives with empirical findings. These texts, particularly *Sport and Social Systems,* represent a more advanced stage in the development of knowledge, because some attempt toward explanation was made.

In addition to the texts, second and third editions of previous publications also appeared; anthologies were updated and included more recent empirical investigations. Content was also expanded and additional topics like economics, sport for children, and religion were included. Although conference proceedings were published on a regular basis by this time, it was during this period that such proceedings were undergoing strict peer review (see, for example, *Psychology of Motor Behavior and Sport—1977,* NASPSPA, edited by Landers and Christina; *Studies of Anthropology of Play—1977,* TAASP, edited by Stevens). Also evident during this stage is the *second generation* of sport sociologists, graduates whose professional preparation included extensive training in substantive areas of sociology as well as an orientation to sociological theory and methodology (Loy, 1980; McPherson, 1975).

According to Loy (1980), "sociology of sport has not yet made the transition to the fourth or specialty stage, nor has it achieved full-fledged status as a legitimate area of specialization in either physical education or sociology" (p. 98). Because legitimation and transition to the specialty stage are closely interrelated, and because these developments encompass the present time as well as the *third generation* of sociologists of sport—those students currently enrolled in graduate programs—the reader might well ask what issues or events have critically influenced the development of the subdiscipline.

Although a matter of interpretation, the answer is not simple; it involves three interrelated factors. For any field to develop, there must be a critical mass of scholars so that social networks can be formed. Such networks are essential because through interaction specific research thrusts or foci become recognizable. To achieve this state of recognition or identification, however, sufficient scholarly productivity must exist. Intellectual progress cannot occur in a social vacuum.

Despite the interest and presence of scholars in sociology of sport, there has not yet been sufficient productivity nor is there a critical mass for the fourth stage to be achieved. In a recent study, Loy (Note 2) identified only 100 individuals in North America who had two or more publications in the sociology of sport literature. Furthermore, only 19 authors who have 10 or more publications could be identified, yet they accounted for 56.5% of all the published work surveyed (Loy, 1978). Hence, Loy concluded that sociology of sport did not have a critical mass of scholars and that the limited productivity from the few scholars in the field may be a factor in integrating the subdiscipline into either physical education or sociology (Loy, 1980). Such notions have received substantial support from other sociologists of sport (Sage, 1979; Snyder & Spreitzer, 1979), and Loy's appraisal has been generally accepted.

To understand the present status of sociology of sport, its perplexing and somewhat paradoxical relationship with physical education should be considered. Whereas many points converge between the two, some points of divergence have also been identified (Sage, 1979). Based on outward appearance, sociology of sport was an accepted subarea in physical education by the early 1970s, as demonstrated by presentations and topics at meetings of professional associations (e.g., AAHPER and NCPEAM). This acceptance, however, seemed to be based on the (mis) understanding that *any study* dealing with sociological variables or social issues related to sport could be classified as sociology of sport. As previously mentioned, scholars in the subdiscipline disavowed the atheoretical, fact-finding research that was superficial in nature. In contrast, their concern was with a value-free science which used theory, concepts, and methods of sociology to describe, explain, and predict the underlying patterns of social behavior in a sport context (Kenyon, 1969; Kenyon & Loy, 1965; Loy, Note 1; McPherson, 1975). Moreover, the goals of the new subdiscipline were focused on theoretically based research and substantive topics relative to understanding social processes and structural, organizational patterns found in sport (McPherson, 1978). As such, these goals created a second point of departure with physical education because they implicitly encompassed a basic research orientation. This position can be contrasted with the traditional research orientation found in physical education which is more applied in nature.

In addition to these differences, another crucial debate received unparalleled attention: the meaning of value-free research. Because sociology of sport was concerned with description and explanation of underlying behavioral patterns found in sport, the objective of the subdiscipline was *not* to demonstrate the social value of sport, justify sport practices, comment on the good, or criticize the evils in sport. Thus, the term "value free" was applied to the philosophical position that values should not interfere with the scientific process by altering one's interpretation of the data. Unfortunately, the meaning of value free was taken quite literally, and one set of critics indicated that such a perspective was impossible. The selection of a research topic implies a certain set of values; therefore, these critics maintained that a value-free perspective was unrealistic and philosophically untenable. The debate was further fueled by another set of critics who were writing about the social ills inherent in sport practices. They argued that the value-free approach was politically conservative and tended to maintain the status quo (Edwards, 1973; Hoch, 1972; Meggyesy, 1971; Melnick, 1975; Scott, 1969, 1971). As such, they believed that important social issues and social problems would not receive research attention.

At first glance these issues seem to be concerned with *how* the sociologists of sport should conduct their research and for what purpose. Embedded in this debate, however, are deeper issues: (a) the type of knowledge to be generated, (b) the kinds of research questions to be asked, and (c) the nature of relationships to be explored (Greendorfer, 1977). Thus, the very nature of knowledge lies at the crux of this debate; it is more than a controversy over methodology. This issue has not been satisfactorily resolved, and it has created distinct cleavages between sociologists of sport and between the fields of sociology of sport and physical education. Although this debate can have the positive consequence of promoting development of the subdiscipline by presenting it with a multiparadigm approach (Picou, 1979; Sage, 1979), failure to agree on mutual coexistence of alternative perspectives may be one reason why sociology of sport currently occupies a marginal position in physical education.

Prior to discussion of future prospects for the subdiscipline, two additional concerns should be mentioned; both encompass areas of neglect or omission, and these "nondevelopments" (for lack of a better term) may also have had a profound influence on the present status of sociology of sport. First, during the early 1970s when the sociology of sport bandwagon was "riding its crest," a formal association or network of scholars was not formed. Secondly, a center sponsoring sociology of sport research as well as a graduate program of preparation was not firmly established.

Specific to a formal organization, scholars in any field need an institutionalized forum or means by which they can band together, identify colleagues with mutual scholarly interests, exchange ideas, and discuss philosophical or research issues. Although each of the other social science subdisciplines did establish viable organizations in North America (e.g., history: North American Society for Sport History; anthropology: The Association for the Anthropological Study of Play; psychology: North American Society for the Psychology of Sport and Physical Activity), attempts to organize sociology of sport were informal, diffuse, and minimal.[3] The presence of sociology of sport sessions held by other organizations did not create an atmosphere conducive to attracting a critical mass of scholars. The impetus in North America was missing, and the only forum for sociologists of sport was at the international level. Whereas several first generation scholars participated at ICSS conferences, attendance for others interested in sociology of sport was problematic. Communication between first generation scholars and others having scholarly interests in the subdiscipline was selective, and the dynamics of exclusion were quite interesting.

The second "nondevelopment" represents a failure rather than an oversight or omission. Although plans to establish research centers and graduate curricula were evident in at least three separate locations—with a definite possibility for additional centers—pivotal events altered the course of their development. One leading factor concerned the careers of several first generation sociologists of sport, while a second dealt with budgetary considerations. Graduate curricula were planned at the University of Wisconsin, University of Illinois, and Michigan State University. Two of these programs

---

[3]Recently a North American Society for the Sociology of Sport (NASSS) has been formed and has begun publishing a professional newsletter, the first issue which appeared in December, 1978. This formal organization held its first conference in October, 1980, and currently has over 100 members—scholars from anthropology, sociology, psychology, and physical education. Perhaps this association will serve as a basis for attracting a critical mass and, by its existence, will lead to a solution of the legitimation problem.

were implemented, whereas the third never did develop. Unfortunately, career mobility, promotion, or change of career paths of some key figures affected program implementation, and development became spasmodic. Secondly, despite the fact that philosophical agreement to develop a sociological thrust was reached by some physical education departments, curriculum growth in higher education became limited because of budgetary constraints. Periods of financial crisis represent a time for retrenchment and reaffirmation of existing programs rather than times for development or implementation of new programs. The net result was a failure to attract and sustain interest from a large number of students. Although this affected the size of the late first and early second generation cohort of sociologists of sport, it also led to the dissolution of some existing graduate programs. These consequences also contributed to the present critical mass problem.

Future Prospects

Although issues related to critical mass, limited productivity, and legitimation have thus far interfered with achievement of the fourth stage of development, the future for sociology of sport can be viewed with some optimism. In the brief 15-year history of the subdiscipline, the rate of growth cannot be discounted. Despite debates that might well have splintered the subdiscipline into nonexistence, it is still intact and the progress made has been steady. Not only are there specialized journals, formal courses, a variety of textbooks, and regularly held sessions at professional meetings, but the quality of theoretical and empirical efforts indicates a definite progression. The future holds exciting possibilities for continued growth and development in the understanding of sport as a social phenomenon. Hopefully, within the next 10 years, there will be more efforts toward integration of empirical results with theoretical conceptualization. Perhaps research questions will be less concerned with discovery (i.e., fewer questions asking whether or not a relationship exists), and more concerned with explanation (i.e., inquiry into specifying the nature of relationships). Thus, increased theoretical and methodological insight would be logical outcomes. Because these are important considerations, each issue will be discussed separately.

In their most recent paper Snyder and Spreitzer (Note 3) advocate the generation of sport theories of the middle range.[4] They consider such en-

---

[4]There are varying levels of abstraction, and many theoretical debates have focused on the desirable level of generality. Whereas some notions are considered too general or too abstract because they seem so far removed from empirical data

deavors a concern for sport sociologists dedicated to the growth of the subdiscipline. Implicit in their position is the applied versus basic research debate, particularly because the development of the subdiscipline is believed to be contingent upon a shift from the accumulation of empirical facts—a pattern typical of applied research—to higher levels of abstraction. The development of useful constructs at a more abstract level should be welcome additions or extensions to the already existing theories of the middle range which pertain to centrality in sport organizations (Grusky, 1963; Loy, McPherson, & Kenyon, 1978a), sport and academic orientation, achievement, and social mobility (Snyder & Spreitzer, 1978), and role conflict (Snyder, 1970; Spreitzer, Snyder, & Larson, 1979). Thus, future endeavors would enhance the theoretical base and provide greater insight into sport behavior.

Relative to research methodologies, an expansion in the use of various research techniques may occur in the future. In addition to questionnaires, interviews, and secondary analyses of data, field studies should become increasingly more popular, and the use of specific methods, such as participant observation, should become more evident. Such techniques enhance the symbolic interaction approach, and actual occurrences as well as perceptions of the sport experience from the perspective of the participant could become part of the data base (Fine, 1979; Koehler, Note 4, Note 5). Furthermore, such tools not only provide additional insight because of the nature or form of the data, but interactional experiences can also be useful as a basis for grounded theory. Another indication of expanded research methodologies could become evident through the increased use of qualitative data collection techniques which are interpretive in nature. The historical-comparative approach may be more subjective than other techniques, but such methods could gain in credibility if more sociologists of sport adhere to a conflict-systems paradigm (Gruneau, 1978; Picou, 1979). Thus, expanded research methodologies and an increased number of theoretical approaches should make tapping more realistic, experiential, and relevant research questions possible. Moreover, broadened research approaches have implications for application.

Although discussion thus far has focused on the generation of theory as one objective of research, improved methodologies and theory are not

---

(and hence are called Grand Theories), theories of the middle range provide a deeper degree of abstraction than do concrete facts of social reality but are not as far removed from empirical verification as are Grand Theories. Snyder and Spreitzer (1980) more fully develop this point, and the reader is referred to their paper for more detail.

the only goals of research. Quite often empirical findings and theoretical principles can be of benefit to the practitioner, and application is also a legitimate research objective. Good theories lead to greater understanding, and good theories can explain real life behavior. Thus, empirical findings obtained from sport settings and the sporting experience can be of use to the physical education teacher and coach. To date, sociology of sport has not ventured too far into the world of applied research, but some indications show this is changing. Unlike other subdisciplines, however, research findings from sociology of sport may not be as easy to apply; simple cookbook answers may not be available. Rather, application of principles will most likely occupy a "middle ground" position; application may not provide solutions to problems but may offer suggested changes in teaching and coaching practices that may ultimately lead to solutions. For instance, in-service training of teachers in the area of sex role stereotyping and early childhood socialization practices may sensitize them to certain facts relative to female motor performance. Perhaps physical education teachers will recognize that motor skill is a product of learning, that many females have not been taught sport skills, are not rewarded for motor performance, and hence are not motivated to do well. Therefore, special care should be given to females in coeducational classes, because closing the performance gap between the sexes falls within the responsibility of the physical educator. Sex differences in motor performance during childhood are not innate; physical educators should not take these differences as natural but should focus their teaching on narrowing such differences. Again, such applications from research findings are not direct, and they certainly are not simple. Nevertheless, the future should see sociologists of sport more concerned with application, particularly because the knowledge base is constantly growing and empirical facts are more readily available.

One unique consequence of continued utilization of qualitative methods would be collaborative research and the use of multidimensional research designs. Hopefully, debate over which methodology is best will recede into the background or completely disappear; then multivariate statistical techniques could be combined with a qualitative data base, thus enriching the possibilities for discussion and explanation. Despite this encouraging forecast toward qualitative methods, however, the quantitative approach will continue to be dominant because it achieves a greater degree of objectivity and relies more on sophisticated statistical analysis made possible by computers.

It is likely that many current research topics will maintain the interests of sport sociologists: sport and social mobility, educational orientations and value structure, sport subcultures, cohesiveness and team effectiveness, and formal structure of sport organizations, to mention a few. Several possibilities exist for new and different research thrusts, however, particularly relative to the following topics.

Multidisciplinary Approaches to Sport Research

It is possible that future research endeavors will incorporate theoretical perspectives from other subdisciplines or will involve collaborative efforts from scholars in other disciplines. For example, in the sport socialization research, it is possible that the social role-social system perspective will include psychological constructs, such as motivation, perceptual interpretation of sport experiences, and notions of cognitive and social development. Similarly, more anthropological perspectives could be employed in the comparison of play patterns of ethnic and cultural groups.

Socialization Research

This topical area can expand into several different directions. Relative to socialization through sport, one area of concentration could be on the analysis of outcomes or consequences resulting from sport participation. Although it is a widely held belief that individuals, particularly children, acquire role and social skills through their sport participation, such outcomes have not received empirical verification. Examination of how the sport experience leads to specific outcomes (i.e., specific social skills or roles) would be a worthwhile endeavor. Moreover, if social learning through sport does actually occur, then research questions could be devoted to identification of specific factors that account for social learning outcomes, under what circumstances such factors become operant, and whether or not the factors always contribute to similar outcomes. (In other words, do all individuals receive the same benefits from sport participation? Do all children learn similar social skills? Are sport experiences for blacks/whites/males/females similar, and do each of these groups acquire the same skills? If not, why not?)

1. Another consideration pertinent to socialization involves research that would examine the process from the perspective of the entire life cycle. Types or forms of sport involvement of the aged or elderly could be considered. Sport involvement of the "middle aged," as distinguished from youth and the elderly, is also worthy of consideration. Desocialization, due to either voluntary withdrawal from sport (e.g., conflicting time commitments, changing interests, etc) or involuntary withdrawal (e.g., injury, forced retirement, trades, or being benched) are other pos-

sible foci. In addition, the social-psychological adjustment of retiring athletes and their resocialization into alternative careers would represent still another potential research topic.

2. The relationship between spectatorship and participation could be examined from the perspective of sport socialization. How one form of participation positively or negatively influences the other is another viable research area.

Sport as a Social System

Although this notion has been consistently mentioned since the early position papers began to appear, minimal attention has been given to empirical studies of this nature. Recent work on the structural analysis of children's games (Lever, 1978) or on the dynamics of sport teams (Dunning, 1979) could provide impetus to types of approaches and research questions pertaining to sport as a social system. Such research could include cross-cultural structural analysis of games as well as incorporating theoretical perspectives from anthropology (Geertz, 1973; Levi-Strauss, 1963).

Females in Sport

Only peripheral attention has been given to this topic; however, recent considerations have shifted from issue-oriented concerns (i.e., what constitutes equality) to more serious research thrusts (i.e., how are females socialized into sport; what attributions do females make when they succeed or fail in sport?). Essentially, the major empirical thrusts that have been thus far applied only to males could be applied to females—stratification and mobility, sport subcultures, team effectiveness and cohesiveness, centrality of playing positions, etc. Inclusion of research pertaining to females would represent a major commitment for sociologists of sport only if they integrate research results into the mainstream and consider sport phenomena from both a female and male perspective. Recently, the issue has been raised that definitions, theories, paradigms, and methodologies are male biased and represent a form of intellectual sexism (Hall, 1978, 1979). If this is true, then theoretical perspectives need to be broadened. Perhaps such broadening would offer alternative explanatory paradigms in the interpretation of sport behavior, particularly that which concerns sex differences (Greendorfer, Note 6).

Sport and Social Problems

It is likely that such topics as deviancy in sport will be revived in the future, especially those relating to use of drugs to facilitate performance, cheating, or moral or ethical sport practices. Despite the fact that each represents an issue-oriented topic, conceptual frameworks could be applied, and empirical investigation of these topics does present an exciting possibility.

Conclusion

The issue of legitimation cannot be minimized nor ignored. Sociology of sport needs to remove itself from its marginal status and incorporate its research thrusts into the discipline—which discipline seems less problematic today than it did 15 years ago. Throughout its brief history, sociology of sport always had proponents who aligned themselves with sociology rather than with physical education (Kenyon, 1969; Loy, Note 1; McPherson, 1975, 1978). Most likely this affinity was related to ideological orientations concerning the definition and purpose of research. The structural-functional perspective was more consonant with sociology than with physical education. Yet, some anomalies do exist, because the pull toward a discipline is in dichotomous and perhaps contradictory directions. The majority of core scholars in sociology of sport have had a background in physical education (Loy, Note 2; Sage, 1979), whereas most graduate curricula in the subdiscipline are still housed in departments of physical education. Third generation sport sociologists will receive greater depth and background in sociology than either of the previous two generations, and most likely they will gravitate toward sociology. They may, however, retain some philosophical commitment to physical education, perhaps, creating some internal role conflict.

The prospects for the future indicate that efforts will be made to incorporate research findings into the discipline (most likely sociology), the quality of research will improve, and productivity of scholars will increase. Whether efforts are achieved by the third or fourth generation, resolution of the problem of legitimation will take considerable time. However, despite its marginality and despite its unspecified affiliation, sociology of sport is a recognized subdiscipline, and whether or not it is institutionalized in a major discipline, it is here to stay.

Reference Notes

1. Loy, J.W. *The nature of sociological theory and its import for the explanation of agonetic behavior.* Paper presented at the 74th Annual meeting of the National College Physical Education Association for Men, Portland, OR, December, 1970.

2. Loy, J.W. *An exploratory analysis of the scholarly productivity of North American based sports sociologists.* Paper presented at the 9th World Congress of Sociology, Uppsala, Sweden, August, 1978.
3. Snyder, E., & Spreitzer, E. *The role of theories within sport sociology.* Paper presented at the American Alliance of Health, Physical Education, Recreation and Dance Convention, Detroit, MI, March 1980.
4. Koehler, L. *The interactional experiences of female high school athletes: Implications for socialization through organized competitive sports.* Paper presented at the North American Society for the Sociology of Sport, Denver, CO, October, 1980. (a)
5. Koehler, L. *Symbolic interaction: An alternative approach to the study of sport and symbolism.* Paper presented at the Sixth Annual Meeting of The Association for the Anthropological Study of Play, Ann Arbor, MI, April, 1980. (b)
6. Greendorfer, S.L. *Gender differences in play and sport: A cultural interpretation.* Paper presented at the Sixth Annual Meeting of The Association for the Anthropological Study of Play, Ann Arbor, MI, April, 1980.

References

Coakley, J.J. *Sport in society—Issues and controversies.* St. Louis: C.V. Mosby, 1978.

Dunning, E. The figurational dynamics of modern sport. *Sportswissenschaft,* 1979, **9**, 341-359.

Edwards, H. *Sociology of sport.* Homewood, IL: The Dorsey Press, 1973.

Eitzen, D.S., & Sage, G.H. *Sociology of American sport.* Dubuque, IA: Wm. C. Grown, 1978.

Fine, G.A. *Preadolescent socialization through organized athletics: The construction of moral meanings in Little League baseball.* In M. Krotee (Ed.), *The dimensions of sport sociology.* West Point, NY: Leisure Press, 1979.

Geertz, C. *The interpretation of cultures.* New York: Basic Books, 1973.

Greendorfer, S.L. Sociology of sport: knowledge of what? *Quest,* 1977, **28**, 58-65.

Gruneau, R.S. Conflicting standards and problems of personal action in the sociology of sport. *Quest,* 1978, **30**, 80-90.

Grusky, O. The effect of formal structure on managerial recruitment: A study of baseball organization. *Sociometry,* 1963, **26**, 345-353.

Hall, M.A. *Sport and gender: A feminist perspective on the sociology of sport.* Ottawa: Canada CAHPER, 1978.

Hall, M.A. Intellectural sexism in physical education. *Quest,* 1979, **31**, 172-186.

Hart, M. (Ed.). *Sport in the socio-cultural process.* Dubuque, IA: Wm. C. Brown, 1972.

Hoch, P. *Ripoff the big game.* New York: Anchor Books, 1972.

Kenyon, G.S. Sociological considerations, *Journal of Health, Physical Education and Recreation,* 1968, **39**, 31-33.

Kenyon, G.S. A sociology of sport: On becoming a subdiscipline. In R.C. Brown & B.J. Cratty (Eds.), *New perspectives of man in action.* Englewood Cliffs, NJ: Prentice-Hall, 1969.

Kenyon, G.S., & Loy, J.W. Toward a sociology of sport. *Journal of Health, Physical Education and Recreation,* 1965, **36**, 24-25; 68-69.

Landers, D.M., & Christina, R.W. (Eds.). *Psychology of motor behavior and sport–1977.* Champaign, IL: Human Kinetics Publishers, 1978.

Lever, J. Sex differences in the complexity of children's play and games. *American Sociological Review,* 1978, **43**, 471-483.

Levi-Strauss, C. *Structural Anthropology.* New York: Basic Books, 1963.

Loy, J.W. The emergence and development of the sociology of sport as an academic specialty. *Research Quarterly for Exercise and Sport,* 1980, **51**, 91-109.

Loy, J.W., & Kenyon, G.S. (Eds.). *Sport, culture and society: A reader on the sociology of sport.* New York: Macmillan Co., 1969.

Loy, J.W., & McElvogue, J.F. Racial segregation in American sport. *International Review of Sport Sociology,* 1970, **5**, 5-24.

Loy, J.W., McPherson, B.D., & Kenyon, G.S. *Sport and social systems: A guide to the analysis, problems and literature.* Reading, MA: Addison-Wesley, 1978. (a)

Loy, J.W., McPherson, B.D., & Kenyon, G.S. *The sociology of sport as an academic specialty: An episodic essay on the development and emergence of an hybrid sub-field in North America.* Ottawa, Canada: CAHPER, 1978. (b)

Lueschen, G. *Kleingruppenforschung und gruppe in sport.* Koln: Westdeutscher Verlag, 1966.

Lueschen, G. (Ed.). *Cross-cultural analysis of sport and games.* Champaign, IL: Stipes Publishing Co., 1970.

Lueschen, G. Sociology of sport: Development, present state, and prospects. *Annual Review of Sociology,* 1980, **6**, 315-347.

McPherson, B.D. Past, present and future perspectives for research in sport sociology. *International Review of Sport Sociology,* 1975, **10**(1), 55-72.

McPherson, B.D. Avoiding chaos in the sociology of sport brickyard. *Quest,* 1978, **30**, 72-79.

Meggyesy, D. *Out of their league.* New York: Ramparts Press, 1971.

Melnick, M.J.   A critical look at the sociology of sport. *Quest,* 1975, **24**, 34-47.

Mullins, N. The development of a scientific specialty: The phage group and the origins of molecular biology. *Minerva,* 1972, **10**, 51-82.

Picou, J.S.   Some comments on the growth of knowledge in sport sociology. *Review of Sport and Leisure,* 1979, **4**, 1-9.

Sage, G.H. (Ed.).   *Sport in American society.* Reading, MA: Addison-Wesley, 1970.

Sage, G. Theory and research in physical education and sport sociology: Points of convergence and divergence. *Review of Sport and Leisure,* 1979, **4**, 48-65.

Scott, J. *Athletics for athletes,* Hayward, CA: Quality Printing, 1969.

Scott, J. *The athletic revolution.* New York: The Free Press, 1971.

Snyder, E. A longitudinal analysis of social participation in high school and early adulthood voluntary associational participation. *Adolescence,* 1970, **17**, 79-88.

Snyder, E., & Spreitzer, E. *Social aspects of sport.* Englewood Cliffs, NJ: Prentice-Hall, 1978.

Snyder, E., & Spreitzer, E. Sport sociology and the discipline of sociology: Present status and speculations about the future. *Review of Sport and Leisure,* 1979, **4**, 1-9.

Spreitzer, E., Snyder, E., & Jordan, C. Reflections on the intergration of sport sociology into the larger discipline. *Sociological Symposium,* 1980, **30**, 1-17.

Spreitzer, E., Snyder, E., & Larson, D. Multiple roles and psychological well-being. *Sociological Focus,* 1979, **12**, 141-148.

Stevens, P. (Ed.).   *Studies in the anthropology of play: Papers in memory of Alan Tindall.* West Point, NY: Leisure Press, 1978.

Stone, G.P. American sports: Play and dis-play. *Chicago Review,* 1955, **9**, 83-100.

Wohl, A. The problems of development of physical culture in the socialist system. *Kultura Fizyczna,* 1953, **6**, 182-187.